MW01537982

TERROR FLIES THE SKIES
(The Diary Of An Air Force Pilot)

by

RODNEY L. CRON

SPECIAL LIMITED EDITION

DEDICATED TO MY COLLEAGUES
OF THE 572ND SQUADRON,
391st "Black Death"[1] Bombardment Group (medium)
9TH Air Force, ETO, WWII,
and to my loving children,
grandchildren and great-grandchildren,
as well as my helpful friends,
notably John W. Brown, Dale Devol,
George Johnson, Bob Mayer,
and Doug McCabe,
all of whom nudged me repeatedly
to record these oft-told stories for posterity.

Well, posterity, here they are!
May you be as thrilled as I was, but not as emotionally scarred by
these vicarious experiences.
 –Rodney L. Cron

[1]**Designated by a black triangle at the top of each vertical stabilizer, pointed upward (▲) and centered in front of the rudder hinge.)**

ISBN: 978-0-9800378-4-5
Copyright Registration Nr: TXu1-336-819
(Dated 22 January 2008)

LoneTree Publishing Agency
1641 N. Memorial Dr. #132
Lancaster, OH 43130

Also by Rodney L. Cron:

NON-FICTION: (Not listed, newspaper articles, "Toastmaster Magazine," IAE, etc.)

What I Can Do For Freedom (1961)
Passive Defense (1961)
Protecting America's Freedoms (1962)
Assuring Customer Satisfaction. (1973)
Survival and Success in a Shrinking Environment. (1974)
Let's Do It Now! (1975)
AIR WEST (Air travel magazine, 1975)
*K*M*T (Egyptian Archeological Magazine, 2002 -2003)*
Terror Flies the Skies! (Autobiography – 2008)

FICTION: (Not listed, miscellaneous short stories.)

ORIGINAL "CODEWORD" SERIES *(1975-1982)*
TWO ROMANCE SERIES (with Ilogene C. Cron)
(1982-1998)
At Cross Purposes (alone, 2004)

DR. ROBERT A. CARSTAIRS MYSTERIES
Just a Piddlin' Little, Two-Bit Murder. (2001)
I'll See You in Hell! (2006)
Murder Tops The Menu (coming–2008)

NEW "CODEWORD" SERIES:
Codeword: Apollyon (2003)
Codeword: Bluefire (coming–2008)
Codeword: Shammash (coming–2009)

Also

Do Your Own Thing! (Write! Write! Write)
(Coming –2008)

(And more . . .)

ACKNOWLEDGMENTS

There is no way to acknowledge the contributions of so many . . . most of whom are dead. Many died on, or over, the once-lush, war-torn fields of World War II. Some we left behind on the glass-shard-like mountains of Korea. Some "bought it" in the steamy jungles of Viet Nam. A number came to their end on the arid sands and savannahs of Africa, and the Middle East. Those who did not die there, returned home to "buy the farm with their boots on" in private aircraft or car accidents, waste away with cancer, drop from strokes and heart attacks, or drain away their once-active brains in senility, Agent Orange reactions, or insidious Alzheimers.

Far too few are still alive today or alert enough to acknowledge anyone's accolades.

To all those–too many to be individually named here–I owe a forever unpayable debt. Their actions not only fought our nation's wars, but kept me alive through untold narrow squeaks and stupid errors. These stories, though centered around my life, are to their honor.

War makes heroes . . . or cowards . . . of us all.

The true heroes are those who no longer can read these tributes to their bravery, stamina and sacrifices. They–along with the veterans suffering at home, in VA hospitals and retirement centers, or forever sleeping in our National Cemeteries scattered around the world and in unmarked graves, unsung, unnoted, and unknown–have been largely forgotten. For these warriors I wrote this record of their inestimable contributions.

Thanks–especially to those who have already gone ahead.

I will be joining them soon.

–Rodney L. Cron

Captain Rodney L. Cron
Kimpo AFB, Korea
(1952)

PREFACE

▲

At dawn, the freezing morning of 13 December 1944, the Group's entire four squadrons of B-26s[2] scrambled upward from our airfield at Royé, France. A grey sky glowered. Storm clouds boiled to the west. Visibility barely met minimums. The briefing for us pilots–at 0400 hours–promised only a small window of opportunity before a heavy snowfall. We *had* to go on this mission . . . *NOW!*

Thirty minutes later our 391st Bombardment Group joined three others. (My Combat Sortie #10.)

Together, we created a black and silver, bomb-laden armada. In one vast assembly we climbed eastward at 250 MPH toward sixteen thousand feet. Our mission: to bomb out of existence–finally–Germany's last major, ball-bearing plant at Dusseldorf.

The highly camouflaged factory enjoyed the protection of the best fighter pilots and ground-to-air gunners left in the enemy's dwindling forces. All former instructors, they shared "killer" reputations.

[2] B-26s: small, medium-type bombers–Martin Marauders–twin-engine, single-tailed, torpedo-shaped. Manned by at least one pilot, a co-pilot, one each bombardier/navigator, engineer-waist gunner, turret gunner, and tail gunner. The letter preceding the number designated the aircraft *by type*: "A" = attack; "AT" = advance trainer; "B" = bomber; "C" = cargo , including personnel; "P" = pursuit (later changed to "F" for "fighter"); "R" = reconnaissance, and a few had only a "T" for trainer. See the next page

A-26, Douglas Invader

B-26, Martin Marauder

Despite the highly negative propaganda not a plane lagged on take-off. Nor did any return to Base for replacement. The climb-out proceeded without incident, except for ever-thickening clouds, dropping temperatures, and deteriorating visibility.

In the beginning, everything went smoothly . . . too smoothly.

Fifty miles beyond enemy lines we encountered our first flak, sleet, ice and Me-109s.[3] Some of our ships dropped, falling away with the lazy aplomb of drifting snow flakes, indicating dead pilots.

Soon we confronted our first rocket planes[4]–*ever*!

We could not believe our eyes. They rode skyward on fiery tails as if providing a fireworks display. Scattering our formations going up, they dove back meteor-like, firing their guns both ways, and reducing more of our bombers to fluttering shrapnel.

The resulting confusion instilled fear into the voices screaming over our plane's interphone: "My God! What was that?"

"Don't know. It went by so fast I didn't see."

"Cripes! Straight up! Through our formation like a rifle bullet."

"Wow! Zip-a-dee-doo . . ."

I asked, "Did anybody get a shot?"

Sullen silence provided the answer.

Two hours later came the really hot flak!

Fired from Dusseldorf's instructor-manned batteries, the shells traced our invisible pathway across the sky as if the enemy knew our flight plan. Their deadly flowers blossomed around us in groups of four, bright, red-and-black explosions. When near enough for us to hear the sharp crack and bang, jaw-rattling

[3] Messerschmidt-109s (German "BF-109s")–German fighter aircraft, resembling our F-51, small, fast and deadly.

[4] These were *not* "jets," but small, one-man planes (Me-163s) propelled solely by rockets. They exhausted their fuel on the way up and could strike again only during their downward swoop. They made the most of it. (Difficult to land and prepare once more for flight, they fell rapidly out of favor.)

tremors shook the plane. The bursts lined-up in front and to each side like orange barrels on a highway–Bang! Bang! Bang! (We always sweat-out the fourth one, certain it would end-up in our bomb-bay . . . sometimes it did.) *BANG!*

Trundling along like massed school buses from the "IP"[5] onward, our bomb-bay doors wide open, we formed double-Vs of vulnerable geese. Right after we embarked on the final bomb run, our lead aircraft exploded in front of us. Seven of our buddies and their ship vanished instantly in a gigantic puff of fire and smoke.

Our plane leaped as if it were the one hit. I fought the controls, regained stability. Aluminum shreds and body parts pelted our wings and fuselage. Hot, wet blood splattered the windshield.

As deputy flight leader, we carried the squadron's back-up navigator, our bombardier, and the squadron's other Norden bombsight. I slid our ship up and forward, assuming command of the now-five-aircraft flight.

During the final bomb run we kept our planes as close together as possible. Crowded in so closely the wing-men bounced and jiggled in the turbulence of their leader's slip stream, flying immediately behind one of his engines. Flying less than two feet apart placed our bomb-bays in the closest attainable proximity, assuring our bombs' hitting the ground in a maximum

[5] "IP" ("Initial Point")–the last checkpoint on a mission before the target, usually an easily identifiable landmark on the ground (a major river curve, another city, a river, railroad or highway intersection). From here the Group, turned and, for the first time, flew a straight, unswerving line toward the target (no more evasive maneuvers nor altitude changes). Here, bombardiers turned "on" their Norden bombsights and began "lining-up" the cross-hairs on the target. From this point to bomb-release (also done by the bombsight itself), the bombardier and the bomb-sight actually *flew* the lead aircraft, turning the ship into the wind to "kill" drift, and coordinating the Norden's internal gyroscopes so the scene the bombardier saw through the sight appeared to be stopped, relative to the aircraft's movement. (The Norden bombsight was so superior, the Air Corps charged each bombardier–if downed–with destroying it or giving up his life, rather than letting an enemy obtain one. Doug McCabe, OU archivist claimed the enemy already had these secrets by this time.)

4

concentration of explosives.

This singular capability of the "medium" bombers over the "heavies"–coupled with our flying at lower altitudes–racked-up higher success rates. Thus our smaller bombers truly "pinpointed" their bomb loads[6].

Then the fighters pounced!

Those predators popped out of the sky at twice our airspeed, unheralded except by the sudden absence of flak. They dived at us from every conceivable angle, guns blazing like winking lights, tracers flowing like streams of flaming steel.

Within our ship the noise grew deafening. Engines roared. Machine guns chattered. Incoming bullets pounded. Equipment fragmented. Shell casings banged the floor.

Excited crewmen[7] began shouting over the interphone: "Look out, Brian, there's one zooming in–six o'clock, low."

"Hey, Tony! Another's about to fly over the top . . ."

"Can you get that bastard coming straight at us, Tony? . . . Brian? . . . Joe?"

The repeated assaults kept everyone on his toes. The throat-rasping stink of cordite began filling the ship. It stung our eyes, choking us, the taste acrid and bitter on the tongue. Usually only wing men used the nose- and fuselage-mounted fifty calibers to shoot forward. Now each gun roared. The bombardier and navigator[7] kept busy, shifting between firing theirs and lining-up the bomb sight.

Naive and green-as-grass on our first missions, by 13

[6] See later pages for drawings of the B-26's "in-flight" arrangement (from both vertical and horizontal perspectives). From this it is easy to visualize the close bomb pattern achieved on the ground.

[7] Group Headquarters assigned navigators, on a one-time basis, to fly in lead aircraft. On most missions, the crew's regular bombardier handled both responsibilities.

December our crew[8] had matured. Now we were a "lean, mean, fighting machine." Our bombardier, Joseph. K. Lasser (for most missions also our navigator), a skinny little New Yorker, later the author of the famous "J. K. Lasser Income Tax Guides," concentrated on his bomb sight. Earl Brow, our older engineer, manned the waist-guns and hailed from West Virginia. Our radioman-turret gunner, Tony Marshall, came from Pennsylvania. Ernie Bryant, tail gunner, was a Texan, I an Ohioan. We made a motley assortment–tall, short, dark or light–all razor-thin, a cross-section of our country's youth.

This mission was our most crucial test. Yet the men braved the enemies' bullets without flinching, and struck back at the incoming attackers without hesitation. Each man made me proud . . . even as I shook in my boots.

Now in our extra-close formation, the Groups maintained a rigidly straight line, no matter what happened. Aircrews remained constantly alert, eager to drop their loads on the leader's triggering signal and head for home.

During those long, white-knuckle sessions of agonizing torture (really only a matter of minutes, but seeming like hours), we were most exposed. Even with temperatures sixty degrees below zero in our unheated aircraft, we all sweat bullets–from pilot to tail gunner. I always felt as if I were a stark-naked puppet, dangling by a single thread high above the enemy, while every hostile soldier took pot-shots at my bare posterior. It put a sickening taste in my mouth and, sometimes, gave me diarrhea.

This never-to-be-forgotten mission on that bleak December day shattered our Group's record for damage sustained and aircraft lost on a single sortie. Since then, I have always marked

[8] In the US Army Air Corps (USA) and US Air Force (USAF), a "crew' meant all the people on a plane–officers and enlisted men alike, without distinction. The Navy meant only enlisted personnel as "crew."

December 13 in red on my calendars[9].

No wonder! Only twelve planes out of our original forty-eight completed the bomb-run. Of those twelve, nine disappeared, one by one, as we ran the return gauntlet, hit by more flak and fighters.

Our ship, luckily, came home . . . one of the only three[10].

* * *

We returned to our base in the early afternoon to make virtually blind, hair-raising landings. We groped our way downward through a three-hundred-foot ceiling. Our fuel tanks registering empty, we had no chance for a "go-around." Red flares warned one plane carried hurt crew members. Two planes slid off the runway. A herd of ambulances and medics off-loaded the dead and treated the injured.

A single truck picked up our undamaged aircrew.

Rapidly undergoing debriefing by Military Intelligence, we gulped down a quick shot of the Flight Surgeon's booze. (Till then I'd been a teetotaler–but not that day!) From there we trucked to the mess hall for warmth and food . . . if anyone could eat. Few did.

Jack Brown, my former pilot[11] and one of the other two returning, approached me there. Hot coffee cup clutched in quivering hands, he edged closer. Yet he remained silent, staring

[9] Beginning 1 January 1998, the day my wife died, I added another red entry. The events on December 13 and my military career gave me the title for this, my autobiography–"Terror Flies the Skies!"–taken from my personal assessment of flying twenty-seven years as an Air Force pilot: "Hours and hours of absolute boredom punctuated by moments of sheer terror."

[10] I deliberately opened these pages with a fast-moving episode. I wanted to put you *there,* as best I could–emotionally and traumatically–so you might share to some small extent what we felt at the time (always a difficult chore).

[11] I went overseas as a co-pilot, right out of flying school, now I commanded my own crew.

blindly into the middle-distance as if he still saw the flak and fighters.

Jimmy Doolittle–*not* the famous Doolittle of "Shangri-La" and the Tokyo raid, but the third pilot to come back–joined us. Grimacing as if sucking on a lemon, he rasped, "That, my friend, was one . . . rough . . . tough . . . son-of-a-bitch!"

I nodded, chilled fingers wrapped around a steaming cup.

Gaining control of my chattering teeth, I managed to squeeze out, "Yeah! I . . . can't . . . believe . . . only . . . three of us . . . came back."

Major Sanford, who had remained behind on this mission, scowled. "Oh, some may have made it, landing at other fields. Or parachuting down. But . . ." He shrugged his shoulders, leaving the other dire possibilities to our already-overactive imaginations.

"The hell you say, Major! I was there!" I squinted over the rim of my mug. "They got iced-up, blown up, or shot up."

The three pilots' expressions chilled. They eyed me as if I violated a sacred trust.

I held up my hand. "Yeah, I know! It's bad luck to say aloud what we believe. But–bull!–we all know . . ." Seeing their increasingly hostile expressions, I shut up, deciding I better leave well-enough-alone. (Flier scuttlebutt contended, "Gremlins will get anyone who talks too soon about his comrades' deaths!" And I was guilty of doing just that.)

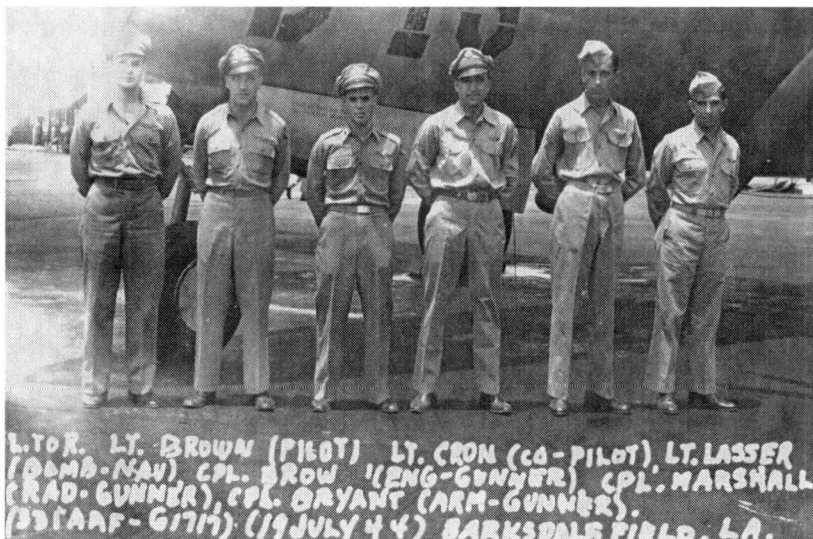

L.TOR. LT. BROWN (PILOT) LT. CRON (CO-PILOT), LT. LASSER (BOMB.-NAV) CPL. BROW '(ENG-GUNNER) CPL. MARSHALL (RAD-GUNNER), CPL. BRYANT (ARM-GUNNER). (33[AAF-G171]) (19 JULY 44) BARKSDALE FIELD, LA.

> My first aircrew, training completed in B-26s at Barksdale AFB, Louisiana, now ready for combat (we thought) in the European Theater of Operations. (September 1944)

A few minutes later our co-pilots, navigators and bombardiers joined us from their hospital trips and special debriefings. We huddled in clusters. Reliving the mission while cradling coffee mugs and warming chilled rears at the red-hot, potbellied iron stoves, our faces sagged lower and lower, growing as long as mourners' at a wake.

Suddenly, I realized, *that's what we are--mourners at a wake!*

I did a quick recount: *forty-five planes times seven crew members . . . all missing!* Again I shot off my mouth, "Hey, guys! If no one else makes it, we just lost 315 airmen!"

Growling, the men crowded nearer, hands working.

At that instant, Colonel Jerry Williams, our Group Commander, banged aside the mess hall's door and stomped his

9

six-foot-two, rigidly erect, West Point frame, straight into the center of our close-knit grouping. He opened with a ringing, "Men, I know, you had a damn tough time today!"

When his statement earned only mumbles, he managed a grim smile. "But it's not as bad as you think." He whipped out a telex. "I've news here on some of our planes. Yes, many crew members are injured and a number are dead, but *not everyone . . . nor every plane . . .* has been lost, as we thought.

"Tomorrow, we stand-down. As soon as the weather improves, we will regroup and get back to killing Nazis." He eyed our wistful, drawn faces. "Buck up! Have a drink. Get a good night's sleep. I'll let you know the full results tomorrow."

Colonel Williams turned to leave, but stopped. "By the way, congratulations! The strike photos show you bombed the hell out of the ball-bearing plant."

Our squadron members slapped each other on the back, though tears underlay their strident chortles. Mine as well.

But the weather didn't improve until later in December. During those anxious days a major event took center stage.

Beginning December 16, and only a few miles to our north, the Germans crept like ghosts out of the mists. This was the covering storm the Nazis had been awaiting and they made the most of it.

Thus began the Battle of the Bulge.

When the snow eased, our replenished Group flew multiple, low-level missions daily, strafing and bombing from dawn to dark in support of the Allied ground troops. Once more we claimed–from throttles-forward to engine shut-down–*terror flies the skies.*

My story starts here, amidst prayer and terror, though it really began many years before . . . when I was just a kid in Piqua, Ohio . . . with my father.

CHAPTER ONE

▲

Frank Sinatra often sang about his "very good years." Like him, my parents heralded 1922 as just such a time, citing my birth as the reason. 1922 was not, however, the first pivotal date in my young life. 1929 was.

In October, 1929, the year I was seven, the stock market crashed. My great-grandfather, first mayor of Piqua[12], Ohio, lost our family businesses (Cron Company and Cron-Kills)—worth some twelve million dollars. With that, Dad also lost his job as the forthcoming general manager of both.

(See accompanying photos of both, next page, in the 1920s.)

What the collapsing stock market did *not* take, the lawyers did.

[12] Piqua had three other interesting "claims to fame," none of which involved our family. The first was Albert McKnight, a slim, grizzled black man, some five-feet, four-inches tall, age unknown (everyone guessed him to be somewhere in his eighties since his hair was white and almost gone). In the early twenties, "Albert" developed a wide-spread reputation for unofficially directing traffic in downtown intersections at every parade. Wearing a tattered set of tails, no shirt, and once-white tennis shoes, he gaily waved cars to and fro, while nodding, smiling and talking to himself. He became such a fixture the people of Piqua and the surrounding area erected over his grave a life-sized replica of him in his "uniform" and gave him a rousing funeral attended by hundreds. People came from miles around to wish this venerable icon "God speed."

At the other end of the spectrum, the Mills Brothers, of stage, film and record fame–from Greenville, Ohio–sang regularly on Piqua's street corners . . . from the time they were children. Though "Albert" scared me with his deranged machinations and wild look, I listened eagerly to the Mills Brothers and, later, bought their recordings.

Piqua's third entry is the still-existing Hartzell Propellor Company. A once-small enterprise, it expanded rapidly during WWII and produced propellers for millions of the world's planes, playing a major role in the manufacture of both small reconnaissance types and larger combat aircraft.

11

Cron Furniture Company, Piqua, Ohio
(Circa 1920)

Cron-Kills Furniture factory, Piqua, Ohio.
(Circa 1920)

By January, we were *poor*. The lawyers owned the plants; "Granny" owned nothing. Thus, without my ever being aware our family was in the chips–we weren't.

At age six, therefore, I went from prince to pauper. Where, one year, I had "all the toys in the world," the next year I was grateful to have a cardboard, Wonder Bread box to play in. I saved a few of my favorite toys–Mom sold the others–in a black, trunk-type container looking like a small military footlocker.

Dad shifted his avid interest from making furniture to anything that flew. Gliders, airplanes, autogiros, blimps, dirigibles, hot-air and gas balloons became his obsession. He instilled in me the same drive.

Taking whatever time he needed to do special things on my behalf, he was not perfect, yet I'd have endorsed him as "Dad of the Year." We played catch in the back yard (ducking the clothes lines). We boxed. (He bought a pair of out-sized gloves so big I swung them like mallets and gave him a black eye when I was five.) To my delight, every July 4th he exploded huge firecrackers. (These were so large the police came by and raised Cain.) Above all, he devoted continuing attention to my welfare and pleasure; so much it irked Mom. But, to Dad, nothing was too good or too costly for me–until we went broke. I loved him dearly and when he died at forty-one (Labor Day, 1941), I was devastated. Mother took his loss better than I did. I arranged all the details of his funeral and (since I had been singing on the stage since I was six) tried to memorialize his death with his favorite song, "Ah, Sweet Mystery of Life!" I broke down, though, in the first measure and had to substitute a recording by Nelson Eddy, whose voice Dad said he liked next best.

When things "went south" in 1929, Dad opened a grocery store across from our home at 122 Staunton Street, Piqua, Ohio, and bought "Learn-To-Fly" books by the dozens. He figured the more books he owned, the better his chances to learn to fly. It did not work! To learn, he set up a kitchen chair with rudders and a

control stick to practice by the hour. (Of course, I imitated his every move.)

Though Dad remained driven by the flying bug, he never once flew at a plane's controls, or took in-the-air lessons. I often imagined how thrilled he would have been to see me pin on my wings and second lieutenant bars, March 12, 1944, in Pampa, Texas. For him, my flying as an Air Force pilot would have been the "cat's meow."

My graduation photo (flying training) taken
in Piqua, Ohio, March, 1944.

Still, for me–despite Dad's kitchen training–my aviation enthusiasm actually began when a sleek dirigible, the U.S.S. Shenandoah, groped its way along a local railroad spur in Piqua, and into our part of town, one summer day. I was barely three years and one month old, but I still remember it vividly.

On a foggy morning, visibility under a hundred feet, the silver tube of an airship[13] suddenly appeared out of the mists, barely thirty feet in the air. It had followed the steel beams of the B&O's rails into "Shawnee," the area where we lived.

That did it for me. I was sold!

From then on–though we seldom had the money to travel– Dad made sure I saw it all! He dragged me on repeated trips to Akron, Ohio, to watch the building of the "Akron" and "Macon" dirigibles. He hauled me off to the Army Air Corp's annual air shows (WWI German, French and US aircraft), at old Cook Field, Dayton, Ohio. He made sure we attended the special visitation of Roscoe Turner and Amelia Earhart at the airport in Columbus.[14] (Graciously, they came to where I was pressed against the steel cyclone fence, nose sticking through an opening. She reached down and shook my little, trembling hand. I remember only Miss Earhart's asking, "Little boy, do you want to be a pilot too?"

(I do not, now, recall my answer, but she had pretty eyes.)

Turner and Earhart were on a nationwide tour, exhibiting one of the world's first, commercially-built autogiros (a low-wing, open-cockpit design, bright red and as awkward as a goose with a

[13]The *U.S.S. Shenandoah* crashed on this same trip, near Caldwell, Ohio, 3 September 1925.

[14] Turner, noted for flying both balloons and airplanes during WWI, became most famous as a showman, barnstormer and National Air Race winner during the thirties. Amelia Earhart may be remembered as the pioneer aviatrix who also gained fame for twice flying the Atlantic–solo–during the early 1930s, then vanishing in 1937 over the Pacific during an around-the-world flight. (Many accounts credited her loss to the Japanese for her having overflown their secret military installations.)

broken leg). They parked this ungainly craft near the old, east-side, two-story terminal where we also–as we did at the Vandalia Airport (north of Dayton, Ohio)–gaped regularly at the mail planes' nightly cross-country flights.

All in all, Dad drove hundreds of miles[15] to show me our new airways' installing light beacons. We went even farther to welcome the inauguration of TWA's first, stately DC-2s and DC-3s, any airports' new runway/perimeter lights, and radio towers with flashing and identifying, rotating signals. (Still in use when I began night flying regularly in 1942.)

My father,
Rodney L. Cron, Sr.
(1900-1941)

My mother,
Juanita Mae (Nedderman)
(1903-1985)

[15] The cars Dad was driving then were not today's sleek vehicles, but those of the twenties – wooden-spoke wheels with split-rims and inner tubes, six smoky cylinders, running boards, tiny trunks, and lumpy seats. The heaters seldom warmed anyone and we had to carry multiple blankets to keep from freezing. The tires also blew out regularly (one about every fifty to a hundred miles), requiring every driver to carry several spares and extra tubes, air pumps, and tube patches. The travel described was also over gravel roads and, in some instances, muddy lanes . . . and hotels had bed bugs.

The huge hangars housing the Macon and Akron dirigibles especially awed me, as they did everyone who saw them. The workers who did around-the-clock welding, high on scaffolds, raised the vast room's temperature so much it was necessary to open the massive doors, periodically, to cool the monstrous building. When the doors slid back, clouds formed instantly near the roof . . . and, inside, rain poured.

From these events, my flying experiences escalated to a first-time-flight (age seven) in a far-too-old, battered, WWI "Jenny[16]," flown by a tall, lanky, half(?) drunk, half(?)-crazy, and aging, barnstorming pilot from Rickenbacker's old WWI squadron.[17] We later made repeated hops with one of Dad's friends, a test pilot at the Waco Aircraft Company in Troy, Ohio. This pilot put me (age seven to nine) on aviation's ground floor with rides in the front-line fighters Waco was then building for the Nicaraguan Air Force. Sometimes, the planes were all ready to be shipped out, guns loaded. (Can you imagine our government allowing that, today?)

Yet my first time aloft I never forgot (like my first sexual experience). On Piqua's south side, soaring out of a tiny cow pasture rimmed too closely by trees, even our short circuit of the city in the old Jenny gave Dad fits. On landing, the pilot "slipped" the plane in over the trees to squeeze the no-brakes-biplane into the short field.

I loved it and cried, "More!"

Dad blindly slapped our fare into the pilot's outstretched palm, then turned and spewed his cookies into the nearest bush.

Oh, I've been "around-the-block." Maybe it's been a small

[16] "Jenny"–a two-seater, WWI training biplane (one wing above the other, held together by struts), built of flimsy fabric, stretched over a wood and aluminum frame.

[17] Eddie Rickenbacker is best remembered as our nation's "Ace-of-Aces" during WWI, and as world-renowned land/air racer, and commercial air pioneer. At one time, he owned the Indianapolis "500" Motor Speedway.

block, but I can truthfully say, "I grew up with aviation." For, in 1946, Bill Prentiss, a veteran flyer of WWI and an aging, fellow service engineer–salesman at the Thresher Paint and Varnish Company, Dayton, Ohio, really made my day.

He introduced me to–and I had a chance to chat informally with–the sole remaining Wright brother in Orville's own home. (Bill Prentiss lived in Dayton, two blocks from Orville, then in his late seventies.) When Bill told me what he was going to do, I thought Bill was a big blowhard. During the next two years, he proved he actually knew Orville Wright, Ted Lewis (the famous band leader of "Me and My Shadow"), and many other notables.

By the time Bill died in 1960, I had developed a deep respect for his statements, claims and stories. By then, if he told me he knew Moses and had been there when he parted the Red Sea, I would have believed him.

Since we worked in the paint industry, as an aside Bill often talked about his earlier job with the Ford Motor Company in Detroit. There, he put the delicate stripes along new cars' sides. (This was back when Henry Ford said, "You can have any color you want, as long as it's black.")

One of Ford's chief executives owned a Pierce-Arrow–the very thing for big wheels to drive in those days. Bill said he brought the car into their paint shop on a Monday morning, asked Bill and his crew to strip the body, and repaint it a different color.

They–as was the usual procedure–removed the body (just a matter of a few bolts) and dumped it into the acid bath to clean off the old paint. Twenty minutes later, they pulled up the huge basket to find the body of the Pierce-Arrow . . . *gone.*

No one had alerted them to the body's being *solid aluminum.* It cost the paint crew several thousand dollars to replace it. (A fortune in those days.) Thirty years later, Bill still griped.

On my first trip with Bill to Canton, Ohio, we were eating dinner in the hotel bar, when he stabbed a fork toward a line of femininity crowding the bar stools. "Choose any girl there, Rod,

and I'll sleep with her tonight."

If Bill had been a young handsome man, such a boast might *not* have seemed so outrageous. But Bill was U-G-L-Y. Five-foot-five, over-weight and round-shouldered, he sported a banana nose, beetle brows, and a graying, unruly mop of hair resembling a cheap wig. The black hairs in his ears clustered so thick they looked like two bird's nests. By no possible reckoning–ever!–did I figure this grisly, sixty-five-year-old man was going to "get" one of those young girls.

When I snickered, he laid ten dollars on the table. "Bet?"

I could not pass that up. I placed another ten atop his.

Dinner finished, Bill lighted a stinking cigar and nodded toward the bar. "Okay, Rod, pick'er out." He leaned nearer. "If you stick close I'll demonstrate my technique."

I selected the youngest, prettiest, and best-dressed woman in the lineup. Looking no more than thirty, she wore a long, white, silky-looking evening dress. I gestured toward her, assured I just made ten bucks!

Bill scrambled from his chair like a crouching spider and hopped up beside her at the bar. He motioned me to the stool on his opposite side. He called-over the bartender and ordered a Stinger (a mixed drink) for the girl and one for himself. (Bill called "Stingers"–"leg-spreaders.")

She turned and scowled at him, shaking her head. "Thank you, but I do *not* accept drinks from *perfect strangers.*"

Bill patted her hand, blew out a puff of gagging cigar smoke, and smiled (brownish-yellow teeth glistening like an attacking predators' in the back-bar light). "That's good, honey. I can see we're going to be great friends . . . because *I am not perfect.*"

At midnight he ran her through our connecting bath and my bedroom–both of them stark naked. After that, as I noted, I believed anything he said.

On another trip to Canton, Bill scared me to death! When he was driving, he drove absolutely uncaring for others. Always lost

in his own thoughts and words, he told stories without a break.

Owning a relatively new Hudson, he habitually shoved the accelerator to the floor . . . and held it there . . . until the fenders shook. He then let the car slow until it bucked like a bronco, then repeated the speeding episode. This time, he did it while driving along a single-lane road where no one could pass.

An irate driver finally managed to swing around us. Once he squeezed by, he slammed his car to a stop across our path, blocking our way.

Bill stopped, nonchalantly smoking his cigar. He rolled down the driver's window when the fuming driver stomped toward his door.

The other driver—a big dude, even uglier than Bill—ducked his head through the open window. Nose-to-nose, he read Bill the proverbial riot act in fiery, very blue, impressive terms.

Bill continued to puff, unconcernedly, on his cigar. When the fellow ran down, Bill took the cigar from his mouth, much like Groucho Marx, and calmly asked, "Are you finished?"

The other guy, out of breath, nodded.

Cigar now in his left hand, Bill reached under the front seat with his right and banged a tire tool across the sucker's forehead. The unfortunate aggressor fell back, spread-eagled on the highway.

Bill calmly replaced the cigar and tool, rolled closed the window, backed up, and drove around the prostrate body. He never mentioned the incident.

From that point to Canton, I kept a sharp eye toward the rear, certain a State Police cruiser must soon catch up. But we never heard a word about the altercation.

In addition, Bill seemed completely unaffected in any way. To me this vindicated Bill's earlier stories of his harsh action and bravery while flying in WWI. Somehow, I believe Bill may have given me a little of himself that day, instilling some of the grit I lacked.

*　　　*　　　*

Yet, I am getting off the beaten trail. Let me begin again by answering an oft-asked question: *Do I remember, after more than sixty years, every mission I flew in WWII or Korea? Not only no, but hell no!* (And my memory is still good!)

Women say, "Put two men together and they'll talk about sex." I say, "Put two pilots together and they'll talk about flying, *then* about *sex*."

I also say, "Put two combat pilots together and they will not only talk about flying, but they will tell each other apocalyptic war stories about their 'hairiest' missions, each trying to outdo the other."

As a joke (like Snoopy's story beginning, "It was a dark and stormy night . . ." when he sits on his doghouse roof, trying to write The Great American Novel), pilots have a standard humorous beginning for their epics too. They hold aloft both hands before their up-turned faces, fingers spread, one hand behind the other, simulating multi-engine fighter planes (P-38s) chasing each other, claiming, "There I was . . . at twenty-thousand feet . . . flat on my back . . . hanging by my throat mike . . . both engines shot out . . . bleeding from my legs, arms and chest . . . when . . ." From there, they embellish their tales with the hoariest, most adventurous experience they can dredge up from their pasts.

I will, therefore, carry on this *tradition–without that opening.*

Every sortie we flew was scary in some way and our lives were on the line (from the moment we pushed the throttles forward until we turned-off the engines), yet they were *not* all ball-breakers. Most missions fell into a pattern–taking-off, easing into formation, climbing out, sliding closer over the enemy lines . . . even closer as the target approached . . . and holding that position rigidly through the bomb drop–then flying home, and landing. Only a few were "milk runs.[18]"

[18] "Milk-run" was the title usually given to any mission with little to no flak, fighters or problems, and no major hassling by the enemy. Common sense will tell

Each trip meant encountering some enemy action, going out and coming back. But our Group navigators, who planned each mission, used the latest Intelligence reports to plot the routes as best they could to avoid *most of the fighters and flak.* Sometimes they succeeded. Most often they did not. When they failed, the mission resulted in heavier losses, more grief, and replacements. (But the USA had plenty of cannon fodder for their aircraft too, it seemed . . . and "we" were the fodder.)

Like a cartoon I once saw showing *nine* Roman soldiers with a tenth lying dead at their feet. A standing soldier was kicking the dead man and saying, "Hey! This decimation ain't so bad," the groups and squadrons took their losses, managed a stiff-upper-lip . . . and bore it. What else could we–any of us–do? This was war. Warriors lived; warriors died. We had to "suck it up."

The memorable missions usually stood out like problem children among a covey of angelic tots. That meant the sorties we remembered were those where an engine quit on take-off . . . bombs hung-up in the bomb-bay and someone had to go in to kick them loose . . . or the enemy shot us down. They also included those not-so-rare occurrences when it was necessary to land at other bases because ours was "socked-in" by bad weather–or we got lost. They all happened to me.

Here, too, I was luckier than most.

The morning my engine quit a few seconds after take-off, the weather was particularly "iffy." But I was flying a twin-engine, A-26 (Invader) and not a B-26 (Marauder). If it had happened in a B-26 (Marauder), I would *not* be writing this. When an engine quit in a Marauder at that point, it tended to roll-over on its back, stick its wheels into the air, and strew wreckage and airmen for a mile along the runway.

In an A-26 (Invader), I had a chance–albeit a small one. Alone in the cockpit (A-26's carried but one set of controls), "loaded for

you this was mighty rare during wartime.

bear" (full tanks, full guns, a six-thousand-pound bomb-load), a quarter flaps for take-off and wheels still down, I barely flew on one engine at full throttle.

I feathered the bad engine, jerked-up the wheels, and slowly eased *down* more flaps[19]. Unable either to drop the bombs (too close to the ground–less than thirty feet away) or climb (too much weight for one engine), I shoved those options aside. (We're talking microseconds to make these decisions!)

One leg fully extended and quivering from the strain, pushing the rudder as far as possible toward the good engine (damn difficult for a short guy!) I managed to hold the plane straight and level, and keep it in the air. In this half-ass configuration, I nursed the plane through a broad, sweeping, gentle turn, in a five-mile radius, at the same altitude, flying under a set of high tension wires barely a mile off the end of the runway. I had neither the time, nor did my crewmen have the necessary altitude, to "bail out." Of necessity, they rode along, mutely (probably running through their rosaries).

I broke radio silence to warn the tower of my dilemma. They cleared the runway of traffic and stopped the mission take-off. I never knew how, or where they put the waiting aircraft.(At that point I had other, more pressing concerns.) But I do *not* believe the controllers expected me to make it . . . no one else had.

Nearing the field, I saw the runway, barely visible in the mist over the snow banks. I waited until the last second to lower my gear, and brought the faltering aircraft "across the fence" about ten feet off the ground and a car-length before the runway's near

[19] Some pilots objected to my putting down more flaps at that point, but it not only let me fly the aircraft at a slower speed, though increasing the "drag," but it also gave me more lift and lowered the nose so I could see. The Davis wing – a wing designed with an extremely thin camber to assure higher speeds–at that point needed every bit of extra camber I could manage to give me more lift. Only the simulated, increased curve provided by the lower flaps, gave me that needed boost." The trade-off saved my life and became the SOP (Standard Operating Procedure) for pilots in similar situations.

end. Banging the gear onto the ground just as they snapped into place, I shoved down full flaps and eased back the throttle on the straining engine, again fighting the changing torques. Sweating profusely, I barely held the plane on the runway, swerving from side to side. I slowed by clamping on the binders (brakes) as soon as possible. Nearing the other runway's end, still moving far too fast, I gunned the remaining engine, trounced only on the opposite brake, and kicked the rudder–hard! This brought my wonderful beast to a slewing, bucking halt, off to one side of the runway, half-turned, nosed into a snow bank.

Since I was now out of the takeoff path, the engineers let the plane sit there while the group resumed its mission take-off. The medics picked up my crew members and me in an ambulance, and ran us to the Flight Surgeon for medical care and debriefing.

This incident taught me a valuable lesson: Yes, I could remain calm and do the right things under extreme stress. *But* I would pay a penalty–in spades–afterward. For the next ten minutes my adrenaline-overload shook me till my teeth hurt. I was so palsied I could not hold the glass of whiskey the Flight Surgeon offered. When I settled down, I *did* swallow the liquor . . . and as quickly asked for another.

This, however, was only one of several such memorable events.

Only a couple months before, on a bomb-drop, a "stick" of bombs had hung-up in the bomb-bay. That time I was still flying B-26 Marauders–thank God! (In an A-26, freeing them would have been nigh-on to impossible.)

On my call, our engineer took off his gloves, parachute and oxygen, went back and slid through the door, stepping into the open bomb-bay. Bracing himself against the battering wind (about 50 degrees below zero), he grabbed a hold on freezing aluminum braces. He leaned forward, out over a fourteen-thousand-foot emptiness . . . and kicked loose the reluctant bombs (a whole rack).

My task was easy–I had to keep the plane on an even keel.

Describing it here on the written page, the potentially fatal incident appears run-of-the-mill. It will never be possible to cover, adequately, Sergeant Brow's bravery, his chore's difficulty, or the inherent risks the bombs' hang-up entailed.

Not only could he have died–blown away or falling when his hands slipped–if he had been unable to dislodge the bombs and we took them home with us, we would have endangered not only our plane and crew, but the entire base. The bombs, very likely, would have released as we touched-down on landing, falling onto our closed bomb-bay doors. (They might also have done that during the flight home, loosened by turbulence or flak bursts.)

Though bombs normally did *not* arm themselves until they fell so many feet through the air (usually a small propeller on the nose set the timer and contact fuses), this was not a secure protection. They often exploded on occasion under exactly the circumstances outlined . . . and, sometimes, without anything but vibration.

The havoc such an explosion would have created on the runway would have resulted in multiple deaths, injuries and aircraft accidents–ours and those near our plane.

Hanging, without a parachute (not enough room through the doorway to wear one) in an open bomb-bay, at fourteen thousand feet, also unable to wear an oxygen mask or a safety harness, hands exposed to sub-zero temperatures and grasping freezing metal while buffeted by two-hundred-fifty+ MPH winds, was no picnic. For that risk, Staff Sergeant Brow received a special, well-deserved Air Medal. It did not really compensate, however. Our gracious thanks were profuse and enhanced by gifts of wine and Scotch. (He preferred those, by far, than the medal.)

Those were not all the "sticky-wickets."

When still a newcomer, flying my first sorties as a pilot (no longer a co-pilot), I thought I was "snake-bit."

Flying Martin Marauders at the time from a British airfield not far from London, prior to our move to France, the enemy shot me down each of my first three missions as pilot. We landed in

Brussels, Belgium.

A vicious anti-aircraft battery, a few miles east of Brussels, just within enemy lines, daily demonstrated its gunners' uncanny accuracy. Three return routes in a row placed our path right across that site . . . to my chagrin.

Each time we flew by, they shot out my right engine. Each time we were forced to land at a tiny, British reconnaissance airbase in the center of the city. Each time we were cordially met and hosted by a most gracious British Army colonel.

The second time we so graced his tarmac, he asked us to go elsewhere. "Please," he pleaded, plaintively, "You are depleting my reserves of special rations and single-malt Scotch." But he grinned. This man served in Africa and India; he knew the ropes.

Each time we had to leave our planes and be picked up by couriers. That wee, little field in the center of Brussels was far too small for a B-26 take-off.

The night prior to the last of those three missions, I dreamt I landed there once more. In the morning, after our pre-flight-briefing–when I first saw our programmed return route was the same–and before our take-off, I bought four bottles of Haig and Haig "Pinch" from other pilots. I loaded those, with three cases of C-rations into the engineering compartment.

Wouldn't you know it! While coming home, outside of Brussels, once more they shot my right engine to pieces.

The British colonel expressed his gratitude for our foresight. When my Group picked us up the next day to fly us home, the courier found us well-fed, happy to be alive, and slightly the worst for the scotch the colonel had foisted on us, drink by drink.

Also, during WWII, in snow, rain storms, and poor visibility everyone got lost frequently. Our crew did that as well . . . sometimes even by accident.

On one occasion, with one engine shot out, propeller feathered, I came across another field (only ten miles from our base, but did not know it). I saw it while groping along in a thickening fog and

scud, three hundred feet above the ground.

When I saw the tower pop out of the mist, I made a quick turn and landed. The tower controller thought I wanted solely directions. Due to "radio silence" I had to leave the plane and climb the ladder to explain, "That one engine, if you notice closely, is feathered. Can you get someone to fix it?"

That night my crew and I went back to our Base by truck, to sleep in our own beds. We returned and flew the plane to our Base the next day.

Yet landing at other Bases was always a "drag." For this, we set up a special internal procedure ("internal" to our crew, that is). All we officers (my co-pilot, bombardier/navigator, and I) began carrying spare rank insignia in our pockets. (During our missions we wore none.)

Once I saw the lousy quarters in which they billeted my enlisted crew members, ever afterward–before we landed at a strange base–we shared our officers' insignia. On landing we presented ourselves as five officers – no enlisted men on board. This afforded us *all* the best facilities available (and they were bad enough). This system would have worked just as well behind enemy lines.

We pulled this little stunt five times before someone questioned me, as the aircraft commander. I squeaked through with a haughty stare and firm lips. But, honoring The Officer's Code ("We do not lie, cheat or steal, nor tolerate those who do"), I said nothing. It worked!

This revealed another facet of my up-to-now concealed personality, perhaps this was a "stain" besmirching my record. I believed in cutting corners for the benefit of the war effort, my crew, and our mission.

Even as a colonel and Defense Attaché during two tours, later, in Africa (I was the first Air Force officer ever given two Defense Attaché assignments; but others followed), I applied the same principles and techniques. For example, out of the millions the

government gave us to run our embassy detachment (for salaries, housing, aircraft fuel, aircraft maintenance, and personnel housing, etc.), each fund narrowly delimited its potential use. This permitted no money to be shifted from one project to another. (Lest someone steal some, I guess.)

Yet, I had a number of houses and offices demanding continuing air-conditioning in the daily, one-hundred-ten- to one-hundred-thirty-degree heat. If my staff (and their families) were to get any rest, be ready to fly, and perform as required, the A/C units in their homes and in our offices (windowless for security purposes) had to run the clock-around. Unfortunately, when our A/C units failed, there were neither spare parts nor qualified A/C specialists available to repair them. Yet, though we had *no money* allocated to buy *new units*, we had *plenty for repairs.* (Odd state of affairs, but usual.)

You got it, I'm sure. I literally "repaired" the very devil out of those units, and had all new A/Cs when we needed them. This, of course, was a no-no.

Again, in Fort Lamy, Chad, I arrived on station to find my most valuable NCO, Master Sergeant Alvin Batman, my administrative sergeant major, living in an old, adobe-type house by the Chari River. Mambas, Gaboon vipers, and scorpions, big enough to challenge the snakes, daily invaded his home. (These scorpions were the most dangerous–eight inches in length and longer, and jet black!)

In a violation of administrative policy, I moved Al (an enlisted NCO) at once into my assigned home (solely for officers, with the swimming pool). My wife and I took the former administrative officer's house (bigger, anyway, with more bedrooms) only three hundred feet away. I continued this arrangement until chastised by my general (back in the USA), then I went on doing it the few remaining weeks until Al completed his tour of duty and returned to the States.

Was I wrong in these instances? Yes–technically. But as an

isolated commander General Lemay expected me to demonstrate ingenuity. And I did–maintaining a happier work force and increasing efficiency, while I eased my staff and their families' living problems in a very hot, semi-hostile foreign country, 7,000 miles from home.

Would I do it again? Absolutely! Without batting an eye lash!

<div align="center">* * *</div>

With Dad dead only three months, World War II's beginning on December 7, 1941 changed everything for Mom and me. To increase our incomes and shift into constructive work for the war effort, Mom and I sold out in Columbus and returned to Piqua. There, we took jobs at Bill Lear's "Lear-Avia." (Yes, the same "Bill Lear" who built the "Lear Jet" and the steam-auto developed at Reno, Nevada.)

Even though I was barely nineteen, Bill gave me the dual-foreman's job over the "Inspection" and "Receiving Departments." In addition he urged me to help with his drafting tasks. Thus I was at his elbow when Bill invented the wire-recorder[20] (he sold it to Bendix), improved his teardrop-shaped, radio-direction-finder for aircraft, and miniaturized his already, highly effective, hydraulic-screw mechanisms for lowering and raising airplane flaps, badly needed by the Navy and Army Air Corps. (I did some of the drawings for him.)

Bill liked my work, and we became close friends. He regularly took me on flights from the Vandalia Airport in his modified "stagger-wing Beechcraft," often letting me fly. But the aircraft

[20] My drafting table sat immediately behind the chief draftsman's. Bill came in one morning and stopped at his table to tell him, "I had a great idea this morning on the way to work – a method for recording sound on wire. Here, take this down and 'bread-board' it for me." Bill proceeded to lay-out every part from the input to the audio output. The next morning he stopped by again. "Get that recorder done?" The draftsman laid a wooden tray in front of him and said, "It didn't work." Bill examined the schematic drawing the man had made from Bill's description and pointed, "Decrease that resistor from sixteen to eight ohms and it'll work." The engineers did . . . and we had our first functioning wire recorder. (Now *that* is genius!)

was so loaded down with direction-finders, Bill had to install a larger engine. Still the FFA limited the aircraft to two people.

As another aside, Bill married the daughter of a famous stage comedian, Olsen, of "Olsen and Johnson." Bill's wife gave Bill two children while in Piqua. These gave him his most outrageous chances to demonstrate his well-known, "odd-ball" humor.

Their first child–a girl–he named, "Crystal Shanda." Her name thus became *"Crystal Chanda Lear."*

Bill's argument? "Aw, that's not so bad. She'll get married and it will be something else, like 'Crystal Chanda *Brown.'"*

Then they had a boy.

This child, Bill named, *"Cava Lear."* The poor schmuck was stuck with that moniker all his life. (He later raced modified F-51s in several Cleveland Air Races . . . before the FAA put an end to the races as too dangerous.)

While at Lear's, I met a girl (again) who gave my life a new direction.

I hired this sexy, little gal (Ilogene Catherine Mays) as one of my five secretaries, to replace an older woman promoted to work for Bill's purchasing agent. Though, at the time, Ilogene was engaged–to an Army sergeant in training to go overseas–in my egocentric assurance I *thought my charm convinced her to dump him and marry me.*

I had gone to school with Ilogene in the eighth grade (when she thought me a "sissy" and I thought her a "Dumb Dora"). This time, though, everything clicked.

Ilogene, however, made up her mind before I did. She went home after her first day at the office and told her parents, "I just met the man I'm going to marry!"

On their question, "But what about . . . ?"

She answered, "Nah! I'm returning his ring." (And she did!)

(I *did* feel bad about her sending him that "Dear John" letter, though–for about ten seconds. No, it wasn't quite that long . . . only two!)

Six weeks later Ilogene and I eloped. With two friends (Jack and Pat Jenkins, married only two weeks themselves), we drove to, and were married at, a pretty little Methodist Church in Maysville, Kentucky, just across the Ohio River. (Ilogene wanted to be married there as the city was named for one of Ilogene's relatives, Major Marion Mays.[21])

Despite the many warnings from friends, we made liars of them all:

"It won't work," they said, "you're too young!" (We were nineteen.)

"It'll never last!" (We were married fifty-five and a half wonderful, happy years until her unexpected death, 0927 hours, 1 January 1998.)

"Marry fast and repent at leisure!" (We *did* have a few narrow squeaks–"loud discussions"–but our abiding love won out.)

Our lengthy, and unusually happy, married life disproved all our critics' warnings and clichés. Among my most heart-rending regrets–something I could do nothing about–was her sudden, unexpected and, to me, "early death" from a brain aneurism at seventy-six.

Marriage, though, changed my life style. Now I had a wife to support.

Then Bill Lear's superintendent refused to give Ilogene the standard, universal pay raise for all employees at the end of her probationary ninety days. He claimed my request to raise her pay exhibited favoritism, "As she is now married to 'the boss.'"

I climbed on my high horse and we both quit. (Too proud to use my relationship with Bill to exert pressure on his superintendent.)

Going to work the following Monday as an Army-Air Corps Inspector at Wright-Patterson Air Base, near Dayton, I tried

[21] Its only other claim to fame is Rosemary Clooney, remembered for her role in "White Christmas" and TV signature song "Come on a My House," who was born nearby (1928) and buried there (2002).

joining the Navy for pilot training. But, in spite of their posters proclaiming, "Fly with the Navy, married or unmarried," only the *unmarried* went to pilot school and became officers. The Navy offered the *married* solely NCO-aircrew slots. (I wanted to be a pilot and an officer.)

I, therefore, turned my back on the Navy and signed on as an Aviation Cadet with the US Army Air Corps. For a few months, while awaiting my call to active duty (in October 1942), I took a temporary job as an inspector, right there in Piqua, with Robbins and Myers, making Norden bombsights. (All this was hush-hush, of course. I could not even tell Ilogene what we were building . . . and I didn't.)

Those jobs–at LearAvia, the air base, and Robbins and Myers – started my "Top Secret" (and much higher) security clearances. Later, those clearances assured my receiving some cushy assignments: as a general's aide, as head of the Air Force's cryptographic school, and my two African assignments as a Defense Attaché.

Soon after I joined Robbins and Myers, Bill Lear called and pleaded for me to, "Come back to my shop across town, we need you." Regretfully, I told him, "Sorry, Bill. I've already enlisted in the Army as an Aviation Cadet and will be leaving any day now." We remained friends, though, till he dropped dead of a heart attack from overwork and stress. Bill, one of the "great ones," died with his boots on.

My flight training, during the hectic forties after Pearl Harbor, was a hassle. Flying schedules called for us to be on the flight line, flying aircraft simulators, or flying in the air, night and day. The Army pushed us to get the maximum number of hours in a minimum amount of days.

This restricted my time with Ilogene. And now we had daughter, Melodie Mae. In Brady, Texas, for both Primary and Basic Flying Training, base schedules seldom offered any chance to go beyond the scope of regular cadet activities. Yet I found

ways.

2nd Lt. Rodney L. Cron, Ilogene and Melodie
(March 1944, on graduation leave,
Piqua, Ohio)

Though only a lowly flying cadet–one among hundreds–I took over and directed the Base's Drum and Bugle Corps, organized a dance band, and sang at two local churches–to earn money to buy food for Ilogene and Melodie. I obtained instruments for the dance band from the local high school music director. This and my other music chores, gave me access to a government vehicle and some extra time off-base. (Ilogene, meanwhile, often lived on an apple a day–not telling me–while I stuffed myself at the Air Base.)

Discovering our dependants' hardships, the base's owner opened his mess hall doors to our families. Also, each month, he generously split his income from the government for the base's rental (less expenses), with the cadets.

As a result I hated to leave Brady. But I had to go on to Advance Flying School at Pampa, Texas, and graduate.

There I had three choices:

(#1) Ask to stay on at Pampa as an instructor. (Some of the

older ones were leaving for combat. And I had both the flying time and references needed.)

(#2) Try for an assignment as a fighter pilot. (or)

(#3) Sign up for one of the bomber pilot slots.

As all pilots do, I thought I was a real "hot rock." I had recorded more flying hours than anyone in our class because I flew a lot of extra time with my instructor between Primary and Basic (in the venerable BT-15s, the fixed-gear, rattle-traps we called "Maytag Messerschmidts"), while helping him practice instrument training.

I had flown under bridges, then looped around bridges[22]. I had engaged in repeated "dog-fights," though I was shocked out of my wits by "hammer-head" stalls while chasing other cadet trainees. I had hedge-hopped so low I frequently brought back grass, brush and leaves in my engine nacelles.

"Certainly," I assured the board, visualizing my wearing a white scarf, the top button of my blouse undone, and flying one of those souped-up, twin-engine, twin-tailed P-38s, "I have the makings of a fighter pilot . . ."(Of course, I skipped my seamier exploits and stressed only those that might "sell" me.)

My instructors resolved one of three decisions right off, "For you, Rod, married with a child, *flying fighters is out!*[23] *We want reckless, single men.*"

That narrowed it to bombers or instruction.

The base hierarchy then cooled the instructor deal further when they added, "Rod, you *may not* be a *great* pilot–yet–but you're a good, steady pilot . . . the safest we've seen."

[22] See Addenda for details of how this was done.

[23] I never had a chance at the P-38 I joined the service to fly. The only fighters I flew were a Navy F4F and a German ME-109. The first, in 1944, when at Barksdale AFB, Louisiana, a Navy friend, ferrying the F4F, let me take it for a spin around the traffic pattern. I flew the German ME-109 when we found it intact at the end of the war, needing only fuel. Both gave me exactly the thrill I anticipated I might have in a fighter . . . like "strapping my fanny to a bullet."

This sounded to me like the "big let-down."

It was! The next day I received my orders and the Army assigned me as a co-pilot, after a thirty-day graduation leave, to combat training in B-26s (Martin Marauders). Destination: Barksdale AFB, Shreveport, Louisiana, then overseas.

As a result, I was at Barksdale on D-Day and hated it. Since I was going into combat, I had yearned to be a part of the "Big Show." I didn't make it.

Following my graduation at Pampa (now a second lieutenant and proudly wearing the silver wings of a pilot), I, along with Ilogene and Melodie, took a train home (from Texas to Piqua, Ohio). Then Ilogene returned with me to the new base at Shreveport, but stayed only a few weeks. She already was carrying Rodney Leonard Cron III, who became our Number One son (born on November 9, 1944, while I was flying combat in Europe).

At Barksdale AFB, as a co-pilot just out of flight school and a newcomer to the B-26, I had to learn (quickly) the entire plane inside and out. Not only to fly it, but also all its systems, electrical, hydraulic and mechanical.

Jack Brown, my pilot, was a funny, lackadaisical, dyed-in-the-wool southerner from Richmond, Virginia. He had gone to VMI and trained in B-26's at Tampa, Florida, where the watch-phrase was, "One-a-day into the bay!" We called those short-winged B-26As we flew both "Widow-makers" (because, if an engine so much as coughed on take-off, "That's all she wrote") and "Baltimore Prostitutes" (because their short wings confirmed their having "no visible means of support").

I lived in awe of Jack's suave, urban mannerisms, his experiences at school and his greater hours in the B-26s[24]. Though

[24] Flying the B-26 and A-26 (the Douglas Invader, which I flew later in WWII), prepared me for flying jets in the 50s through 70s. Both 26 types had easy stalling characteristics, high landing speeds (170+), sensitive controls, and the Marauder's inherent instability taught me to think ahead of the aircraft and stay on my

slightly aloof, he appeared to be a good pilot.

Lucky in the extreme–or we said our prayers right, often and fervent enough–we squeaked through our training and qualification boards. When finished, the Army shipped us, as naive aircrews, to the ETO (European Theater of Operations).

The five-day, uncomfortable trip over on the Queen Elizabeth, crowded twelve to a tiny cabin with only sea water to bath in, is best remembered for my having met the sister of a fellow cadet, Julie Cummings. She sang with a USO troop. The moment I heard her sing, I dashed to the stage. "You're Julie Cummings, Shepherd Cummings's sister!" (He and I had been flying classmates.)

She smiled. "Yep, and I'll bet you're Rod Cron, the baritone."

For the remainder of the voyage we sang jointly with the USO troop, rehearsing daily in the lounge and giving nightly shows for the massed soldiers. But, from the time we landed in Liverpool, I never again saw or talked with Julie, though her brother and I both worked (from 1960 to 1963) in the Inspector General's Office, Norton AFB, California–he in flying safety, I in management inspection.

Going overseas as a copilot, I soon advanced to pilot. This involved another rare happenstance.

On one of our early missions, while flying between clouds at high altitude, we were on Colonel Williams's right wing. At the time I was doing the formation flying, eyeing the colonel's lead aircraft from across the cockpit, when we passed through a moisture-laden cloud. We instantly iced up. Wings, props and fuselage over-loaded.

The plane stalled.

Instead of letting me make an easy, smooth recovery with two fast moves, the pilot grabbed the controls and sucked them against his stomach. The plane rolled, flipped and spun . . . out of

toes–always a requirement for piloting a jet.

control. Jack refused to relinquish the controls or counter the spin. I begged, but no dice!

Realizing he was scared into paralysis, I reached up and removed the small fire extinguisher on the bulkhead above me. Making one final futile request, I lifted his flak helmet and hit him across the forehead, then shoved him back, helped by the engineer.

At the same time I jerked closed the throttles, dropped some flaps, and advanced the props to slow us. (Mighty hard to do, while also holding the pilot until Brow strapped him in.)

It took several turns to stop the spin and we were still diving. The airspeed went beyond the red line (somewhere over 450 mph, maybe more). I envisioned our wings tearing off any moment, but they held.

Ringing the alarm bell for everyone to bail out, I continued the plane's recovery. As soon as possible, I jerked the ball on the piano-wire cable designed to blast open the bomb doors with compressed air and toss-out our bombs. The ball broke off in my hand. (The 2500-lb.-test wire snapped as if it were rotten string!)

Easing up the nose, very gently to protect the wing structures as best I could, we came flashing out of the clouds between two hills just before we leveled.

Using the plane's huge momentum, we reversed direction. Shooting back, upward into the overcast, we climbed almost as fast as we had dived. When we popped out of the top of the clouds like one of the rocket planes, I added power and chased our squadron. (We were not about to remain alone in enemy territory, if I could help it!)

Within miles we resumed our place in formation. It was even necessary to slow down to make the join-up.

Checking with the crew, they astounded me—they were all still in place. I asked, "Why didn't you bail on the signal?"

One and all replied, "We couldn't. First, we couldn't peel ourselves off the sides during the spin. Then, we were squashed to

the floor in the dive and pull out."

The engineer placed our unconscious pilot on the floor in the engineer's compartment. The medics took over on landing.

I intended to say nothing, but the crew and medics reported the incident. The Intelligence Officer took down our stories and said nothing either. I did not know what to expect: *Reprimand? Court-martial? Dismissal? Permanent grounding?*

The next morning, Colonel Williams drove out to our squadron and talked with my commander while I shivered in my boots. They then called me in and the colonel shook my hand. "As of now, Cron, you are no longer a co-pilot, but a *full first pilot and I am promoting you to first lieutenant.* You will have your own crew starting tomorrow." (Wonderful words . . . but that meant a promotion even ahead of my original pilot.)

<p style="text-align:center">* * *</p>

All of which brings us full circle, back to the fateful day of the mission I first described, in France, 13 December 1944. There we stood in the mess hall after that nightmarish mission–my tenth sortie–with all three of our returning aircrews in shock from the raid and the colonel's statements.

Our three crews went as one to the window, sipping now-cold coffee and staring at the rapidly falling snow. Outside, the church and air field gradually vanished under the increasing blizzard-like conditions.

Though mentioned before, this period–while the German's took advantage–set-up another of those once-in-a lifetime experiences for my crew and me. Since this heavy snow fall provided the very cover Hitler's troops, those few weeks ended-up being very memorable.

Our Group officially stayed on the ground for about ten days. The ground-hugging fog, continuing snow, and dearth of available aircraft made group missions impossible. At the end of this delay, our engineers cleared the single air strip, but only a single aircraft managed to get off on Christmas Eve morning . . . mine.

For some unknown reason[25] the colonel chose me to fly our major Red Cross nurse (everyone suspected she was the colonel's "main squeeze") to London, England, to shop. She wanted to buy Christmas presents for the men. (Really, for just him and his staff.)

The offer appealed to my crew. We all shared visions of a day free of our dreary quarters (in a partially destroyed German hospital). Becoming "stir-crazy, we hated the mile-long trudge–each way–three times a day, through knee-deep snow, and eating in the drab mess hall, with its ersatz food and worse surroundings (an old, modified barn, across from the Catholic church). Facing that, each of them eagerly volunteered to brave the lousy flying conditions just to make the trip.

Though we executed a zero-zero take-off and a difficult landing in London rain, the trek offered an unexpected consolation. While we waited in Operations at the London airport for the Red Cross nurse to return from her buying spree, we met Major Glenn Miller and his entire orchestra. They were preparing to leave for the continent as well.

After a while, the famous band leader waved off his crew. They climbed into a C-47 with their instruments and headed for Paris. Every fence post already boasted circulars announcing their Christmas-Eve Concert, later that night, scheduled for broadcast to the US troops, worldwide.

Major Miller stayed behind for a brief discussion with a ranking officer from ETO headquarters. He left a couple hours later, alone with a pilot, in a single-engine Norseman. When he finally took off, we all stood on the tarmac and waved "goodbye," not knowing this was the last we–or anyone–would ever see them. (This is portrayed differently in the movie about his life. We, however, were *there*.)

[25] I always accredited the colonel's choosing me to two facts: (1) My "safe pilot" record, and (2) the incident for which he earlier made me a pilot and first lieutenant.

A few minutes later, we, too, departed London.

Flying between cloud layers and faster, we caught up with the Norseman when it was only part-way across the English channel. Although we were on a beeline for our airfield's radio beacon, north and east of Paris, Glenn's Norseman was angling even farther toward the north.

We wondered why, but could not question the pilot by radio for we were still under "radio silence" restrictions.

Everyone now knows Glenn Miller, his pilot, and his aircraft were never seen, heard from, or found. The military announced his loss at the special concert broadcast.

Later, I wrote a short fictional account[26] based on this incident. At Doug McCabe's suggestion (Ohio University's curator of Ryan's "The Longest Day" data) I titled it, *"And the Band Played On . . ."* In the story, we fictionalized finding a dying Major Glenn Miller in Holland, protected by a Dutch girl who lost her husband. In the story, respecting her wishes and Glenn's hopeless situation, we never reported the discovery.

On our return from London, the continuing inclement weather forced us to make three tries at the field before we got on the ground. Visibility was less than a quarter-of-a-mile. The five-hundred-foot, variable ceiling and our repeated, haphazard approaches from the field's beacon provided only one vector. The rest was, "By guess and by *God!"*

That day, though, *God* was truly riding in the *pilot's seat — right where He always belongs*–not in the *co-pilot's*. (Despite what General Scott's book title says.)

We did not learn about Miller's vanishing until the evening broadcast. Mourning his loss, we immediately reported what we had seen and surmised. Obviously, nothing came of it.

<p style="text-align:center">* * *</p>

The next day the weather improved. A few of our planes (those

[26] See Addenda for this complete short story.

repaired, crews recovered) returned from the other bases where they landed, plus new additions (planes/people).

Our Group began, at once, making 'round-the-clock, one-hour, low-level bombing missions, nose-to-tail, in support of our Allies a few miles to the north, struggling mightily in the Battle of the Bulge. Often flying three and four sorties a day (sometimes more), only a rare aircraft sustained damage from ground fire. The enemy's air cover appeared almost nonexistent. At last, we controlled the skies.

A few weeks later we moved our group, now flying the faster A-26s (Douglas "Invaders"), to a small, emergency field just outside Maastrich. There we lived in tents. Engineers cut our new field from the thick stand of forests and we flew off PSP (pierced-steel-planking). The PSP, laid flat on the ground, interlocking at the sides, in long, twelve-foot strips, literally chewed-up aircraft tires on every landing.

With planes landing at 160+ mph, the stationary tires hit the eight-inch, circular holes in the planking and their edges sliced the tread away like huge meat grinders. Virtually every landing left behind a spraying trail of flying rubber. Our Group began replacing tires at an unprecedented rate . . . and aircraft tires were already in short supply.

Seeing this, from my first landing I elected to prevent it. On my approach, I held my aircraft about eighteen inches short of the ground and eased my wheels into the tops of the tall grass a few yards short of the runway. This started my wheels turning before they reached the PSP and before touch-down. I did not replace a tire.

Colonel Williams saw what I was doing. He asked me to explain my technique to the group and demonstrate it.

The men then cut our new-tire-need by 96 percent. The colonel also made me Squadron Engineering Officer on the spot and put me in for immediate promotion to captain. (This required 9th AF Hq approval. The war ended; I never got it.)

Our stay among the trees proved to be short-lived, however. While we were there, though, we made the most of our visit. Daily, we sneaked through the forest to the nearest town and gorged ourselves on pastries and ice cream. The Dutch made their delicacies as rich, sweet, attractive and tasty as the French . . . but the area was rampant with tuberculosis. (We did not know that at the time.)

When the Flight Surgeon found out what we were doing, he posted big red notices, forbidding our eating any local foods. Most of us ignored the warnings.

We figured, "If we're going to get it, we already have it by now." We thumbed our noses at the signs and went on.

To stop the practice, Colonel Williams ordered our group back to Cambrai, France. But that's another story . . .

CHAPTER TWO

▲

No matter what official records may show, the war in Europe started running down as early as the end of March, 1945–for the US Army Air Corps. Though the fighting went on for the ground troops to the north and east of us, a number of us pilot types completed our combat tours during March and April. Then we were at loose ends. (Not good for pilots!)

Now flying out of Cambrai (France again), we played horseshoes, went to school, hiked, rode canal boats, and explored the local vicinity, when on the ground. Our squadron lived in town in what had been the city's *Gendarmerie* (police barracks). The Army fed us at a local restaurant (French cooking, um-um-good!), located but two blocks away on the south side of the city's public square. (It also boasted a bar, and its presence caused a few problems.)

Living in the Gendarmerie had its drawbacks (in my opinion–some may not agree).

Three of us officers, assigned a back room on the ground floor in the rear, shared one window, situated between two of our cots. The third officer's cot lay against the opposite wall beside the door.

One night, this arrangement proved to be a source of embarrassment (at least to me). That night the moon was full. The officer's cot, sitting against the opposite wall, lay fully revealed–spotlighted by the moonshine through the window.

The officer climbed in through our open window well after midnight. (He must have assumed we were asleep, or did not care.) From behind him he helped over the sill a slim, French girl

43

and proceeded to undress her at the foot of our beds in the bright moonlight.

I coughed. Now realizing we were awake, instead of stopping the officer deliberately turned the girl around in the light to display her charms, meanwhile talking to us as if admiring her, "I had no place to take her, guys, so keep quiet and I'll give you an eyeful. She speaks no English."

He proceeded to lay her on his bed and they "had at it," to the tune of five minutes filled with sighs, groans and finally screeches. I never believed sex was a spectator sport, and this was the first–and only–time I ever saw this type spectacle.

In the morning, I told the officer not to do it again or I'd "blow the whistle," whether it shamed him and the girl or not. He never did. But our third roommate enjoyed the show and called me a "Party Pooper."

Cambrai's "Town Mayor," a military post held by a US Army major assigned to the duty, lived in a sumptuous home one block north of the central square. He entertained the local constabulary and the Air Corps officers, every Sunday afternoon. He also had a live-in mistress–French, of course. A lovely girl, I met her again a few months later in the States when I was mustering out, at Wright-Patterson AFB, Dayton, Ohio. (She had married an Air Corps first lieutenant right after we left Cambrai. Very likely he served merely as her "ticket to the USA.")

Remember the comment about, "When pilots' did not have anything to do it was not good?" Here's where it showed up.

While at Cambrai and no longer flying missions, our Group daily patrolled the Rhine (our planes still loaded with ammunition and weapons, but no bombs), playing "air tag," and chasing each other and P-51s. (See next page). We hedge-hopped over hills, up and down the Rhine river as if we were cadets again, and flew into, over and around Paris. (Some of us did stupid things, like flying under the Eiffel Tower. Some got caught and court-

martialed. Others were luckier.[27])

During this period, a few of us did more stupid things as well:

For one, three of us, while patrolling the Rhine one morning and flying a "follow-the-leader" game, popped-up over a hill and overflew four German farmers loading a hay rick. The farmer on top of the load threw his pitch fork at our lead aircraft . . . and the fork almost hit the next one.

The leader saw it and could not let that pass. He turned on a dime and aimed directly at the side of the hay rick, pulling up only at the last second. The rear of his airplane skidded forward, momentarily, and slammed the side of the hay rick.

The horses, farmers and wagon went rolling down the hill. (The farmers had obviously forgotten they were still "the enemy.") Though the US Army did not tolerate such aggressive moves, we would have done nothing if the farmer had not thrown the pitch fork. I seriously doubt the German farmer lived through the incident.

Also, every day we flew the Rhine in our A-26s, a P-51 pilot came by and "bugged" us. He flew up from behind, took a position just off to one side, thumbed his nose at us, then added full power and streaked away in a cloud of smoke.

Finally, sick and tired of his insolence, I asked the colonel if I might use his ship to shake-up this guy. He said, "Sure, Rod, give 'im hell!"

So we stripped the colonel's plane of every unnecessary part (guns, ammo, bomb racks, internal equipment, etc.). We then countersank every rivet and screw, washed, waxed and polished the entire aircraft, filled its engines' water injection systems. We also reduced the fuel load to the minimum I believed needed to do what I had in mind.

Sure enough! The P-51 pilot edged up beside me while I was flying along at about 250 MPH. When he lifted his hand to give

[27] See Addenda ("Flying Under the Eiffel Tower").

me the old "finger wave," I shoved the props, throttles and mixtures full forward, kicked-in the water injection system, and slowly eased back on the props. I left him behind when I reached 413 MPH. Though only a few MPH faster than his capability going straight and level, I caught him completely flat-footed. He never "bugged" any of us again,

Colonel Williams[28], suspecting I might have been the brazen young pilot (*moi?*) who flew an A-26 under the Eiffel Tower and got away with it, assigned my crew and me a small vehicle. He then gave us orders to drive to the front lines and "liaison" with an Army brigadier general for a few weeks. (I always thought he wanted to get me out of his hair and let things cool off a bit. His decision may have been my salvation.)

We loaded our stuff and took off the next morning. The roads we drove over, at first rough as the proverbial cob, were mere mud-hardened paths created by the tanks and supply trucks. Each one was heavily rutted and pock-marked by shell and bomb craters. The few good highways drew us like food to a hungry dog.

The trip to the still-fighting front lines took us eastward through Cologne and across our Army's pontoon bridge there (where we had earlier taken down the original without hitting the cathedral). We then drove on those magnificent autobahns to the Magdeburg area.

Our liaison stint–that we thought would be such a blast–turned out to be both heart-breaking and gut-wrenching. While we were up there with the general and his staff, we were "privileged" to join him in opening atrocity sites at Gardelagen and Dachau, and

[28] After the war, Colonel Williams received an assignment as Air Force Attaché to a South American country. On returning from a trip with his entire family aboard, he crashed when he ran out of gas over the mountains–having flown seven hours and fifty minutes in a C-47. Everyone on the plane was killed. It was days before searchers found the wreckage strewn along a remote peak. I and others mourned his loss.

several dreary POW camps.

The Gardelagen site consisted of a barn on top of a small grassy hill only three miles from town, and behind it, two, one-hundred-foot-long, five-foot-wide, eight-foot-deep pits. Burned bodies filled the pits to overflowing, now largely ash sprinkled with lime. The bodies once had been Allied military and a host of unknown civilians, some identifiable solely by the remnants of uniform insignia, others by their burned clothing.

Opening the large, side-door to the barn, we found the interior still crammed with burned bodies, now only white ash. I was standing but a few feet behind the Time Magazine's photographer who snapped the first pix with his camera.

That picture made the front page of Time and was seen world-wide: a kneeling officer, head bowed to the inevitable. From that angle nothing but the white ash of his body showed against a black background. Beyond, among the shadows, we found dozens more incinerated airmen and soldiers, and even more unidentifiable civilians, whom we guessed had been slave laborers from the local villages and factories.

The general asked me to go into Gardelagen and bring back the Town Mayor (Burgermeister). I located him hiding in his home.

I brought him back at gun-point. My hand, holding my .45 automatic, shook so much from emotional trauma I feared I might lose control. For the first time in my life–and it may have been the only time–I was so enraged I wanted nothing more than to plunge the snout of my handgun deep into his big, fat gut and empty the clip.

The general, therewith, charged the town leader and his city with "Eternal care of the site and all its victims." He also insisted every able-bodied Magdeburg citizen come out, help dig up each body, prepare and bury it with the utmost consideration, then create and maintain a perpetual shrine at the site.

When I returned the German to his home, a young boy ran up to my side. In halting English he informed me, "That 'Nazi

bastard,' he has a Mercedes stashed in the barn behind his house."

Urging the reluctant Burgermeister into his barn with my .45, I demanded he personally pick up a pitchfork and remove the hay from the huge pile in the center of the floor. His abject pleas went ignored.

Soon, a beautiful, black Mercedes convertible with a white linen top emerged from under the haystack. I insisted on the keys. My crew and I then used the German's own cache of oil and gasoline to drive it to the nearest military base. There, I insisted they paint it olive drab while I typed-up a sheaf of orders, using my serial number. We also placed my serial number on the hood and bumpers, and added military designations, copying those on our vehicle from our Group's motor pool. (When we left the front lines, we drove the Mercedes back to our home base and gave it to our squadron commander.)

Our front-line excursions also took us to several Allied military prisons, where we removed hundreds of emaciated, mere skin-on-bones, POWs. We then released several hundred Jewish, Polish and Gypsy slave girls found nearby, freeing them from their German-enforced lives of prostitution.

The girls, assuming we, as conquerors, would simply use them like the Germans did, had to be convinced we had no such intent. We assured them, repeatedly, and demonstrated this, providing "without any ties" meals, clothes and considerate medical help. Only then did they begin to understand we were *not* there to abuse them further. We wanted solely to free them, feed them, care for them, and send them back to their homes.

The most heart-rending cry came from a young, former native of Krakow, Poland. She lamented, "But we have no homes, now, to go back to."

Another little, dark-haired, wasted-away Jewish girl, no more than sixteen, but already looking thirty, pleaded for us to take her along and use her any way we wanted . . . just so long as we gave her food, companionship and a place to sleep. Her–and the

48

others'—cries were pitiful as we departed.

Though we left behind piles of food and clothing, and places for them to live for the time being, the memory stayed with us. Worse was the feeling of helplessness from our inability to do more. Like those memories of the POW camps and the atrocities at Dachau we carry forever these as indelible nightmares inscribed on our minds.

In Dachau, we found masses of human bodies—old and young, men, women and children—stacked like cord wood outside the ovens. That find, alone, forever made false anyone's insane claims that, "There was no Holocaust." Those of us who were there can attest with heart-breaking conviction and experience, that, "We know differently. We saw it. We smelled it. We tasted the acrid film of all those deaths on our tongues, and felt the dry, cold skin of their decaying flesh. We carried out the hundreds of bodies. We helped bury the men, women and children still lying there, waiting to be baked, minus fingers where rings had been removed and missing teeth once containing gold.[29]

The former POWs we released, equally a sad lot, seldom weighed a hundred pounds each. With little to no food for themselves, the German guards, of course, had none for prisoners.

We carried-out stretcher after stretcher filled with the few still-living POWs who remained, most unable to walk. Tenderly we loaded those who had survived the ordeal into the waiting, make-shift ambulances—mere trucks with shelves for the stretchers.

Many of those who lived, spent the rest of their lives fighting the extensive and remorseless, physical and mental aftermath of their prolonged incarceration, torture and starvation. But a large

[29] *But what, I wondered, will happen when we too are gone? Who will attest to these horrors, then? Who will defend the weak, help the helpless? Who will feed the hungry? And who will lift up the down-trodden? Will there be any "Good Samaritans" . . . or will the entire world continue to pass by on the other side of the street . . . until it's too late—as too many of us did before WWII?*

number did not even endure the short truck ride to the nearest military hospital. Though medics gave them intravenous fluids and nutrition en route, administering as best they could to their needs, only about one in three made it.

One of those weak, near-dying prisoners whom I carried from a POW facility, was a French major, Jacques Hascöet. By another unusual happenstance, I served with him again in Africa, twenty-three-years later, when we were both colonels. He was then the French military assistant to the Chadian President, and I was the US Defense Attaché to Chad. (This story is included in a later chapter.)

R to L: Colonel Jacques H. Hascöet (Ret.);
Ilogene Cron, Suzanne Hascöet, Colonel Cron.
(US Military Cemetery, Normandy, France, 1978)

CHAPTER THREE

▲

In the front lines, even my aircrew got on my nerves.

After what we saw at Gardelagen and Dachau, I grew so unstrung I nightly tramped the streets of the small German village in which we were staying, trying to recover my mental equilibrium. *How*, I asked myself, *can anyone be so cruel?* It took hard work to regain a positive perspective about mankind. When depressed too much, I cried. It required miles of walking and praying . . . and hours of introspection.

One night, when we were billeted upstairs in a tiny, two bedroom house owned by an aging German couple (who might have been our own grandparents), my men went exploring while I was out. They found a wall of shelves in the basement loaded with food-stuffs from their garden: home-canned beans, potatoes, cabbage, kraut, etc. Another wall held a few carefully preserved, glass-enclosed, canned chickens. With the desperate situation anticipated for the remainder of the year, this was very likely the only food this couple could count on to keep them alive during the coming winter.

My men were gleefully removing the cans, about to destroy the entire cache, when I walked in. Irate, I scolded them for their lack of foresight, humanity and commiseration. Not much younger than I, they apologized and replaced the plunder.

Throughout the rest of our trip–other than their "acquiring" examples of German weaponry, daggers and insignia–I endorsed only one spoils-of-war retrieval. When they discovered a set of brand-new, artist's pastels in another house, I let them draw lots to

51

see who, among them, would take the collection home intact . . . *providing* they in turn promised *not* to vandalize anything else they discovered.

To my knowledge, they stuck to their word. (Yet I often worried about that old German couple in their little house back there in that tiny village. *Did they survive the winter? Did other Allied soldiers destroy their hard-earned food cache?* I'll never know.)

<p align="center">* * *</p>

When describing wartime actions and events, it is difficult *not* to dwell on the bad, the worst, and the depraved. Death, injury, illness and perversity lay to every side.

Yet, even at the worst of times, we found time for humor and joy, hope and love. All one had to do was look for it. I tried.

Though a Methodist, I directed the Catholic choir made-up of airmen from our Group and sang the solos in the Masses and oratorios, as well as the responses to the priest. (See next page.)

Father John Graff later became a colonel as the number two man in the Air Force chaplaincy. (The number one spot rates a two-star position.) John let me sit in on instructions to new Catholics. Afterward we talked, played cribbage by the hour, and sipped select, French wines.

Occasionally, in my naivete, I interrupted Father Graff's instructions to ask some very stupid religious questions. These prompted lengthy debates–after the priest's new people went back to their quarters. He, however, was always kind and generous, allowing me to broach fairly heretical and caustically searching arguments (at least from a Catholic's viewpoint).

I was intrigued–still am–by different perspectives and how each religion sees its path to God, compared to others'.

In keeping with this, recent changes in Catholic dogma made me yearn to consult John Graff again. I would like to know what he thought about scrapping all those long-worshiped saints a few years ago. I also would like to hear his explanation for "dumping"

Purgatory. Those once-central parts of their centuries-old tenets, are gone.

Our WWII Catholic choir, Royé, France.
Father John Graff is to my left, in a dark robe,
I am centered.

We sang a special mass on Christmas Eve, and
again on Easter, Notre Dame Cathedral,
Paris, France.

In this regard, I have earned a reputation–not always good– for being a critic, voicing my questions and doubts. Too often, these make me appear negative, when I simply want to know.

For example, all churches are changing. Society's shifts, economics and rising costs have closed churches, forced consolidations, and caused delays in planned new structures.

Congregations are aging. It is difficult to attract youth . . . and even more difficult to lure them away from their new electronic toys, golf, and their weekend rest.

Foremost, though, I see the Catholic church changing more every day, and with every new pope. Like those with "inquiring minds," I am eager to see what's next–*Ordination of women?*

I heard some nuns tried it a few months ago. They ordained each other under a female "Bishop's" supervision. But the Vatican did not let that "fly."

Yet there is still hope. Someday, the all-male Vatican hierarchy may address the issue of women's ordination with a more positive attitude. Though many "old-liners" will hate it, the action may serve to move the church closer to women's equality. In the process, its actions may have a salutatory effect on their sin-service-areas of priestly sexual misconduct. (A recent thorn in their sides.)

Already, the Pope has dropped Latin and adopted the local language for Masses, which I thought a grave psychological mistake. There was a time when a Catholic could attend Mass in Japan, or elsewhere in strange countries, and participate actively. *Now, he can't. (But I hear this, too, is changing back.)*

The last time I attended Mass, I was lost. With its new English Missal, all that running around down-front, the guitars, zithers, saxophones, country-western-style singing, and jumping-up-and-down music, for a moment I thought I strolled into a "Holy-Roller" service.

Father Graff and I would have a good laugh at my "warped" perspective, as described above, just as we did so often in France.

Yet, all we soldiers looked anywhere and everywhere for humor and laughter.

Probably it is no longer funny, but I will always remember the first story told by Jack Brown at Royé, France. I went into hysterics. Let's see how it affects people now:

"It seems a lion, all 'full of himself,' went charging through the jungle one day, challenging every animal he met.

"He ran up to a zebra, beat himself on the chest, and roared the zebra into a near-panic. Then he asked, 'Why am I so big and

strong . . . and you're so weak and puny?'

"The zebra cowered. 'I don't know, O great Lord of the jungle.' He skittered off into the trees–glad to get away with his life.

"The lion next confronted a wart hog, again beating himself on the chest, roaring, and asking the same question, 'Why am I so big and strong, and you're so weak and puny?'

"The wart hog also bowed before the lion's might, saying, 'I don't know–just don't eat me.' He too slunk away, scared witless.

"The lion continued throughout the jungle, accosting animal after animal, roaring them into a state of shock, and asking the identical question. All gave the same answer, tucked their tails between their legs–those that had tails–and sped off, full speed.

"Disgusted, the lion finally came to a teensy-weensy, itsy-bitsy, skinny mouse and went through the same routine, 'Why am I so big and strong . . . and you're so weak and puny?'

"The little mouse looked up timidly and in a high, thin, squeaky voice said, 'I . . . been . . . s-i-i-i-c-k.'"

I don't know why–maybe I was afraid of imminent death and this gave me a moment's respite–but Jack's joke floored me. Even now, if someone walks up and says in a high, thin, squeaky voice, "I . . . been . . . s-i-i-i-c-k," I erupt into paroxysms of laughter. (Did it do anything for you?)

At Royé, the Group Commander had scattered the other squadrons around the town, often in bombed-out houses and barns. He billeted our squadron in a former hospital, a mile east of town. To get there required our traipsing along a winding dirt road between fields the Germans had planted with cabbage (to make sauerkraut, I presume).

When it was cold and snow covered the ground, we were happy. But when the weather warmed, the rotting cabbage produced a stench best left undescribed. The fields were supposed to be mined, so we were unable to plow-under the rotting vegetables. (In the spring, far too late for us, the engineers found

no mines, anywhere!)

That odor gagged us so much we often foreswore meals to avoid trekking the mile to and from the mess hall. And, if we wanted to eat, we had to do it three times a day. The group provided transportation only when they called us to headquarters for mission briefings, debriefings, or the missions themselves. All other times we walked, trudged, plowed through the snow, skidded on the ice, or kicked pebbles up the gravel before us.

We believed the former Germans had deliberately blown-up their hospital when they left, so we could *not* use it. But they failed to do a good job. Destroying only one wing, the other three wings and one large room, plus a kitchen, some large closets, and several smaller rooms, remained intact . . . or relatively so.

We scrounged steel, double-decker beds and flat, screen-like springs from the hospital wreckage, put our down-filled sleeping bags on rolled-up blankets, and we were in business. Adding a pot-bellied iron stove to each room drove off the chill when the snows came, and we took turns keeping the fire going and fuel stacked nearby.

When we needed ice for our drinks, we went outside and scooped up the freshly-fallen snow. There were so few operating stoves in the vicinity the snow was pristine.

A group of us dug a latrine behind the building on the north side (the approaching road came in on the south) and built an old style "Chick Sale, four-holer," over the pit. This became a source of amusement and embarrassment when French girls from nearby farms (who washed and ironed our uniforms for a pack of cigarettes, a bar of chocolate, and some cakes of bath soap) began to use the latrine too.

One night, I was hunkered there in the dark and cold, when my laundress flew through the outhouse door, flipped up her skirts, dropped down beside me, and began grunting right along with me. I immediately lost all capability, grabbed up my trousers, and hurried back inside.

Much more of that, I reasoned, *and I'll be suffering from the world's worst case of constipation.*

My fellow pilots, finding out I was a prude, elected to "get me." Soon thereafter, when my laundress brought back our laundry and the guys knew I was sleeping nude, they unzipped my sleeping bag. Quietly, they stuck the girl inside with me–stripped naked–then zippered my bag closed and locked it, so I could not open it from inside.

After I begged for an hour, they finally released us. But I had to wash my sleeping bag lining at once, and hang both my lining and bag outside in the open air to cleanse them. (I don't believe that poor girl had taken a bath since the beginning of the war! Maybe not then.)

Our next project was bringing showers and water inside for shaving and bathing in our hospital quarters. We selected a small room, one of those former, large closets, removed the shelves, and made shower heads from sprinkling cans.

We "borrowed" two large, 250-gallon tip-tanks from our fighter-pilot friends ten miles up the road, put them on the roof, and asked the base engineers to fill them with water every day. After running copper (gasoline) tubing from the tanks to the shower heads and water taps, we had a "going concern." The water might have been cold, but it felt like ambrosia when we took our first baths and shaved without using our helmets.

Even Colonel Williams came out weekly to use our facilities. Within days, we became so popular we had to add two more tip-tanks, and have all four filled twice daily. Then in an enthusiastic burst of youthful fervor, we busted our buns to develop a "flash" heating system with which we surrounded the incoming water line. Now we were in Heaven. (I began to worry the colonel and his staff might "ace" us out of our domicile, but they never did. He still came regularly, though, to use our hot water.)

Another noteworthy benefit derived from our being in combat (if there can be such a thing), every week we received a special

ration from Ninth Air Force headquarters. It cost us, each, two dollars and seventy-five cents. (I never did figure how they arrived at that figure.)

For that paltry sum, they gave us two, one-liter bottles of French wine (one red, one white), six cakes of bath soap, four candy bars, a bottle of outstanding cognac (sometimes eighty-year-old Napoleon brandy and sometimes equally aged Courvoisier VSOP–that's when I learned to like cognac), and a carton of cigarettes.

Not being a smoker or drinker I used my cigarette rations to buy laundry, ironing, eggs and bread (baguettes) from the French. I traded the wine to the other officers for their candy, soap and cigarettes.

Some of the guys used their rations to lure the girls into their beds. Not only was I married and true to my wife, but there was no way in the world I would ever find anyone attractive enough to sleep with who stank so badly . . . and they all did!

This was also true when I was in Korea. I walked down a Korean road one day, south of our Air Base at Kimpo, toward Seoul, to find the rank aroma emanating from the nearby "hooches"(all of a hundred or more feet away) made me instantly sick to my stomach. The stench, a combination of kimshi, the National dish of Korea–consisting of marinated, rotten cabbage, spices and garlic–unwashed body odors, feces and urine would have knocked down a strong mule.

Yet, every week, one of our airmen and, sometimes, even an officer, reported to the Flight Surgeon with something he did not want to take home to his wife and kids. Some got over it; some didn't.

<p style="text-align:center">* * *</p>

After our first weeks in France, since we had done such a good job knocking out bridges and German factories, 9th Air Force selected our group to be the first to go into Paris for a seventy-two-hour pass. We scrambled to get ready.

Like the others, I stoically endured the 75-plus miles of rough roads and pontoon bridges in the back-end of a truck, eager to see Paris on the sky line for the first time. It was all I ever read about it: the "City of Light," the Eiffel Tower, the Arc De Triomph, the Champs Elyseé, wine, women, song . . . and Chanel Number Five to send home.

That night, on the streets of Paris with its streets blacked-out, I quickly found I might close my eyes and still avoid running into any Frenchman, woman or child. I smelled them from twenty-feet away – a mixture of wine, garlic and body odor, covered by strong perfumes and scents. Everyone seemed really "ripe." (I have always had a sensitive sense of smell, often to my dismay.)

After dinner in a French bistro, rabbit and more garlic (which I love), hot French baguettes, sweet butter, cooked vegetables, and even fresh tomatoes, I felt ready to "hit the rack." But my crew would have none of that.

"The colonel's going out to the Rue Pigalle to see the shows at the 'Bal Tabarain' and 'Eve's Club,'" my crew exclaimed, "ya gotta come along."

I did, and proceeded to create a near-international incident.

The show at the "Bal Tabarain" kept us on our toes with fast music, fancy costumes, near-naked girls, first class and high-caliber dancers and singers, and a raunchy comedian who considerately spouted most of his spiel in English. The drinks came rapidly–largely champagne–and the club's prices seemed reasonable.

From there we stumbled a couple blocks in the dark, to the "Eve's Club." Inside the black-out curtains, when my eyes adjusted to the light, I discovered why they called it "Eve's Club." No women working inside–hat-check girls, girls dispensing cigarettes and cigars from a tray before their bare little tummies, waitresses, dancers and singers–wore a stitch of clothing.

The colonel, his staff, my crew and the others quickly found "companions for the night." Declining, I was left to find my way

back to our hotel, downtown–about two miles away–on my own, in a strange, darkened city, in a foreign country, still populated in places by pockets of hiding, vicious and ruthless German troops.

This was not the best prospect to consider at one in the morning.

Outside, I buttoned up my top coat and sighted on the stars, heading–I hoped–toward the "Centre de Ville." Within two blocks I realized I had picked up a tail[30].

To protect myself as best I could, I moved to and strode steadily onward, down the middle of the street. I also took out and cocked my .45, holding it by my side in my right hand. (I had already, before leaving the hotel, jacked a shell into the firing chamber and refilled the clip. I liked having "one up the spout." It afforded me as much fire power as a weapon can give me, when in a jam.) *Now*, I realized, *I'm in a jam!*

Soon the steps behind drew nearer. As, out of the corner of my eyes, I saw approaching darker spots to each side, indicating alleys between buildings, the person behind me whistled. Feet pounded from behind and from the darker areas toward me.

I went to my right knee, fired to my rear, first, as that assailant seemed to be closest, then I shot in rapid-fire toward my right and left. A matter of seconds–and eight shots–later, I was alone on the street and there were five dead men lying around me on the cobblestones.

Thinking I had been attacked by a German patrol, I did not investigate, but trotted all the remaining distance into town, guided solely by starlight and my peripheral vision. Panting, I undressed and climbed into my waiting bed, certain a covey of Gendarmes would be awakening me the next morning with enquiries. *It never happened!*

The next morning, the English version of the Parisian newspaper, "Le Monde," reported "a gang war" right where I had

[30] I heard persistent footsteps and knew someone was following me.

been walking . . . and the "happy elimination of five French footpads whom the city had been seeking for some months for 'rolling' and killing members of the American military . . . and making it appear as if done by Germans."

I was sorry it had not been Germans I killed–as I thought. Still, I breathed a sigh of relief and did not mention the incident to anyone until now. Flying under the Eiffel Tower might be one thing; killing five Frenchmen was another. I preferred not to be associated with either incident. (And I wasn't.)

CHAPTER FOUR

▲

The "footpad" attack made our three-day visit to Paris another milestone in my life. It did not warrant another red mark on my calendar, though–I didn't want anyone asking why! But, for some crewmen, Paris *did* create a red-letter day.

One officer returned to base from our Paris trip with an incurable case of syphilis. It proved so fast-moving he died within weeks, right there on base.

Another officer–and I saw this while in Paris–found a little shop selling Chanel #5. He bought a whole gallon. (Think how much *that* cost!)

Running up the street in celebration, he held the glass jar over his head, shouting, "I got it! I got it! A whole gallon of Chanel #5." Then he tripped on the cobblestones and threw the jar about ten feet.

It smashed to smithereens on the cobblestones, perfuming the thick Parisian air with many hundreds' of dollars . . . maybe thousands' . . . of the most sought-after fragrance in France. The officer sat on the curb and sobbed.

French women gathered around the puddle of liquid like rummies around a whiskey barrel. Squatting down they soaked their skirts in the fluid, then took them home, I am sure, to wring them out and save the expensive distillation they could not afford, for special affairs.

Also certain Parisian landmarks none of us had seen before. Back then, in the forties, "pissoires" dotted most street-corners in Paris and other major French cities.

When a man felt "the urge," he went inside, to be blanked by steel sheathing from knee to chest, while he relieved himself. (The "pissoires" are no longer there today. Paris retains only one as a relic. But, when available, they made for humorous jests and clever remarks.)

Americans, born prudish about necessary bodily functions, hunkered behind the flimsy barriers, red-faced, refusing to acknowledge what they were doing, ashamed when anyone saw them. If someone they knew happened by, they looked down, or the other way, or closed their eyes like a child putting his hands before his face to make others disappear. None of those strategies worked.

Frenchmen, in hats, gloves, spats, canes and ascot ties, stood there in total nonchalance. Smiling at the passing ladies, they occasionally tipped their hats to passing attractive or known faces, remaining utterly at ease.

The best act of this French-type affability I caught on the way into Paris the very first morning. No one ever topped it.

A very distinguished-appearing French gentleman, dapper in a rich brown suit and pencil-thin moustache, a hat, gloves, spats and ascot, carried an ornate, gold cane. He, too, must have suddenly "felt the urge." He stopped, moved to the edge of the sidewalk. Carefully, he removed his right glove and placed his cane very delicately over his left arm. He began urinating into the street, using his bare right hand to guide the stream.

Behind him a lovely young lady approached on the sidewalk. Politely, he turned to her, changed hands, aiming his output to one side with his gloved left . . . and shook her extended hand with his bare right. When she passed, he again turned back to the street.

Once finished, he assiduously tucked himself in, buttoned up, donned his glove, and strolled on. His smug smile while readjusting his hat to a more jaunty angle, made me chuckle and think of Maurice Chevalier. Probably assured, I mused, *"I handled that very well and didn't get any on either of us."* It also

made think of Shakespeare's passage, *"What fools we mortals be . . ."*

During the afternoons in Paris, our aircrews largely chased willing French girls, ate pastries, and drank wine, coffee (terrible) or cognac at the sidewalk cafes. More often the men slept in, readying themselves for another night "on the town."

Jimmy Doolittle–the only other married squadron member true to his wife–and I visited the Eiffel Tower, the department stores, the museums, and the Arc de Triomphe. We tramped along the Champs Elysée and toured Les Invalides, where Napoleon's beautiful maroon, marble sarcophagus is located, as well as the tombs of Marshall Foch and several other French notables.

We too sampled the wines and excellent French cuisine, but generally rubber-necked like typical American tourists. Happy and free-wheeling, the French treated us like the saviors our troops had been. (This was long before "The Ugly American" became our signature title worldwide.)

I also explored a different "Metro" route daily, riding to the very ends of the subway lines. Going to the farthest terminals, I strolled through the seldom-seen outskirts of Paris, far from the tourist traps. There, in small pawn shops, I loaded up, buying scads of unique and practical items to ship home to Ilogene, mother, and my mother-in-law. *No gaudy crud for me*, I vowed. Carefully measuring out my stash of money, I selectively invested in "before-the-war" costume jewelry, unusual serving dishes, soup ladles, tureens and carving-knife sets. They later repaid their purchase price several times over. I was just lucky, I guess. I really did not know what I was doing, but I enjoyed the unexpected.

<div align="center">*　　　*　　　*</div>

The war in Europe finally ended and, soon after VE Day, my crew and five others received orders to fly our planes home (those A-26s, Douglas Invaders). Orders directed us to take them, via a short visit in the USA, around the world to Japan, to help our final

effort there.

The proposed route called for a stop at Marseilles, others at Dakar and the Azores. Then we were to make a long, hair-raising flight across the south Atlantic into Trinidad, go north to Florida and–for me–to Wright-Patterson AFB, Ohio.

By then, I figured I'd be gone thirteen months. (Some men in the Pacific Theater were away seven years!) I yearned to see Ilogene and Melodie. And to see my new son, Rodney III, for the first time.

Our homeward bound take-off from Cambrai, going south, went without a hitch. Climbing to fourteen thousand feet, we assumed a heading to Marseilles, the major port of southern France.

The entire trip, flown between cloud layers or above a thick undercast (a layer of clouds beneath us), masked any possible evaluation of the winds. Without land marks and radio beacons, the navigators bit their nails, trying to calculate where we were.

Finally, when our fuel began running low, my navigator said, "We ought to be over the Mediterranean now, you can start your let-down."

I told him over the interphone, "I like everything you said, but the word 'ought.' Is there a chance we are *not* over the Med?"

His answer came too hesitantly to satisfy me. He said, "Well, sir . . . we . . . er . . . um . . . *should* . . . uh . . . be over the Med. *If* the winds held up, in strength and direction . . . *If* there were no errors in the weatherman's guesses . . . *If* the wind predictions were accurate in the first place . . . and . . ." His voice trailed off as he lost confidence.

Here is where my second paranormal event raised its protective head. I said, "Okay, cross your fingers, Joe, we're going down." I "pulled the plug" to descend, but *something urged me to turn forty-five degrees to the left and hold that heading.*

In thirty-seconds we broke out of the clouds, descending into a valley between two lines of towering Alps, each line vanishing

into the clouds. I yelled, "Gun'er, guys, and hold on."

Leading the flight back to our original flight level, I made a turn to 220 degrees and flew for an hour before letting down once more. This time we were about ten miles off shore from Marseilles.

Unlike my wing men—the five others flying with me—I had visited Marseilles some weeks earlier to see my "third cousin, once removed," Technical Sergeant Rodney J. Slover. I had flown him and his captain around the western Mediterranean. That flight also had been graced by another Gremlin attack—we accidentally flipped over a small sail boat by flying too close, when we were hugging the surface.

Coming in for a landing now, en route to the USA, the gremlins "got me again."

Approaching Marseilles' runway that began two hundred feet out in the clear blue water, I made the mistake of looking down. Instantly, I lost my depth perception and had to make an emergency "go-around." Now, I was the last one on the ground.

Major Stanford ridiculed me. "Tomorrow, *Rod, I* will lead the next leg."

Once more, the following morning, our take-off came early and with no problems. The sun was just clearing the haze to the east.

Major Sanford led us in a quick, joining-up circle. Once we were all in formation, he pointed his nose south again, across the Mediterranean, toward Rabat and Africa.

Flying on his right wing, I saw Major Sanford suddenly lurch forward across his control column. His plane immediately entered a steep dive.

His sergeant reached over, frantically trying to pull Sanford back and bring the plane to level flight. *Too late!* The plane, less than a thousand feet above the water, did not have enough altitude to recover. Sanford's plane and crew hit the surface going more than three hundred mph.

Helpless, I radioed the other crews and took them back to

Marseilles. Once there, I telephoned 9th Air Force headquarters and told them what happened. Meanwhile, search and rescue teams from both sides of the Med crisscrossed the sea over the accident site, looking for survivors. A hopeless task. The plane was too deep. No one exited.

Mourning Major Sanford and our buddies, we waited two days for approval to continue our transatlantic flight and return to the States. Instead, the answering telex ordered us back to Cambrai.

Once again in Cambrai, another directive forced our Group Commander to give our ships to the French. Despite my pleas, they promptly bulldozed them over a nearby cliff into a pile of worthless rubble.

My ship had never been flown by anyone but the original test pilot and me. I would gladly have paid the costs to bring it home . . . but no one offered me the chance.

The next orders we received, cancelled our flying to the States. By truck, train and, finally a Kaiser-built, concrete Liberty ship we were on our way again. This trip did not go smoothly either.

We sat around various shipping points, waiting. To keep up my flying time, I flew a small reconnaissance plane (a Taylorcraft) at a nearby field near the French coast. It took another couple weeks to get us onto a ship.

In mid-ocean, the concrete ship encountered a massive, destructive hurricane. The weather was so bad–(I can imagine someone's shouting, "How b-a-d was it?")–that enormous waves snapped our rudder and the ship's crew had to put out a sea anchor to keep us from turning turtle. An hour later, we had bounced around so much the concrete hull began splitting at the front cargo hold.

Virtually no one felt like eating, except the captain and me. Stuffing down a biscuit filled with sliced ham, he foraged through his less-green-faced members, amassing enough who could still stand, and ordered them to place cables around the two front masts to tie them together . . . and around the raised lip of the hold

to keep the crack from worsening.

The crew, roped together on deck, sick, weak and bleary-eyed, finally got the job done . . . just in time. The hurricane "eye" passed over the ship, and the winds shifted, blowing even more strongly from the other direction.

In this shift, the ship heeled over so far the desk seemed vertical. For seconds, decks awash in monstrous waves, the ship became more submarine than surface vessel. (My son, a Navy submariner, told me it is not unusual in the North Atlantic to experience waves two-hundred-feet high, and sometimes higher. I believe we exceeded that range,)

The captain assured me, "The repairs should now keep us afloat until we get through the worst of this." (He and my navigator would have made a good pair, with their not-so-confident "ought-to's," "if's," "maybe's" and "should's.")

What happened? I wondered, *to those cheery words, "Everything's okay now . . . we'll soon be home, all safe and sound."*

As a result of the increasing tension, neither the captain nor I slept until the next day . . . and we did not breathe any sighs until two tugs came out and hauled us into Hampton Roads, Virginia. (To give you an idea how far off course we were blown, our original destination had been New York.)

I'll be honest, during this hurricane I was pretty callous and uncaring. In retrospect I recall I did *not* so much as turn a hair, worrying about my crew. They were zonked out, anyway, on sea-sick pills, vomiting or sleeping. (For all I knew they might have been dead.) But, concluding I was unable to help them (my excuse), I worried about the ship and gave the severely harassed captain my full, worthless support.

CHAPTER FIVE

▲

Between wars, out of the Air Corps and working for Threshers Paint and Varnish from 1945 to 1947, Ilogene and I arranged to buy a house in Marietta, Ohio. The day we received the loan approval and finalized the papers, with the deal ready for signature . . . a minor glitch at the last minute stopped the transaction–cold! The next day I received the Army's telegram offering me a Regular commission. (Happenstance . . . again?)

Ilogene hesitated, still uncertain about the military. But, she finally agreed to return to the service with me. The bank, the house owner, and the realtor let us withdraw at no cost.

Ted Hardenbrook, a friend and Ford dealer in Piqua, obtained a new car for me at no extra cost, to replace one ruined in an accident. (Only someone who went through this period will appreciate this feat, its timing and rarity. A new car–virtually any car–was all but impossible to obtain from 1945 to 1947, no matter what one did.)

One of my former Piqua classmates bought a new Hudson at about the same time, and took delivery. He did not receive either the front or rear seats for six months! He drove it, sitting on a box. Passengers crouched on pillows.

A second acquaintance sneakily obtained a car via the "black market." (Oh, yes, there was a "Black Market" then–in cars, gasoline, tires and steaks–just as there was during the war. It lasted several years after the war's end, while industries geared-up again for civilian production.) This buyer was not so lucky, he blew the engine in a hundred miles. He never, to my knowledge, received a replacement.

Where was Nader, we wondered, *when we needed him?* No matter what Nader said about Corvairs' being "death traps,"if they had been available during those years, they would have sold like the renowned "hot-cakes."

My new Ford, not only carried us through the remainder of my brief return to civilian life, but back into service–and multiple cross-country trips to and from Ohio, Texas, and New Jersey. I can not say much, though, for the tires. Any lengthy trip assured at least one blow-out, and biannual replacement of at least two out of five. Gasoline came cheap, however–twenty to thirty cents a gallon. Oil sold at twenty-five cents a quart and a complete oil-change-lube-job cost no more than three bucks. When I hear someone talk about the "Good Old Days" . . . this is what I think of, not some rapturous, Eden-like period of wine, women and song. (I don't even envy a return to the "Eve's Club" in Paris. Of course, maybe I am just getting old.)

Yet, during those first months back in the Air Force, in Texas, the civilian years took on a rosier glow in retrospect. (Reference our first Christmas, 1947, when the military separated us, our lousy living conditions, the snakes and scorpions, Rod III's asthma, my going to school after school, and my being gone so much.) Yet, once we were settled, with on-base housing, things looked up–somewhat–but that took months.

In the meantime, we hopped from the frying pan into the fire, time after time.

At our first pilots' meeting after I returned from Flight Safety school, I concluded my initial lecture with a warning, "Be extra careful when pulling up the flaps after landing the B-25. The flap handle is located right next to the gear handle. Be sure you know which one you have when you lift it. Or, you may find yourself, like many other careless pilots, sitting on the runway, gear up, engines ruined . . . and, very likely, a one-way ticket home awaiting you at headquarters."

General Johnson, base commander, sitting in front of me in the

first row, leaped to his feet and turned to glare at the assembly of our Base's pilots. He shook his fist, shouting, "And I will accept no excuses. There are none. Any pilot who does such a stupid act is O-U-T! You hear me? OUT!" He thrust a thumb over his shoulder as if calling "out" at a baseball game.

The next day it was my "day in the barrel"–I had the duty as Base Airdrome Officer. This meant, for twenty-four hours I greeted all incoming notables, checked the runway and taxi lights every hour . . . and handled all in-flight and ground emergencies involving our Base's aircraft–plus a hundred minor tasks filling a large notebook.

General Johnson landed his B-25 about four-thirty in the afternoon and I prepared to welcome him at Base Operations. He turned his B-25 off the runway . . . *and pulled up his landing gear* . . . right where a pilot normally raises his flaps.

Since it was my duty, I got there first. I hurried onto the field even ahead of the ambulance, fire trucks, and engineers.

Johnson climbed out of the squatting B-25, saw who was on duty and wiggled his index finger under my nose. "Don't say one damned word, Lieutenant Cron. Everything I said yesterday morning still applies. That was stupid."

Though he did not cashier himself from the service, he called a special "Flight Safety" meeting the next morning . . . and took it on the chin in front of the assembly. The old guy died six months later. (Looking back, I should never say he was an "old guy." He was fifty-five. To me, now approaching eighty-six, he was a kid.)

General Johnson, all during the years after the war, also kept a captain close by him on his staff, giving him positions and according him a deference he normally gave only other general officers. No one understood why.

One evening at the Officer's Club when they were both at the bar and well "into their cups," I had occasion to wheedle out the answer. It seems this captain graduated from West Point with General Johnson, but, early on, ran afoul of General Arnold. On

this officer's dossier in Army Air Corps headquarters a red tag read, "This officer will *never* be promoted as long as I am on active duty," signed General Hap Arnold.

The day Arnold retired, Johnson's lifelong buddy jumped from captain to colonel. He made brigadier general the following year, soon after Johnson died.

This also happened to the French Colonel Morlet the last man out of Dien Bien Phu, Viet Nam. DeGaulle put just such a marker on his dossier too.

One week after DeGaulle lost the French Presidency, Morlet wore two stars. His only complaint? "I had a good job lined-up for retirement as a colonel. As a retired general it may now be 'dans le chute' ('out the window' or 'in the toilet')."

All military services have their prima donnas, I guess. Ours too.

<div align="center">* * *</div>

When I was a kid, often, to my parents' dismay, I asked detailed questions showing I was a true "Doubting Thomas." (And much too precocious.)

At the age of five, for example (because it was important to me, I can still remember precisely where I was when I asked this question–I was outside the screen door to my grandmother's dining room, at 122 Staunton Street, Piqua. Ohio, standing on the concrete slab, looking up at my mother, just inside), I asked, "Mother, where do babies come from?"

Now, remember, I was but five. I presume mother tried to be careful when she answered, "Well, Buster (they called me "Buster" for years . . . and I hated it!), your father and I prayed to God . . . and he sent you."

This might have worked for some kids. It did *not* work for me. Not even at age five.

I immediately did some mental calculations, probably far beyond my years, but here is what I concluded: *Mom's answer is simply so much "doggy-do-do."*

I prayed for a new sled. Did I get one? No!
I prayed for a red bicycle, with a bell that went ding-ding. Did I get one? No!
I prayed for a lot of things . . . and actually received only a few.

Internally, I shook my head. *Nah! There are too many people in the world. Why even here in Piqua there must be thousands–for simple prayer to produce 'em all. There's gotta be a better way.*

I squinted at Mom, knowing she lied. But, like all good little kids, I nodded as if I "bought" her fantasy, and went back to playing in the back yard.

The next day, I asked the same question of a fourteen-year-old girl who lived down the street. Wow! Did I get my eyes opened!

She not only told me–she *showed* me. What's more, she let me touch "it" . . . that funny-looking, black-hairy thing between her legs. (Later, as all men eventually do, I found out this little gadget was the major source of man's primary motivation and pleasure, as well as the source of our greatest problems.)

I also believed this girl's story, far more than my mother's. She not only grabbed me–my tiny little protuberance–while she went on explaining in colorful detail all the how's, what's, why's and wherefore's.

That was my first "intimate" lesson in female anatomy, sexual reproduction, and what the French exclaim about when they say, "Viva la difference!" (Yet, for all my early training and excitement, I remained a virgin until married. Quite a feat, even then.)

Upon reading, in Europe during WWII, Henry Miller's books, "Tropic of Cancer" and "Tropic of Capricorn" (both banned at the time in the USA), I discovered many other older girls introduced young boys to the same mysteries, and in the same manner. Miller's education went much further than mine–or, I should say much "farther"–for his nursemaid took him, when he was just a lad, "all the way," then on to cunnilingus and fellatio.

Since we are now talking about "sex"–and my friends often

ask, "Are we going to talk about sex now, or work up to it gradually?"–let me pull together my major experiences of this type. (This will, most likely, be the section of greatest interest . . . yet, even more likely, the most disappointing.)

Unlike many men, my life has *not* been strewn with lurid affairs. Instead, it has been more or less colored by a series of narrow escapes, abstinence and celibate episodes, rebuffs, refusals and rejections. Few will stir anyone's libido.

In addition to my first sexual indoctrination, as described (the fourteen-year-old's introduction to the more titillating aspects of "the facts of life"), there were also other, well-remembered "checkpoints." (That *is* a double-entendre!)

No one who knows me now will ever believe I was once both naive and shy. Just as my current friends have difficulty visualizing me "with hair." (But I was innocent once. I also had hair once, too. Honest! Cross my heart!)

In some ways I'm still shy. Aggressive women scare me.

My second shocking encounter occurred right in our Bijou Theater when I was eleven. (I may still suffer from this trauma. Perhaps it "stunted" my development.)

Madge Kinsey's[31] husband, obviously a pedophile (I know that now; I did *not* know it then), caught me back stage, between scenes, one night during a performance. He dragged me behind some curtains and took me in his arms. (I came nowhere near his shoulder height) He kissed me, strangling me with his whiskey-laden breath . . . and fondled my genitals.

I squirmed out of his arms and got away. But, then, I did not know what to do after that. I was just a kid!

Madge never acted as if she knew what her husband was up to, but I believe she had her suspicions. I know she thought it strange when I suddenly stopped hanging around and rarely performed with them again.

[31] Madge owned the "Kinsey Komedy Kompany." (More on this later.)

Since I recommended and urged Dad to bring Madge's troupe to our theater, I felt responsible. Thinking, somehow, this incident was all my fault, I kept silent–never mentioning it to a soul, until now. (Since then, I discovered instilled "guilt" is often the pedophile's best protection. Such monsters rely on it.)

I never allowed myself, after that, to be caught alone by this aggressor. Yet, I learned the same year, (to me, at the time) a shocking and dismal fact, during the company's stay with us. Two of the actors whom I liked best ("Paul" and "Dave"–I will not use their last names) lived together and had for years. In the thirties we called them "queers," now we call them "gay." I learned from this "couple" a deep and heartfelt appreciation for the wide spectrum of noteworthy talents shown by many homosexuals. They, like all others, can also be most compassionate. These two men taught me a number of valuable acting "tricks" and smoothed my performances with skilled criticisms. (*And they never "made a pass" at me.*)

My third "eye-opener" occurred when I was about to leave Logan for Tipp City. A girl whom I barely knew, elected to give me a going-away party one afternoon when her parents were working. She invited my friends to her home and arranged for the whole schmear–a cake, ice cream, and presents.

An hour into the party, a storm deluged the city. Realizing I left the windows open in my parent's car, I ran out in the heavy downpour and jumped in. Slamming shut the car door, I frantically began cranking up the windows.

My hostess, virtually a stranger, still in her school band uniform, followed close on my heels. "I'll help!" she exclaimed, hopping in beside me.

When the rain continued–a downpour so heavy the house was only a blur–she slid closer and asked, "Well . . . aren't you going to kiss me?"

I hadn't thought about it, but kissing her suddenly sounded like a grand idea. I took her into my arms, ready to plant a big, wet

smackeroo on her waiting lips.

She stopped me, saying, "Wait!"

Not knowing what she wanted, I waited. After all, I was pretty awkward at this, unskilled and only fourteen. Up till then, I had indulged solely in some hand-holding and putting my arm around girls at the movies, thinking it was "hot stuff" and "real risque." And I'd kissed girls no more than ten times.

While I waited, she unzipped the top of her band uniform. Sliding nearer, she took my hand and slid it inside her blouse, squeezing my open palm onto her bare breast.

I had never touched a girl's breast! Certainly not a bare one. The nipple popped up against my palm, I began sweating and experienced instant arousal. But what did I do? *Nothing!* I did not know *what* to do.

So startled, I forgot I was supposed to kiss her. Turning a violent red, I hung my head and slid quickly out the car. Ignoring the soaking rain, I dashed back into the house.

Now I know my reaction was not typical! It seems, in this area of my life as well as some others of note, I got hit often by the seven plagues: near-misses, lack of knowledge, reluctance, naivete, shyness, shame and fear.

Yet as a boy and man, I have always–even today at my advanced age–felt all the normal desires and male responses. I just did not act on them for the reasons given.

I would like to say, "I was religiously 'saving myself' for marriage." But I can't–not honestly. Nor can I say I was in any way repulsed, revolted or turned-off. Never! (Except by the cold, icy rain.) Oh, there may have been elements of religious perspective involved, too. Yet I believe I was most motivated by respect for girls, and stifled by fears of pregnancy and disease. Whatever, I always maintained control.

For this, another quote (Leon Blum, French statesman, 1872-1950) applies: "Life does not give itself to one who tries to keep all its advantages at once. I have often thought morality may

perhaps consist solely in the courage of making a choice."

My courageous choice was to opt for chastity.

The next occasion on which I faced temptation came during the week of high school graduation. I drove from Columbus back to Tipp City to graduate there, and sing Malotte's "The Lord's Prayer" at the school's Baccalaureate Services.

Out of the blue, the most desirable girl in our class phoned me where I was staying with Jim Clingenpeel. The girl, a shapely, seductive brunette we boys all drooled over, had been going steady with our "BMOC[32]" throughout her high school years. She asked me if I would come by her house at the edge of town.

Again not knowing the reason—but interested—I hurried to her house.

Greeting me in snow-white sneakers, a pair of white, short-shorts, and a form-fitting white T-shirt (if I can remember such detail after more than sixty-six years, you know she was impressive) all accenting her olive complexion and flowing black hair, she invited me to walk with her out into the country (a two-mile circle). She led me along a path on a single-lane, seldom-used road, by a grove of trees, with a pond at the midpoint.

On the way, she really set me back on my heels. She abruptly turned, stared me in the eye, and said, "Rod, you could have 'had' me anytime you wanted, you know. All through school. If you'd just asked."

I gasped. "You were going with Bill. I never stood a chance."

She batted lovely lavender eyes, reminiscent of Elizabeth Taylor's. "It's not too late."

But it was.

I was already deep into college (begun while still going to Columbus Central), had a full schedule of singing engagements plus other plans, and really had no time for girls. (My refusal

[32] "BMOC"–"big man on campus"–the leading football, basketball and baseball player. In this instance, not smart or handsome, but "BIG," heavily muscled . . . and mean. Better to leave his girl alone.

made me worry, "Am I gay?")

Seeing her again at our fiftieth class reunion in 1990, she explained explicitly, "Rod, that day we took a walk, I didn't plan anything serious. I simply envisioned a quick 'roll in the hay' out there in the woods . . . nothing more."

That was exactly what I did *not* want. Even then, at seventeen, I was not looking to have an affair. I wanted to find a soul mate and make a lifetime commitment. Where I saw a "no-win" situation; she saw a pleasurable "win-win" goal, with no regrets.

This high school episode ended my personal record of specific girls' throwing themselves at me . . . until much later. (I evidently was not much with the girls.)

College life came next with all its multitudinous temptations–everyone remote. Yet it was some time before I supposedly encountered the truly subtle offers.

Working (two jobs), singing (vocalizing, memorizing and rehearsing) and doing weekly church services (four solos and choir work), coupled with Louis Dirks' demanding schedule (as head of the Ohio State music department) all mitigated against me. Result: I seldom dated.

In Europe, during the war, I saw the worst side–sex was cheap and an easily available commodity. In London and Paris prostitutes propositioned every passing military man.

In Paris, girls took men to hotels. In England, they often performed "the act" on the streets, backing a man into the corner of a building or hauling him up an alley, hoisting their skirts and "having at it," day or night. I bumped into one such couple in a pea-soup-fog. The man thanked me for the boost.

A few days after our arrival at our English Air Base (Matching Green, seventy-odd miles northeast of London), the colonel asked (when a colonel "asks" second lieutenants, that's an "order") our squadron to provide male escorts for a dance at the central town hall. Being one of the newest members of the officer group, they commandeered me for the duty.

At the dance, I met a pretty little, pregnant English girl, married to one of our Air Corps sergeants. He left three days before for the London docks, en route to France.

A vivacious companion, she quickly told me her life story, then asked me if it was okay to stop dancing. Her reason–"I'm all knocked up."

I stepped back and raised my hands. "It's not my fault!"

She giggled and explained the many ways Brits used the phrase, "Yeah, I know you Yanks say that when you impregnate a girl . . . well, I actually am 'knocked up' by those terms too. My husband doesn't even know it. I didn't find out till this morning." (The next day, I used our military communication system to make certain he found out.)

She went on to tell me, "I can also be 'knocked-up' in the morning, meaning someone awakens me. Or it can mean I am tired, like I am now . . ." She went on, giving several other examples as we sat at a table and talked.

Before we left that night, she hugged my arm and calmly informed me, "Yank, you can come in and stay overnight with me anytime you're off-base." But I didn't.

I never saw her again. Yet I worried about her and her baby. With such a free and easy attitude, she could pick up a disease and lose the sergeant's child. Also he might *not* be coming back. How would such round-heeled activities make her feel then? (I always wondered if he made it back.)

On another afternoon, in London, an eager female usher working at a downtown theater put me in the top, back row of the lower balcony, hidden by curtains. When the audience finished singing "God Save the King" and the movie began, she joined me . . . and nearly raped me right there in the seats.

I eased to one side, pushing her away. "What is it with you English girls?"

She slapped down her skirts and jumped up. "We don't have any men . . . that's what! They're off to France and India, or on

the high seas." She squinted at me in the semi-darkness. "What's it with you? I thought all you Yanks were 'hard-up' and 'after it,' wherever you can find it. Or are you one of 'those?'"

I wasn't . . . and I am not. But it did seem that way.

Once more, in Paris, only five minutes into our three-day pass, Sergeant Brow and I ambled along the broad sidewalk in front of the Grand Hotel, gawking at the people near the city center. A young, attractive brunette (about seventeen-years-old, I guessed) dashed up from behind, out of nowhere. She ran between us and grabbed an arm of each. "Voulez-vous 'zig-zig?'" ("Want to have sex?")

I spoke some French, but never heard that phrase. Perplexed, I asked her, "What did you say, mademoiselle?" (I asked that in French.)

Like the fourteen-year-old girl in Piqua when I was just a child, she not only told us, in fractured English, but showed us, using her two hands. (She used the classic gesture–a circled thumb-and-forefinger, the other forefinger pumping through the circle.)

Brow and I got it. What's more, he was hot to trot.

They scrambled back down the avenue to a local hotel, her pulling, with me along in tow. I sat in the lobby, waiting.

They signed-in, rode up eight flights in a slow-moving, creaking elevator, and walked down the hall to her room. There, she washed him, undressed part way, and they "zig-zigged." They then reversed the route and came back . . . gone less than eight minutes.

In the lobby, the girl then tugged at my arm, wanting me to duplicate the "trick." When I refused, she pouted like a spoiled child. (Which I believe she was.)

Outside, I punched Brow on the arm. "Eight minutes! Must be a world speed record."

He looked sheepish. "Well, it had been a while."

<p style="text-align:center">*　　　　*　　　　*</p>

Earlier, I stressed "subtle offers." Years after the afore-cited

incidents, when my wife and I attended or conducted daily a whole slew of military and diplomatic cocktail parties, Ilogene kidded me about the "come-on" glances I ignored.

I told her, "Honey, I am completely unaware."

Because of this, we discussed "signals." She contended I had been getting winks, smiles and little strokes intended to tell me certain women were "available."

I contended, "I'm a friendly person. That's all they are being."

Admittedly, I am a "touchy-feelie" type. And I try to be friendly. Regularly and inadvertently, I place a hand on a person's shoulder, or press an arm or a hand when talking to someone I like. With those I do not care for, I allow a greater distance.

Ilogene said those innocent "moves" sent out mixed signals and women misinterpreted them as "come-ons." I tried to stop . . . and succeeded . . . for a few years. (I still do it, even now, but less often.)

As I aged, I felt certain I no longer held any attraction for the opposite sex. (I had mirrors. No one had to beat me over the head.) But, after I partially recuperated from my wife's death (having lost sixty pounds)–and felt I could, once more, at least go out in public–a few ladies warmed up to me. Still keeping an eye on my mirror, I was now more cynical than ever. I believed they were not so much captivated by my not-so-handsome and bald, grey brow, as enthralled by the erroneous assumption I "HAD MONEY!" (I put those two words in capitals, for they seemed to be the primary motivating entrancement of widows for widowers–and vice versa–drawing them toward their counterparts.)

These ladies saw my Cadillac (though my latest, an old 1994, *was* a Fleetwood Brougham), the paid-for, tiny, two-bedroom home and furniture, the multiple computers and printers (obsolete the minute they left the store), the assumed bank accounts, my son's and my editing/publishing businesses, and the mounting list of my published books (some fifty-nine, but few still paying

royalties). They, then, obviously thought: *"Aha! This guy is really 'fixed!'"*

Little do they know how close the "fixed" comment comes to reality–like a male dog "fixed" by a veterinarian. But careful evaluation might tell them otherwise about the money. For, even if I had any, they are unlikely to get it–my four children will!

I began protecting myself, though, by disclaiming romantic interest ("I'm still mourning my wife, you know") and talking-up "Pre-nuptial Agreements" whenever anyone edged close. *It worked!* Now I am actually too much alone. Though I have a lovely lady with whom I dine, travel and watch movies on occasion. I love her, yet our relationship remains platonic. She is erudite, charming, full of wit, quick at repartee, and works cross-word puzzles faster than I. I yearn for no more than a continuation of our warm friendship, nor does she. (One major exception, I'll describe her later.)

My lifetime review, therefore, disclosed no "behind-the-barn" episodes, nor any exotic or steamy affairs for readers to enjoy vicariously. In this respect, I led a boring life.

Even when young, my friends knew I was a "Straight Arrow." This became obvious when a friend's wife accused me of raping her (thinking this might protect her after I caught her with a fifteen-year-old boy, en flagrante delicto).

Her husband (we sang together for ten years), told her, "You're lying. I know Rod better than that." (I later testified to the viewed incident, described above, at their divorce trial.)

I will not discuss my married life in detail. It was forever earthy and remained mutually satisfying, I believe, to the end.

The military developed a number of jokes about our men being "horny" and "hard-up." We, in the Air Force, handled the situation after a long absence from our wives–usual for Air Force pilots–by applying the "jelly-bean system."

After a lengthy trip, all of us brought home a bag of jelly-beans. Tossing the beans on the floor for the kids to pick up–the

longer the absence, the smaller the bag–the horny returnee grabbed his wife and dragged her into the bedroom, locking the door. (Norwegian ski-troops were so eager they removed their skis . . . "afterwards." And the wives of Army foot-soldiers sometimes had time to remove their panty-hose, but not always.)

Recently, the "jelly-bean system" has been identified as the primary reason for the large "baby-boom" in military families after WWII.

CHAPTER SIX

▲

Early in January, 1945, General Patton gave those "Battle of the Bulge" GIs the Christmas gift they most desired–too late. To reinforce their buckling lines, he scrambled up from the south, dragging across those miles of snow-covered fields all his tanks and entire Army, to reach the fighting front in less than twenty-four hours. Even Generals Omar Bradley and Eisenhower thought it impossible.

Our Medium Bombardment Group, the closest to the action, had begun flying as soon as we could get the squadrons in the air again. Bombing and strafing as if we were flying fighters, we stayed in the air from dawn to dark, providing needed troop cover.

Keeping low, hugging the ground, strafing, hedge-hopping, we saturated the enemy with one-hundred-pound anti-personnel bombs, carrying sixty at a load. Our fifty-caliber machine guns–some of our aircraft carried as many as eighteen–and seventy-five-millimeter cannons played havoc with the massed enemy troops. With Patton's Army at full blast, we put the enemy into retreat.

The Germans quickly expended their ammunition and their gasoline reserves. At first, by the hundreds, then by the thousands, they stranded along the road, tanks, treaded-trucks, personnel carriers, and richly appointed staff cars. Burning and wrecked, they were abandoned. The smoke curled into the low-lying clouds, adding to our decreased visibility. Still we dived down, guns blazing, giving no quarter.

General Hoyt S. Vandenberg, wearing the two stars of a major general on his open shirt collar (and now our 9th Air Force

commander), came down from headquarters just to address our Group, personally. He briefed each squadron individually, then asked us to go on a special, one-time, all-out mission for the next day.

"Tomorrow," he said, sitting casually on the edge of a table in our little hospital dining room, "each of your aircraft will drop bombs on separate targets–oil, ammo and gasoline dumps, military encampments, railroad spurs, and warehouses. Then you'll descend to tree-top level and strafe an assigned village or city near that target.

"I want you to shoot-up every street, house and person you see–men, women and children." He paused to frown, letting us absorb his earth-shaking declaration. "I know, this is contrary to the Geneva Conventions. But we are going to put the fear of God into every damned German from hell to breakfast . . . and bring this war to a screeching halt."

He jumped to his feet and raised both hands like a football referee after a touchdown. "Are you with me?"[33]

All caught his enthusiasm. To a man, we also leaped to our feet, raised our hands, and shouted, "Yes, sir!"

The next morning we dropped the bombs and made the descent as ordered. But, flying up the streets of the small village assigned to us, we saw an old man on a ladder painting a house. We then came across several old ladies strolling along the already broken sidewalks . . . and groups of small children playing on the lawns.

Noncombatants all, they each turned toward our low-flying, roaring aircraft, mouths and eyes wide open in fear. Since we were their enemy, they expected death!

My aircrew then made me forever proud. Without any contradictory instructions, not one man, nor I, fired a single bullet. Not a single person in our tiny, assigned village fell.

[33] I visited this village after WWII. It lies just north of Eltman and is still a sleepy little town with the same working brewery (brass vats shining in the sun). It seemed the same as I remembered it from 1945.

In silence, we climbed to our assigned altitude and headed homeward. En route, the intercom, usually filled with aircrew chatter, stayed so silent I thought it failed.

Only when we were nearing our home field, did the tail gunner use it to whisper, "Sir, will we be court-martialed?"

"No, Brian, we'll just keep it to ourselves." I paused, then added, "But I want everyone to use up a lot of shells when you 'clear your guns.'"

That night, I learned other crews returned from the strafing part of the mission with unfired fifty-calibers, just as we did. Later, I mused about this, *Did our humanity result in a trade-off? Was this the reason our aircrew was never injured or killed?*

No one told General Vandenberg we had not strafed. When the Army Air Forces became the US Air Force–a separate service–in November 1947, General Vandenberg became our first chief-of-staff, though his serial number was but #4. (They awarded three other retiring generals lower numbers, Hap Arnold, for example, got #1). Mine was #15483 at the time–only that many numbers from the "Top Gun." (When I retired, we had more than 16,000 colonels, alone, not counting some 434 general officers (brigadier, major, lieutenant and four star) on our rolls.)

Hoyt died a young man, from cancer, his tour as our Air Force Chief-of-Staff barely completed. (*Was there a connection?*)

<div align="center">* * *</div>

Everyone reminisces. Sometimes, even now, I wonder why I ever accepted my Regular commission in 1947. (At the time I was not yet able to see ahead to the benefits of multiple promotions and a military retirement with its medical plan.)

I had not had a good tour in the ETO during WW II (1944-1945). There were too many of those "hairy" missions (except I did not get hurt or killed), plus seeing Dachau, the POW camps, and what the Nazis did to young girls, left a bad taste in my mouth (as it did to everyone who was there). I also expected, unrealistically, to return home at least a major.

My training had not gone too well either, from Basic through graduation (1942-1944). I resented the hardships Ilogene suffered. And she hated the service–at first.

Now, looking back, I believe I embraced my return to active duty in 1947 largely because I became so disaffected with civilian industries and their stupidities. I still find what happened impossible to understand.

During the year before I received my second (Regular) commission, while selling for the Thresher Paint and Varnish Company, I brought in a single purchase order and proudly placed it on the desk of the President. It was so outrageously huge, instead of rejoicing, he complained.

His argument? "Why, I'd have to turn-over the entire company to the making of this one shipment . . . and you want this much *every month!*" (This one sale assured a five-year-minimum, continuing income for the company, while earning me more than $100,000 a year–exceeding even the company president's salary. Maybe that was the reason he was so unreasonable.)

"Why not divvy-up the orders each month throughout the entire company?" I asked. "As a subsidiary of Pittsburgh Plate Glass you have access to a dozen major manufacturing facilities nationwide?"

He still refused.

In a pique of anger I quit and gave the orders (and the paint's name–"Chromagray"–as well as the formula, which I developed in the lab) to Devoe-Reynolds in Kentucky, then accepted the Army Air Corps commission. (Devoe-Reynolds made a "mint." Neither my former company nor I made a cent. Now, the Thresher Paint and Varnish Company is no longer in business. I often wondered if this resulted from the president's shortsightedness.)

But that was all back in 1947; we have yet to examine the earlier years. They, too, had their "moments."

From 1942 to 1943, (like my first year in Piqua's grade schools, 1927-1928), all kinds of difficulties plagued my first year

in the Army. Later, I discovered practically every enlistee, even draftees, suffered the same guff. I saw it as insurmountable catastrophes.

<div align="center">* * *</div>

Called to active duty at Fort Hayes, Columbus, Ohio, the end of October, 1942, the Army sent us south by "milk train." We crowded into a long line of dirty chair cars, so hardbacked no one sat comfortably. So cramped there was no place, time or opportunity to sleep. So old they were heated by wood, burned in two, pot-belly iron stoves per car. So ancient we mused about the likely possibility the train transported Lincoln's body from Washington, D.C. to Illinois in 1865. So wretched the windows would not open – or close – and we languished day and night, in heat and cold, smoke, cinders, grim and misery. And so slow, kids and dogs passed us, trotting alongside.

During the trip, the Army fed us two meals a day. We ate standing up, from mess kits (the first time we ever saw a mess kit, much less used one). The cooks prepared our food (?) on open fires in a wooden box car. We gathered the burnt and sad offerings from an array of buckets lining one side of that same makeshift kitchen, in that same box car, then dunked our dirty mess kits in tubs of "supposedly" boiling water.

Everyone developed "Montezuma's Revenge." The few toilets rapidly became stinking cess pools. In those days, the "refuse" dropped straight onto the tracks. (No nice, clean, sparkling sanitary equipment there.) Since we never stopped – not even once to pick up food or download ill recruits throughout the three-day grind south – our aged cars painted a trail of brown stench along the railroad ties from Ohio to the Gulf Coast.

At 0230 hours, on the morning of the fourth day, we arrived at Biloxi, Mississippi. In the dark, the railroad cars finally came to a grinding stop on a siding by the Gulf.

Exhausted, having had no sleep, no exercise, no place to wash off the stickiness, stink and grime, too few "facilities" for doing

the necessary, and nothing to do or read . . . we descended and fell-in, half-asleep. Still in our civilian clothes, we began Basic Training.

"Why 'Basic Training'?" we asked. "We're 'Aviation Cadets,' not GIs."

The Army told us. "There are no pre-flight schools open, right now. We're trying something new." (I hate that phrase as much as, "We've always done it that way.")

The brass decreed, "Here, you get six weeks Basic Training, then go to a university for classes and learn to fly in Cubs and Taylorcrafts, all before formal cadet training."

Out of the dark, on that beach at Bilox, a host of wide-eyed, alert, well-dressed drill sergeants (we believed they came out only at night, like vampires) met us at the train. Marching us through the black, in the chilly wind off the Gulf, they led our rag-tag, smelly, shivering group up a maze of sleep-darkened streets to a warehouse. There the Army outfitted us in those "little brown suits" so popular after Pearl Harbor Day.

(Note: still no food, no clean up, no sleep! Sleep came later in tents and cots, after shots, vaccinations and indoctrination lectures. Most slept through all three.)

Naturally, the Supply Sergeant had no shoes to fit my 9/AAAAA measurements. The only nines he had on hand came in D, DD, EEE and wider. (Made for "Yeti" or "Big Foot," no doubt.) I showed him I could not wear even his narrowest by putting both my ski-slim feet, side by side, in one shoe.

He bent over the counter and squinted. "Okay! Wear your civvies."

By the time I received the special-ordered pair, my civilian shoes were completely shot . . . and my feet had widened. I then wore a 9½C. Later, they reverted a bit and I have worn 9Bs ever since.

The Army explained to us the details of its new program the same morning (still no sleep). We listened bleary-eyed, in a

stifling auditorium. "From Basic Training, here," they said, "some of you will go to the University of Alabama at Tuscaloosa, others will go to other universities scattered across the southern states. There you will learn among other things, Morse code, first aid, military justice, how to parade and march."

The year-long stay at Biloxi (really only the promised six weeks) introduced us to callouses and bunions via a thirty-five-mile hike from Biloxi to Groveport – and back – along the then-new Gulf Coast Highway. (Torn up by the hurricane years later.) We also left on a first-name basis with sand fleas, scabies, athlete's foot, and "crotch itch."

Another train ride similar to the first transported a hundred of us to the University of Alabama. As soon as possible I enrolled in special classes, and began singing in local churches. (This earned money to send home. Ilogene was about to have our first child.)

The school housed us at first on a hill behind the school, in separate cottages formerly used by affluent students. After our Basic Training experiences, we thought we had fallen into the lap of luxury. *Until the wind changed!*

Tuscaloosa operated two paper factories near the school, twenty-four-hours a day. The rank stench from a paper factory has to be smelled to be believed. It curls the hairs inside your nostrils and attacks your nasal membranes like sulphuric acid. You acquire a continuing sickening taste, your throat burns, and your stomach revolts.

With our first whiff, we cadets knew why the school so generously gave us those cottages on the hill. They were right in the normal wind stream from the paper plants . . . and we had to try and sleep while breathing those odors. (We complained so much they finally moved us to a barracks on the lower campus. Yet it took weeks to wash the scent of rotting paper from our lungs and uniforms.)

On the other side of the teeter-totter, those little Cub airplanes were a snap to fly, especially after Bill Lear's training and my

dad's kitchen tutelage with chair, stick and rudder. Yet, we were not allowed to solo.

The airfield owner was a massive five-hundred-pound Alabaman (and that weight figure is no exaggeration). Every morning he waddled out of his office (barely squeezing through the three-foot-wide door) and personally started the engine of every airplane. Grabbing in one hand the end of each propellor, he gave it a mere flick of his right, one-hundred-pound arm . . . and the prop spun, the engine roared, and the pilot taxied out.

On a chilly morning ("Alabama chilly" – meaning the temperature was about fifty degrees), he had trouble starting one of the aircraft engines. He stepped closer and jerked down on the propellor even harder than before. The engine caught, then backfired. The prop swung in reverse – once! – it struck his huge rear, somewhat like encountering a concrete abutment. (I didn't intend that last word as a pun, but it fits!)

The shock broke the engine mounts on the engine. Engine and propellor flew out of the nose of the aircraft and dropped to the ground. This so damaged the aircraft it never flew again.

The airfield owner rubbed his hip. Later, it turned purple with a massive bruise, but that was all. No broken bones, no serious injury . . . except to the plane.

A couple weeks later, a terrific windstorm blew-in just before noon. All the aircraft were in the air with students aboard. The storm brought such a gale (actually reaching hurricane force) only those planes up-wind of the field came home. By easing off on their throttles, the instructor pilots backed their planes carefully, holding a five-hundred-feet-altitude until they centered our field. By careful jockeying, balancing their throttle power and glide angle against the wind, they managed to descend vertically into the arms of waiting ground crews. The men immediately stuffed the tiny aircraft into the hangars. The planes flying downwind of the field did not return until the next day.

Continuing rains followed on the heels of the windstorm. This

forced cancellation of our remaining flights and we, thus, received less than half our scheduled flying program. But that had a good side–for me. It meant more time for classroom studies and singing.

One early episode at the University of Alabama produced some laughs. My second cousin (Aunt Hazel's son) had been a "ham" for twenty years. During the war he was the Chief Radio Operator at the Navy's Great Lakes Training Center. When I was just a youngster, he taught me Morse code. In high school, I had become–like him–a "ham." (We built 20-meter, then 5-meter units so small we put them in cigar boxes[34].)

Before our first code test at the university, I claimed I had a code capability . . . *then failed the test.* I recorded nothing but a series of "Es", "Is," "Ts," and "Ms." (Single dots, double dots, single-dashes and double-dashes.) The sergeant realized at once what had happened and cranked-up the tape's speed to twenty-words per minute (we needed only an eight-word capability). I then passed the test with flying colors.

Out of all those I can recall, I have only one good memory of our time at Tuscaloosa: I strived so hard as a Cadet Sergeant the military faculty named me "Cadet of the Class." No medal or awards, but they allowed me a special dispensation–a trip home

[34] A friend and I built two of these small, 5-meter transceivers when attending high school. I gave one to the friend then sat in the study hall while he took his math and English tests. He whispered the question into one end of the cigar box (where we installed the microphone) and I gave him the answers. He passed his tests, graduated and become an electronic genius in the Army, as a radio technician. The only time we got into trouble with our radios (doing a one-hour radio show from his house to the school, for the Radio Club), we transmitted in the room containing his 20-meter transmitter and aerial. The 20-meter aerial picked up our signal from the tiny 5-meter radio and resonated it at a higher frequency into the middle of a commercial station's broadcast in Washington, D.C. The next morning we had a visit from two FBI agents. They were about to confiscate our equipment and put us in jail . . . until they discovered we were but high school sophomores. They let us off with an oral reprimand and a warning never to do that again. Scared to death, we didn't. (I guess I can say, though, this was the first time I sang on a commercial station doing a nationwide program. But I did not brag about this to the agents.)

on "leave" (at my expense) when Ilogene gave birth to Melodie. I was the sole cadet granted any time off without a family death as a basis. Even then only one other cadet had a similar week's respite, to visit his dying wife in Columbus, Ohio. (This cadet and I trained north together and found– another happenstance–we had sung together in the Columbus Grand Opera Company, 1940-42.)

In the spring, the Army tossed us back into another of those time-hoary trains. Again crammed into "cars of misery" we rode the rails (same old, wooden seats, same dining methods, same absence of facilities) all the way to San Antonio, Texas, to the SAACC (San Antonio Aviation Cadet Center). As much time as this passage required, we figured the route really went via Alaska. It seemed another year of sustained misery.

Our prolonged stay at "SAACC" also began to appear permanent. Week after week dragged by. We stayed in place. No progress. No encouragement. No information. No flying training. "Much ado about nothing!" (Old Shakespeare knew what he was writing about.)

What did we do there? Not much! Merely drilled, drilled . . . and drilled.

The Army gave us lots of lectures (military history, law . . . all dry as a bone), and KP! We drilled – marching back and forth, four hours a day on a special grassless field, in the boiling sun, no shade, no wind, no respite. We marched there, to and from our barracks, three times a day. We marched to the firing range (one mile, to and from) once a week; to classes (another mile in another direction, to and from), twice a day (sometimes four times); We marched (three times a day) to KP and the mess halls, then to the athletic fields for PT (one mile). On weekends we participated in two massive, multi-thousand-man parades to entertain every dignitary who came within a hundred miles . . . marching another two miles to the parade ground . . . through the lengthy, complicated parades . . . then we tramped wearily the two

miles back again to our barracks[35].

Is it any wonder that, each night, we fell onto our double-decker cots, exhausted, despite the mouse-sized cockroaches and sweltering 102+ degree weather? We lay nightly on wet sheets, gasping for breath, swatting mosquitoes, and ducking roach attacks. (Those things had wings! Not only did they fly, but they bit . . . and they relished human flesh[36]–ours!) In the morning, our sheets were not only sweat-soaked, but bloody.

Ah, but no one ever forgot the "drill and parade field" activities pursued daily!

Every morning we did our "PT" (physical training) – all that jumping up and down, squatting, push-ups, chin-ups, arm-swinging, and running five-mile obstacle-courses, leaping over coiled rattlesnakes and dodging mesquite limbs. Then we scoured every inch of the ground (called, "going ass holes and elbows"), picking up every rock, pebble and any item bigger than 1/16th inch. If we saw it, we removed it.

Of course, the next day, we did it again . . . and the day after . . . and the day after . . . ad infinitum. What was worse, each day we found as many rocks strewn across the fields as we found there the day before. (We were convinced our Tactical – Drill – Sergeants came out at night and "seeded" the area.)

While we awaited assignment to a cadet class, some of us were lucky, or lied convincingly enough, to get jobs working in the mess halls (this excused us from some of the interminable

[35] Since I was a singer the sergeant chose me to lead the flight's and squadron's singing, and we sang everywhere we marched. (Remember the Green Beret chants . . . we did 'em all.) This might have been good vocal exercise under some conditions, but dust and dry-air played hob with my throat.

[36] No enterprising cadet ever stood that for long. We discovered we were able to thwart the little buggers by placing the legs of our cots in small cans of kerosene–then they could not climb up to our beds. But they fought back by climbing to the ceiling and dropping on us from there. (Without mosquito netting we were open game. We were still working on a barrier when I left.)

marching). Another friend from Columbus suckered our mess sergeant into taking me on as a meat-cutter. (I had never cut a piece of meat in my life bigger than a small steak for dinner, but I got the job. I left SAACC a pretty competent meat cutter.)

I also had a chance to sing with Gordon MacCrea at SAACC. He was a class ahead of me (I don't believe he made it through flying training, though, as I never heard from him again.) Pat O'Brien came visiting one weekend, along with a string of other celebrities from Gordon's most recent movie, and a few of us had a chance to meet them all. They gave a round of shows for the cadets.

On weekends I sang, like Gordon, in the Base Chapels' services. (No pay, but a way to keep our vocal chords well-oiled.) I also earned a bit doing weddings and funerals. Again Ilogene needed the money–we sold our 1938 Ford to pay for Melodie's delivery and the hospital. (Another of the sacrifices servicemen made every day.)

At long last–and this is a meaningful description–at very "l-o-o-o-n-g l-a-a-a-s-t"–the Air Corps assigned us a class number, 44-C, (which meant 1944, third month, thus they scheduled our class to graduate with wings and second lieutenant bars, 12 March 1944). The military then shipped us to PFS (Pre-Flight School) . . . fifty feet across the road to the north. But we were still at SAACC. Now, though, we were finally *really on our way.*

Yet in PFS, contrary to our hopes, there were no weekend passes. We marched less and studied more, still they managed to fill our time from morn till night. In addition, here we got our first taste of demerits and "walking tours" (one tour for each ten demerits). Each "tour" meant mutely carrying a rifle, and tramping back and forth on a forty-foot ramp, for fifty minutes. (I never walked any tours here–thank God!) But I did receive some demerits.

We "earned" demerits from improperly-made beds, unbuttoned or unpressed uniforms, unpolished shoes, unshaven chins, uncut

hair, and all the other "un's" our Tactical Sergeants could think of. (And they were quite imaginative.) Some cadets busted their buns to avoid walking those dreaded tours, yet every week they were out there tramping that ramp, rifles on their shoulders.

We also cleaned those self-same rifles, our uniforms and parade sabers, spit-shined our shoes, and generally pretended we were West Point cadets. We even endured (unflinchingly, of course) our upperclassmen's hazing–answering stupid questions. A failure to do so meant, "sweating our shadows into the barracks' walls."

My sole change-of-pace at PFS came when Ilogene[37] also climbed onto one of those old, nineteen-century trains. She then suffered the same discomforts–almost!–demanded of us soldiers. She rode more than three days each way (from Ohio to Texas), sitting up, not sleeping, to visit me for my first weekend off . . . our long-awaited "two-day leave."

To us cadets, the "two-day leave" turned out to be a different reality. Yes, we were freed each of the two mornings, at 0800 hours. It seemed a grand release, an unexpected taste of freedom . . . until we found out we had to return to base each night, no later than 2000 hours (8 PM). No time for hanky-panky. (Well, not much! We had to learn to be quick about everything.) No sleeping all night with a wife or girl friend! We quickly discovered the Army thinks of everything and finds some way to foul-up even the "best laid" plans of the most astute.

Ilogene found a room in a downtown hotel near the bus line terminal I took into town . . . and looked like a dream when I saw her. (I can describe to this day her dress, her smile, the cut of her

[37] Ilogene considered bringing Melodie with her, but decided against it since she was still very tiny and train conditions were so miserable. As it was, Ilogene barely got tickets. The government largely limited travel to only "that which was necessary." They allotted seats mostly to troop movements. Troops crowded her trains, all eager to help her . . . of course, why not? She was a pretty girl, traveling alone.

hair, the small, shining brown shoes she wore.) Going straight to the hotel room (do you need to know why?), we stashed the candy I brought her and some food for snacks in her ice box (no refrigerators in hotel rooms in those days).

When we returned from our stroll along the River Walk and our visit to the Alamo, we found the candy hosting an invasion of red ants and intrepid cockroaches. Not only did we "toss" the food, but did not try again. Yet those few hours in her arms made up for many of those hard months of training and loneliness. Her leaving for home left me with two avid desires: to see her and Melodie again, and to graduate, as soon as possible.

At SAACC we again paraded weekly for dignitaries, but now I was a cadet officer and carried a saber (a cause of one of my major "stumbles"). Our cadet colonel, some seven inches taller than I, had been given a saber several inches longer than mine. (I always was cursed with a short "saber.") This difference in our sabers caused one parade to stand out above the rest.

The Base Commander called upon us to perform, at the last minute, for a visiting Bolivian general. Everyone scrambled into his best uniform, hurriedly grabbed-up equipment, strapped-on his sword (cadet officers, that is), and ran out the door. Everything hectic to the extreme.

During the parade, the military band played; we marched. Our squadron approached the stands where the dignitaries sat. As required, our cadet colonel shouted, "Eyes right!"

We cadet officers, two paces behind him, saluted by raising our saber handles up in front of our faces, then, facing right, we swung the blades down and to the right, pointing the tip at a 45-degree angle toward the ground (and, thus, toward the visiting dignitary). I jabbed my sword (the saber really belonging to the cadet colonel and much too long for me) deep into the parade field. A quick twist showed it was stuck. I straightened up and, ignoring it, marched on.

It stayed back there, vibrating in the dust . . . right in front of

the generals.

A following flight sergeant, pulled it out and tossed it ahead of me on the next turn. I grabbed it up and returned it to my scabbard.

For that little fiasco I got a hearty dressing-down. But our captain–not a cadet officer on this occasion–spoiled it when he broke into laughter as he recalled the startled expressions in the stands, caused by the quivering saber.

"Do you know, Cadet Cron, the Bolivian general actually thought we arranged that display as a special tribute to his high office? He complimented our general on his unusual presentation."

I did not receive a single demerit. (Talk about luck!)

<p style="text-align:center">* * *</p>

The next time I saw Ilogene was in Brady, Texas, three months later. She brought Melodie with her and Ilogene's mother came along to help.

Assigned to Primary Flying Training (in PT-17s[38]) at Brady (the city billing itself as the "Heart of Texas"), I finally got into the air again. I will always remember my solo take-off. (Does anyone ever forget that? Mine is forever engraved on my mind.)

On that first solo take-off–I had barely reached the field's halfway point, not yet in the air, filled with excitement–when a truly sobering thought hit me. *You know, I can kill myself doing this!* I never again approached any aircraft without due consideration.

Yet I made those initially required three take-offs and landings with no problems. (Okay, maybe I sweat . . . and trembled . . . a little .)

[38] PT-17s, built by Fairchild, painted bright blue and yellow, with an in-line, six-cylinder engine and a single, low-wing. Though not very powerful, they were excellent planes for the novice and neophyte trainee. Their wide-spaced landing gear and rear skid tended to discourage a cadet's ground-looping them (losing control and swinging in circles while taxiing, taking-off and landing). I saw it happen only once.

Primary Flying School introduced me to two instructors. One proved to be a maniac (and lost his job while we were there). The other was a rarity–a noteworthy and considerate helpmate, who graduated many fine flyers.

Our first instructor (the maniac) already had earned a "sub-rosa" reputation (among the cadets) for his cruelty. He used his control stick, regularly, to beat the knees of every one of his students, including those the head office assigned him solely to give "check-rides." He often did this until the cadets' legs turned black and blue . . . then laughed.

No one had ever reported this unusually cruel and maniacal instructor. Our class took a different approach . . . we vowed to "get" him.

One student not only reported him, but also lifted his legs and used the control column to beat the instructor's knees. That's when the instructor caught his foot in the trap.

The instructor reported the student. Ten of us came forth at the cadet's hearing and attested to what the instructor had been doing (among other things).

The board gave us new instructors. (And fired ours.)

Here also, at Primary, is where I began my "under-the-bridge[39]" exploits. I quickly developed a reputation for trying anything (among the cadets, that is). But no matter what I did, I never bettered the gutsy acts of our oldest student.

We had one classmate (Harlan Crowder) who, though married, had an "eye for any skirt." Ten miles from our airfield lived a girl whom Harlan came to "know" (Biblical sense) very quickly.

When Harlan found her parents left her alone every day at their ranch (both worked in a nearby city for the war effort), he vowed to exploit the possibilities this situation offered . . . to the utmost.

[39] And who taught me? My second instructor! He was a real dare-devil, He also taught me how to do "loops-around-bridges." But that was in Basic Flying Training, my next class. We stayed at Brady for Basic Flying Training too, and I had the same instructor for both Primary and Basic. (Discussed later.)

He did—and quickly.

The next day, he flew to her ranch, landed and parked the plane in the shade, next to the house. After spending an hour or so with her inside, he flew back to the base.

This immediately raised questions at the Base, "How could he fly so long and use so little gasoline? What was he really doing?"

The first time he explained, "I wanted to hide the fact I had engine trouble. I landed on the sand and cleared my carburetor. It took almost all my scheduled time to get the engine started. Then I flew back to base." (They let him off with a mild oral reprimand for not radioing the base, but complimented his ingenuity in making the repairs.)

The next day, undaunted, he again flew to the girl's house. On this occasion, he landed nearby, then taxied to and parked the plane inside the central opening of her huge barn (so no one flying over could see it). He braced the plane's wheels and tied down the tail, ran-up the engine and let it grind away while he did the same thing inside the house. (Later, he merely drained the tanks and gave the fuel to the girl for her parents' tractor. Gas was not expensive, but required hard-to-get ration stamps.)

He did this virtually every day and managed to escape detection until a week before we graduated Basic and I left for Twin-engine Advanced Flying Training at Pampa, Texas. (Harlan went to fighter training, for obvious reasons.)

On Harlan's final "goodbye" visit, an instructor doing instrument training in the area saw him take-off from the girl's ranch. Again Harlan squeezed by with only a reprimand. (This guy deserved to be a general officer—he had a gift of gab unequaled in our group.)

The base commander proposed setting Harlan back a class, but Harlan had demonstrated he was such an outstanding pilot and setting him back would have precluded his commissioning. (Harlan teetered at the upper-age-limit and would have exceeded it before graduation if he had been held up even two days.) He

settled down later, with another wife, and we served together again in the USAF Inspector General's Office. But he still sported–even at the age of forty-eight and then a lieutenant colonel–an errant twist: he drove a beautiful Jaguar XKE . . . fast and recklessly . . . top down. And, as proof, he bragged about the stack of speeding tickets in his glove compartment.

Back in Brady, Ilogene's mother returned home, alone, after a week's stay. Ilogene and Melodie lived in rented rooms through the remainder of my Primary, Basic and Advanced Flying Training (Pampa, Texas). Ilogene pinned on my wings and bars, when I graduated and received my commission.

"Advanced Flying Training" came easy to me, compared with Primary and Basic. In "Advanced Flying" we trained on two types of twin-engine aircraft, both with a door to the cockpit over each wing. One type, built on a skimpy aluminum frame, was covered with a thin covering of fabric. (Little different from the original WWI "Jenny.")

The other type had aluminum wings and a fuselage consisting of a thin, round, aluminum cone, open behind the pilots all the way to the tail. On the ground, the tail wheel acted like the needle of an old-style record-player and the cone-shaped fuselage behind us served as a horn, focusing and magnifying the sound until our heads ached. (We always hurried to get into the air and have some quiet–where only the engine noise was deafening.)

The fabric model flew like a kite and was about as easy to handle. The aluminum "cone" of the AT-9 was treacherous. It stalled easily and demanded constant attention. No one ever relaxed when flying it.

Early in our advanced flying we did a great deal of "night cross-countries." Going north into the winter snow belt from our field[40], we daily planned to fly a route of checkpoints and land at

[40] Pampa's standard cold weather joke was, "There's only a snow fence between the Base and the North Pole . . . and it blew down ten years ago." Snow, sleet and variable winds, mixed with blizzards, marked our 1943-1944 winter calendar.

three or four "strange" airfields. (All good training for new pilots about to receive their wings.)

During the daytime such flights seldom caused problems. Night flights revealed last-minute pilot weaknesses . . . if the cadet lived.

Two of our class's cadets flew north one night into a blinding snowstorm, into an area where more than three feet of snow already lay on the ground. They began the flight at five thousand feet (ample clearance for our field at Pampa, Texas). But they continued maintaining the same altitude while flying north where, according to our charts, the flat terrain gradually rose higher and higher with every mile traversed.

They, of course, should have planned for this during their pre-flight preparations and climbed ever higher as they flew north to compensate. Their instructor also should have caught their lapse when he checked their paperwork, prior to their take-off.

They didn't. He didn't.

Two hours later they were flying merrily along when both engines abruptly quit. They each jumped out the door on his respective side, and jerked his parachute ripcord. Only then did they realize they had landed and the plane was sliding across a vast field of snow, so deep they were on the ground, unhurt, propellers stopped by the snow.

The next morning after the storm, the scout planes looking for them found the two cadets sitting on the airplane's wings, their parachutes strung out behind the plane on each side. These two potential pilots . . . and their instructor . . . were cashiered.

Another night, closer to graduation, two gremlin visits set our class on its collective ear.

Though I had long-since achieved my flying time requirements to graduate*, several other cadets had not. I volunteered to fly as an instructor with two of them to help them meet requirements. (*All the extra flying I scored with my Basic Training Instructor added up, plus I volunteered to fly any extra trips headquarters wanted. I graduated with twice the average cadet's time.)

That night I flew with two students. Three-quarters of the way down the runway on our take-off into the stygian dark-ness[41]–with one of the cadets flying as pilot–the wind abruptly changed 180 degrees. (Now it was a *following wind*, instead of a head wind). In addition, the wind speed abruptly increased dramatically (the tower claimed the wind speed actually exceeded hurricane velocity–more than seventy-five knots).

Too late to abort the take-off, we went racing down the runway, the wind further accelerating our ground speed. And we were flying one of those twin-engine, aluminum-cone "jobbies" requiring a higher air speed[42] to get off the ground than the fabric ships.

The cadet in the pilot seat faltered, unsure what to do. Sitting in the right seat as "instructor," I took over, dropped a quarter flaps, and pulled-up the wheels just before we came to the fence.

We staggered into the air . . . and the wind gust quit as quickly as it began. We stayed aloft . . . barely.

Two others behind us did not. No one was killed, though their planes crashed into the fence and their injuries postponed their commissioning with our class.

The worst incident occurred the last night before our

[41] North of Pampa, Texas, at night, when the sky was overcast, we could not see the ground, i. e., we flew as if in a blacked-out cave. This is one of the reasons our new pilots tended to make turns too tight on the approach . . . so they could see the runway lights for orientation.

[42] To the non-flyer this may sound like a contradiction in terms. So let me explain: to take-off an aircraft must reach a certain air speed–with respect to the parcel of air in which it exists, not necessarily with respect to the ground. This is needed to achieve the lift it must have if it is to rise from the runway and go forward. In this case, the parcel of air in which we were flying began accelerating WITH US . . . and thus, though we were going faster with respect to the ground beneath, we were having trouble achieving the required speed relative to the parcel of air in which we were now trying to fly. Though we were literally racing faster and faster, the parcel of air also raced along in the same direction, and therefore we were actually flying slower compared with it.) In short, the fence loomed ahead, while we were still on the ground.

commissioning ceremony—an accident spoiling our non-fatal class record. At the last minute, the Base Operations' clerks found two more cadets who needed three hours, night-flying-time, to meet graduation requirements. One of those was the son of an Air Corps brigadier general who arrived that morning, with the boy's mother, to conduct their son's (and our) commissioning exercises.

Everything went well during the two cadets' take-off and throughout the three-hour flight . . . until they reentered the landing pattern for their final landing. Periodically, for training purposes, tower operators were required to change the landing pattern from a standard entry, whereby the pilot flies into the invisible box-like, traffic pattern at a 45-degree angle, then turns onto a straight, down-wind leg, makes a 90-degree turn thirty seconds after he passes the runway end, flies a crosswind "base-leg," another 90-degree turn onto the final approach, and ends-up directly aimed at and descending toward the runway. (This creates a box-like pattern[43].)

The tower operator, this night, requested cadets use a 360-degree, straight-in, overhead approach. This required them to fly straight at the runway while staying 1,000 feet in the air, then make a descending circle, lowering their gear and flaps – usually in a left turn so the pilot can be the first to see the runway lights—and rolling out of the circle about five hundred feet in the air . . . the aircraft's nose pointed at the runway, ready for landing.

Unfortunately, too many novice pilots became disoriented in this type turn. Too eager to see the runway, they pulled the controls into their stomach—thereby increasing the rate of turn.

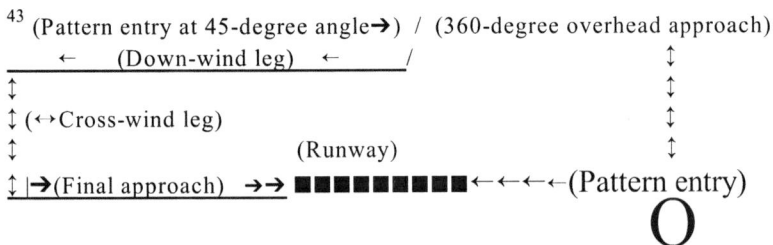

[43] (Pattern entry at 45-degree angle→) / (360-degree overhead approach)

 ← (Down-wind leg) ← /

↕ (↔Cross-wind leg)

(Runway)

↕ |→(Final approach) →→ ■■■■■■■■■←←←←(Pattern entry)

O

Sometimes, this put them into a descending spiral. The aircraft then stalled and they spun into the ground.

These two cadets spun-in on the final approach. This killed them both mere hours before graduation.

The general and his wife were so devastated, he was unable to conduct the graduation exercises. Our Base Commander, a colonel, handled the ceremonies, with a pall of sadness hovering over the theater. All of us had been close friends, so the class dedicated their yearbook and class motto to the two dead boys.

Our class was more fortunate than most, however. Those two were the sole fatalities suffered throughout our twin-engine class's training. Oh, there were many close calls, a number of major injuries, and half those who began did not graduate . . . as predicted.

Back at Pre-flight School (SAACC), the first time we stood in formation as official flying cadets assigned a class number, the ranking officer had told everyone, "Cadets! Take a good look at the man on your right. Now, look at the man on your left. When you put on your wings and 'butter-bars' (second lieutenant's insignia) a year from now, one of you won't be there."

Our class exceeded that challenge when more than seventy-five percent graduated.

CHAPTER SEVEN

▲

Ilogene and I (with Melodie, Rod III, and Pat) rejoined the military ranks for the second time in October 1947, when the Air Corps came through with its offer of a Regular commission–as a first lieutenant. I accepted, exactly two years after I demobilized in Pennsylvania.

With the usual Army foul-up, my recall orders did not arrive until 20 December and directed me to report to Headquarters, 14th Air Force, Brooks Air Force Base, San Antonio, Texas, on–(Come on, what did you expect?)–*no later than December 24.* There was no way Ilogene and our three children could get ready and drive there that rapidly.

I went down alone.

Speeding like a demon from hell across the fifteen-hundred-miles, I barely made the arrival date. Once I signed in, I found virtually everyone gone. And not a soul knew I was coming. (I did not expect a brass band, yet I *did* expect a reception and some information.)

The headquarters building lay empty . . . except for the lonely Duty Officer. On the entire Base, a mere ten people, forced to stick around, held the fort until after the New Year. They were partying . . . of course!

Not at all happy, to me this meant another unnecessary Christmas without my family. I could just as easily have come down after the 1st of the year; such an adjustment would have meant nothing to the Fourteenth Air Force Headquarters to which I was assigned.

But, even so, it was still a far better year-end than the one in

Europe two years earlier, in 1945, with the Battle of the Bulge, the snow, and that flurry of last rough/rapid missions. At least, this Christmas, I had a chance to talk on the phone to Ilogene, the children, and her parents.

At the New Year's Eve party, given by a kind, older WAF captain, (her family name, "Starbuck," became famous long after she died) this firecracker of a lady proved the high quality of service women. My first indoctrination into working with female troops, Virginia showed me women had to be smarter, better educated, and harder-working than men . . . just to keep up. In a few weeks, Virginia received a well-earned promotion to major, and replaced her male boss. (He detested the change . . . and her.)

She was also tough! During the party, Virginia went into the kitchen for some crackers and cheese. She moved a damp dishcloth on the sink. A hiding, four-inch scorpion stung her on the finger. The sting left not a mark, only the initial, temporary pain–but the scorpion promptly flipped over on his back and died. (Now that's tough! We never let Virginia forget it, either.)

The next day I began scrounging a place for Ilogene and the kids. The only one available was a furnished, three-room, partial segment of an adobe house, five miles out in the wild desert, south of the city. The place was furnished all right–with one bed and sagging springs (we had to buy bunk-beds for the children), handmade furniture, leaking sinks and toilet . . . and a full, highly active complement of fire-ants, scorpions, rattlesnakes and cockroaches. (The cockroaches were so monstrous the Texans called them "Palmetto Bugs" because they flew like the ones in Florida. Some years later, Rod III told me South Carolinians voted them their "State Bird.")

To top that, Rod III, in 1947, then just a skinny little tyke, developed asthma[44] while we lived in that adobe. Ilogene and/or I

[44] Never having seen asthma, I called a doctor during Rod III's first attack (when Rod was choking) and told him I believed my son had diphtheria. I was wrong, of course, and the doctor chastised me for scaring him . . . *but* the doctor made an

spent night after night with him at Brooke General Hospital, Fort Sam Houston (Melodie and Pat in tow–no place to leave them).

Other new arrivals to the area (military, that is) lived in chicken coops[45], attics, basements and garages. I guess our snake-rat-and-bug-infested housing might be considered luxurious in comparison.

(In response to such housing complaints, an ironic cartoon appeared in the military newspapers about this time. It showed a table surrounded by six, four-star generals. One stood at the opposite end, saying, "I am having no trouble with housing . . . are any of you?" The others were shaking their heads and saying, "No.")

We stayed in this adobe "prison" only until our furniture arrived (in three weeks) then the Army moved us into a tiny, two-bedroom house on the Base. This was really a step-up–at least we five were no longer crowded into one bedroom.

The new Air Force (still acting as the Army Air Forces) during those initial weeks and months, resembled the renowned "chicken-with-its-head-cut-off." Confusion graced every new day. My assignments provided a good example: In an attempt to cut-back and restructure, the military had ousted by the thousands, colonels and generals, lieutenant colonels and majors. I, but a first lieutenant, held two positions that, before the first of the year, full colonels filled.

A few months later I found myself working also in the Twelfth Air Force Headquarters (Orlando, Florida), holding the same positions there–Director of Ground Safety, Director of Flying Safety, and Director of Special Services (to name only three). As

immediate house call far out in the country, and gave Rod III instant relief. (If I hadn't called it diphtheria, the doctor might well have ignored us.)

[45] These deplorable conditions received nationwide publicity via the newspapers. As a result, the government launched two major housing projects. We benefitted (?) from one of them, for a while, when at Lubbock, Texas, after I returned from Korea.

a result, I commuted between Texas and Florida, The flying gave me hours of extra time and exasperated Ilogene—until we moved again.

To worsen an already bad situation, the Air Force elected—as a way to qualify us for our new slots—to send everyone off to school . . . all at once. We scattered like roaches when a light's turned on. (We were familiar with that!)

Though I cannot say what others did, I went to Ground Safety and Flight Safety Schools. I attended the Military Administrative School. I drove two thousand miles to the Army's Special Services School, Fort Monmouth, New Jersey. (I know there were far more, but they became a whirl and some have fallen through the cracks. Somewhere, in my records there's a pile of graduation certificates and my three-inch, 201-file shows the times, dates and places.)

The Special Services School I really liked. It offered rare opportunities fitting my profile. Students learned to sing, play instruments, teach crafts, run service clubs, and direct soldier-manned stage productions. There, I directed the chorus.

Rodney L. Cron

My chorus's lead singers (Special Services School, Fort Monmouth, NJ)–hamming it up prior to our two-hour Soldiers' Revue. (1948)

The Army Special Services School sent us into New York where we worked with the major Broadway plays and musicals in the theaters of the Strauss brothers. We sat in on and saw the shows, then had a chance to direct the weekly improvement sessions of such hits as "The Little Foxes" (where I met Helen Hayes) and "Oklahoma" (starring John Raitt). Miss Hayes graciously added one of my "business" suggestions to her performance. (A trick I learned back at our "Bijou" theater from "Paul" and "Dave.") While at Fort Monmouth, I won the leading role, sang four solos and the lead chorus numbers in the class's graduation musical–with some 150 officers in the cast. As close as I came to Broadway.

Returning to Texas, I still held those four "colonel" jobs in two headquarters, sang in churches and the base chapel to make extra money, developed and directed the choir at the Orlando Catholic

Church . . . and, oh, yes, in between, I requalified in four types of aircraft (A-26s, C-47s, C-45s, and B-25s). It seemed every day I underwent new and intensive instrument flight training in my sleep. Yet, somehow, I found opportunities to love Ilogene and our children, and introduce them to the local points of interest.

Ilogene and the children adored San Antonio's River Walk, a highly decorated ten-block-long strip of the river, eight feet below street level. In the very center of town, it had walkways on each side of the water, and (in those days) only a few old-timer restaurants. Cadets once rented boats and played war games on the river, fighting to dump each other in the water. In 1947, the city was just beginning to see this area's potential as a commercial enterprise and started renovating it. (Today, it is one of San Antonio's primary tourist attractions and the river uses more of the available water than any other enterprise. Occasionally, it is also–as it was then–the site of murders, assaults and muggings . . . but the city down-plays those aspects.)

What most astounded Melodie and Rod III was the Alamo's setting. Located a few hundred feet to the east of the river and right downtown, it sat just north of Joske's Department Store, on the east side of the street from a Murphy's Ten Cent Store . . . and (this is true too) beside the "Davy Crockett" motel, billing itself, like the song said, "Across the Alley from the Alamo." The kids (and later my mother-in-law, Mercedes Thaddora "Babe" Mays) expected to see the Alamo located out of town, on a grassy hilltop surrounded by acres of open space, with a river at the slope's foot. (Okay, maybe that's the way it once looked–during the siege in 1836 and in the movies –but no longer.)

Moving to Florida (no "Disney World" or "Epcot Center," then), we drove the seventy miles, regularly, one-way, to the beach. The kids loved the ocean and Rod III's asthma vanished whenever we came within twenty miles of the water.

Rodney L. Cron

Brigadier General
Ralph N. Snavely
(1949)

In Florida, also, I fell into a pot of luck. Within weeks, Brigadier General Ralph Snavely selected me as his aide. The personal training General Snavely gave me, during my assignment, not even a military academy[46] could have duplicated. He insisted I sit at his left side during every staff meeting. Ostensibly there to take notes, he suggested I also "take note" of the proceedings. (See his picture, above.)

He regularly queried the ranks of his staff, all colonels, for problem solutions to his Twelfth Air Force's tasks and goofs. Once he milked their brains, he turned to me and asked, "Okay, Rod, what would you do about this if you were in my shoes?"

His initial question caught me flat-footed. I blushed and stammered, "General, sir . . . these . . . uh . . . men are all . . . um . . . colonels . . . I - I - I'm just a lieutenant."

[46] Though I was fairly good at writing, every letter I wrote had to pass through a captain, a major, a lieutenant colonel, then two colonels, before it reached the general for his signature. One day I took my original letter, plus the five changes, and obtained permission to speak to General Snavely. I showed him my original letter, then the others (with their repeated changes), and my final letter. The last was exactly the same as the one I wrote the first time. Not only did my letters, after that, go directly to the general, but I believe this motivated General Snavely to make me his aide. (One of the aide's jobs was to read, and precis, the Congressional record each morning prior to the general's arrival at the office, at 0800.) **See photo of General Snavely, next page)**

The general stared at me–hard. "Son, if you want to be a general, you have to learn sometime. You won't learn any younger . . . now give!"

In time I developed the capability to make the right decisions, ones he approved. He would then say, "All right, gentlemen, that's the word. Go do it."

I was not too popular among his staff, but I learned valuable–if not priceless– management techniques. I never got to be a general, yet I carried those lessons with me into later life, everlastingly grateful, and used them when writing my three management books for business. [I sang at General Snavely's son's wedding (Ralph Jr.), in the Catholic Chapel, Randolph AFB, Texas–gratis–in minor repayment.]

<p style="text-align:center">*　　　　　*　　　　　*</p>

In an earlier chapter I said I have had only a few regrets.

I lied. My life is strewn with regrets. Largely for actions I took–or did not take–because I had no choice. These often hurt loved ones, friends, associates and colleagues, sometimes irrevocably, sometimes disproportionately.

While I was in military service, for example, I sat on literally hundreds of General and Special court-martial boards[47], initiated a few of my own as well as Articles Fifteen, wrote letters of reprimand, and gave oral chastisements. I feel little regret for most of those decisions, especially those we rendered as a panel. A court-martial is so carefully investigated in advance, prepared and supported with a preponderance of evidence and witnesses that,

[47] At Lackland Air Force Base, we adjudged cases across a broad spectrum–murder, rape, assault, desertion, AWOL, domestic and military violence, homosexuality, even child pornography, and pedophile attacks. All types of criminals end-up in the armed forces, just as in civilian life. But in the not-so-distant-past it was worse: civilian judges once gave criminals a choice between prison and "joining up." Sometimes this "made a man" of the convicted civilian; more often, it simply gave him another field for his depraved activities. At Lackland AFB, we sent our convictions off to die, to be incarcerated for various lengths of time (in either local stockades or federal prisons), to be drummed from the service, or to return to their outfits with fines and restrictions–to name a few of the decrees we handed down.

by the time the case goes to court, the perpetrator is usually guilty and pays the assigned penalty. The differences arise mostly from technicalities. Yet, even here, there were some I would have avoided if I had been granted any leeway.

Without naming names, let me cite some heart-breaking "for-instances":

Immediately on arrival in Africa, I had to recommend for court-martial a fellow Army attaché who invited a French officer into our secure offices at the embassy . . . and showed him some secret documents. Our officer's argument was, "He traded me their classified information as a result." Though the Frenchman probably did, that was beside the point. My colleague violated sensitive security US directives. It cost him a fine, but more importantly, it cost him his promotion to full colonel. (I told him, if only he had asked the previous Defense Attaché, he could have obtained permission. The data the officer revealed was actually of comparatively little value to the USA, could have been declassified by the Defense Attaché for this purpose, but he acted without thinking.)

If my assistant had not filed formal charges before I arrived, I would have handled this differently. But, once submitted, it was too late. My predecessor waved off the "hot potato"and it landed in my lap . . . the day I signed on as Station Commander. The only way to resolve the issue, then, was via a military tribunal.

Again, in Africa, it was necessary to court-martial another excellent officer, take away his grade, status and retirement-- and send him home to spend years behind bars. We caught him dealing in clandestine currency exchange (highly illegal) between nations. He made, on this deal, about four thousand extra dollars a month, for about six months. (Having diplomatic passports and immunity, all of us had available a multitude of black-market-means to line our pockets, if we so chose.) This man had a lovely wife and two delightful children. I considered both this officer and the attaché mentioned to be personal friends. (The extremely bad

elements of this latter case arose from, first, his being very close to me and my wife, and second, he and his wife were *black,* living in a black country–Ghana. I cried over this.)

A third attaché (one of my young, Air Force assistants) pulled a boo-boo while I was confined to bed with a bout of malaria. He moved our offices in the embassy–as we had planned–from one floor to another (to achieve greater security), but then he signed-off on a "locked filing-cabinet" *that was not locked.*

His action went beyond any protective measures I might have instituted, when the Marine Guards assigned to the embassy discovered the security violation in their daily checks. They immediately and officially filed it with the State and Defense Departments. This took it out of my hands.

Potentially, since this "open" cabinet contained top secret material, the Department of Defense had to assume the open lock compromised every Navy submarine location, as well as the Strategic Air Command's routes and codes throughout the world. Though the cabinet remained in a locked room, inside a closed embassy, secured by those same Marine Guards, our immediate instructions required everything inside the cabinet be scrapped . . . at once. This cost a bundle!

The officer, a young, eager, brilliant and devoted pilot with a high potential, did not warrant a court-martial. (That I prevented with special messages to General Lemay.) But my immediate commander, through whom my report had to pass–another four-star general–insisted the incident be reflected on the young officer's ER (Effectiveness Report).

I argued, "Our rules, sir, specifically discourage reporting one-time, isolated incidents on an ER. This is not this man's typical or standard performance."

The general replied, "I said, 'Do it!' So *do it!*"

I did . . . but I bent over backwards and eased the wording.

The general then, personally, lowered my evaluation of the lieutenant (making it far worse). This slated the officer for a "no-

promotions" future which he did not deserve. (The young officer and his wife hated me ever afterward. But I heard he was able to have the offensive ER removed from his file after a few years, and eventually became a full colonel.)

While at Lackland, for some unknown reason the base "legal beagles" (our legal arm, called the "Judge Advocate's Office") repeatedly assigned me not only to sit on court-martial boards at all levels, but also ordered me to act as investigating officer on case after potential case. In this capacity–while only a major–I investigated two complaints against the general commanding the base. (NOTE: This was not Bob Stillman, but his predecessor.)

The first involved the Base Exchange, the base's outlet for merchandise sold to the airmen (good quality at reasonable prices, other than groceries–the Base Commissary sold groceries and related items). A civilian "whistle-blower" in the BX system accused the general of using the Exchange's profits in a non-prescribed manner, meaning "for his own personal benefit." (Although we found possible indications of this, we could not develop the necessary proof, as no other employees testified for fear of losing their jobs.)

My second investigation handled an accusation against the same general–saying he derived personal income from a skating rink he insisted the government build on the base for young airmen. This one we *did* prove. We documented his getting a cut . . . plus his ordering every new enlistee to spend so many hours there, each week, skating (and at the airman's expense). This constituted several major violations: ordering subordinates to perform a duty for which they had to pay, receiving monies therefrom, and ordering other subordinates to make certain this happened.

The last of the above three caused the "fit to hit the shan."

The general's vice commander, a colonel–a real go-getter and himself frocked for promotion to brigadier general–refused to comply. He told the two-star, "This is an illegal order, sir. I cannot

direct our airman to roller-skate and pay for it as part of their training."

The general promptly announced, "You shall, Colonel . . . or else."

This debate went on, with a deadline set by the general. The colonel still refused.

The general initiated court-martial action, then relented. Instead, he offered to let the colonel sign an Article Fifteen (pay a fine), admit he was wrong, perform the assigned (illegal) task, and get off virtually "Scott-free." The colonel refused again.

This case went all the way to the Secretary of the Air Force. The secretary called in the colonel and made him the same offer the general had. The colonel again refused. (So would I!) The secretary tossed the court-martial and Article Fifteen into the waste basket and reassigned the colonel to Spain. The colonel complained to the Inspector General's Office.

That is where I came in. My investigation proved the general was totally out of line and the colonel was right. (In the meantime, the general was still ordering each airman to skate–and pay! He had developed a real "cash cow," and was not about to give up the milk it produced.)

My report recommended the general be court-martialed . . . but the "good-old-boy" network stepped in. The colonel never made general, and the two-star was assigned overseas, to Italy.

Yet, still arrogant, in Italy, the two-star really "stepped on his crank." He left his wife behind in the USA and took his sister-in-law to his Italian assignment, introducing her to everyone as his legal spouse.

The four-star commanding our European Forces went down to Italy to visit them–and, since he knew the two-star's real wife–there was no fooling him. The two-star, not remembering this, tried to carry it off . . . but failed.

Finally, after three times at bat and not taking a hit, the inning was over. The four-star court-martialed the two-star, sent him

home, and retired him in his permanent grade of colonel. (If I'd had the four-star's clout, I'd have slammed the two-star's butt in prison. The two-stars' actions blackened the name of all Air Force officers. I also would have given the colonel who refused to carry out the original illegal order both a medal and this idiot's two stars. Maybe that's why I was never a general or Secretary of Defense.)

I detest besmirching the history of our generals as there were only a few who deserved having their hands slapped. (For those mentioned here–unnamed–I can reference other hundreds of honest, hard-working officers of flag rank who were never appropriately honored and never dishonored the stars they wore. Many gave their lives for their men.)

Yet I must cite one more wayward soul. This one may be revealed by the time and place. Before I left Chanute AFB, Illinois, its two-star commander, near retirement, saw a way to provide for it most adequately. He affiliated with an insurance company, and required every airman on base (usually assigned there for aircraft-engine training) to buy insurance.

This made the general a mint. No one complained until he retired. Then our investigations revealed he made millions on the incoming airmen.

The Air Force, aghast, called him back to active duty to court-martial him. He remained on active duty during the investigation, trial and sentencing–a period exceeding six months. During this period, he was paid about $2,500 a month (salary, benefits and per diem).

The court-martial convicted him . . . and fined him $500. *That was all!*

My calculations indicated he made at least $15,000 on the deal. (At that rate I might volunteer for a court-martial, with a known conviction and such a fine, twice a year.) In addition, the conviction did NOT take away his retirement. It did NOT reduce his monthly retirement pay by one cent. Nor did it adversely affect

his standing in his community one iota. (If I had been so convicted, I would have been on the streets the next day, begging, with none of the perks cited above.)

Lest you think I am "down" on generals, let me assure you *I am not*. My investigations and court-martial experiences actually ran the gamut from the lowest ranking airman through colonel as well. These just happened to be noteworthy enough to enumerate in detail and I was involved (usually as investigator or on the court-martial board). It would be impossible to cover the other cases in a similar fashion . . . and most would be boringly alike. I will say this, however, when investigating officers turned in a report indicating a basis for a court-martial . . . *there was usually a conviction.*

Our military tribunal system worked better than the civilian courts'. For example: Just a couple years ago, Hocking County assigned me as an alternate juror to a robbery case in the local court. I sat and listened, then the judge called me in to his office and talked with me while the remaining, full jury decided the case. Since he knew my background, he asked what I thought of the court action.

I told him, "In a military court we would have taken about fifteen minutes to handle it, including the time needed to hear the witness, examine all the evidence, make a determination of his guilt . . . and sentence him.

"You took four hours and had ten witnesses say the same thing. The prosecution presented identical evidence over and over until everyone was bored. Now the jury is deciding the case–and already they have been out an hour. Plus you still have to sentence him after his conviction. Why so long?"

The judge said, "We have to do all that to make certain jury members are firmly convinced. Remember, we aren't dealing, here, with well-educated people in all instances, and some are slower than others. But what do you think of the two charges?"

"The prosecutor presented ample evidence to convict on the

first. The prosecutor fouled up the second charge and it should have been dismissed."

He nodded. "I agree. But I predict they will convict on both charges."

(He knew his jury panels. They did.)

"Anything else?" he asked.

"Yes, you made one ruling I didn't understand. The defense attorney objected when the prosecutor asked, 'What was the other person thinking at the time . . . and what was his opinion?' You overruled the defense's objection and I saw the prosecutor's question as absolutely unacceptable."

The judge looked thoughtful for a second, then answered, "I shouldn't have done that. Are you sure?"

He called in the court stenographer and asked her for a rereading of that portion of her trial records. (Her reading verified the situation.) He waved a hand. "I was wrong."

"Won't that be a valid basis for a retrial or reversal by an upper court?"

This time he laughed. "That guy is so guilty it will never get that far. His attorney will wash his hands of the whole thing and be glad to get it out of his hair. As for the defendant–he knows he's 'hung' and will say nothing."

(The judge was right on those two points, too.)

Interested in obtaining answers to several other observations, I said, "The defendant looked as if he were a hardened criminal. He was completely at ease, wearing handcuffs and shackles . . . despite his nice suit, white shirt, and tie."

"Aha, you caught that? How?"

"He sat there too nonchalantly. He cleaned his nails, not bothered by the shackles, apparently unconcerned about the trial's outcome. I figured he'd been there before . . . and knew he was going back into the slammer."

The judge smiled. "This will be his fifth conviction. His record shows –" (He thumbed through a stack of papers on his desk)

"–he already has spent five years in three different prisons. He'll be there longer this time."

I grinned too. "But he was so stupid–taking a credit card and trying to use it locally at Wal-Mart . . . a credit card belonging to a lieutenant on Logan's Police Force. For Cripe's Sake, that was just plain dumb!"

The judge rose from his chair and ushered me into the next room. "Rod, that stupidity is what's keeping me in business and our jails so full."

CHAPTER EIGHT

▲

Throughout my entire career I never preferred court-martial charges against any enlisted man under my immediate supervision. Yet I *did* warm numerous rears on occasion, with reprimands–giving them Articles Fifteen through some hearty "chewings-out." (I tried to follow the rule: compliment in public, reprimand in private.)

In Abidjan, an NCO–my aircraft engineer–yearning to make master sergeant asked for my recommendation as his commander. I delayed giving him an answer, either way.

I had suspected this, but the next day I actually caught him working on our aircraft engines while our radio operator read to him from the engineering manuals. A little quick questioning verified the NCO wanting the promotion could not even read! (How he got that far I do not know.) It saddened me because he was an eager, hard worker. (Okay, so maybe he needed some "jacking-up" occasionally, but that was typical.)

I called him into my office and told him, "Sorry, Bill, no way! I can't promote you to master sergeant if you can't read. You cannot lead nor teach other NCOs. If you learn to read . . . I'll add that extra stripe." (All of us pitched-in to help him, but he never managed to do it. I had to send him home at the end of his tour, ready to retire, still a Tech Sergeant.)

Earlier, I reprimanded this same NCO for chewing tobacco and spitting out the window when sitting in the co-pilot's seat. (He had streaked the side of the airplane with brown.) I made him clean and wax the aircraft as well . . . all of it . . . by himself . . . forbidding any other NCO or his household servants to assist.

After that he showed more respect for our special aircraft.

This NCO then married the ambassador's secretary. A wonderful girl.

I translated the French for them at their wedding in the Abidjan Mayor's office (warning them they were marrying under Napoleonic Law and, therefore, the husband could take the children and dispatch the wife, at any time, without recourse). Pulling some strings, I also arranged for President Houphuet-Boigny's motorcycle escort to provide a roaring accompaniment during their short honeymoon trip in the country's only limousine, from the City Hall to the Hotel Ivoire (in Cocody, Abidjan's most affluent area). Despite my refusal to promote him, both remained my friends.

I also lost another valuable NCO, some years before, while at Recruiting Group Headquarters, Chanute AFB. This master sergeant typed at a rate faster than any court stenographer and helped me publish three books[48].

One day he came into my office highly agitated, hands flitting, face dour. He said he needed desperately to borrow some money. I refused. He then asked a captain in the next office who promptly wanted to know, from me, if he were good for it.

I told him, "I have no idea. But I make it a point never to loan anyone anything–and certainly you know it's illegal for officers to lend money to enlisted staff members."

The captain ignored my hints and made the loan. He also made out a contract, charging the sergeant an usury-level interest for the $2,500. (I told the captain the contract would never stand-up in court.)

That very night the NCO deserted. He left his wife and four children in Rantoul, Illinois, and ran off with a local divorcee with

[48] Air Force Management, The Air Force Recruiting Guide, and the Air Force Recruiting Supervisor. (None of which carried my name and for which I received no credit, no monetary return, and no benefit, except in my Effectiveness Reports.) This also happened to me later, working with another author who made millions from his books. Later, I began charging up front for editing and writing.

five children. *Five children!*

No one has ever seen or heard from them since, nor did the captain ever see any of his money. As far as I know the NCO is still on the loose to this day.

I have always hoped it was worth it . . . to the sergeant!

Before this man deserted, we stayed late in the office one afternoon when a Major Kissel and I were having a bit of a "go-around." After lengthy discussion–some of it at the top of our lungs–I saw Kissel and I were not going to resolve this disagreement easily or quickly. I called in the sergeant and told him he could leave for the afternoon. (I didn't want anyone else to hear what I was about to say to the major).

He showed an odd expression when I said, "Take the rest of the day off, Sergeant. I'll see you in the morning."

The major and I continued until late at night . . . and, in the end, we gave up. This one had to be adjudicated–finally–by our group commander.

In the morning, I confronted the sergeant, "Why the strange look when I said you could take-off yesterday for the rest of the afternoon?"

He laughed. "Sir, it was already nine o'clock at night."

Taken as a whole, our Air Force NCOs earned mostly compliments. From my combat aircrews, to the many others I worked with, at Lackland AFB, in Florida, Chicago and ROTC. I was happy to serve with each of them. Most had earned high school diplomas, many Bachelor's Degrees, a number had gleaned their Masters', and a few boasted Ph. D.s. Many were far smarter and better educated than I, and fully as dedicated.

Among the officers with whom I served, many were good, several were outstanding. My first attaché assistant, Air Force, in Abidjan, Captain LeBaron Whittier, bested me as a pilot, and proved to be an outstanding administrator. He retired years later, a lieutenant colonel.

In Chicago, one young captain–intelligent, multi-skilled–stood

out above the rest on my Recruiting staff. Byron Hetherington learned quickly and was always eager to improve. He showed a rare and gifted promise, and enjoyed the support of a lovely wife admired by both my wife and me. During his work with me we discovered another odd happenstance.

We found his father flew as a pilot with my B-26 Group when we were stationed in Royé, France. One morning, a day I was not flying, we members of the 572nd Squadron stood behind our hospital, a half-mile from the runway's end, watching the takeoff in bad weather. When the wind required a departure to the east it was always "touch-and-go,"for–just beyond our hospital–a series of high-tension electrical lines ran across the climb-out route. (The very ones I flew under when I lost an engine.)

While we watched, an engine failed on a plane just as it left the ground. The pilot tried desperately to climb above the wires on a single engine and saw he couldn't do it. He elected to fly under them. His propellers struck a fence. The plane crashed, splattered across the landscape, and began burning mere yards from where we stood.

Aghast, we ran into the burning debris. I saw the pilot still strapped in his seat, ran forward, grabbed up pilot and seat, and sprinted from the smouldering wreckage. All of us feared the over-heated bombs might explode any second. (None did!)

When I put down the pilot, I found he was dead. The pilot was my friend, Lieutenant Hetherington.

Later, in Chicago, while Byron and I were talking one evening I told him his name was familiar. He explained his father had also flown B-26s during WWII, and where he died.

It was Byron's father, I pulled from the crash site.

My wife and I visited this young man and his wife after I retired. At the time, he managed his father's meat packing plant in Hobart, Oklahoma.

Just recently, out of the clear blue sky (to coin another cliché), he really "made my day." He telephoned to say he was moving to

Duncan, Oklahoma (we had not talked in years). He exclaimed how he remembered my management and writing help in Chicago, and how he applied them. (It is deeply moving to find your assistance and guidance have been truly helpful, actually remembered and used. I assured him his accolades gave me a new lease on life. They did.)

<div align="center">* * *</div>

Our flying–especially mine–came hot and heavy during the years after WWII, before and after Korea. There also were several noteworthy "Nightmare Alley" flights among the many hours of tranquil boredom. Let me consolidate a few to show you the ones coming closest to nailing the lid on my coffin.

Grant Swartz, my former commander in Korea, flew a B-26 (a former A-26, now called a Douglas Invader) from Shaw AFB (South Carolina) to Kelly AFB (San Antonio, Texas) just to give me a weekend at home in Chanute AFB (Illinois). This was very generous and thoughtful.

A-26 and I, flying out of Chanute AFB (1953) Grant's ship had a glass nose.

At the time, I was taking special training in Texas. Ilogene and the children were up there in Illinois (Chanute AFB) at my permanent base. But the results of this flight kept Ilogene and me (and, maybe, Grant) awake for days.

Preparing to leave for home, I helped refuel the bird while Grant obtained the flight clearance. (We used to joke about "increasing regulations meaning we could no longer take-off until the weight of the paperwork equaled the weight of the aircraft." Originally, we had only to hop in, call the tower, and blast off. Now, that was a thing of the past!)

No one told either of us that afternoon, but the man refueling our aircraft knew nothing about B-26s. To speed things along, I refueled the two outer, auxiliary wing tanks, when I leaped up on the plane to help.

The refueling truck driver filled the main tanks, checked them, and sealed the gas caps. (If the caps were not sealed and locked tightly in place, the air flowing across the wings and creating a negative pressure, sucked all the gasoline out of the tanks. How big a problem this unexpected lack of fuel can cause . . . we were about to find-out, first hand.)

The crewman on the tanker handed me the fuel line and I filled the central, main fuselage tank. When finished, I asked him–again–if he had filled the main tanks.

He reassured me with another, "Yes"–and a "thumbs-up"– before driving off.

Grant came out of Operations, bringing along one of the chaplains from our Chaplain Training School who also wanted to go to Rantoul. All of us climbed in. We locked the canopy, and Grant taxied to the runway, assuming take-off position.

Grant took the pilot's seat. I sat on the jump-seat to his right–with no controls. To watch the take-off, the chaplain crawled forward, through the passageway, into the glass nose. Grant had told him that, from there, it was awe-inspiring. (The

landing was even more unforgettable.)

While Grant taxied out, I noticed the fuel gauge needles on the two main tanks remained in a position indicating less than half-full. I called this to Grant's attention.

Grant tapped them–they did not move. "Don't worry," he said. "They stuck there on the way over. The refueling operator assured me he filled them to the brim."

This gave me chills. But on this trip I was not the pilot, merely a passenger, and I was not about to look a gift horse in the mouth. (Grant had flown more than a thousand miles to do me this favor, and I was eager to get home for a few hours with my family.) Besides, I had already called Ilogene and given her our ETA.

The take-off and climb-out went smooth as silk, over-awing the chaplain. Taking-off on the two main tanks (with the stuck needles)–which is SOP–we shifted to the wing tanks and exhausted them, then went to the fuselage tank and eventually back to the mains.

Over Illinois, nearing the middle of the state, fifty miles southwest of Rantoul (Chanute AFB) and about ten miles southeast of Springfield, the right engine abruptly quit. No coughing, no surging, no warning–one second it was humming like a watchmaker's dream, the next it went absolutely silent.

One quick glance at the fuel gauges showed no change. The needles were still stuck (?). I sensed at once we were about to run out of gas.

Grant looked to me (I taught him to fly the B-26 in Korea and had logged more than two thousand instructor hours by this point in time). "What do I do?" he asked.

"Feather the right engine. I'll put all the gas tanks on the left one." (The reason: this engine carried our electrical generators and inverters.) I handled all the prop and gas controls while he adjusted the tabs and flew. I called the chaplain out of the nose and told him what was going on, and how to prepare for a crash landing. I also asked him to pray. (*Boy! Did he ever!*)

I then turned back to Grant and pointed him toward the Springfield airport . . . we barely saw it in the distance . . . and I made my instructions very clear, "Aim for the north-south runway, straight in, across that tiny lake, I'll keep shifting the gas pumps from tank to tank to milk-out every drop.

"You do nothing but fly. I'll handle the wheels and flaps, if we get across the lake. If we aren't going to make it, put her down in the water, still holding 160 mph air speed."

He eye-balled the distant runway as if it were manna from heaven, and asked out of a corner of his mouth, "Why 160?"

"That'll give us our maximum gliding ratio . . . and we need every inch."

The remaining engine began wind-milling, quietly. We were now flying a glider. "Okay . . . feather the other engine!"

He gasped. "Feather *both* engines?"

"Yep, now the propellers are providing only drag . . . which we do not need."

We had been flying at ten thousand feet when the first engine quit. Now we were at six thousand. The plane kept dropping lower and lower while the runway seemed to remain the same distance away.

I called the tower to alert them to our dire emergency. But it was a civilian airport and did not monitor our frequencies. Over the military channels I began calling "May-Day." (The flying equivalent to an "S-O-S" at sea.)

Into cyberspace, I broadcast to all who might be listening. I begged someone–everyone . . . anyone!–to notify the Springfield tower. (The Springfield airfield was currently flying aircraft off another runway, 90-degrees from the one we were approaching.) Springfield never got a single message!

We crossed the lake getting lower by the second . . . with Grant shaking so hard the controls seemed about to fall off. But we made it over the fence.

I slammed down the gear and flaps.

Grant "pranged" the B-26–dead-stick–onto the runway's initial two feet, where the boundary line was still painted white and lights marked the threshold. Reaching the intersection, we slipped between two, taking-off Cubs.

Screeching to a halt at the other end of the runway, Grant palsied from having made it alive. I clasped the chaplain's shoulders and bent forward to whisper, "I guess your prayers did it, sir."

He looked up, eyes rolling. "It sure was quiet those last few minutes, no engine noise, only the sound of the wind over the wings."

I too began shaking now (from the overdose of adrenaline). "Ever think those might have been angel wings you heard?"[49]

Before this, though, I had become very well acquainted with another airfield–Wright-Patterson AFB. Not only had I worked as a civilian and enlisted there as an Aviation Cadet, but I had another of those once-in-a-lifetime events on that Base, while flying General Snavely's B-26.

Finishing a conference one morning, my sergeant and I buttoned-up for take-off and home. It was a lousy day. Thunderstorms, frequent lightning, heavy rainfall coming down by the bucketful, visibility zilch, thick clouds right down to the ground.

If I had not waved my green instrument card at the Operations Officer–assuring my authority to fly under virtually any conditions–and I were not heading for Orlando (where Ilogene and the kids were waiting, all of whom I had not seen for several weeks), this would have been a "no-brainer." I would have stayed in Ohio. But the general had also called earlier and wanted me back at headquarters ASAP, another *big* incentive.

I took off in zero-zero conditions . . . no visibility . . . right into

[49] The "Incident Reports" Grant and I filed after the near-accident episode burned a few tails at Kelly AFB and resulted in a radical change of procedures as well as greater strictures on the training of all new refueling operators.

the clouds hugging the ground. On instruments (even before take-off), I got off the ground, pulled up the gear, and eased up the flaps. Everything seemed to be working fine.

But we barely passed the location of the water tower on the hill (which we could not see), when we sustained an electrical fire in the switch board to the left of my instrument panel. The fumes began choking us.

I called the tower, declared an emergency, and asked them to clear the area . . . "I'm going to make a time/distance approach with no radios or electronic equipment to tell me where I am."

I also said, "I'm shutting down all transmissions and reception–*now!*" I cut off every electrical switch.

Fighting the acrid fumes making breathing difficult (I opened the tiny, triangular window to my left, but it helped only a little), I flew straight ahead for one minute, a thousand feet above the ground, still in solid rain and clouds. I then made a careful, 90-degree turn to the left, flew what would normally be a "cross-wind" leg and a "down-wind" leg past the field–I hoped! Constantly calculating wind speed, time, distance, air speed, acceleration and deceleration, I turned left again 90-degrees (praying the winds were steady) onto an imaginary cross-leg, and finally turned left once more, another 90-degrees, to line up on an invisible approach heading, hoping the twelve-thousand-foot runway now lay directly ahead.

Blind as a bat in the rain, I put down the wheels, added flaps, (hydraulically operated), and proceeded to descend. Now it was "Katie bar the door." We were either going to land on the runway or crash . . . into buildings, the road ahead of the runway, the fence, or houses short of the field.

Sight unseen, when my altimeter indicated we were fifty feet off the ground, I eased up the nose, and pulled back the throttles. The water was so deep we never felt the touch-down, only the aircraft's slowing as we entered the water's surface . . . and landed. Out of the corners of my eyes I saw lights flashing

by–they had to be the runway lights. Very dim, very obscure.

We came to a halt. Two crash trucks approached, one from each side. I opened the canopy into the heavy downpour, so we could breathe. A pump truck immediately swung a sprinkler over our heads and filled the cockpit (to the brim) with sticky white foam.

The Base really jinxed the wiring. It took four days to clean-out the foam. It took another three to replace the "short."

The Base Engineering Officer phoned General Snavely to explain my extended absence. (No one, but I, explained to Ilogene. She understood. The general? Well, maybe!)

In all my years of flying that was my sole zero-zero landing, without any visibility or ceiling, with no radio communication, without any external electronic or oral guidance, solely on guess and calculations. (Nor did I want–ever!–to do it again.)

The next incidents were both in jets.

Colonel Hosmer, years later, had to go from San Antonio, Texas to Wright-Patterson AFB, Ohio, near my home town (Piqua), for a meeting. As my boss, he asked me to go along and help fly. This entire flight was one huge conglomeration of near-disasters and freaky luck.

Going north toward Ohio at forty-thousand feet, our pitot tube froze-up with ice, therefore we had no airspeed indications. Its electric heater failed.

Before leaving, we had agreed to share the flying. He would do the chores going up–flying from the front seat with good visibility; I would ride in the rear, barely able to see around his body and glimpse the runway ahead. On return we would reverse the procedure.

About to land at Little Rock, Arkansas to refuel, Hosmer did not want to risk landing the bird without an airspeed indicator. He asked me if I could do it . . . from the rear.

Good old, over-confident me, I said, "Sure, Colonel. No problem."

I made the instrument let-down and landing, using solely engine rpms and a sense of relative speed as my guide. I eased the plane onto the ground just as if I knew what I was doing. The Base rapidly installed a new pitot heater and refueled our T-33, and we were, once more, off on our trip.

When we landed at Patterson Field, an emergency-crash truck followed alongside all the way from the runway to the hard-stand. I thought it was some kind of new requirement.

We opened the canopy and the truck driver came forward, uneasily edging nearer our plane. He pointed at it. We looked, mouths dropping open.

Behind our rear seat–from there to the tail–the fuselage had largely burned away. Only a few bare struts held the engine in and the tail on.

The crash truck driver said, "Why didn't you bail out when you got the red emergency light in the cockpit?"

"There were no red lights. Every dial indicated normal, in the green all the way. Still do."

This time the Base replaced the majority of our aircraft during Hosmer's conference, and I had a short visit with my parents-in-law. Saturday next, both of us once more readied for take-off, eager to return home.

The colonel sat in the front cockpit, radios on, waiting to record our clearance and departure instructions; as the return pilot I stayed on the ground to do the external "walk-around" inspection.

After our previous experience, I was skeptical of the pitot[50] heater. During my usual check, I called, "Pitot heater off."

He shouted back, "Pitot heater off."

[50] The pitot tube" consists of two small metal tubes, one facing forward into the wind and the other, shorter and twisted, facing downward at an angle (both contain an internal, electrical heater). These two tubes provided wind-speed data to our gauges. Attached instruments gave us readings in the cockpit regarding our aircraft's air speed relative to the air cell in which the aircraft was flying. (A rather primitive method . . . but it worked (still does!) . . . as long as the tubes do not fill with moisture and freeze-up.)

133

I removed my right flying glove and reached out, preparing to tell him to turn it "on," so I could feel it warm up, as required. When I grasped the pitot tube it was already red hot.

My hand literally baked to the surface. I screamed and pulled away, leaving a lot of skin and some muscle.

The fireman standing-by to protect us while we fired up, drove us instantly to the hospital, my hand outside in the cold wind. On a hot day, or even a warm day, I believe the pain might have put me in a coma. On this cold, winter day I was in the emergency room before the lights began to turn color and fade.

The doctors shot me with a pain-killer, then bandaged the hand (with my coat on, because the bandage was as large as a boxing glove). They stuffed me with more pain killers (and gave me a bottle to take along). They then cleared us to make the return flight to Texas for further treatment . . . *if Hosmer flew.*

Of course, the colonel was equally over-confident. He said, "Sure, let's go."

I have no idea how the flight into and out of Little Rock went. Throughout those first hours, I huddled in the back seat, giggling, chewing on pain-killers, playing with my fingers, and blithering like the village idiot. The medications alternately depressed, then lifted me to places I had never been–literally. "I was feeling no pain." (Cheech and Chong never had it so good, even with their entire van of marijuana.)

Approaching San Antonio, Hosmer snapped me alert.

Around us the sky growled, flashed and boomed with thunder storms, lightning, rain, more lightning, and violent turbulence. We needed to make an instant instrument approach to Kelly Field and a jet let-down, in this stormy onslaught.

The colonel once more waffled. "Can you make the let-down and land, Rod? I don't think I can do it."

By now I rode so high, I'd have tried a brain transplant with an axe and shovel.

"Sure," I told him. Silently, I added, *Whoop-de-do! Why,*

Colonel, I'll lay this little old T-33 right thar on that landing spot . . . and grease it in like you've never seen before.

Halfway down our vertical dive to a lower altitude, the heater vents (blowing air into the cockpit to prevent the canopy's fogging and freezing) flipped the contact lens from my left eye.

No sweat! Tonight, I'm superman. I'll make the landing with my right eye.

But my hand in the boxing-glove-sized bandage prevented my handling the controls with ease.

No sweat there, either! I'll fly left-handed, shifting from the control column, to the throttle, to the flaps, to the gear, and back to the control column. Why! This is easy–I thought–*like sitting in the living room at home, changing TV channels.*

Then the tower switched our approach from west to east–a 180-degrees reversal–when the winds on the ground abruptly changed direction.

Hey! No problemo! I can make a "back-side" approach as well as anyone. (Har-de-har-har!) But I'd never done it under these conditions, nor practiced Kelly's recently changed, complicated procedures.

Meanwhile, Colonel Hosmer sat in the front seat making radio calls, as happy as if both of us had good sense. Throughout the host of bumps, grinds and whipping turns, he remained completely calm–externally–and he gave me the confidence to do the impossible.

The funniest part of this . . . though I was damned near "out of it," could barely see, kept hopping around the cockpit like a Mexican Jumping Bean shifting the controls from hand to hand, and back again . . . I *did* make the let-down, approach and landing (in a thick rain squall with low visibility and gusting winds). And I did it better than I made any before, or since. (Hosmer suggested I get drunk after that, before every flying.)

On the ground, Hosmer told me he came back to pull me out of the rear cockpit once he parked the plane . . . and found me

completely unconscious. Medics had to help him drag my frame from the plane and ease it into his car.

Ilogene was shocked to see my condition, I heard later. Of course, the next day I remembered nothing of our return flight (except vague, dreamy snatches).

<p style="text-align:center">* * *</p>

For another look at flying's problems, parachutes and "bailing-out" must assume central roles. Often, when flying passengers, they asked, "Did you ever bail out?"

I told them, one and all, "No! But if you fly in any military aircraft carrying chutes, you must be ready to do it at all times."

While giving my passengers thorough pre-flight, emergency instructions (what the various bells mean when I ring them, and how to crouch for crash landings, how to don the chutes, and how to bail out), I always added this final admonition, "When the alarm bell rings three times, don your chutes . . . immediately!

"When it goes into full ring (ringing continuously), hurry to the rear door–and *jump*! Don't hesitate! Don't waffle . . . *JUMP!*

"For, that streak of blue you will see sailing by you . . . will be me. If you wait around, you will be alone in the aircraft!

"When I indicate, 'Bail out!' I mean 'Bail Out!' *So go!*

"Then is not the time to debate the issue. Make the decision right here, and now, before we climb into the plane. If the answer is 'no,' or even a 'maybe' . . . stay on the ground."

Sometimes a potential passenger elected to remain behind. A good decision! Only seldom did passengers yearn to leap from a plane. Still, there were exceptions.

My youngest son always wanted to don a chute and jump. He even begged; I was hard-nosed. The answer was always, "No!"

While we were in flight training, the Army originally insisted all pilots have actual practice bailing out and using parachutes. Later, evaluating the statistics of killed and wounded, broken legs and worse, the hierarchy decided this was too costly. Pilots could learn to jump when they had to bail out.

I was not, therefore, about to let Mike "hit the silk" unless we were forced to leave the ship. (I argued. "It's better to stay aboard.")

That too was a lucky decision for Mike. There was no way in those wet, tropical climates for us to adequately store or protect our parachutes.

My assistant and I flew them once to Dakar, Senegal, so the French could open, hang them up, dry and repack them. Aghast, they showed us what we had been carrying: the chutes' silk canopies were mildewed and rotten, sticking together like clumps of glued rags. The risers also had deteriorated. The pins were rusted in place, locking the chutes closed. They would never have opened if needed in an emergency.

I obtained permission from headquarters to destroy them and carry no parachutes thereafter. No need loading-up the aircraft with useless equipment that might lead someone down a primrose path . . . and using any of them in that condition would certainly have killed the user. After that, we flew like the airlines – without parachutes.

When Mike grew up and joined the Army, they offered him Paratrooper Training. He declined. I believe he made an even better decision then.

Looking back on twenty-seven years of military flying (plus civilian experiences), it seems to be a sea of lower waves punctuated by some white caps and a small collection of unexpected tsunamis. If this record appears to report only one near-miss after another, one crash, one failure, and one stupid mistake piled one atop the last . . . this is a false impression.[51] True, we had them all . . . and flying *is* dangerous, but . . .

An airline pilot landing in Los Angeles said it best, "You have

[51] Perhaps, because of my mystery-novel-writing, I have subconsciously injected a disproportionate number of those episodes solely to provide my readers with page-turning suspense. But they are all true.

just completed the safest part of your journey. Now you must battle the death traps of the freeways, high speed, huge semis, drunken and inept drivers.[52]"

Flying, despite my compilation of problems (and I did not cover them all), is still–statistically–far safer than any other form of transportation . . . even with terrorists doing their best to scare the hell out of us. Today, only airport congestion, the down-to-the-skin-search of belongings, the repeated delays and the general hassles detract from its one-time speed, beauty, majesty and relaxing attractions.

Admittedly, it was better when airlines served gourmet food even in the coaches, when drinks came fast, frequent and lavishly fulfilling, when the hostesses were all female (shapely, smiling, youthful and attentive), when there was room in a seat to squirm, lay back, and close one's eyes, and when a passenger did *not* feel like a steer herded into a pen for branding. In those days the hours flew-by faster (Sorry! I just could not help inserting that pun), the miles seemed smoother, the cabin air cleaner and fresher, and passengers did not take four "carry-ons" when entitled to one, and hot towels eased tired eyelids and dry faces.

None of this occurred in the military except on VIP flights. I flew Air Force Two (never Air Force One, with the President aboard) in D.C. and when bringing President Maurice Yameogo to the States from Upper Volta. [The gift he brought our president had been ours a few weeks earlier (a large oil portrait of a native African girl in full, white regalia). It hung in my living room until we sold it back to the studio so the president might take it to President Johnson. It is nice to be able to say we once owned–and had hanging in our home–something later gracing the White House walls, even if it did so for only a short period.]

[52]There was a time when airlines experimented with rear-facing seats–to protect passengers' necks and shoulders during rough landings. One airline still jokes about its hard landings. Its cabin servers announce, "When our pilot finally parks what's left of our aircraft, please remove your luggage from the overhead compartments and pick your way through the wreckage to the front door."

Colonel Cron, Ambassador Thomas Estes,
and President Maurice Yameogo
Ouagadougou, Upper Volta (Now Birkina
Faso, West Africa) (1964)

Of course, Air Force One and Two have all the amenities, including some you will never know about. A small number of planes used by senators and representatives, high–ranking civilian and military officials also have unexpected luxuries–but, why not? Their civilian counterparts, CEOs, Bill Gates's contemporaries and the like, do not "stand short."

I don't begrudge any of them their perks. That's what the perks are there for–to reward money, prestige and power. If I ever had any of those, I, too, would want the rewards going with them.

Down deep, a person might resent them (because they are not his), but I doubt anyone would reject them given the chance.

These "special arrangements" for VIPs, introduced me to many of them.

I frequently stood in the VIP lounge at Andrews AFB, drinking repeatedly with John F. Kennedy on his arrivals and departures. I shook his hand, talked with him, and experienced his almost incredible charisma. Yet, I saw, too, the contracted pupils in his eyes. I noted his frenetic, virtually desperate, movements. I felt the tremble in his fingers.

Though I never ceased to enjoy his humor and sharp responses, all the while I wondered if this could–or would–last. Obviously, he was hurting, on pain pills–and, perhaps, "speed" –his mind and body going a thousand miles a second.

Did I resent his climbing into the expensive luxury of his Air Force One (then a Boeing 707)? Did I envy his dashing off across the country–or around the world–to represent us to friends and enemies alike (and doing it while he was still hurting)?

No! But I *do* resent and abhor the smallest government official (the French call them "petit functionaires") who takes one single dime from our USA's coffers and does not extend himself or herself to the maximum on our behalf, and our constitution's.

CHAPTER NINE

▲

Critical junctures in life often inspire pauses for self-analysis and a philosophical review. My return flight from Korea proved to be just such a juncture.

By then, I had completed two full combat tours in two different wars. (Ignoring the so-called epithet–"Police Action" –as applied to what occurred in Korea. I figured, in anyone's book when people shoot at you and you shoot back, a reasonable definition says. "This is war.") Thus, this was the time to reassess my place in the "Grand Scheme of Things."

It is as easy for inflated egos (I speak from experience) to assume grandiose personal characteristics as it is for them to take-on nonexistent responsibilities. As easy as assuming, for example, that celebrity status rubs off by association, and a person, thereby, is also a celebrity.

In neither WWII nor Korea, did my squadron, or even my group start the wars or end them. We played a part–Yes!–but we were _not_ pivotal characters or forces. Together, we did our little bit, like tiny cogs on a clock's wheels–carrying the action along, while acting as merely contributing factors.

As individuals we did even less. None of us stood at the center of the whirlwind. Our loss, like "the nail," would have been but a "nail," it would not have meant the domino-effect of losing "a shoe, a horse" and, by implication, "a war." In Europe, more than three million Americans fought during WWII to free people from tyranny. At best, unless a person were General Dwight David Eisenhower, President Franklin Delano Roosevelt, Winston Churchill, Stalin . . . or one of the other notables . . . he exerted

no more than one/three-millionths of the energy applied in that campaign. And those are both reasonable computations.

In spite of all this, when a person finds himself constantly in the midst of enormous and earthshaking events, one begins wondering if, perhaps, "Am *I* making history?"

The answer is seldom, "Yes!" Most often it is a more realistic, "No! Yet you may have existed at a time and place where history was being made . . . around you . . . and often despite you."

My family has often said, "We're like Al Capp's cartoon character who always has a cloud over his head, rain pouring on him, lightning shooting down, and thunder blasting his eardrums." Paranoid? Sure . . . but some truth lies there as well.

These questions raised their ugly little heads and bared their teeth on my return from Korea, largely because I–from my childhood, throughout my life, and now notably two wars, with what happened soon after–always seemed to be nearby, if not a part of, central events. I can, therefore, merely report them as I lived them, leaving the judgment regarding my proportional responsibility and/or credit to others.

<p align="center">* * *</p>

My speedy and unexpected early return from Korea, early June,1952, appeared to confound the Air Force. Seemingly they did not to know quite what to do with me.

Yet the USAF dreamed up a quick assignment as an instructor–both for flight- and ground-school duties, involving cadets and commissioned officers in flight training–and shuffled me off to Lubbock AFB (back in Texas, again).

At Lubbock, following a 30-day, post-combat leave, I was assigned to teach students meteorology in the classroom, and how

to fly T-28s[53] and B-25s[54] in the air. But, first, I had to attend Instructor Flight Training School for six weeks, in Selma, Alabama.

Does that sound familiar? Of course, I had only been flying these aircraft now for about eight years, and was already a "Senior Pilot.[55]" I had been an "IP" (instructor pilot) for both our squadron and group in Korea, during my time as a general's aide, and while at Ohio University . . . so what did I know about instructing? I had only two thousand (plus) instructor hours.

First, I saw Ilogene and my family situated in new government housing built[56] among former cotton fields infested with the usual rattlesnakes, multitudinous scorpions and–on this occasion–pie-plate-sized tarantulas. I then left for school at Selma, Alabama. (I

[53] A small, single-engine, tricycle-landing-geared, two-pilot, low-wing monoplane in which the student sat up-front and the instructor flew from the rear cockpit. Easy to fly, it served as an excellent and stable flight platform for new cadets, before we introduced them to the B-25.

[54] The twin-engine, twin-tailed, tricycle-landing-geared aircraft best remembered as the plane General Doolittle's team flew off the aircraft carrier code-named "Shangri-La," on his famous Tokyo raid, three months after Pearl Harbor. A very forgiving bomber, used as a trainer and executive transport, the B-25 also was an excellent aircraft for newcomer training.

[55] A formal designation given competent pilots after they completed a set number of flying hours and years in the US Air Corp/US Air Force. This designation came on official orders from Washington, and permitted pilots to wear the usual silver wings topped with a star above the central shield. (In other words. "Senior Pilots" were no longer "rookies" or–as we called them–"Slick-Wing Pilots" (i.e., those not yet allowed to wear wings with either a star, or the star and wreath granted "Command Pilots."

[56] This new housing looked nice, but hid a million problems. Sand storms in this desert area came frequently. Obviously, they occurred often during interior painting–the painters had varnished the sand right into the paint (it was like sandpaper), and the walls were mottled with streaks of sand in their light enamel and wood work. The windows and doors were so loose the wind blew through the house as if a person stood in a wind tunnel. Every morning an inch-deep pile of sand and bugs lay beneath each window and before the door jambs. The appliances and wiring were questionable. A captain's wife across the street became a drunk, and blamed it on her environment. The flight surgeon endorsed her argument.

had been there before–for Ground Safety School and a couple other short stints.)

On this trip, though, I fought a new adversary–"Love Bugs." Evidently they hibernated for a number of years (somewhere and variable), then came forth in all their glory only at periodic intervals. Thank God!

The first Tuesday night I drove into town to attend a choir practice, Love Bugs splattered my windshield, swarmed about the street, road and car lights, and, when dying, covered the ground like a thick coating of axle grease. They made such a mess, driving became a severe challenge.

First, a driver could not see through their splatter on his windshield. Second, the bugs' dead bodies made an oily, slippery surface. Driving was "iffy" . . . at best.

Steering tricky and braking impossible, to my right and left headlights pointed into the sky as if they were searchlights, showing where cars lay in the ditches. Solely by dint of extreme care and foregoing use of brakes I let my Ford slow down gradually . . . and eased forward into Selma.

Then the stench hit me! Nauseated, I gagged, stomach trembling.

Handkerchief over my nose, I dashed . . . as if I were a drunken, broken-field runner . . . across the ice-like sidewalk, into the church, and slammed the door behind me. Inside, the choir director called-off practice, but warned us to give the bugs a couple hours to burn themselves out in their initial frenzy.

I asked, "Why not, then, go ahead with practice?"

He smiled grimly. "By Sunday, the odor will be worse. Probably no one will come to services. Oh, yes, and I recommend some strong deodorants around your rooms . . . it will be quite unpleasant for about a week."

He was right. The situation became so bad the base grounded our aircraft. (That assured us of another week away from home. Having just returned from combat in Korea this did not go over so

well with us trainees.) We holed up in our quarters, sniffing candles and evaporating aromatic fluids. Few of us went to the mess hall. I ate practically nothing, and had a hard time keeping that down.

This was also a critical period for Selma and Montgomery in other ways as well. Civil Rights marches (the devoted following of Martin Luther King, Jr.), sit-ins on buses and in restaurants (this was the time Rosa Parks' made her admirable stand), created a sensitive populace. The military, which had been trying to integrate, was suspect and glared at with jaundiced eyes.

School completed, I received a "Certified Instructor Pilot[57]" diploma, and endorsements on my Commercial Pilot's License as well as in my military records (already growing thick). I headed home to Ilogene, my children, and Lubbock. But fate again reached out a bony finger and pointed it at my family.

Back again on Lubbock AFB, I saw warning signs posted on every wall, pole and bulletin board. Alerting-type handbills had been passed to every household and office: "Beware! Rattlesnakes and tarantulas are rampant. Pick up no 'ropes' anywhere . . . and leave crawling creatures strictly alone."

At least neither Ilogene nor one of our children was bitten by snakes or tarantulas. But I saw two neighboring six-year-olds tossing between them what I thought was a Frisby. Yet, somehow, it did not look quite right.

Approaching cautiously, I found them tossing a six-inch-diameter, brown tarantula from one boy's bare hands to the other's. "Whoa!" I whispered, afraid I might startle the spider into biting someone, "better put that down, kids . . . that's dangerous."

The nearest little boy glared at me over his shoulder. "Nah! We been a-teasin' 'Joey' all week. He ain't abit us t'onc't."

[57] These enhanced my already FAA-endorsed "single and multi-engine land, and instrument ratings" showing my pilot qualifications. The only major endorsement missing was "Airline Pilot." I really had no need for that. Although my last squadron commander in Korea (Major Grant Swartz) carried that rating and had flown for one of the larger airlines, he did not have an Instructor rating.

I watched for a few minutes, still apprehensive. What startled me next were the spider's actions. If a boy missed catching it, the spider crawled to him so he could pick it up. *Unbelievable!*

They went on playing and I left them to their new toy. (But I did talk to their parents about it. They took immediate action–no more spiders!)

Our dire family problem showed up within a month of my completing instructor training–Rod III once more came down with asthma. Much worse than before, now the doctors said it was life-threatening. With his being deathly allergic to Lubbock's brand of dust, the doctors urged us to get him out immediately. To do that required my either resigning my commission or motivating Headquarters Training Command to move us. (And such a transfer movement under a year was supposedly impossible.)

<p style="text-align:center">* * *</p>

Given a plane for the purpose of finding out what could be done, I flew to Air Training Command Headquarters and explained my dilemma. (I carried the doctor's report on Rod III–and my request for transfer–in my hot little hands).

They read the data, and listened. They nodded their heads sagely. (Translation: they acted as if they were about to say no.) Then they again examined my portfolio and file.

"At the end of this year we have you slated to be an Aviation Cadet Detachment Commander, north of Detroit, visiting universities and recruiting new flying trainees." That said, they put their heads together and mumbled some more. (Sort of like the midgets in "The Wizard of Oz." Come to think of it, they looked like the "munchkins," too.)

The upshot came quickly, "We're taking an exception to the 'one-year-in-one-place' rule and shipping you to Michigan, right away, as commander."

I flew home as fast as the little T-28 could go. We packed and were gone in a week. But, once more, the dark rain cloud over my head, spewing lightning.

Ilogene, the children, and I drove madly for fifteen hundred miles to Chanute AFB, Rantoul, Illinois. Once there, we were to check-in with the local group commander before going on to my detachment's site north of Detroit, Michigan. (Our furniture was already on the way to the new location.)

At Chanute, the commander took one look at my file . . . and changed my orders. "We need you here, Captain. That current commander up there in Michigan will have to stay put for a few months longer."

"But . . . but . . . sir . . . my orders . . . our furniture . . . ?"

"Don't worry about that. We'll change those too."

(Hah! I learned, right then: Beware of such glib revisions of destiny.)

The group spent three months shifting my furniture from Michigan to Chanute—and it looked for a while like I was going to have to pay the thousands of dollars for the change. It took two more months to straighten out my orders and pay checks. In the meantime, I had to leave Ilogene, Grandpa and the kids in government quarters, with furniture from the Base (like the wife whose husband was in Korea). With no recourse, I was ordered to take-off on a previously established, tight schedule to visit twenty-five universities (Illinois, Indiana, Ohio and Michigan).

If my detachment staff had not been such jewels, this period could have been a disaster. They covered for me while I handled details, arranged money for Ilogene, and helped her get the kids started in schools. I also had to buy another car, which we could ill afford right then.

Cooling all the bubbling cauldrons and picking up loose ends were, for a while, Ilogene's and my full-time jobs, while the children struggled with new schools. Into this seething kettle of fish the Air Force abruptly stirred another condiment altering our life's flavor and direction.

Now some six years (plus) after it became a separate entity, HQs USAF elected to separate Air Force Recruiting from Army

147

Recruiting. This decision precipitated major procedural changes all up and down the line.

In its infinite wisdom, USAF sent selected experienced people–officers who had been in Recruiting and *Aviation Cadet Detachment Commanders*, as well as enlisted men who had been front-line recruiters and supervisors at several levels–to San Antonio (good old SAACC, again). Their job was to set up an Air Force Recruiting School. So . . . again . . . off I went to Texas.

Barely settled, Ilogene and the children suffered. My problems were minuscule beside theirs, yet I left for another six weeks.

Colonel Alexander tried, but floundered, running the school. Instead of waiting for the "pilot class" (our designation) to make suggestions and contribute our experiences, they went ahead. Thereby they created a monster.

The first day, the first class, we laughed the instructor, off the podium. It was not his fault, but he tried to tell these many-years-in-the-field, hardened men, "Don't sell young, potential enlistees on a four-year enlistment . . . sell them, immediately, on a twenty-year career!"

That went over like a "lead balloon." The class erupted into a shouting brawl.

Colonel Alexander came in to stop the melee. The class explained.

The class halted right there. The class then went to their rooms to write the curriculum and lessons for the entire course. Their results proved to be a roaring success. When, a few years later, I took over as the Recruiting School commander, the basics remained virtually unchanged. [Later, when I was the Group Training Director, 1958-1960, I took charge of *all* the Group's schools (Cryptographic training, Instructor training, Recruiting, Administrative, Air Police/Guard Dog training, and Chaplain training). In this position, I had the opportunity to write and conduct our first WAF Recruiter and Recruiting Supervisor courses. With five officers, we took the Supervisor Course around

the country to all six of the Recruiting Group headquarters.]

That initial "pilot class" activity, however, resulted in my subsequent reassignment to Lackland AFB permanently (meaning for at least a year), as noted in the previous paragraph. The base commander, Major General Robert Stillman, soon learned about my speaking experiences with, and writing articles for the National Toastmaster's Club. (Colonel Clark Hosmer, my Group commander, told him). One evening, General Stillman called to ask if I could substitute for him, speaking the next morning at a Breakfast Club, downtown in the Gunter Hotel.

Flattered, I said, "Sure, General! Be glad to."

That worked out well, for him. I did virtually all his service club and off-base speeches thereafter. For me, it meant getting up early and driving to far-off locations, giving a speech . . . only to return and find my desk piled with unfinished work.

Stillman liked this arrangement. It worked so well by the time I left for Command and Staff College, I was giving *all* his school graduation speeches. The only ones he kept were the graduation exercises for the Basic Trainees–involving thousands of young men and women, new members of the USAF.

At Lackland, too, I had the pleasure and privilege to meet and get to know intimately our NASA's original seven astronauts[58]. I had lunch with them regularly in the hospital . . . and cocktail parties, night after night, at Doctor David Wiltsie's house, next to mine. A cardiologist, David ran their "base line" checks at the hospital, prior to their intensive training.

Among them, I liked Carpenter, Cooper, Shirra and Slayton, but Gus Grissom best. I liked Shepard least, the man who became an admiral. He always sat in a corner of the sofa at David's parties, knees up under his chin–the "Great Stone Face." John Glenn seemed overly arrogant. [Later, when he was our Ohio

[58] I'm a bit confused here–I always remembered "eight" were in the original group. Maybe I was including Dr. David Wiltsie or one of the men who accompanied them. (Or perhaps I'm just getting old–huh?)

senator and I went to his office, hat in hand, trying to wrangle a West Point appointment for my son, Patrick . . . Glenn literally "blew me off." (I wanted to give him "the finger," but he *was* a senator, so, instead, I never voted for him after that.)] Also Gus's death came as a shocking blow. He was mourned by all who knew him and millions who never had the privilege. They all attended one of my speeches when I was on the road for General Lemay, adding their prestige to a rather boring evening.

Brad, the son of my Group Commander, Colonel Clark Hosmer, was a cadet at the newly developed Air Force Academy while all this was going on. He eventually ended-up at Colorado Springs and graduated number one in the first class. He closed out his career as Commandant of the Air Force Academy, wearing three stars (a lieutenant general). This boy was brilliant. I wanted to see him as the USAF Chief-of-Staff. (So did his father.) I always enjoyed his Jaguar XKE and his fiddling with it to keep those three carburetors in synchronization.

Brad's sister retired recently as a military nurse, with the grade of lieutenant colonel. (See! The military *does* run in families! See below.)

In our family, not only did all three of our boys "join up," but Melodie– shown here as she graduated from Nurse's Training, a sweet, innocent, young girl–became a 2nd lieutenant, in the Army Nurse Corps right after her graduation.

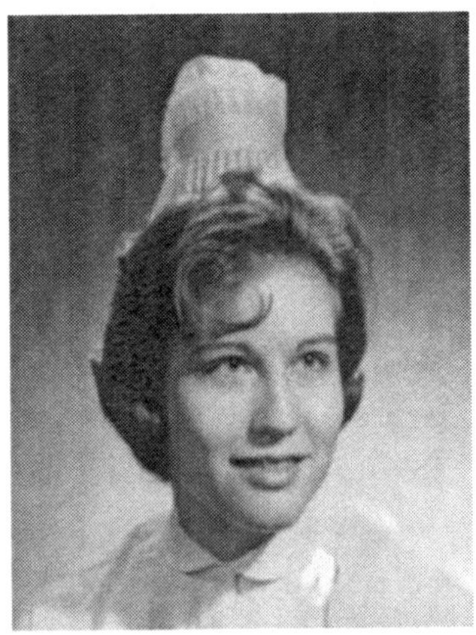

CHAPTER TEN

▲

The inauguration of the United States Air Force in November 1947, when it split from the United States Army and became a separate, individual service entity unto itself, promised much. It began with all the right ideas. The generals' aims were sound, innovative and needed. One of their objectives was to scrap all the complicated Army regulations–two hundred years in development–and create a simple, easy to read and easy to understand set of directives. Their aim: *Only* Headquarters' USAF regulations and no sub-command would be allowed to issue any modifications. ("The best-laid plans of mice and men . . ." and all that.)

From this ostentatious opening, a fiasco resulted. This resembled the description in the opening lines of the poem, *Dangerous Dan MacGrew*–"A bunch of the boys were whooping it up, in a Malemute saloon . . ." For that is how it seemed.

Everyone thought USAF HQs had gone nuts! Each officer and airman received a new serial number based on where he stood relative to the top-ranking general, who was awarded "Number One." Each was given direct orders, but few funds, to buy the newly prescribed, powder blue uniforms, without belts . . . and the new, all-silver insignia. Ranks remained the same, but there were many a lengthy, knock-down-drag-out discussion about adopting the English nomenclature for grades–from "Flight Officer" to "Group Commander" and "Air Marshal." Congress shot that down. (They did adopt "airmen," and so forth, however.)

The concept of a single set of directives also rapidly "flew the

151

coop." Within one year, every numbered air force, wing, group, squadron and detachment was busily publishing its own regulations under the guise of SOPs ("Standard Operating Procedures"), or some variation thereof.

USAF Headquarters hand-picked a few officers to create new guidelines–from manuals on Management (my chore[59]), to Officer and Enlisted Effectiveness reports, flying training guides, detailed (objective) measurement systems for efficiency, cost reduction, and inspection, to calendars of events (and this list does not touch the broad spectrum of work attempted, but failed, abandoned or cancelled). What it took the US Army two hundred years to achieve (and streamline into their leadership procedures), we, of the US Air Force, were charged with completing . . . *yesterday!* (Dan McGrew had it easy.)

Also, our giving up the "pinks and greens" of our Army Air Corps dress uniform made it tough on the "fatties." (I was still slim, then, but always fought my increasing weight–diets, exercise, even amphetamines . . . before the world labeled Dexadrine as tabu and it became a "controlled substance.") Our earlier uniform belts hid a lot of pounds. The former colors concealed what advancing years (and good living) generated. The older officers and even some generals hated the uniforms and the new, form-fitting profile required.

Let's face it, only General Hoyt Vandenberg and his "gold-dust-twin" looked good in the new get-up . . . so they became the "poster boys of the Air Force." The rest of us hid out in raincoats, topcoats and flight clothes.

[59] Here is where I not only applied what I learned from my education and civilian job experiences, but also put to work General Snavely's "staff-meeting" training lessons. Ralph Snavely Sr. never knew he influenced the management techniques of so many thousands of officers after his death.

All Air Corps officers wore "pink" trousers with the regular Army's dark green jacket ("blouse"). Fighter pilots wore their top blouse button open (a uniform "no-no!") and some flouted regulations completely by adding a long, loose, white silk scarf around their necks (á la World War I–this was considered "really hep"). All Air Force pilots removed the metal ring giving the billed officer's cap its rigid-round appearance (sometimes referred to as "The West Point Look"). It sagged into a slouch (called the "Fifty-Mission-Crush"). Pilots also affected the wearing of Wellington Boots, in the new USAF black (those shoes came to just above the ankle), rather than the standard, Army Officer's brown, low-cut shoes. Some sported hand-made boots and modified cowboy boots ("Chuck" Yeager did this even after they promoted him to Brigadier General). Each flying Group added individual touches to these idiosyncracies to differentiate their "Fly-Boys" from those of other, "lesser" Groups.

Squadrons went even further. In Korea, for example, our Weather Reconnaissance Squadron wore black silk scarves, all the time we were in uniform, even on missions. The 4th Fighter Wing, with which we shared the airdrome at Kimpo AFB, wore scarves with black and white squares, tucked into the tops of their blouses, black, twelve-inch-high, highly polished boots, lined with fur inside and zippers on the outside, with higher heels than most. (This outfit was "the heppest"–so they thought. Colonel Gabreski, their commander, flaunted regulations right and left, uniform-wise, and ignored air traffic control instructions, endangering other aircraft, even after his return to the States. A real maverick.) Of course, as a bomber pilot, my perspective may be a trifle warped. But all fighters pilots, as a rule, felt they were a different breed from us. I suppose we envied them their *savoir faire*, arrogance and elan. Down deep, though, we knew WE were the coolest . . . regardless. Anyway, more of us bomber pilots lived to return home and boast, than fighter pilots (percentage-wise).

General Vandenberg realized his dream for a separate Air Force, co-equal with the Army (a dream once shared with Generals Hap Arnold and Tooey Spaatz, but too late for them). Yet this dream for many became a rotating nightmare.

Later, I served in the Headquarter's USAF Inspector General's Office as head of the management team delving into pay scales, perks and bonuses of the Martin-Marietta Corpor-ation. We examined every form of remuneration for their employees, including all their officials and top-level brass. We inspected

every tier of each, still-growing, artificially created, management level (the usual work of the "empire-builders'"), examined the rapidly heaping mounds of regulations (written by the "nit-pickers"), and scrutinized every level's infinite conflicts, discrepancies, and deficiencies (resulting from the two previous actions). We also did this for several other civilian organizations as well.

By the 1960s–barely fifteen years after the Air Force's inception–the paperwork molehill had already grown into an unbelievable mountain. The proposed "simple, central, original" regulations had proliferated like computer viruses. Most of our management team's recommendations, given directly to General Curtis Lemay, urged streamlining, eliminating and simplifying. We urged everyone, at every level, to apply the "KISS" principle. ("Keep It Simple Stupid!") For a while they did and those procedures, along with the name, were on every commander's lips, if not in his heart and actions.

Our team was the first, ever, to work with a major civilian contractor (named above), inspecting its sub-contractors down to the thirty-second sub-sub-level. Upon completion of our nine-month mission we flew to D.C. to brief the general on our findings. [Anticipating backlash, we prepared two debriefings. Since I was a member of the Chief of Staff's (Lemay's) eight-man speakers' bureau[60] and knew him personally, I was elected to present the "short" (touchy) version.]

I took my place on the dais before Lemay, my easel loaded, my pointer in hand. I flipped the first page, pointing at the picture there. "General, this is the 'short version.' It is our concerted conclusion the Titan II missile is a waste of the government's

[60] A total of eight officers–no more–chosen from among the few "outstanding" graduates of the Command and Staff College, and the War College, served for one year each, speaking for the Chief of Staff, across the nation at assigned sites and events. My Freedom's Foundation Award and "jail time," both of which gave me national publicity probably accounted more for my selection than any so-called "outstanding status."

money. We do NOT recommend any improvements in its management or manufacturing systems . . . we recommend, instead, *it be discontinued at once.*"

The silence was deafening.

General Lemay sucked on his ever-present cigar creating a sudden fog of smoke. Our two-star boss sat in the back of the room, squirming.

Lemay hopped to his feet, put his arm around my shoulders, and faced the Inspector General and their mutual staffs. "Rod, we can't do that. General Shott, sitting back there, knows that. This country must make sure our scientists and engineers stay here. You inspectors better think of our missile programs as a massive WPA project–we gotta keep their brains on *our* payroll . . . or they'll end-up working for the Russians, Chinese, Japanese, or someone else." He returned to his seat, still smoking his cigar. "Now, go to your other report and tell me what you *really planned* for improvement." He even smiled.

We gave him the "other" briefing. Obviously, though we worked directly for him as Chief of Staff, we were not privy to all the ramifications of government at his level. We spent the next two hours giving him the desired and lengthy "nitty-gritty," page, chapter and verse . . . and the music to go along with them.

At the end, he nodded and again stood. "Those are good recommendations. We can put *them* to work." He pointed his cigar (now his fourth or fifth) at me. "But, if you try to pull that again, Rod, I'll see you make airman first class." Once more he smiled . . . and two weeks later I was a lieutenant colonel. (Lemay also kept me on his speaker's bureau for a second and third year. The sole member so chosen.)

Publicity photo for General
Lemay's Speakers' Bureau.
(1960-1963)
Major and Lt. Col.

Major General Shott, director of the Inspector Generals' office at Norton, chaffed, however, at my having to do such double-duty. He had to give me time off, when I was called to speak. He had to provide me with a private sedan and plane, when I was called away. (Norton AFB assigned me both a military vehicle and a jet for my exclusive use.) He had to allow me flexibility in my working hours and on my mission assignments. Another officer had to cover for me during mission preparation and, sometimes, I flew to the inspection site on my own, not with the inspector group. General Shott did not like any of those.

General Lemay's office phoned me virtually daily–and followed up with faxes–assigning me my speaking engagements (dates, hours, places, people and events). I also received a distinctive briefcase, an original speech outline (which I never used; instead, Lemay's office reproduced mine to send to everyone else), a projector, slides, boxes of miniature planes, missiles and space craft (one was made with real re-entry materials). In my two years and a half years, I spoke to more than ten million people–in person, by radio and television . . . from the prestigious Winter Night Club at Colorado Springs and on the major, network television talk shows, to small breakfast, lunch and dinner meetings of service groups, at local restaurants in major cities.

These speech episodes, too numerous to enumerate here, involved a brace of outstanding ones worth singling out.

Assigned to speak at a breakfast meeting of a large (130-member) Kiwanis group in Sacramento, CA, I arrived the night before. As it was my established procedure, I appeared the next morning at the restaurant an hour before my scheduled appearance to "set-up." I worked fast and had everything ready.

No one came! Not one cotton-pickin' soul showed for the breakfast!

The restaurant owner had prepared food for a full chapter gathering and was extremely unhappy. He called the group's president.

The president was aghast. "Why, we had a 100 percent commitment for this meeting and the colonel's speech. I don't understand this." He phoned his members.

He called back to tell me that everyone, including himself, had encountered a scheduling conflict, but no one worried, believing, with a 100 percent commitment, one person would not be missed. He promised, if I rescheduled for the following month and would speak at an evening dinner, he assured a superior turn-out.

When I returned, all the Kiwanians attended, so did the City Mayor and his staff, the local government employees . . . and everyone's wives. I had a total of 1200 listeners.

At the other end of the teeter-totter, I also accepted an invitation to speak at a local Rotary dinner in Logan, Ohio. My lifelong friend, Ralph Owen Moorehead, introduced me.

Acknowledging his introduction before beginning the body of my speech, I wanted to emphasize how long Ralph and I had known each other. I ran on and on, struggling through, "We went to school together. We've known each other for more than forty years. We double-dated. We are as close as brothers. We shared bowls of soup when we were virtually penniless. (He was now the President of the local bank.) He married one of my high school girl-friends, Margie Morley . . . tuh-yuckity-yuckity-yuck." But,

for the life of me, *I could not remember Ralph's name!*

I leaned over and in a loud stage whisper asked, "What *IS* your name?"

Startled, he told me. Everyone roared; they thought this was an opening speaker's ploy.

After the speech, I told Ralph, "I'm sorry, but, momentarily, I really *had* forgotten your name, already mentally deep into my speech-preparation mode." (I don't believe Ralph believed me.)

These speeches and our inspection missions, however, triggered my next assignment . . . and made General Shott even more angry with me. (I knew it, first, when he bunched his jaw and gritted his teeth as he pinned on my new, lieutenant colonel insignia at my promotion celebration. The promotion that came out of the blue– unexpected, but gratifying.) Then at the end of my second year on the speaker's bureau, General Shott actually growled at me.

Our team had gone to the D.C. area, earlier, to inspect the Attaché organization Headquarters and its methods for controlling our Air Force (and Defense) Attaché system, worldwide. Sited way-out in the "boonies," at Fort Belvoir, far more remote than its civilian counterpart, the "Company" (CIA[61]), at Langley, Virginia, this tiny outfit actually did a splendid job and earned our compliments. While there, however, the director astounded me by citing my known connections with General Lemay, my speaking, and French training. He asked if I were interested in going-out as an attaché.

"I hadn't thought about it," I told him. "Anyway, I have another year in the Inspector General's Office . . . and no one ever–*ever!*–leaves before the end of his three-year tour."

He insisted, however, I fill-out the application forms. So I did.

[61] As if you did not know, "CIA" means "Central Intelligence Agency." We also worked hand-in-glove with the National Security Agency, the European Commander's staff, the Air Force Chief of Staff, the Intelligence organization at McDill AFB, Florida, and all other pertinent, intelligence/police communities, Le Surete at Quai D'Orsay, Interpol, MI-5 and 6, the Israelis' Mossad, etc.

A month later, he called me at Norton AFB, CA. "Hey, Rod! We have an assignment for you–just what you wanted: a French-speaking country, actually more than one, even more than ten–and in Africa." (My first choice.)

"Next year, I presume."

"Nope! *Right now*. The colonel assigned to the post proved to be a dyed-in-the-wool, closet-bigot. When he discovered he had to work with blacks, he resigned his commission. We need you, here, to begin training in three weeks. We'll expedite everything."

"You're wasting your time," I told him. "General Shott will never let me out of here early."

"Hmm! We'll see."

The very next morning General Shott called me into his office and told me to shut the door. I anticipated a chewing-out for some infraction. He glared for a full fifteen seconds before saying, "I don't know what in hell you've got, boy. But General Lemay just called me on that there phone." He waved a hand at his desk. "I've been ordered to ship your ass out of here tomorrow, no argument! You're going to D.C., then to Abidjan in the Ivory Coast, as the Defense Attaché." He reddened as if about to explode, but, saying nothing further, futilely motioned for me to leave the room.

From that instant, the pace grew steadily more hectic till the Kennedy mourning period was over. We next relaxed in Africa, in December, 6,000 miles away on the other side of the globe.

<p style="text-align:center">* * *</p>

An attaché's job is like none other in the military. He goes through extensive (and intensive) military intelligence training to become an overt spy ("open spook"). He gathers the intelligence the USA (and especially the military) wants, using his ability to ask questions, take photographs, and observe. He works for several bosses (also a departure from the norm). Other military personnel–usually and most often–have a clean-cut, single line of command above them, all the way to the president (the soldier's

<p style="text-align:center">159</p>

immediate superior, his boss, his boss's boss, all the way to the Secretary of Defense, and Commander-in-Chief, the President of the United States).

An attaché, however, has a convoluted path of many bosses. One is the Commander, Defense Intelligence Agency (DIA) in D.C. He also works for his service's Chief-of-Staff, directly–in my case, this was General Lemay, again–and can report to him directly, by personal (one-time-pad) communication. Things may have changed drastically in the thirty-some years since I retired. But, then, we also worked for the Commander of our European Forces (another four-star, headquartered then in Wiesbaden, Germany) within whose sphere of influence our station fell. There were others, too, that I will not enumerate.

This made for conflicts. Many and often!

This contrasts with the job of the CIA (Cental Intelligence Agency), our government's only, or at least primary, *covert* intelligence-gathering organization. Often the CIA receives unwarranted criticism for performing tasks put upon it by the president and congress (and, for which, those elusive sources wish most often NOT to be accredited with initiating).

The CIA is charged largely–and virtually exclusively–with covert intelligence tasks *external* to the USA. The FBI (Federal Bureau of Investigation) and other government agencies perform those tasks, solely and supposedly, *within our borders*. All our attachés' data–and the CIA's–like the raw intelligence accumulated by our entire intelligence community, ends up at the National Security Agency (if handled correctly and in accordance with their established charters).

An attaché has a "choice" assignment. It is sought after by many, approved for only a few. It demands an officer: (1) pass extremely exhaustive FBI background investigations (military, civilian, family, associate and school-performance histories); (2) obtain the cleanest references (a noteworthy personal record); (3) show language skills (and/or fluency in at least one foreign

tongue); (4) be in above-average physical condition (especially where non-modern countries are involved); (5) have some command experience; (6) if a plane is on-station and he is a pilot, his flying record must be unblemished; and, finally, (7) demonstrate basic speaking, writing and observation capabilities. An attaché also must be of exemplary honesty and integrity to earn the highest security clearances available. (Some cannot even be discussed outside a "vault.")

This assignment is a rare commodity in that it also directly and officially involves the attache's wife. Together, they must undergo thorough background checks and training. Many potentially excellent officers are regularly denied such assignments because their wives are foreigners.

Arriving on-station–meaning once in place at a US Embassy, somewhere in the world–the Defense[62] attaché works with and assists the ambassador as a member of his staff. He keeps him/her and the staff abreast of local military situations, while satisfying his assigned Defense Department requirements.

Where the State Department works with the "client" (using the State Department's own terminology)–usually the President of the country or the equivalent of that country's Secretary of State–the Defense, Army and/or Naval Attachés deal with the country's military counterparts (the Defense Secretaries, generals and military leaders).

Attachés live "high on the hog." Often resented by the embassy staffs. Their quarters, furniture, staff cars and other vehicles, manpower, offices and aircraft (if one is assigned) are "general-officer" grade. They also receive a rare and special "perk"–an annual expense allowance, with which to entertain potential information sources and contacts. (They receive nothing for the great amount of entertaining they must also do for friends and/or

[62] The "Defense Attaché" is the ranking attaché on station. He may be Army, Navy or Air Force. The other attachés are his "Assistant Attachés"–for example, "Air Force Attaché," etc.

USA embassy personnel.)

An attaché's primary job (and his wife's) is to be the eyes, ears and hands of the intelligence community in that area. Since the attache is usually as much as half-a-world away from any command jurisdiction (guidance and advise), he must make daily decisions, often of a highly sensitive nature, as well as those normally required of any commander in a remote location, using solely his acumen, ingenuity and experience.

In short, the attaché's job is not easy. He is constantly under the scrutiny of his multiple commanders as well as his various ambassadors (in my two assignments I averaged at least ten, each tour). Ambassadors, by the way, also file reports contributing to an attaché's annual Effectiveness Report (determining his future promotions)–though he does not, in effect, work for them. (A touchy situation–at least, it was then.)

In D.C., for the job of attaché, the military services groom a potential candidate as if they were about to be judged at a county fair. They stuffed me, for example, with protocol data, detailed Emily-Post-type instructions on dress, deportment, societal functions, table settings, uses of wine and liquor glasses by type, size, shape and function (all of which I had grown up with, knew before, and used as a general's aide), language lessons, intelligence training (an attaché IS an acknowledged overt spy, as noted previously), and photographic training in the use of hand- and other types of cameras, and an assortment of lens. To run completely through the list would require an extra chapter with a thousand footnotes . . . and some of the data can still *not* be released. Let me say only this: though attachés do not work FOR the CIA[63], they work closely and constantly coordinate WITH

[63] This is not quite true. Some of us "ran" clandestine organizations for the CIA when our American ambassadors would not permit them "in country." Supposedly we did it without the ambassador's knowledge. (That was to protect him if the activity were exposed . . . then the attaché "took the hit" as if he had been doing it solely on his own. I am reminded of a certain North who, but a lieutenant colonel, working for an admiral, supposedly "ran" that sticky Iran-Contra deal. No way! Not

them (meaning we made many trips to Langley and received covert, classified, requirement/equipment briefings, cross-training briefings, and detailed lectures on the array of equipment available, plus mutual funding and procedures' instructions). We also coordinated with the intelligence agencies of our allies, both here and in foreign countries. (To this day, I always check-in and out with our embassy and those of our allies when in other countries.)

when brigadiers in the Pentagon are mere "go-fers.")

CHAPTER ELEVEN
▲

Attaché schools, on the other hand, are a gas. A former attaché (an old Army colonel from Texas, about to retire) coming back from a remote country in Asia, gave us our "break-in" briefing.

"Gentlemen . . ." (There were no ladies present at this one, for obvious reasons.) " . . . you-all are a'goin' to make boo-boos. Lots of 'em. You're gonna bust your balls, sometimes, for nuthin'. You'll have all the ass you ever wanted shoved in your face. You're gonna be offered money, power, drugs and rewards you ain't never thought of–all for a chunk of the US of A's secret info.

"Like the Devil did to Jesus, the enemy will haul your pretty little butts to the top of the mountain and offer you the world–and try to get you to sell your soul." He paused and eyed officer after squirming officer. "If that's your *thang* . . . go for it, Bubba! But you're gonna pay the price. Big Brother WILL BE awatchin'! An he'll have you by the ying-yang. You gotta be careful all the time . . . about what you do and what you say.

"Let me tell yuh a story. A bright, young, snot-nosed assistant attaché, trained in the French language, arrived at his new station. That very first night he was invited to attend the President's ball–held to welcome all incomin' diplomatic personnel.

"This young buck approached the President's wife in the receivin' line. He bent over her hand, kissed her finger tips, and spoke to her in *the most intimate form* of French. . . used only for conversations with mistresses, children and servants."

"The President heard. The next mornin' the dismayed new attaché was on his way home."So, rule number one is this: 'Always play SYA!' (Save your ass!) Look before you leap, or

you may end up in a viper's nest."

The colonel had us all on edge when he ended with, "Yeah, you-all will make boo-boos . . . ever' one of yuh . . . lots of 'em. Just make sure they're small ones or ones someone can correct–preferably you–before others find out."

My first weeks in Abidjan, I remembered his words when I began pulling my own boners. (Also see next chapter.)

I guess, if I strung all my stupid bumbles together they would make a long line. I would prefer *not* to dwell on them at length. Still, I want this to represent both sides of my history's facets, so I will neither gild the lily nor pull my punches. My goofs began in D.C.

Leaving our apartment doors locked only on the door lock, not the dead bolt, cost us a bundle while we were still in training. Someone broke in and took our money, my wife's wedding ring, two automatics (a .22 and a .45), our TV, and a whole pile of minor stuff. The policeman who responded said, "Forget it . . . you'll never see those again."

I was only happy the looters missed several thousand dollars worth of hunting rifles I was taking to Africa for a planned (really only "hoped for") safari. The robbers walked right by them, though they were plainly visible. (Those guns belonged to Ted Hardenbrook, my friend who owned the Ford Agency in Piqua. He came over, later, and we did a safari in Upper Volta.)

<div align="center">* * *</div>

Sometimes it is easy to determine what prompts a dream. My reading Edgar Rice Burroughs's *Tarzan* series even before I entered first grade obviously stimulated my desire to go to Africa. From then on I yearned to see those tall, towering trees along the hot, humid coast. I wanted to stroll the beach and visit the hut where "Lord and Lady Greystokes" lived, and died. I eagerly sought the place where intelligent apes substituted their dead baby for the Greystokes' human, and raised him as theirs.

My wife's, Ilogene's, reasons for wanting to go to Africa did

<div align="center">165</div>

not lend themselves so easily to analysis. But she, too, had a similar dream. On one of our earliest dates we found we shared this common goal.

Africa, then, became part of our plan for the future we built together. To satisfy this desire, truth again became stranger than fiction, when we accomplished it.

Not only did we visit Africa, we *lived* there–for eight years. And not just *any place* on that enormous continent–three and half times the size of the United States–but we lived initially in the Ivory Coast and its capital city, Abidjan. Its beaches, jungles, 300-hundred-foot (plus) trees, rain forest, heat and humidity fitted to a "Tee" those of the "Tarzan" stories. *And* we lived in Africa not just for one tour of duty, but for two. Yet, we never saw an ape in the wild, never saw a gorilla, and never saw "Tarzan," though we had a Green Monkey, we called Sam, as a pet.

When I applied[64] for attaché training in Washington, D.C., we were given a choice. We could polish up our French and go to one of the newly-emerged African countries . . . or we could learn Spanish, Russian or some other exotic tongue . . . and go elsewhere. Ilogene and I did not even have to discuss this: we chose French and Africa. (Of course!)

The training did not come easy. Our children had to attend schools some distance away from our apartment. They had to ride school buses from dusk to dark. The other students were not accommodating. The only available apartment–one we could afford in the district–was remote. The streets were crowded . . .

[64] Note here the use of the word "we"–not "I." This is *not* a misspelling. Ilogene also underwent intelligence and diplomatic protocol training just as I did, as well as intensive language tutoring. This is one of the few military assignments in which wives are fully as important as the husbands. In many ways–as quickly discovered when Ilogene had to return to the States when her mother became seriously ill during our tour in Chad–an attaché cannot function well without his wife's help. She is his closest confidant and assistant. My young son, Michael, performed extraordinarily, acting as my maitre d', running my household, conducting dinners and parties, and supervising our household help. Yet, Only Ilogene received the training to do the intelligence duties. Without her, I was handicapped and not nearly as effective.

and crime-filled.

Ilogene's and my class hours in the intelligence and "special" schools (some still classified) were lengthy, but at reasonable hours. Our French tutoring, however, downtown in D.C. at 0600 hours, strained our capabilities.

To enumerate all the difficulties encountered in our short D.C. stay, would require another, complete volume. Let me summarize them: we were robbed (not mugged) in our apartment; the schools hassled our children for a variety of reasons; I tore the bursa in my right shoulder and, until they performed corrective surgery, I flew, lived, ate, slept–when I could–and studied in intense pain. Ilogene carried the burden, not only handling her studies and trips to the schools, but the unrelenting domestic chores . . . without a murmur. Since I was the principal, Ilogene made certain I had undistracted time to study, while she shirked hers to solve the myriad family problems.

The crowning blow came when we were leaving for Africa, driving two cars east from home (Piqua). Just outside Logan, Ohio, on the way to pick up our airline flight in New York, en route to Abidjan, we heard via the radio the saddest news: President Kennedy had been shot (this was on Ilogene's 41st birthday), 22 Nov 1963.

Kennedy's death created repercussions around the world in diplomatic circles. His death, funeral and their aftermath colored our entire trip and first tour, undermining our effectiveness as attachés. (In many aspects we never "caught up.")

Arriving in Dakar, Senegal (two days later), en route to Abidjan, Ivory Coast, we discovered the travel office had billeted us in the "Majestic," a tiny, old-fashioned hotel in the center of town, beds sagging and bug-ridden (with a bathroom forty feet away down the hall, shared with thirty other guests on that floor). At the time the Majestic was the best hotel in the city! But its French restaurant served a magnificent couscous and peanut soup. Those helped make up for the missing amenities . . . sort-of.

Nothing eased the shock of our President's assassination.

My assignment orders called for my handling our travel arrangements from Dakar to Abidjan. In consideration of the tragedy represented by Kennedy's assassination (and how it might affect our new job), Ilogene, Pat, Mike and I gave serious thought to renting some native pirogues (those hand-cut, hollowed-out-log canoes sharing a name with similar boats used in the Caribbean),leisurely paddling the thousand plus miles around Africa's coastline, and seeing it all . . . from here to there.

We should have done it. At least we might have had some fun.

Our initial introduction to our "base" country came through the windows of a Boeing 707, twenty thousand feet up. Here, in Abidjan, we were to live for the next three years, at least. All of us gaped at the sight.

Beneath us the sprawling city first appeared as a distant, isolated oasis of dazzling whiteness (walls) and bright orange (roofs), set amidst a field of verdant green. From here it belied what we knew about it, appearing glamorous, clean, modern, mysterious and exotic. Yet, under this appearance of fresh-washed innocence, we knew from our training the area reeked . . . and seethed.

As the jet descended farther, the city emerged more clearly from the surrounding hills. Perched on the edge of a huge, half-moon lagoon stretching fifty miles to east and west, it resembled a precious gem shining under a diamond light. The sun's overly-bright gleam, now barely a few miles north of the equator, blurred details.

Nearer, the buildings turned into glistening splashes of white glare, with one tall apartment tower standing out above the rest. The entire scene sat amidst an exuberant spread of foliage, the rain forests of tropical West Africa.

I told Ilogene and the boys,"It's easy to visualize Tarzan of the Apes in this lush jungle, isn't it? Just as Edgar Rice Burroughs imagined him?"

Ilogene nodded. "Uh-huh. Everything fits, even the few remaining elephants lumbering trunk-deep in the marshes out there, twenty miles to the west." Though sleepy, she had done her homework too. (Both of us had studied hard in D.C., poring over the State Department's "Station Reports" on the countries we were now accredited to.)

From up there, though, we saw only the surface brilliance of the complex mosaic. A mix of aqua tints among the whites, an occasional, lustrous, flowering red (frangipani groves) amidst the array of lush greens. The large inland lagoon, threading its arms among the house- and tree-covered hills, predominantly on the city's south side, bestowed the darkest blues and a superior seaport, after yearly dredging. Boats hugged the shores and crowded the docks, ranging from those tiny, native-built pirogues to the latest ocean-going liners. Many of the smaller varieties flitted across the face of the open water in simulation of excited water bugs.

I nudged Ilogene with an elbow. "There! See that! That's the Vridi canal, France's last gift to its former African colony. That canal is a mile-long arrow of clear teal, pointing straight as a sunbeam from the lagoon to the Atlantic's Bay of Guinea."

She compared her readings with the sights below. "Yes, exactly as described. The boys in the backroom did a good job."

We continued to watch avidly while the 707 swung out over the Atlantic, reversed its direction under a cloudless sky, and dropped those final feet to the runway. The jet came to rest on the concrete with an ease masking the turgid heat.

When the outer door opened, hot air flooded in as if from a massive blast furnace, instantly overwhelming our previous coolness. The wave of scorching heat also brought a wilting humidity and a nose-wrinkling compilation of alien stenches— the acrid, pervasive odors of frying fish, rancid fats, and hot, fresh feces mixed with urine.

Ilogene gasped and held a tissue to her nose.

"Get used to it, Hon," I chided. "That's all human, coming from the beach. Each airfield in Africa has its own distinctive aroma[65] . . . and this isn't the worst. Wait till you get a whiff of twenty thousand camels! I hear that'll knock our socks off."

Gathering up our carry-ons, we left the plane atop a tall landing platform (no enclosed terminal here). Looking down, there was a billowing sea of black covering the tarmac. The black showed a mere sprinkling of whites, an enormous dark fabric spotted with polka dots.

On some unseen clue the fabric surged forward. In an instant it became the upturned faces of a hundred, varicolored humans, black, white, black, brown, black, yellow, and more black. The mob greeted the aircraft's arrival with ear-shattering, high-pitched, ululating cries, the snapping splatter of clapping hands, and the chant of native songs, punctuated by the rapid heart-throb of small drums.

There is where the beauty ended . . . for at least a month.

When we flew into Abidjan, 26 November, we discovered our ambassador (Wine) to the Ivory Coast had been a dear friend of and campaign manager for Jack Kennedy, appointed by him. Devastated at his death, Wine had ordered "no parties for thirty days, no flights, nothing."

This severely restricted–No! It actually *prevented!*–our doing our intelligence job! There was, therefore, no way to transfer any of my predecessor's assets or contacts to me. I, finally, had to pull strings in D.C., calling General Lemay, or we would never have been able to fly to my other countries and meet anyone there. [I was also accredited to Upper Volta (now Burkina Faso), Niger, Dahomey (now Benin), Togo and Ghana, with a secondary responsibility for the surrounding nations and even Liberia . . . all

[65] I soon learned to identify each city by the smell of its airfield. Each was different. Each was distinctive, All were stench-like. I swore I could fly into any field within my area and positively identify it– blindfolded. (No one ever challenged my claim.)

the way to the Atlantic seaboard.]

Working under this initial handicap cost us extra energy, money and time (none of which we had in abundance). My staff and assistant attachés (Air Force and Army —my Naval attaché lived in Liberia and was unaffected) did their best, but my predecessor left us seven days later, without revising his departure date (more eager to get home than to help us do our job). He left us stranded, literally, on that beach I had so badly wanted to see. As a result Africa initially and immediately acquired a distinctive stink and not just from the drying fish and human excrement, the clutter of huts, fishing boats and nets, and the bites of sand fleas and mosquitos, all of which instantly disaffected us.

Yet, to be a good little attaché family, we "soldiered" on[66].

[66] I sensed a sub-rosa animosity in Ambassador Wine's words and actions. It proved to be true, but it eventually backfired on him. Soon after I arrived in Abidjan he had a huge parcel delivered to my office. It had a note affixed saying only: "Tell me what you think of this?" (No background data, no clues as to its importance.) Inside were extensive maps and engineering drawings showing a sketchy layout for an airfield at Yammassoukro, President Houphuet-Boigny's home town. Since it was in French, other than the ambassador's note, I thought the French were considering building a new airfield for the Ivory Coast and he wanted my comments. I went through it carefully and dashed off a highly critical condemnation. The plan proposed using a current roadway for the sole runway (in a valley between two hills where there were extensive fog records, angled 90-degrees from the prevailing winds), the roadway was inadequately stressed (the plan called for landing huge commercial aircraft), and a hundred other, minor deficiencies regarding lighting, avionics and approach patterns, etc.

The ambassador had my notes typed and translated into French—exactly as I wrote them—and sent them straight to the President, over my signature. Since they were so negative I believe the ambassador thought I just signed my death warrant as an Attaché. Instead, the President was ecstatic and invited me to his home in Yammassoukro for lunch and dinner, sent a French helicopter to fly me up there and back, and around the area with charts. During our detailed discussion, he asked for my specific guidance on building the airfield. After a series of such discussions, I ended up designing his new field in toto. (It is now complete, just as I laid it out.) But the ambassador *did* stifle my receiving the "Order-of-a-Thousand-Elephants" (a beautiful and massive medal worn around the neck, made of gold, ivory and diamonds) that the President wanted to award me for the job. But Houphuet compensated us by repeatedly inviting my wife and me not only to his home for dinner, but to a special private performance of Miriam Makeba, the famous singer from Kenya (and the ambassador was not invited). The President also wrote letters of commendation to the State Department and US Air Force.

Flying into Upper Volta (and its quaint little capital called Ouagadougou ("Wah-gah-doo-goo"), a radio beam directed us. Though a clear day. Barry, my assistant, suddenly said, "Look ahead, Colonel . . . see if you can find the city."

Thinking this would be a snap–at least to find the airfield–I leaned forward and stared down . . . at an expanse of unbroken brown. From horizon to horizon I saw not a single identifying feature.

Barry chuckled as he dropped a wing, circled, and pointed. "Almost impossible, isn't it? The houses are brown. The streets are brown The fairgrounds are brown. Even the runway is brown. If the sun is just right, though, you can see the President's Palace–it is white, but usually covered with brown sand as well. If you squint you can just make out the river. Sometimes, in the early afternoon, you can see the mist where the water percolates into the dry atmosphere."

In Upper Volta, Tom Estes, our ambassador there, did everything he could to help us, in contrast with Ambassador Wine. Tom, a man who came up through the State Department and noted for his humor, named one of his dogs, "Wah-Gah," and the other, "Doo-Goo"–both ugly, ungainly hounds. He and his wife loved them like the children they never had.

Our other ambassadors, one a former television talk show host/newspaperman (Dahomey), and a second, a movie star (Shirley Temple Black, later, in Accra, Ghana) did their best. But Tom Estes had a grasp of the situation no political appointee ever managed. (Tom had been a Marine guard and seeing what the State Department was doing, vowed to become an ambassador. Tall, rangy, rather gruff in a friendly way, he went back to college, qualified to work for the State Department, and built its current State Department Building in D.C. For that feat President Kennedy appointed him our first US ambassador to Upper Volta.) Behind the scenes, I connived to fly Tom down to Abidjan every year for the Marine's Anniversary Ball. He was "Semper Fi" to

the core. (And the corps!)

Ambassador Wine did *not* host the usual Thanksgiving Dinner for the embassy families in 1963. He left that to his second in command, Rudd (Chargé D'Affairs in Wine's absence). Everyone called him "Rude Rudd," for good reason. Where Wine appeared aristocratic and aloof, his assumed ambassadorial demeanor, Rudd came across as a cold, arrogant, martinet. The embassy staff to a man–and even "to a woman"–detested him. Still, under Wine and Rudd the embassy ran well and efficiently, though it did not show the same warmth of others I served.

The Defense aircraft was the biggest problem a Defense Attaché (DA) had, when in a location where he had one.

C-47, Defense Attaché aircraft
Abidjan, Ivory Coast, West Africa

Usually this resulted from a misunderstanding by the ambassador, but even more often by the embassy staff. The aircraft was assigned to the Defense Department, not to the embassy staff (State Department, SD). The USAF aircraft, therefore, was *not* on-station to haul the ambassador or his staff around the country at the ambassador's or staff's whims, but solely to satisfy the IR ("Intelligence Requirements") of the Defense Department. The DA must explain this quickly to the embassies or they wanted to schedule the aircraft as if it were their personal source of transportation. This made for some nasty spats.

The ambassador could always demand an exception (in an emergency) and request a special flight. When he did this, however, the SD had to pay the DD the full going-rate. In 1963 this meant more than $1800 an hour–for the plane's use (fuel and maintenance) and the pilots' and crew's salary–from the time we began preparations until we finished refueling at the end and replaced the aircraft in its original hard stand on the ramp. [When I explained this, and my willingness to help by searching for a legal excuse (one of those "IRs") to justify a desired flight, most people went along with it. No one, in contrast, ever insisted on ordering a flight and paying the tariff. (No matter how badly they yearned to go somewhere–to see a bull fight, attend a dinner, or visit another country.)]

Those Intelligence Requirements (IRs), we received daily, also inspired some hot communications between attachés and headquarters in Washington. Unfortunately, the IRs we received were not always well-thought-out nor totally realistic. Our corrective responses sometimes put us in hot water.

Our aircraft carried built-in cameras for photographing ground sites (airfields, etc.) and our crews toted 35-mm Leicas with a broad variety of short- and long-range lenses for photographing everything else. Knowing this, soon after I arrived, headquarters in D.C. sent us an IR directing us to photograph, map and record the exact location of every–repeat E-V-E-R-Y!–water hole, well,

stream and river, across our entire assigned territories. In our case, this meant the entire Sahara from the Atlantic Ocean (the beaches of Senegal and Mauritania), on our west, across two thousand miles of barren desert, to the far eastern boundary of Chad (its boundary with the Sudan).

We sent back a request for reconfirmation, with our explanation. We told them, "To satisfy this requirement will require roughly twenty years, and our forming a line of people, ten-thousand-men wide, to walk arm-in-arm across the entire distance from the west coast to our eastern boundary. *Yet* five miles behind their passage the data will no longer be valid. In the Sahara–as in all deserts–water holes and wells, streams and rivers, appear and disappear regularly and without reason. Only a few remain visible at all times."

We received an answer *a month later* (evidently it took them a while to evaluate our complicated observations). The message said, in essence, "If you can't do the job, let us know."

Though I thought we already had–we did it again. This time we wired them: "And this is an impossible task with our small contingent of eight NCOs and officers."

They withdrew the request.

Another IR was equally as stupid. It demanded our office *immediately* photograph each one, and submit a report on the full complement of arms (regardless of size, shape, cost and purpose) *manufactured and developed by each of our countries.*

This time we responded with a simple, straight-forward, "Not one of our countries is sufficiently or technologically advanced to produce significant weaponry, and none worth forwarding. They buy it all elsewhere."

A fiery message came back, "No excuses. Send the photos!"

Now convinced "a picture is worth ten thousand words," and an asinine request demands an equally asinine answer, we placed a clean white bed sheet on the ground. We carefully arranged a collection of the local natives' handmade knives, small spears,

bows and arrows, axes and assagais on the sheet. We made several large photographs, in color, with diagrams, annotations and detailed measurements. We submitted them, along with our equally-detailed assessment of how many of each the natives produced annually. We also referenced our previous wire and their response thereto.

Our report elicited a reprimand from the department head in D.C., "This is foolish and unacceptable!"

To this I merely repeated our first answer. No further communications came through and subsequently headquarters dropped the subject.

I also, as an aside, sent copies of both reports and our answers to General Lemay, USAF Chief of Staff, to whom I could report directly if I so chose.

Not surprisingly, the quality (at least the realistic demands) of the IRs drastically improved after that.

CHAPTER TWELVE
▲

At Ohio University, teaching ROTC (see photo below), my orders came in before the end of the 1951-1952 academic year. They directed me to leave at once and enter retraining, preliminary to being shipped to Korea. My first training assignment sent me to Denison, Texas to requalify in B-26s[67].

Chosen the national,
"ROTC Poster Boy"
for college recruiting.
(Ohio University, 1951)

[67] This is confusing, even to us pilots. The USAF after WWII, scrapped the original B-26 (Martin Marauder) and redesignated the one-time A-26 (Douglas Invader) as the B-26. I was still, therefore, really flying the last type aircraft in Korea that I flew in the European Theater of Operations (ETO), as a general aide, and at OU–just renamed.)

With Ilogene about to bring forth our fourth child (she was seven months pregnant), the one we had so longed for, it was difficult to just pack-up and drive to Denison. Yet, biting the bullet, off I went. (I even had to buy an old car to get there.)

By a happy happenstance (another of "those things"), my instructor at Denison AFB saw my name on the list of incoming students. A friend and former flying student, whom I had trained to fly this very aircraft a few years previously, he selected me as one of his students. I had gleaned more hours in the B-26 (formerly the A-26) than anyone on the base. (For that matter I had more time in the B-26 than anyone in Korea, as we discovered when I arrived there. This made for some amusing incidents and a few personal benefits.)

At Denison, my instructor and I spent those weeks and flying hours (required by statute to qualify), playing games with the aircraft, hedge-hopping, chasing cows, diving under bridges, and testing its newly-configured limitations. (A game of, "Hey! That's good, but now let me show *you* . . ." The days flew by.)

When I finished in Denison, the Air Corps next assigned me–back across country–to Shaw AFB, South Carolina. Again, since I had so much time in B-26s, they trained me there as a photo-reconnaissance pilot.

At Shaw, with Ilogene moving ever closer to delivery, I exercised a new right of military personnel assigned to wartime duty (inaugurated only after WWII). I requested a thirty-day leave, called a "Hardship-Delay." If granted, this leave would permit my remaining in Athens, Ohio, until Ilogene had our baby.

I received the delay and Ilogene gave birth within the period. Although Dr. Larry Goldberg had to hurry Mike along with medications to make the deadline.

This delay set me back one full class at my last training base before Korea. I flew into Reno (the location of the Survival Training School), further delayed by a lengthy snow storm grounding all aircraft west of Denver.

Grimy, tired, having tried to sleep on airport floors for more than four days, and dragging through a round-about series of intermediate flights, south, then west, then north–I finally tromped into Reno a full week late.

Once more the military hierarchy had no knowledge of my forthcoming arrival or my assignment (much like my recall, in December, 1947). Giving me *no training whatsoever*, the survival instructors grabbed up my B-4 bag for storage, loaded me with snowshoes (I had never worn snowshoes) and a ninety-pound backpack of unknown items (as an officer, I had never before carried such a backpack), then hastily pointed me toward the nearby mountains. "Hurry, Captain! You can follow the other students' tracks. They left about four hours ago for Squaw Valley."

Oh, yes, I also had no map or any idea what I was to do in the mountains–camp-out, hunt buffalo, knit booties for North Koreans, "kill myself or go bowling." If I had not been a former Boy Scout, this trek might have been the last anyone saw of me. Laboring up those snowy, slippery slopes, I visualized the Army's not finding my body in a melting snowdrift until the spring thaw. Without realizing it, I came nearer predicting my demise than I thought: the snow, now three-feet-deep and wind-driven by the preceding storm into drifts of ten- to twenty-feet, posed a continuing hazard.

Since no one had shown me how to use snowshoes, I lost my balance in the first ten miles (pulled down by the heavy backpack). I tried to regain my balance by stepping backward. (An absolute "No-no" in snowshoes.)

I vanished into a snow bank.

Get the picture? Here I was, completely alone, left to my own devices, ten miles from any help by base personnel . . . and I had no idea how far ahead my crewmen and the other students might be. I can assure anyone who asks–upside down in a fifteen-foot snow drift, slowly smothering, is not the place to learn new skills,

no matter how resourceful one is.

Struggling around in the snow, I righted myself, used my snowshoes like shovels and after an hour's hard work slowly mined my way back to the surface. Then and there I vowed, "No more stepping backward in snow shoes . . . and I need people if I am going to do this–so I better catch up."

I also decided, *I do not have to wait until Korea to be killed, I can die right out here on these Rocky Mountain trails! In broad daylight, too!*

Tramping as fast as my short legs managed, I reached the last stragglers in another three hours. But I did *not* catch-up with the main contingent until they were high in the mountains, had already pitched their para-tepee tents (made of old parachutes) for the night, and had cheerful (and warming) campfires to cook what little food we had been given (solely for the hike into the survival basin between two remote, towering peaks).

This made for an restless, freezing night.

Too exhausted to eat, I drank a little chicken broth and sought my bedroll. (My crew kindly shared their hot food and para-tepee, and even placed my bedroll on some leaves and boughs from nearby trees, as a mattress.)

I froze to death during the night, almost literally. I did not get any sleep, despite being so tired. I could not understand it. In the morning I asked my engineer-gunner, "Why so cold?"

Shivering too, he said, "I don't understand it, either. We cleaned off the snow all the way to the perma-ice and put leaves and boughs on that."

My Boy Scout training screamed. "Oops! Let me explain: snow is an excellent insulator; ice is not! Next time, leave the snow."

Among our training group there were a number of other former scouts and a few men who had paid attention to the survival training (the week I missed). Later, I heard the training had been thorough, pertinent and saved a bunch of the boys who went down behind enemy lines.

The students demonstrated a high level of competence while in Squaw Valley. We former scouts killed so much game, using shoe-string traps and dead-falls, the Game Warden came up and begged us to, "Knock it off, guys! You're stripping the forest. More men have to use this area."

In consideration, we stopped eating prize venison every night and squirrel for breakfast. We restricted our diet to rabbit and porcupine.

One porcupine we shook out of a tree was so huge he looked like a bear coming at me. Scared, I drove my ax not only through his skull, but also a foot into the hard-packed snow. We dined on him for the remaining days we spent there.

In turn, we were "Fair Game" on our return to base. The instructors waited for us, hiding under every snow bank and behind every tree. Any students they captured when coming back, they interrogated (hard!). They then subjected the crewmen to North-Korean-like prisoner treatment. The Base deliberately made it as rough as possible for us Korea-headed students–using sweat-boxes, third-degree, "Good cop-bad cop" questioning techniques, chains, ropes and water-boarding methods under cold shower heads.

Almost every student was caught on return and hassled. Of my crew, I was the only one who got through unscathed. I must admit I gave the instructors the finger and rubbed it in, "And I didn't even take your stinking course. You just shoved me out in the cold to swim or sink . . . or, in this case, to hike or perish in the snow." I made it plain I was unhappy with their "Go forth and multiply" directions I got on arrival.

From Reno, we drove over the mountains to Los Angeles and, from there, flew to Tokyo, Japan (via Hawaii and Midway), for our specific squadron assignments. Once more, happenstance reared up.

Our touching down at Haneda Airport (Tokyo) precisely at twelve midnight, New Years Eve, must have put shining halos

around our heads. From our airport reception by the Japanese, to our hotel assignments by the Japanese representatives of the military, through the week we spent in Tokyo, nothing was too good for us. Unlike other newcomers, we were *not* given billets in downtown military hotels (a dozen men to a room and hard cots), instead we were sent by taxi to the suburbs and placed in a small, intimate, Japanese hotel. As the ranking man and aircrew commander, I received a three-room suite and private bath. My crew each had a large room, but had to share the "facilities" with the other hotel guests. (They did not mind, though. They bathed every day in the hot tubs with the young Japanese girls, their brothers, and parents. Nor did they refuse when the Japanese girls of the hotel staff insisted on providing a "thorough," prior-to-bathing, hand-administered, soaping, washing and massaging.)

Though my first night in Japan, after flying across the Pacific I was ready for bed as soon as we had rooms. But the hotel proprietor (who spoke no English) insisted on bringing all my men into my rooms and serving drinks.

He then ushered in a group of girls, ranging from about twelve to thirty (?) years-of-age. Lining them up in front of us, he gestured at the girls.

In unison, they flung open their kimonos. This displayed their slim, sleek, naked bodies for potential patrons.

Again he waved his arm toward the girls and looked askance at us men.

Each crewman selected a girl and took her to his room. (I found later, this, too, was a perk for our having arrived in Japan at the stroke of midnight on New Year's Eve. They apparently had some kind of fetish about that time and date.) Unable to explain in Japanese that I was married, I managed to convey to the proprietor I did *not* want a women in my bed.

He smiled and bowed repeatedly. Ten minutes later, as I was slipping into the sack (alone!), he led another group into my room. This time they were all young boys, ranging in age from about

twelve to twenty.

Now I made really violent gestures of refusal.

The hotel owner shooed out his entourage of young boy prostitutes, then stood in the doorway undecided. He left shaking his head. I figured he chalked-up the experience to "another white man's stupidity."

When, the next morning, I told my crew what happened, they kidded me for days. One even asked, "Are you sure you're not . . . ?" He made a limp-wristed motion nearly earning him a sock on the jaw.

Our brief, one-week stay in Tokyo netted us solely a detailed orientation by a ranking representative of the theater commander and physical exams by the Flight Surgeon. A quick flight in a four-engine cargo ship took my aircrew and me across the narrow intervening body of water to Kimpo Air Base, Korea, ten miles northwest of Seoul.

There, on being introduced to our Group commander, the colonel took one look at my thousands of hours in the B-26 and pulled me from my photo-recon assignment. He gave me two jobs on the spot: "Squadron Operations Officer" (second in command of the only Weather Reconnaissance Squadron in Korea) and "Assistant Group Operations Officer" (a staff job in headquarters, running the Air Corps' reconnaissance and weather programs in the Korean combat theater). Good jobs!

In the first position, I checked-out *all* newly assigned pilots as soon as they arrived. In the second, I rewrote the Group's flying regulations. (This last extra duty was a Group mistake. The Group found out a mere four months later when I returned home, all my missions and tour completed.)

I flew my missions with the Weather Recon Squadron. This meant mostly routine trips over North Korea . . . and regularly flying when the weather was too bad for any other aircraft to take-off. In addition, I designed and created the squadron's official insignia, and acted as Squadron C. O. (Commanding Officer) in

his absence. The "Weather Reccie" missions, though not quite as horrendous as those in Europe during WWII, nevertheless, painted these memories in bright, red letters.

Our Weather Reccie outfit lost not a soul to the North Korean warriors while I flew with it, but suffered millions of dollars' damage from flak and fighters (MIG's, now jets), and hundreds of injuries ranging from minor to severe. We also recorded some weird "doings" during our flights over the Korean peninsula and Yellow Sea.

One night, while flying north and west out of Kimpo to evaluate a storm developing over the Yellow Sea, we encountered a meteor. It dropped from the sky right in front of our plane's nose. Since we were flying in the darkness between two solid cloud layers (an undercast and an overcast), and the object was falling extremely fast . . . only those of us in the pilot's cockpit and nose (my two weather observers and I), saw the meteor's rapid transit.

Unfortunately, these conditions also prevented our making any objective determinations as to its size and distance from the ship. It could have been two feet in diameter and ten feet in front of us. Or it could have been a quarter mile in diameter and five miles away.

The meteor's most interesting characteristics rose from its mottled appearance. Its surface looked precisely like the tiny ball from a ballpoint pen, highly magnified, all covered with squiggly grooves, surrounded by raised random lines, plus an odd, greenish-yellow fluorescence. In toto, it seemed ghostly.

When I asked the two observers NOT to discuss it between themselves, or with me–and to make separate reports–we all described precisely the same appearance. Each of us said it might be a new type weapon, or even a UFO. But no one else, other than we three, saw it. Thus there was no confirmation.

Another of our missions into North Korea required us to report, in detail, the changing temperatures, air pressures, and other

significant weather phenomena at ten thousand feet.[68] On our first leg, flying northwest from Kimpo, the skies were clear. We reported no clouds anywhere.

At the edge of the Yellow Sea, many miles deep into enemy territory, I reversed our direction 180 degrees to retrace our route, now flying to the southeast. Once facing southeast, we were shocked to find, behind us, like the huge wake of an ocean liner, a rapidly broadening layer of stratus clouds.

This flat, thin, tenuous stratus, gradually thickened into a new cloud system and required us to revise our report. Our engines and propellers, enhanced by the engines' heat, had stirred up and mixed the fragile invisible water particles[69].

Our ship had actually *created* a rapidly spreading cloud mass in that large parcel of air. Before the afternoon was over, both North and South Korea were covered with an overcast of solid stratus clouds at ten thousand feet . . . all our fault.

The Korean tour also red-lettered two major paranormal experiences for me. On my first mission, leaving the peninsula and heading out over the Yellow Sea, I discovered I knew at once when we passed–sight unseen–from land to water (and as quickly knew when we returned and crossed back over land). It became a sort-of internal warning system: my feet grew cold on our venturing out over the water, and instantly warmed on return to land. (My crew even tested my sensations by triangulating our positions with three radar sites on the ground in South Korea.) This sixth-sense (?), however, never served to warn me of this

[68]Actually, we flew at the 700-millibar level. This altitude was determined by a delicate measurement of the air pressure, using a metric system and two, cross-referenced instruments, rather than our flight panel's aneroid altimeter, measured merely in hundreds of feet.

[69] Our flying through the region triggered the mass. A minute piece of solid matter–a microscopic mote of matter, sand or mere dust–for example, is necessary if water droplets are to form, making clouds or rain. In addition, some mixing action and temperature change must occur, the reason rainmakers seed clouds with small particles to cause rain. Other conditions can cause it too, but they work only rarely.

after we returned to the States.

During another night mission a second type ESP showed.

There was a heavy overcast and not a light to be seen—no moon- and no star-shine, no boat lights on the water, no campfires, no lights in huts—nothing. This route required our going out at the ten-thousand-foot level, spiraling down in a controlled descent, very slowly, far south over the Yellow Sea. Our men took meteorological measurements every five-hundred feet, until we were three-hundred-fifty-one feet above the water (determined by a radio altimeter measuring our exact distance above the surface). We then flew all the way homeward—almost to the mainland—using solely time and distance calculations, at that three-hundred-foot height.

That night, too low to be tracked by radar from our Korean stations, or use our land-based radio beams to cross-check our guesses on wind speeds and direction, we headed northeast across the Yellow Sea. The first hour or so went by uneventfully. In the stable air I had no difficulty maintaining the very low altitude within the altimeter's "needle width"—about ten feet.

Suddenly, I jerked back the control column sensing a barrier ahead. *We flew through tree tops on the hill of a small island supposedly some hundred and fifty miles to the north!*

When we returned to base we found our engine nacelles crammed with leaves and small limbs. Another millisecond later and we would have crashed. (After that incident I no longer doubted any of my hunches, urges or spontaneous motivations. Though my crew swore I could see in the dark, I was convinced an angel rode my shoulder.)

Three weeks after this incident, we were again—at night, fortunately with a sliver of moon showing—returning from our route into North Korea. Our radar trackers warned us a MIG (jet fighter) was on our tail obviously about to attack.

I asked them to keep a close watch and inform us of his relative position as he closed. I then began a steep dive toward the

mountains.

The MIG, with his speed far exceeding ours, eased into a firing position behind us. My rear observer warned me at the same time the radar stations shouted, "He's ready to fire!"

When he did, I slammed the prop controls full forward and jerked back the throttles, simultaneously dumping flaps and gear. Our plane virtually stopped, relative to the MIG. He screeched by us going flat-out, unable to hit us, and flew right into the mountain-side just ahead.

During my short Korean combat tour, however, I probably spent less time on the peninsula than any other Air Force pilot who completed a full tour of combat missions. (That is pure speculation, though very likely true.) There was a good reason: as the Assistant Group Operations Officer, I rewrote all the flying and training regulations for our B-26 Group. The Group Commander and Operations Officer approved them.

These regulations set forth pilot-instructor requirements for qualifying newcomer pilots to fly the B-26 within our Group–combat, reconnaissance and weather. Ostensibly, I wrote them for safety reasons. I actually wrote them so only I, with my high number of B-26 flying hours, could perform certain functions. I, therefore, was the only instructor-pilot with the qualifications to check-out each new pilot who flew the B-26 (giving me whole scads of extra flying time). I, also, was the only one who could go out with a newcomer on his first combat flight (giving me mission after extra mission).

When any newcomer flew, therefore, I flew. When any newcomer went on his first combat mission, I went with him as his instructor-pilot (no one else was qualified). In just a few months I completed my mission requirements, built up a heap of flying time, and the Group cut orders to send me home.

This ploy on my part did not come to light until my next to last mission, when I returned with severe hydraulic problems from flak damage (reported earlier). Our Kimpo controller held me in

the sky, briefly, claiming he needed (by regulation) to find the best qualified B-26 pilot to guide me through the crash landing.

After screwing around for twenty minutes. searching for this elusive character, the tower sheepishly informed me, "You, Captain Cron, are that person. Land as you will." (This alerted the Group Ops Officer.)

Even then it was not until I was leaving for Tokyo . . . and home . . . orders in hand . . . that the Group Operations Officer awoke to what my little set-up with the regulations had accomplished. (Here, *he* had been in Korea more than a year . . . and *he was not yet ready* to return Stateside. I had been there five months and I was leaving.) That was the reason this appointment had been a mistake on my arrival.

He suddenly drooled to prevent my departure, but dared not raise a fuss with the colonel. Since he had approved each regulation–and so had the colonel–each shared some of the responsibility. Both were then at fault for missing my manipulations.

The Group Operations Officer thought he got even with me a few years later when he "arranged" for my assignment to the Air Force Inspector General's Office (Norton AFB, CA) on completion of Command and Staff College. Instead of hurting me, I advanced from captain to lieutenant colonel in less than three years. The same year, 1961, I won the top "Patriot's Award" and met Raymond Burr, Ward Bond, and General Medaris, while there. (See next page.)

<p align="center">* * *</p>

I left Korea reminiscing like most soldiers when departing a combat zone. There were a lot of tears . . . and a few laughs.

My first flight to Miho[70], Japan, my squadron commander took me to the Golden Bear nightclub. We were early, intending to dine there. Several young girl prostitutes, eighteen to twenty years

[70] Miho, pronounced, "Mee-Ho." Periodically, we flew our planes over there for fifty-hour inspections and engine changes.

old, who plied guests with drinks preliminary to charging for their services, immediately swamped our table.

I told them, "You may sit here and talk, if you want. I will not, however, buy you drinks, nor hire you for the night."

They agreed to wait with us until more willing American servicemen arrived. (During this period, right after the Pacific War, the number of Japanese men remained in extremely short supply.)

Four of the girls joined us. Immediately they began chattering like magpies among themselves, part in English, part in Japanese, occasionally asking questions.

Observing they were talking about their menstrual cycles, I asked, "Doesn't that hurt your business?"

"Oh, no," one answered, "we bleed one day . . . two . . . three at most."

I must have winced for the same girl asked, "Why you shocked, Captain?"

"My wife menstruates a full seven days . . . sometimes longer," I told them.

Now *they* were shocked. Gasping, the first asked, "How can she afford it?

Raymond Burr, movie star, 1961.

Ward Bond, movie star, 1961.

General Curtis Lemay, USAF Chief-of-Staff,
and I ,
discussing my top "Patriot's Award"
from the Freedom's Foundation,
Forge, Pennsylvania.
(1961)

The answer took some explanation These girls, already married with husbands who knew what they were doing for a living, thought nothing of it. They could not understand our "white man's" prudishness.

Also, on that first visit to Miho I ordered a pair of handmade flying boots with zippers, lined with rabbit fur. When I went back to pick them up on my next trip, the man making them asked if I

would like to see his new child, born a few hours before.

Liking children, I gave him an enthusiastic, "Yes!"

He brought out his new daughter, displayed *in a shoe box*. She was a living doll, "cute as a button" (as people used to say and "no bigger than a minute"), her black hair already cut straight across her foreheads in the traditional bangs.

On returning to the States, I told Ilogene she was the only thing I saw in Japan I wanted to bring home.

Her answer was concise: "Over my dead body . . . or yours." That seemed to be what all American wives fear most.

The baby was so small she must have weighed no more than three pounds, but healthy. Today, eating like we do, the Japanese deliver much larger children.

On the other side of the coin, in Korea I crash-landed a number of times, suffered severe structural damage, narrowly escaped flak and MIG fighters . . . and not one of my air crew or I sustained so much as a single scratch. Same as my combat tour in Europe.

This seemed more than mere good luck, skewing the usual statistics. Though I might suspect a reason, I could but speculate.

Around me, others had died, been injured, and others remained unscathed. Yet there appeared to be no rhyme nor reason to Fate's selection.

It was not because of piety–most of us prayed and many went to chapel. Yet those who did, fell by the wayside as often as those who did not.

Nor did there seem to be any positive dispensation for Catholics, Protestants, Buddhists, Moslems, or Jews . . . or any prejudices against them.

It was not clean living either . . . as many teetotalers went down as heavy drinkers, and as many smokers, womanizers, drug addicts, clandestine homosexuals as those who restrained, refrained or were straight. (My friend from WWII, Jimmy Doolittle, was killed the day after I saw him in Tokyo . . . and he was the only other married man I knew who remained true to his

wife, in Europe, Korea or Japan.)

It was not honesty, loyalty or any form of visible integrity . . . the crooks passed the test of combat as well as those who wore white hats.

It seemed to be simply a Divine "roll-of-the-dice" whether a person lived, died, was injured, or escaped. I was never much of a winner at gambling. Maybe, I reasoned, it's like comparisons balancing love and cards? (Lucky at love . . . unlucky at cards.) I had a wonderful wife. I loved her and she loved me, of that I was confident. Perhaps this carried over to my risking so much and being hurt not at all? Perhaps I DID have an invisible protective angel riding on my shoulder?

I doubt anyone will ever *know* the answer to that one on this earth. Yet, I survived–though even on the homeward commercial flight from Japan to Seattle two engines failed mid-ocean, requiring emergency replacement in Alaska, and we barely made it into Attu. Evidently the odds were still in my favor. (Up until then, anyway.)

An officer in my squadron whom I knew quite well, was a good example of the wayward. He came through WWII and Korea unscathed. This man flouted every moral issue.

Married, with several children, over the years he had accumulated a private airplane (large enough to fly his family around the country), an old Rolls-Royce limousine (he often used it to take his trash to the dumpster), a Bentley Continental (younger than the limousine, but one he had wired a tin can around its stainless steel exhaust and drove with virtually no brakes, to avoid spending money), a 1944 Lincoln Continental (a collectors item), two hydraulic-leveling, big-eyed, ugly Renaults (one with a Ferrari engine), and an Oldsmobile (the first of the front-wheel drives). One might suppose a person of this affluence would take good care of his wife and children.

But, no, he did not!

His wife, in the States, was wearing shoes with large holes in

the soles filled with cardboard. Though living in Base housing, she was forced to use carpets and furniture furnished by the AFB, and to scrounge food from friends for her kids and herself.

Meanwhile, he spent twice a much as he sent home monthly on a young Japanese prostitute, renting her a room, buying her food, and sending her to school. Yet, he saw this girl, at most, once every six week or so, when he flew B-26s to Miho, Japan, for engine replacements.

Within our Flying Group, more than a dozen others, all married, engaged in the same "horny"foolishness.

CHAPTER THIRTEEN

▲

The oft-quoted phrase, "Into each life some rain must fall . . ." may explain and prepare an individual for a number of dour situations. It might even comfort a few who are grieving. For others it does nothing. No words, no actions, not one thing helps . . . not when one loses one's soul-mate after fifty-five and a half years.

I will not dwell on this. I will describe only briefly the extent to which I was devastated, knowing others have been hit as hard. The life of an attaché (and his family) did not consist solely of flying, intelligence reporting, and embassy work. Ilogene and I used to put our right hands in front us, waist high, as if holding a drink . . .and extend our left as if reaching for a canape . . . then say, "We attaches have but one stomach to give for our country." (In my case that was true, I came home to a hospital from both tours with gall bladder problems from the rich sauces and wines of French cuisine.)

What others saw as "partying"–and for many members of the embassy staff actually *was* (those who had no "intelligence reporting" responsibilities)–to attachés meant "doing the job." For Ilogene and me, an evening often included attending as many as six cocktail parties (called "doing the rounds"), followed by a lengthy dinner (which often began at eleven and extended until two or three in the morning).

Our schedule filled, daily, with written, formal and informal, invitations. Diplomatic circles were tight–we were on their lists even before we arrived "on-station." (A six-inch pile awaited us on

195

arrival.)

From the day I arrived in Abidjan and Fort Lamy, we set new procedures. Regardless of how late Ilogene and I stayed up the night before, I would open our separate offices in the embassy, personally, at 0546 hours. I dialed open the sixteen combination locks in a given order, remembering each combination. (I am not bragging–I had to do this. We could not record any of them!)

During our initial meeting each morning of my attachés, we reviewed the results of our previous day's information-gathering. We sifted the results (separating the wheat from the chaff), prepared reports for transmission to the USA, and planned our duties to obtain whatever else we needed–by questioning, photographing, observing, or flying.

We did not manage much sleep, but "we got'er done."

Ilogene stayed at home and slept . . . for a while. But our servants[71] arrived at eight in the morning, six days a week (and, sometimes, seven). They cleaned, made the beds, did laundry, ironed and pressed clothes, cooked breakfast, prepared the remaining day's meals, and readied the house for our parties.

Servants, as mentioned earlier, were both a help and a hindrance. It was common knowledge among attachés that all our servants were "covert spies." Each of us assumed most worked for the local government, but we were certain some also worked for the USSR, the Israelis' Mossad, etc. (And they did!) So we never discussed any pertinent data[72] in their presence.

[71] We hired and maintained a cook, two "houseboys" (sometimes more), a gardener/guardian (who kept the other natives from robbing us blind and lived-in, twenty-four/seven), a chauffeur, and–for a while–a "chief honcho" whose job was to supervise the others. As Ilogene's language skills improved, she found out the "Honcho" was cheating our other employees, so we narrowed our retinue to five.

[72] Nor did Ilogene or I engage in "Intelligence-type pillow-talk." We all had to assume our bedrooms, phones and houses were "bugged." Though we had the instruments and regularly "swept" each room and all our equipment, we pretended at all times our conversations were heard and acted accordingly. We conducted serious discussions only in my "secure" offices or the vault. If you think about this, this made for some fairly embarrassing situations.

Obtaining good servants was also difficult. Ilogene and I, being gone so much and entertaining so frequently, needed reliable, capable, household assistance. Ilogene, who daily attended ladies' luncheons, bridge games, "teas" and outings during the afternoons, also accompanied me in the evenings, and still regularly conducted our cocktail parties and dinners. A good cook and staff, therefore, became imperative.

By searching and sifting, Ilogene discovered a Nigerian chef (Raphael) who had served as a cook in the British Army. This man spoke English, and–wonder of wonders–could even read and write in more than one language. He also knew how to use cookbooks, calculate and write-out what he needed so we could buy it, having determined the precise amounts required (based on how many and whether the attendees were to be American, British, French, or whatever[73]). For anyone, not in our position, this may seem of little importance. For us, Raphael was a jewel.

Yet, what we were unable to understand was, if he were so very valuable, why did his work history show so many hirings and firings?

When we sent him to our American doctor for the required physical checkup to work in our kitchen, we learned the reason –he had second-stage syphilis. (We said, "So what? He will cook for us, we're not going to sleep with him.") Nevertheless, unlike the French *who raved about him, then fired him*, we sent him, his wife, and his two daughters to our doctor and had them cured (at our personal expense). Not only did we gain a very valuable household assistant, but a devoted friend. (He had been unaware of the reason for his repeated dismissals–*no one had ever told him.* Therefore, he and his family were dying, like millions of other

[73] Raphael always based his needs like this: more food for Americans and Germans, more wine for the French. But the Americans and Dutch drank more liquor than anyone. Arabs, though forbidden by their religion to drink alcoholic beverages, skillfully drank them under the guise of fruit punches and orange juice–so we bought for them too. (They were–and are–even more devious in other ways as well.)

Africans, completely unaware and without the financial or medical means to effect a cure.)

Raphael showed his devotion by actively helping us gain information about our other servants and the local populace. (From his work in the British Army, he knew what we were doing without being told.) When we returned to Africa for our second tour–assigned to Chad–we received a message over the "African Grapevine" that he was willing to move his family (at his expense) the more-than-one-thousand miles from Abidjan to Fort Lamy to work for us again. We could not permit that, however, as we had no place for them to live in Chad, and we feared for their lives. As Nigerians in Chad, with Ghadaffi threatening a war–which *did* occur–they would have been constantly at risk. We might get away; but they would not. But Raphael and his family were so devoted and such good workers, we considered bringing them home to the United States with us.

Early on, working with our household help, Ilogene made some funny boo-boos (nothing serious). But she quickly learned the ropes.

The first morning she asked our boys[74], in French to, "Make the beds." The boys giggled. They were unable to work for minutes. I had to explain to Ilogene how, to get the boys to "make the beds" (as we say in English), the French equivalent meant "prepare the beds." There are other ways to say it, but the boys acted as if they thought she wanted them to go out, find saws, hammers and wood, and actually "make (build) the beds."

Ilogene, always loving, warm and considerate . . . not pushy . . . was uncomfortable around those who were. In one of my earlier commands, the ladies crowded about when she attended the first

[74] I am not putting down our help when I call them "boys." These were not only very young men, but this was the name by which they called each other and the French called them (and these countries had only recently been their colonies). We did NOT say, "Come here, boy!" for example. We called them "boys" only in a group. To us, they were, "Raphael," "Paul," "Adamah," "Abraham," and "William."

"Ladies Group" meeting and probed her for the name she wanted to be called, "Shall we call you Ilo? Gene? Ilogene? Or Katie?"(Her middle name was Kathryn.)

She thought for only a second and gave them an answer I consider to be a classic. She smiled and said, "Until we get to know each other better, how about just calling me, Mrs. Cron?" (That, I admired.[75])

When we arrived for our second attaché tour in Fort Lamy, Chad, as usual my new staff tried to milk Ilogene for information about me as their commander. One officer, representative of the group, asked, "How is the colonel to work for? Is he easy or hard?"

Again Ilogene grinned (I can still see how her eyes must have sparkled). "You'll get along fine if you just remember: *Do everything he tells you . . . and quickly.* If he asks a question and you do *not* know the answer . . . just tell him, 'I don't know, but I'll go find out.' Do NOT try to fool him!"

My staff, their families, and we got along fine after that. In both instances they followed Ilogene's instructions.

<p style="text-align:center">* * *</p>

If we had been allowed to record our first months in Abidjan, they might have made a good book on their own. (We were forbidden, however–for security reasons–to keep any notes or diaries, either the husbands, wives, or dependents, while on an attaché tour.)

One reason: like all modern cities, Abidjan was a study in contrasts. We lived on the highest hill in Cocody–the most affluent part of town other than the "centre de ville" housing the

[75] Ilogene delivered another of her classic one-liners when queried by a military mother who asked, "And how many children are you raising, Ilogene?"

She smiled graciously and answered, "None. I am raising adults." (Think about it . . .)

President's Palace.[76] Less than a hundred yards from our house, just over the hill so we could not see them, all our Cocody servants had built huts, hovels and shacks . . . and lived there.

These were squalid dwellings–built of mud, packing crates, even cardboard. (Very similar to the quarters our American homeless build in parks and alleys.) None had sanitary facilities, water mains or sewers. The women walked a quarter of a mile for water. (That was "women's work." Men never turned their hands to domestic tasks *in his own home*, though they cleaned, cooked and performed those duties daily, for pay, in our homes.) The natives who lived in the "over-the-hill" area were squatters. The land belonged to the city, and the surroundings became their public restrooms. (We were glad the prevailing wind usually blew *from* Cocody across them toward the lagoon.)

This hidden area came to an end one afternoon, however, when one of the native women went to the police station and complained. Her complaint? *"My husband is a cannibal."* He had recently killed an enemy also living in the same site, dismembered him to eat at his leisure, and had *hung his body parts from the ceiling in their hut.* She grumbled to the police, "I don't mind his murdering his enemy, but I do *not* want to duck arms, legs and torso parts when inside my home."

The police arrested her husband . . . and bulldozed *all* the huts.

[76] In the countries to which I was accredited, most of the presidents' residences were called "Palaces." Yet they varied widely in style. In Dahomey, General Soglo's was a one-floor, what we Americans would call a "bungalow," though extra large, with sweeping, front and back concrete patios. President Houphuet-Bougny's in Abidjan (he had another in Yamouassoukro) was massive, ornate, multi-storied, done all in white with crystal chandeliers and–of all things out of place–a huge fireplace in the enormous livingroom. (Seldom were either used, the room or fireplace.) In Upper Volta, President Yameogo's predecessor had built an enormous white, graceful and Arabic-type structure looking somewhat like the castle at Disney World. The notable item there was his dual, city-block-long circular drives from the outer gate to front steps and its upraised patio. In the center of the drives (one in, one out) three massive ponds, fifty-feet in diameter, each had a thousand sprinkling, surging fountains. When he entertained, the entire city went black as his palace, air-conditioners and fountains sucked-up all the electricity produced by the nation's only power plant.

(That was when we provided a place for our servants as long as we were there, on our lower floor.) Until then, we had been living amidst an enclave of multi-million-dollar houses, while cannibals squatted among dead bodies only a few yards away.

Another contrast showed up in our aircraft. I had been flying jets when I received my attaché call. The aircraft assigned us in Abidjan was not only old, but it had seen better days.

Roughly thirty-five-years-of-age, a veteran of WWII, its top speed never exceeded 135 knots (those are nautical miles per hour–about 150 MPH). Our C-47, also called a Dakota, a Gooney-Bird, or a DC-3 (by civilian airlines), was a tired, twin-engine cargo plane. Though a real "clunker," it sported some noteworthy modifications and served well for attaché duty in Africa. It may have been slow, but we were able to land it virtually everywhere–and often did. We put her down, regularly, on sand, lava, lake and river beds, on reasonably level grassy fields (in the Sahara–hah!), and only occasionally on runways (of which there were far too few in Africa and those too widely separated).

The cockpit sat high off the ground (about twelve feet). The engines also were mounted high–that kept them aloof enough so they did not suck-up debris like smaller, more streamlined aircraft did[77].

Requiring two pilots (by regulations), one could fly it in a pinch. It carried enough fuel to provide an endurance of seven and three-quarters hours. (A capability meaning we could fly, as I did–once!–all the way from Tripoli, Libya, across the Sahara, to Fort Lamy, Chad, non-stop . . . but I had a strong tail wind too). Externally, it was painted a gleaming white. The tail displayed an American flag and the aircraft fuselage was boldly emblazoned with a large-sized "UNITED STATES OF AMERICA," painted

[77] In a generous gesture soon after elected, our President Kennedy gave each of these backwater countries an AeroCommander for its president's use. They sat so low, they were usable only on major airfields (usually one in each country) and most were soon trashed by their engines' sucking in sand and debris.

on both sides in blue and black letters. We carried a supply of small blue flags with white stars to put out on landing, signifying we had an ambassador on board[78]. When the passenger door opened, a sign thereon proclaimed to viewers, this as an "Avion Diplomatique" (a diplomatic aircraft), supposedly assuring immunity from national and international search and customs requirements[79], as were all of us–including our wives and dependents–all of whom carried black, diplomatic passports.

Inside, in the central cabin, we carried twelve airline, recliner seats, wall to wall, thick, dark blue carpeting, and two, single-sized beds[80], one to each side of the center aisle. Immediately behind the engineering compartment a set of four facing seats surrounded a table.

As an aside, since I commanded the Defense Department contingent in every embassy to which I was accredited, I was always Number One, *next to the ambassador.* But I could never replace him when he was gone. Since I was Defense Department, that job fell to his first secretary in the State Department. In the

[78] An ambassador merits four stars in his assigned country, two stars when in another country.

[79] A new American ambassador (a political appointee) assigned to the Cameroons, once allowed the local officials–over my prohibitive instructions and pleas–to board our aircraft and ransack its interior. I filed an immediate, official (and top secret) complaint with both the State and Defense Department while still in the air returning to Fort Lamy, Chad. (This one got General Lemay out of bed.) The ambassador was recalled within two weeks. He had violated not only the State Department's most sensitive diplomatic protocols, but also highly classified Defense Department's security directives, His action might have cost our country dearly in international relations. (He never went out again as an ambassador.)

[80] Under the beds we carried our emergency water (canned Evian) by the case) and emergency food supplies, our weaponry with munitions, and four cases of Johnny Walker, Red Label (scotch). These last two items were illegal, of course. Yet, we needed the guns and ammo–as was demonstrated when attacked by Ghaddafi's insurgents–and we needed the scotch everywhere for bribes. Africa is a continent that runs on bribes. We, too, had to play the game . . . or be left out. Without that scotch, we could never have done our job, acquired the information our country needed, or kept the local machinery oiled.

ambassador's absence, this secretary became the "Chargé D'Affaires." (At least I was always Number One, never *Number Two,* like Avis, with an even worse connotation. Although I am sure several of the embassy staff thought I deserved the epithet.)

Behind the "front office" (the pilots' compartment), in the one-time engineer's cubicle, we installed our long-range, single-side-band radios and a galley, a refrigerator, a small hot plate, and a coffee maker (plus a supply of dishes and cups). In the very tail there was a tiny urinal and chemical toilet, with a vent (no lavatory for washing, however). We also carried other devices and equipment (much of which is still classified).

This aircraft's major handicap–especially in Africa–was its lack of air-conditioning and inability to fly at high altitudes. Often, on entering, controls and metal equipment were too hot to touch. Pilots and passengers literally boiled until we reached ten thousand feet. We flew at that altitude, or higher, therefore, most of the time.

Because of the heat, we tried to fly extremely early in the morning or late at night. I always preferred being at ten thousand feet when the sun came up. Over Africa, with its dust and other suspended particles, the dawns and sunsets were spectacular from the ground. From the air they took on a grandeur unequaled anywhere. This decision also put us at our destinations, normally, before the ground grew too hot to land. (There was always the possibility of an exploding tire in the extreme heat–and no repair facilities anywhere nearby.)

All airfield runways in our area, from the Sahara, not too far north of the equator, all the way to the equator, which lay a couple miles south of Libreville, Gabon, were largely unusable from eleven in the morning until sometime after seven in the evening, winter or summer. I landed only one time in Ouagadougou just before noon. (It was an emergency.)

We had been called north by an embassy "flap" in Upper Volta. When I touched down, my plane slowed as if I had slammed on

the brakes. I had to add considerable power to force it along the runway, then up and onto the concrete ramp before the terminal. The reason: the runway had melted, the tar running like treacle. Behind us I left ruts more than a foot deep in the blacktop. But, within five minutes, the surface reflowed and was as smooth as glass. Airlines, avoiding that problem, never landed until two in the morning, except at Abidjan, with its concrete runway.

These areas, too, seldom showed little climatic changes. This entire region, for example, supposedly had four major seasons–a long wet, a short wet, a long dry, and a short dry period. None of us were ever able to differentiate between them. In addition, the temperatures stayed pretty much between ninety-five and a hundred-twenty during the day, dropping only a few degrees at night. (My crew twice recorded unofficial temperatures of one-hundred-forty at Ouagadougou, on a thermometer suspended under a wing, *in the shade.*[81])

In Abidjan, it rained daily; in Ouagadougou it seldom rained at ground level. While flying over Ouagadougou airport one morning, practicing instrument approaches, it suddenly began pouring at my flight level. We were at 6,000 feet and, with the city at about 1,000 feet, we were less than a mile above the ground). The rain was falling so hard we could not see our wing tips. Yet, when we asked the tower to change my flight to an instrument clearance, the controller said not a drop was reaching the ground. (That's how dry it was.) My aircrew vowed it was so dry in the Sahara that, when they threw out a bucket of water, the liquid evaporated before reaching the sand.

Africa, though, offered an assortment of experiences. Some of them will never be forgotten.

Six weeks after I arrived in Africa, my Air Force Attaché,

[81] The record books, contrary to our findings, claim the highest temperature reported was at Al Aziziyah, Libya–136 degrees. (We often recorded higher readings as a matter of course, even in the shade and protected areas. Another Arab inconsistency?)

Captain LeBaron (Barry) Whittier and I flew Ambassador Thomas S. Estes (of Upper Volta) north into the Sahara. At a powerful sheik's request, we landed far out in the desert. The sheik at once invited Ambassador Estes, Colonel Damba (the country's minister of defense), Barry and me to have dinner with him.

The sheik's central, square tent, covered roughly a hundred feet of sand on all four sides and was surprisingly cool inside, despite the desert heat. (It was built with thick, insulated walls.) Since I had never seen one before–either a sheik or such a tent–he gave me the grand tour, except for his harem. He carried with him several wives, plus an unknown number of concubines and hand-maidens. (I thought I might never get a chance to see any of them. But I was wrong. *Really wrong!*)

The dinner that night was spicy, though not as spicy as the entertainment.

During and following dinner–served communally in circular, three-foot-in-diameter, brass containers resembling up-turned wheel covers–a small band of drummers and musicians played, unobtrusively huddled in a corner of the tent. This group, using a type of lyre, wind instruments, and tabors (drums), produced an unbroken cacophony of screeching tones and pounding rhythms.

We dined sumptuously on couscous, lamb, vegetables, raisins, sweetened drinks (no alcohol), and assorted sweet meats (sugared dates and other fruits, including a sort-of baklava). Dinner finished, the sheik clapped his hands.

A team of ten, nubile young maidens, thirteen- to fifteen-years-old (?), skittered out of their quarters through a tent flap. Slithering into the shimmering lamp light of the open central space, they began dancing for us.

All well-oiled . . . and stark naked, except for a narrow waistband of jewels[82] with one gem dangling strategically down

[82] The girls' attire–or lack thereof–was most interesting as I never expected to see such nudity among Moslems. The girls wore nothing visible in their hair. Their heavy black tresses hung loose to their shoulders on each side of their faces, showing

the front . . . they wiggled, pranced and stomped, paced to and fro, and strutted back and forth, almost hypnotically, like a disturbed nest of giant cobras.

When the dance concluded on an ear-splitting drum beat, the girls threw themselves to the ground before the sheik. Prostrate, hands over their heads toward him in obeisance, they lay flat on the tent's thick carpets like so many carved statues, barely breathing.

With a majestic wave of his arm over their heads, the sheik offered us our choice. In Arabic (Colonel Damba translated), he said. "Honored guests, my tent is your tent. For tonight, you may have any of my beauties you wish."

The ambassador immediately chose a girl, as did Barry. I was married (as were they, so their quick acceptance astounded me), and refused to "take" any of the girls. The chosen girls came forward to sit by her chooser and proceeded to feed him the candied fruits and refill his drinking cup.

The remaining girls scurried from the tent.

The stoic sheik clapped his hands and whispered to his aide. The other Arab bowed to the sheik and ran from his side, hurrying through the opposite tent flap.

Colonel Damba, sitting behind me, leaned forward and whispered, "Now, Colonel, you've done it!"

obvious care and heavy brushing for the hair shone in the light almost as if oiled like their bodies. The waist band of jewels appeared to be silver-wired into a narrow flexible belt, with numerous precious stones woven-in. The one hanging jewel swung freely on silver filigree, and extended downward about six to eight inches (varying in length somewhat from girl to girl), centered about where each girl's clitoris might lie. At most, this central jewel was no more than an inch in diameter (it hid nothing). Pubic hair unshaven, their dancing exertions revealed the outer labia and clitoris from time to time as their legs spread. The girls danced with fiery exuberance, lithely and agilely, as only young girls can. This dance also included some movements wherein they turned away from us and bent forward, thereby revealing their anuses and vulvas, intimating anal intercourse was not foreign to their culture. The girls' small, budding, to ripe, pear-shaped breasts, and a minimum of pubic and underarm hair, attested to their youth. I have a very sensitive sense of smell and even over the odor of the oil lamps, I caught the scent of the perfumed oils covering their bodies, the heavy perspiration their exertions produced, and the musk of their femininity.

Dumbfounded, I asked, "What? Why?"

Damba smiled, teeth gleaming against his dark face. "You'll see!"

Within ten minutes, a huge, three-hundred-plus-pound lady appeared, equally as well-oiled and equally as naked. Only difference, this woman wore her hair up, not down, in a complex headdress of woven pearls, surmounted with a tiny tiara.

She danced briefly in the center of the tent, fat jouncing on her huge belly and hips, breasts swaying like two great pumpkins; then she, too, prostrated herself before the sheik. (She lay there panting, gasping and sweating.)

Again the sheik waved his arm. This time, he offered the lady solely to me.

Damba warned, "That's the sheik's favorite wife. You can't refuse."

I pleaded, "There must be something I can say or do?"

Damba nodded and told the sheik, "Colonel Cron apologizes, O Great Emir, but he has a social disease."

The sheik smiled warmly and bowed his head in understanding. Then he insisted, "The very next time you visit my kingdom–after you are cured, of course–you *must* sleep with my wife!"

That did it! From then on, until I left three years later, we flew miles out of our way to avoid the sheik's territory. I was scared to death I might have to land out there somewhere.

Later, when I told my officers about this in Chicago, after the laughter died, one asked, "But what about the ambassador and captain? How were those little Arab girls–good, huh?"

I answered as best I was able, "No one found out. The ambassador and Barry knew they had merely to spend a few minutes talking with them and playing some childish games. Hell! They were just kids! Then the girls returned to the sheik's harem, satisfied they did not have to service huge white strangers. No one told *me*, though . . . until I was leaving for the States."

Another time, our Abidjan ambassador's wife invited ten

French couples plus the families of the embassy staff for the annual Thanksgiving Day dinner. When the African servant brought in the huge turkey, he tripped and the turkey slid across the floor.

Without batting an eyelash, Mrs. Wine said, "Pick it up, Adama! Take it into the kitchen and bring us *the other one*." (Now, *that was fast thinking!*)

There was also another story about an infamous New Year's day dinner. In this instance, the ambassador's wife carefully, in advance, instructed her servants precisely how she wanted them to serve the roast pig . . . centered on a silver tray, parsley sticking from its ears, an apple in its mouth.

When the servant served the main course, he waltzed in with the suckling pig on the tray, as directed, but *he* wore the parsley sticking out of *his ears* and the apple in *his mouth*.

In a third apocryphal tale, a high-ranking French lady of Abidjan's diplomatic community, noted for her Coquilles St. Jacques, one afternoon hosted a ladies' bridge party. During the first break, they pleaded to learn her secret.

Raising both hands, she exclaimed, "Oh, I never go into the kitchen, but I'll ask my cook. Perhaps he will tell you his technique."

She led them to her non-air-conditioned kitchen. Inside, she directed her massive, heavily sweating, black chef, stripped to the waist to cook, "Emile, will you please show my guests how you make your wonderful Coquilles St. Jacques."

He bowed his head. "*Oui*, Madame."

Dropping his other tasks, he carefully laid out the small, special dishes with their little handles. He measured the condiments, cream and cheese, and stirred them into the sauce on the stove. He took his time, explaining each step. He, then, *chewed up the clams and spit them into the dishes!*

The ladies left, hurriedly. I also heard no one ate at her house again.

CHAPTER FOURTEEN

▲

In Abidjan, my major stumble had to do with my first ambassador. I duly appreciated his close friendship with our recently assassinated President Kennedy, and felt for him and his grief. But I had a job to do too. This ambassador's decree directing us to do nothing during the mourning period of thirty days stifled my capability from the git-go. With many more countries than the Ivory Coast, and more than ten ambassadors, other than him to contend with . . . I *had* to get on the move.

I pleaded, to no avail. I explained, but it did not alter his ruling. To gain some elbow room, I contacted General Lemay and the Defense Department, creating a breach from the beginning.

Our next confrontation arose over the use of the aircraft. The ambassador and his staff seemed to think it was assigned to the Ivory Coast as their personal "run-about," to be used any time, at their beck and call. Apparently unknown by the ambassador, my instructions from headquarters dealt specifically with limiting the aircraft's use, henceforth, to Air Force business. This went over like "a turd in a punch bowl." From then on, the ambassador adjudged my predecessor (Colonel Miller) to be God's gift to the world, while I was the lowest of the low. Nevertheless, I stuck to my guns.

If the ambassador had enjoyed the authority, I believe the ambassador would have, (1st) cut me off at the knees, and (2nd) had me relieved, right then. He may even have tried. Though General Lemay never said a word, he gave me the highest possible ratings every year.

Still, if I were called upon to choose the most ticklish decision I ever made as an attaché, I would have to say it was when I refused a direct order from both a well-known United States Senator and the Defense Department. This situation earned me a personal telephone call, in Africa, from General Curtis Lemay, Air Force Chief-of-Staff.

Out of the clear blue one morning we received a classified telex (via the CIA's secure communication system). The telex, from the Secretary of Defense, directed us to set aside everything we were doing and fly immediately to Dakar, Senegal.

In two days–about how long it was going to take us to make the trip from Abidjan, west along the African coast, past Liberia, Sierra Leone, French New Guinea (it was then), Gambia, etc. (the equivalent of flying across the United States)–we were to pick up a senator there, along with his family and eight members of his entourage. From Dakar, we were to fly them to Bomako, Mali, thence to Ouagadougou, Upper Volta, and around a prescribed five-day tour of our countries, then take them on to Libreville, Gabon. (Where a fellow attaché from South Africa was to pick them up and do the same for his area.)

I fired back a terse message: "Sorry. No can do. Both of our C-47's alternators have failed. We have no spares. Defense supply says it will take seven days, even using commercial jets, to get us replacements and another day to install them. Until then we cannot fly. Suggest senator and people use commercial airlines."

This message earned my first call from General Lemay.

The phone rang; I answered. I heard a deep voice, somewhat garbled by static, declare, "This is Curt. I want to speak to Colonel Cron."

(Here's where the "fun" began.) "This is Colonel Cron. Who's 'Curt?'"

"This is General *Curtis Lemay*, Rod." (The static immediately

cleared–probably afraid to continue[83].) "What in hell's the problem, over there?"

I told him.

"Can you fly to Dakar, if we get the French to give you some alternators?"

"Sir, I already tried that . . . and I also have queried all the airlines flying into and across Africa, from everywhere. None have the type alternators we need."

He knew we had no avionics nor electronics without those alternators. We could fly, but solely in the daytime, under clear weather conditions . . . and anytime a pilot flew in Africa–anywhere–those conditions could *not* be guaranteed. Weather reporting was spotty. Sand storms appeared without warning. Tornadic winds and typhoon rains often came in off the Gulf unannounced. I heard him mumbling to himself–he knew this.

"Can you fly VFR, along the coast as far as Dakar, if we assure your receipt of the alternators on your arrival there?"

"Yes, sir. *If* the weather remains good all the way. *If* you give us your permission to violate several regulations. *And if* the French or an airline in Dakar will agree to install our alternators on a priority basis the instant we land in Senegal."

I heard a, "Hmmph! I'll get back to you." The phone went dead.

Ten minutes later the general called again. "You have my permission. We have TWA primed to make the change at Dakar. We are sending every alternator available from every place we can

[83] An apocryphal story of the general made the rounds for years. My experiences tend to verify its validity. When he was Commander of the Strategic Air Command, already wearing four-stars, one day he stood under the wing of a B-29 smoking his trademark, a big black cigar, while the plane was being refueled. A refueling sergeant approached, "Sir, you can't smoke here during refueling . . . the aircraft may explode."

Lemay took another puff, removed the cigar, and stared briefly at its glowing end, then returned it to his mouth. In his typical growling rasp, he said, "It wouldn't *dare . . . !"* (He continued to smoke near refueling aircraft while SAC commander. No aircraft "dared" explode.)

find them, directly to you at Dakar. How does the weather look?"

Suspecting this might happen, I had already checked with the French weather service. "Fairly good locally, but questionable beyond Sierra Leone."

"Are you willing to take the chance?"

When I hesitated, he said, "Now, what's the problem?"

"African weather is treacherous, General. This can blow up in our faces . . . why can't these people fly commercially until we can have those alternators shipped here?"

"Rod, this senator is a key member of the Appropriations Committee–he swings a big stick. The Secretary of Defense says we gotta kiss his fanny for next year's dough. Get the picture?"

"Yes, sir. You send the alternators; we'll try for Dakar. I'll leave yet this morning. But we may be late leaving Dakar going into Mali if we have any kind of delay." (I was tempted to sing a few bars of, "Give My Regards to Broadway . . ." for a little birdie told me this trip would be no romp in the park. But I didn't believe the general was in the mood for humor.)

His answer confirmed it, "Go for it, Rod! I knew you would. Do what you must." The line went dead again.

In less than an hour, my crew and I were in the air, starting our intensive, inch-by-inch map-reading course, flying west. We passed Monrovia without a qualm. We gassed up at Freetown, Sierra Leone. While there, the French Flight Control warned us storms were coming up from behind us, off the Gulf of Guinea. Pondering only a bit, we elected to try and "give it a bloody go."

We took off, flying to the northwest now. The visibility decreased and scud appeared. We kept going.

Nearing Senegal, the visibility diminished drastically and we had trouble seeing the ground. We went on.

I began to think we might have to land in a tiny, little country called Gambia, in Southern Senegal. But the wind shifted and our path cleared somewhat. We plunged forward.

I warned the French flight service and Dakar tower we were

coming in and would be flirting with regulations, flying under minimums. They assured us they would keep the surrounding area clear if we believed we could feel our way in, find the airport, make an approach, and try a landing. (They offered to give us what was known then as a "Ground-Controlled Approach," with their tower telling us by radio which way to turn and our height, etc.

I told them, in return, "That approach requires us to be on instruments . . . and we have none. Our lack of alternators is forcing us to do this solely by eye-ball and magnetic compass. If we lose sight of the ground, for more than an instant, we will be unable to maintain level flight and may spiral down."

The scud thickened and moved further in. It started to obscure our visibility completely. I dropped lower.

Now we were risking, not just hitting other aircraft, but hitting tall buildings and radio towers. I even began to worry about the trees.

But our luck held!

We turned inland, solely following my instincts. (I had flown into Dakar a number of times and had a fairly good feel for the landscape and airfield setting.) When I was about ready to give it up, call a halt, turn around, and ditch our ship in the ocean, I caught sight of an airfield boundary marker.

We called the tower, dropped our gear and flaps, and made a straight-in approach on the only runway in sight (down-wind . . . another definite "No-No!"). I could not have cared less.

I taxied up to the TWA hangar and turned off the engines. Before I could say "Jack Robinson," "General Curtis Lemay," or any of the other epithets I had been suppressing, the ground crew began stripping the engine nacelles.

Then, we got the big jolt!

Not one of the nine alternators they had received, fitted! Shipped in from Europe, the middle-east, and South America, they were all for other types of aircraft.

213

At once, I sent more messages via the phone and the embassy's CIA for the correct ones. But they could not arrive for another two days, at least!

But the senator was *there*. He awaited me in the VIP lounge, pacing to and fro like an angry, hungry, caged tiger.

He forever endeared himself when he ran up gesticulating. "Well, fly-boy. It's about time you showed up. We're ready to load. What time will we get to Bamako?"

I must admit I derived a great deal of pleasure (which I tried hard not to display), when I said, "Sorry, Senator. We're going nowhere . . . not for a while." I told him the story.

He growled at me, got on the horn (no cell phones then), and, I think, called everyone in the world, complaining. I know he again stirred up General Lemay.

The senator and his "troops" languished in the French Base's VIP quarters, while Barry, our crew, and I went into town. We climbed quickly out of our hot, wet clothes and into a brace of cold, very dry martinis. Two day's later, we left . . . the senator and entourage in tow.

This story, however, does not end here. This senator and his staff were known "dead-beats." (The reason I am mentioning no names.) A Dakar embassy official alerted us to their ploys.

Under the guise of time restrictions and meetings, the senator and his people had been asking the military and embassy personnel to purchase for them,"take-home" gifts and local artifacts, promising to pay when leaving. Then they took off and the poor suckers were stuck.

They tried to do the same thing to my men and me. We did it for them in Dakar, in Bamako, and again in Ouagadougou. But in Ouagadougou, I refused to take-off, until they laid the total–in cash, travelers checks, or bank checks–into my men's empty, pleading hands. (The senator made a formal complaint through channels, while still in Africa, saying I was both "arrogant and uncooperative.")

When General Lemay called about *this* complaint (he had already ignored the one from Dakar), I explained and referred him to several embassy people whom the senator had stung. This, too, I never heard about again. (Oh, that's not quite true —what I meant was, "there were no repercussions." For, on my return to the States, when I stopped by the general's office during my debriefing session, he cited the incident and slapped me on the back. "Smart move, Rod, with the senator." That was better than any medal I ever received.)

Unlike my father, who showed compassion and generosity, I believe I derived my often hard-nosed attitude from my dad's father. He could be granite when a condition demanded it.

Leonard Jackson Cron
(my grandfather)
A man who, though kind,
also stood fast in the face
of adversity and took no
crap off anybody.

In later entries at the appropriate places I enumerate my other mistakes, and the places where I tread on toes, all of which were sensitive in one way or another.

These reports may sound overly self-aggrandizing . . . but I can record them no other way. Often I—and other attachés as well—felt as if we were playing a never-ending game of "king of the hill." It seemed as if we were standing on a hilltop, sword in hand, fighting

off the snarling dogs biting at our ankles. Only General Lemay[84] appeared to be on our side, against the State Department and its ambassadors, even the Defense Department and DIA. He pulled many of my hot chestnuts—and other types—out of the fire. Here, he did it again.

An attaché soon learns all ambassadors come in two types: political appointees and State Department promotees "from-the-ranks."

The political appointees get their jobs as part of a president's pork barrel, "nose-in-the-trough" perks following an election. The election of a president sets off a prescribed chain of events. Every US ambassador, world-wide, must submit his resignation (having served at the president's discretion.) The president can then appoint (and usually does), first, a new Secretary of State. This opens the door for him to appoint his election helpers to fat-cat, ambassadorial positions.

What do these naive, political appointees know about running an embassy, conducting international diplomacy, dealing with "clients," and representing the president and the USA to foreign countries?

Zilch! De nada! Rien! (They are frequently worse than the proverbial "bull in the china shop.") These people with a "little knowledge" often believe they can run the world . . . and here is where "a little knowledge becomes a truly dangerous thing."

If these political appointees do *not* rely on and heed the advice of their State Department and Defense Department veterans . . . all hell can break loose. They can—and often do—put our country in

[84] Experience showed no officer went very far up the ladder without a senior officer as his invisible sponsor. For me, there were several (General Snavely, Colonel Hosmer, General Stillman, General Tom McGeehee, and most especially, General Lemay), I even had some help from the State Department— Ambassador Thomas Estes sticks out predominantly. Then they all retired . . . at about the same time . . . and I was left high-and dry. (No stars for me!) There were other reasons, too, discussed in later chapters.

serious jeopardy[85].

Only the people of the State Department who come up through the ranks with their language skills, their vast experience on each rung of the advancing ladder, are adequately trained for the job of ambassador. (This "pork barrel" scheme has outlived its usefulness. In today's world of great sensitivity, ICBMs and nuclear weapons, a single diplomatic misstep may do irreparable harm.)

In addition to the episode cited before (see footnote), I was involved in a number of others, all of which left me in untenable positions and placed our country in both ridiculous and touchy situations.

The first occurred when the president appointed a new ambassador to Dahomey (now called "Benin"). Unfortunately, this new man was black[86].

General Soglo had his aides invite the new ambassador to a private dinner[87] in his home the night he arrived, then he called me in Abidjan. (The general's rear lawn backed up against the ambassador's, separated by an adobe type wall about five-feet-high, with a gate in the center.)

[85] Reference the incident with our ambassador in the Cameroons, who risked our diplomatic immunity by insisting I permit the customs and immigrations inspectors to enter our aircraft. Nor was this an isolated episode.

[86] This indicates no prejudice on my part, but African bureaucrats usually see our blacks as former slaves and beneath them. This was not true for General Soglo, President of Dahomey. He was eager to welcome the new man, but wanted me to "brief" him first and accompany him, on his presentation of his credentials. (General Soglo and I, and our wives, had become close friends. He met me at the plane on our arrivals, held my hand when walking, hugged and kissed me in greeting, so did his wife). I describe this solely to show our closeness and his lack of any prejudicial bias.

[87] I also wanted to warn the ambassador about dining at the general's. Nowhere else did I ever see this done–but at Soglo's I had to ask for a four-inch cushion to sit on–for the general's wife insisted ALL dishes to be used during a meal be placed, one atop the other, at each place setting. The stack (with the soup bowl on top) reached higher than my nose. Without a cushion, I had trouble eating the soup and the first several courses. Even then it was a delicate task.

He explained, "You new ambassador is black, I hear. I want you to meet with him, first, and brief him on my habits before I meet him . . . and I want you to come to dinner with him. You can perform the introduction. I don't want to embarrass him."

I agreed. Obtaining an emergency clearance, we hurriedly flew the three hours or so to Dahomey. Soglo[88] met us at the airport and drove me directly to the ambassador's residence. As usual, we embraced, kissed, and held hands like two lovers throughout the trip while he explained further.

After a few minutes at the residence I went to the ambassador's home and introduced myself. I then tried to alert him to General Soglo's eccentricities.

He blew me off. "Forget it. I know how to handle these Africans. I'm black too."

I tried again, "But, sir . . . I doubt you've ever met anyone quite like Christophe Soglo . . or his wife." I told him how affectionate they were and how he liked to touch and hug and kiss. I also told him how–underneath–he was tough as tempered steel, how he and his wife had personally, and virtually alone, quelled an early uprising by standing back-to-back in front of their home, shooting Thompson machine-guns and leaving some thirty dead insurgents lying in the street. (Soglo and his wife did not sustain a scratch!) I also told him how the general and his wife kept a fifteen-foot python under their bed–the reason I never stayed with them, though they always invited me to make their place my residence when in the country.

Again he waved me off. "Garbage! I'm the ambassador. *I –and only I–*will decide what needs to be done and what needs to be stressed. Come along, if you must. You may do the introductions,

[88] I no longer have photos of the general so I will describe him–imagine a black Raymond Burr, three hundred+ pounds, six feet-two-inches tall, huge hands, head and feet, with a broad grin. That was General Christophe Soglo. His wife, in contrast, was white, five-two, weighed about 120, with an equally bright smile. She was an native-born Israeli with a captaincy in their Army. And she was as tough as he was!

then I want you to stay out of it."

Following meekly behind him (I had no choice), we went through the rear gate and around to the front of Soglo's presidential residence. His home was a nice, but non-affluent adobe cottage of eight rooms, a wide patio in front and rear, sitting only a foot above the ground.

The ambassador stomped ahead like a conquering hun.

On seeing his approach, Soglo on the front patio rushed forward to meet us, his wife a few feet behind him. Not waiting for a formal introduction, he hurried toward the ambassador, his arms outstretched, a broad smile showing an expanse of white teeth in that huge black countenance.

The ambassador stopped and frowned. He stuck out his right hand for a handshake.

Ignoring the hand, General Soglo wrapped the fragile-seeming ambassador in a tight bear hug. He then planted two wet kisses on his cheeks, one on each side.

When released, our ambassador shrank away, cringing from the show of affection. He then took the back of his hand and wiped off the moisture on his face with a revolted expression.

I won't detail the remainder of that tight-assed evening, but I will report this: the ambassador was gone the following week.[89]

A similar event occurred in Upper Volta. On my first tour as an attaché in Abidjan, an Upper Voltan lieutenant colonel, Sangoulé Lamizana, was our main contact. He had served at length in the French Army and now commanded the entire Upper Voltan military.

My other attachés, Army, Air Force, and I, along with him and

[89] General Lemay informed me, when I came home to retire, that Soglo had appealed to the State Department to appoint me as ambassador to his country. I had heard that as a rumor, but Soglo, typically, had said nothing, wanting it to be a surprise. (He did not understand I was Defense Department, and ambassadors were State Department. Although several admirals and generals made the switch, I know of no colonels who did,) Sangoulé Lamizana of Upper Volta also made the same request, I heard later.

his staff, dined and had regular cocktail parties together. We grew quite close. I even flew him to his home and met his parents, his grandmother, and his great-great-grandmother, still living. They had no idea how old she was, but thought she must be well over a hundred. She was blind and spoke no French, so he translated. She wanted to "see" me, and I agreed to it. She reached out her trembling, skinny fingers, traced my face . . . then exclaimed how handsome I was. I had him tell her she misinterpreted what she was feeling, "I am balding, jowly, too fat, and too short." Her laughter–more of a high-pitched cackle– ended with her saying, "I believe he is a wonder with the ladies." (Sangoule always was a kidder.)

On my second tour, in Fort Lamy, we traded airplanes with Abidjan (ours was ready to give up the ghost), so we met at Ougadougou for the transfer. The new ambassador there was also black.

The driver who met us at the field had been Sangoulé Lamizana's driver when he was Chief-of-Staff (now Lamizana was the President). On the way to the embassy to check-in with the new ambassador, the driver asked if I were going to go see President Lamizana while there. I assured him I was and showed him the special box of cigars and bottle of cognac (Lamizana's favorites) I brought along to give him. (I surmised he'd tell the president I was there and about the gifts.)

The ambassador, though, would have none of it. "No! Absolutely not! I don't want you to go near the president. He's my client. I will deal with him . . . no one else."

He was the ambassador and commanded what we did in his country. I acceded to his wishes. But, when we climbed back into the staff car and headed for the Hotel Independence, the driver asked when he could take me to see the president.

"Sorry, but the ambassador said I could not visit the president." I handed the gifts across the seat. "Will you take these to him for me, with my apology, and give him my best wishes and

congratulations on his presidency, please?"

The driver nodded and said nothing more.

Fifteen minutes later, we had barely signed into our hotel room when I received a phone call from our ambassador, "I just got my ass royally chewed. The President insists he wants you in his office right way."

I went. I delivered the gifts. Sangoulé and I had a merry old time, talking about his election and the problems he had . . . one of which was our new ambassador. In essence, he concluded with, "This is the last straw . . . he's got to go." And he did, too.

On the other side of this sordid coin, every ambassador who earned his stripes coming up in the State Department was invariably a winner and a joy to work with. Knowledgeable, well experienced, and well-trained, they handled affairs adroitly and with the diplomacy the job demanded.

There were certainly exceptions to the political appointee rule, but the only one I can vouch for was a lady by the name of Shirley Temple Black, who served as our ambassador to Accra, Ghana. That lady had it all the smarts, the looks, the tact.

* * *

Before leaving for Chad, one of the final briefings I received at CIA headquarters, Langley, VA, had to do with a certain French captain who was now working with the Chadian President as his military assistant. The CIA had seen his name listed on some Intelligence Reports as a "source" and "contact." They suspected, however–having cross-checked his data with several other sources –that this smart young captain was selling the same material to all available buyers. They promised to fund me (whatever it required), to keep him on our payroll, while I did some cross-checking on my own after I arrived "in-country."

They left the decision like this: "If you determine he's playing both ends against the middle, it might be better if he were 'removed . . . with extreme prejudice.'"

Once I was "in-country" and began working with Colonel

Hascöet, General Morlet, the Chinese Ambassador, and an Israeli colonel (Oozi Rigai), we quickly verified this man *was peddling the same stuff to each of us.* (Via a special contact, I also found the Russians were paying him as well.) This internal, double-spy had a real money cow going and was feeding us all the same worthless crap.

Together, we decided this man "had to go." (I wondered if we were to draw straws, hire a hit man, or gather him in our nets and drop him into the Chari River for the fish to eat.) But I did not get to participate in carrying-out the final action. The very day he was found dead I flew to the military hospital in Wiesbaden, Germany for evaluation and treatment of my gall bladder. (I knew it was gall bladder . . . but would they take it out? No!)

On my return, Jacques Hascöet told me–first thing–the matter had been resolved. The former French captain had been found dead the morning of my departure, shot through the head with a 9mm. The time? Sometime the night before. The murder site? Within a hundred feet of the Club du Chari, near the river. The captain, Jacques, Oozi, the Russian and French officers, Ilogene and I, were all members. (Only the Chinese ambassador was not.)

Jacques thought I had done the dirty deed. He believed that was why I left so hurriedly for Germany. I, in turn, thought he had killed him. The French were certain one or the other of us had (but would not ask), and the Russians and Chinese did not care, or ask . . . as long as it was a "done deal." The Israeli colonel merely smiled enigmatically and said nothing (until I pushed his buttons, later).

Now that our double-spy was out of the way . . . permanently . . . our intelligence product immediately improved. And I began to "run" some operatives who generated really good material.

Many wondered what Fort Lamy[90] had that made it so popular

[90] Fort Lamy resembled Ouagadougou more than Abidjan. There were only a few two-story buildings in the city (mostly our American houses), The highest structure was the airfield control tower. (Even then, when Ghadaffi's troops finished

with the host of intelligence agents running around in the nation's capital. Simple: First, the French Foreign Legion headquarters were there; second, it was the major communications' crossroads between west and east Africa, and north and south Africa, with inroads into the middle east.

Remember the movie, "Casablanca?" Well, Fort Lamy (at that time, I cannot speak for today) had all the intrigue of the movie and more . . . because this was real, not fiction.

The Russians maintained a large compound in Fort Lamy, filled with people. Yet seldom did we see them on the streets. It had a vast, complicated, radio array that would not have been out of place on the PanAm building in New York. The only three people who went out regularly were the ambassador, a first secretary, and the ambassador's driver. This driver did not live in the compound, but in the native quarter. Actually he was the highest ranking official in the embassy. (We were not supposed to know that.)

The Chinese also had a small contingent "in-country," the ambassador and a group teaching the natives how to dry farm. (This ambassador we knew before, in Abidjan. He and his wife were a delight. They lived behind us, about three hundred feet away. If they had had their druthers, we would have dined with them and their family–five bright-eyed little dark-haired darlings like stair steps–every night.)

The Israeli force in Chad consisted solely of the colonel and a

with Fort Lamy after the war, they left not one stone or brick standing on another.) The only paved streets were in the center of town, the remainder were laterite or sand, with one exception: the road south, to the bridge and across the Shari river to an Italian restaurant built on the other side, was paved . . . by its Italian owner. The houses and buildings, largely of adobe-style bricks, showed varied colors and some tile roofs. (Our tile was orange, the walls partly wood paneling, partly white-stucco over brick.) About ten houses attempted to nurture a lawn–one of them was ours. But that tended to attract insects, scorpion-spiders, and snakes. "Downtown" consisted of a square surrounded by a double row of stores and restaurants, and one gasoline station. The entire city housed no more than fifteen thousand people, including the natives in their outlying quarters. (The statistics claimed more, but they exaggerated.) Without the French military, who were not counted, there were not many people around. The populace, again excluding the French and diplomatic personnel, were largely Moslem . . . black, brown and semi-white.

woman, whom we originally thought was his wife, since they lived together as such. She was a captain in the Israeli Army (actually they were both Mossad, Israeli Intelligence Officers). Israel has the only military I know that actually does what we always kidded about in our forces. (We said, "If you were supposed to have a wife, the military would issue you one." Israel does!) This captain was his subordinate, his mistress, and his intelligence colleague. He told me all this straight out as we traded current info on our then-deceased French captain.

Naturally, I asked if he were the one who "took care" of our problem.

He merely smiled, then frowned. "If *you* did, would *you* tell *me*?"

I shook my head. "I guess not."

He spread his hands as if to show they were empty. "There you have it." (Colonel Rigai was clever. My son, Mike, called him "slick." And he was.)

The local intelligence activities were ludicrous. We all knew the boys and cooks who worked in our homes also doubled for the local government. It got to be so much of a joke that, when we were leaving to go to Europe on a trip, I gathered them together and gave them a complete briefing on our route and plans, whom we planned to see, and when they might expect us back. We laughed to see them struggling to memorize the complex details for their reports. (Since only one could read and write, this was a difficult chore.) The next day, the leader asked me to repeat some of the figures he had not retained. I did.

I flew regularly into Bangui, Central African Republic to replenish my "contact" money. (The Air Force had cut me off, saying none produced anything worthwhile. The CIA thought differently.)

In Bangui, I went to the CIA agent's home to get "pumped-up" for another month. He dragged a good-sized briefcase from under his bed, tossed it on top, and sprang the clasps. "Take what you

want." He waved his hand over the neatly wrapped currency.

The case was filled from side to side and top to bottom with hundred dollar bills. "How much is here?" I asked.

"Two million."

"What if I took it all?"

He waved an arm in dismissal over the case. "Be my guest. It's yours."

I pulled out two bills. "This is all I need. Where do I sign?"

He lifted an eyebrow. *"Sign?* We never *sign."* He started to close the case. "You sure you don't want more . . . or the case?"

I shook my head, suddenly scared by the temptation. "What would happen if I did?"

"Nothing. District headquarters would send me another caseful in the next diplomatic pouch– tomorrow."

That was my trip to the mountaintop where I heard the voice of Satan.

I must admit I gave a lot of thought to what we could have done with those two million dollars–for the kids, for the family, for retirement. But it would never have bought happiness and I know I could never take it. Guilt would have strangled me. (But, there . . . for a moment . . .)

CHAPTER FIFTEEN

▲

While stationed in Abidjan, on one of my earliest trips to Upper Volta, my initial attempts at kindness and politesse pertaining to the natives, got me into deep trouble. It taught me a valuable lesson. (This was a real boo-boo.)

On this trip we took with us four of Ambassador Estes's staff, including a native girl from the village we were visiting. When we deplaned, the ambassador's girl ran forward. From the assembled crowd, she joyously brought back a younger sister, introducing her to each of us.

I smiled. In an attempt to be gracious, I took her extended hand and told her in French what a lovely girl she was. Then I inadvertently gushed. I added how lucky the village was to have two such attractive ladies, she and her sister, one of whom represented them on the ambassador's staff,

The young sister became excited and began spouting in her native tongue. This left me aghast as I had no way of knowing what she was saying.

Her sister translated into French, "She is saying, 'I will return to Ouagadougou with you and be your wife.'"

I shook my head and carefully explained I was already married, acting as if this made me sad. (BIG mistake!) This in no way stifled her enthusiasm.

She grabbed my arm and hugged me close to her more-than-ample bosom. (Thank goodness she was wearing a western style blouse, bra and skirts . . . or this might have been even more embarrassing.)

While I was tactfully trying to dislodge myself, she replied,

"That is all right. You can have your white American wife . . . I will be your black African wife."

Her sister explained to her again and again, and, finally, the girl unhanded me. But she followed like a lost puppy, tagging along for the rest of our visit, looking soulful.

In the meantime, the embassy secretary relayed to the ambassador what happened. When we boarded the aircraft and everyone was waving goodbye, the younger sister stood in the forefront of the native tribe, waving frantically, lips curving downward as if in sorrow.

The ambassador nodded toward her. "Rod, she'll probably hike to Ouagadougou in a couple days, looking for you. Best you stay in Abidjan for a month or so. Let her come and go. And let her sister and family convince her you are a lost cause."

She did. I did. And they did. The next time I went to Upper Volta, Ilogene went with me . . . also, after that, I kept my mouth sealed shut. No more compliments to young native girls!

Also during one of my earliest trips to Upper Volta, Ambassador Estes and Barry arranged for me to meet the current "Mahdi," living in Ouagadougou. Wives not invited, Ilogene stayed with Mrs. Estes.

The "Mahdi" (Islam), Ouagadougou, Upper Volta. Titular head of West African Moslems in 1964.

This man reputedly was a direct descendent of the famous

227

Mahdi portrayed so well by Lawrence Olivier in the movie, *Khartoum*, about the murder of the British General "Chinese" Gordon. What's more interesting, this same Mahdi is supposedly the hereditary religious ruler of all Moslems living in Africa.

This visit was no mean affair. The ambassador timed it to coincide with the Mahdi's monthly audience, conducted so the Mahdi might hear and adjudicate his subjects' complaints. (African kings, emeers and presidents pretty well acceded to his demands when he voiced them as the Mahdi, much like the Catholics do for the Pope when he issues a decree.)

He quickly finished with his audience (an assortment of petty "beefs," none requiring a Solomon's wisdom, nor the splitting of a baby to satisfy the claims of arguing mothers). Waving us toward a wall behind his throne, he led us behind heavy, ornate draperies into his elaborate quarters.

Here we encountered several contradictions. While outside and in front of "his Islamic people"–as he called them–he acted as their spiritual leader and Mahdi, and wore the traditional robes, ornate turban, and odd-looking booties of an Arab emeer. Behind the scenes, he donned an English suit, including white shirt and "school tie," neatly pressed trousers and coat, with brown wingtip shoes. (Real spiffy!) He also had his many servants prepare for us samples of his well-stocked bar, complete with ice from his hard-working freezer. (Moslems are supposed to be teetotalers.)

Before his people he spoke only Arabic and their hundreds of dialects. Behind the draperies, he spoke fluent English, French, German and Spanish. His English, since he held a doctorate from Cambridge, showed heavy British overtones, but his many, lengthy stays in the USA had added some American idioms.

Once our glasses were filled, he toasted the US State Department and US Air Force, with a hearty quaff of scotch and soda–his avowed favorite–and a ribald declaration. He then explained the monthly ritual about to take place outside his palace.

"Many, many years ago . . . we believe this may have been in the early seventeen hundreds, as the exact date has been lost . . . a preceding Mahdi, quite the stud, married a very young and very beautiful Arab girl of great renown (to be his fourth wife[91])." He stopped to chuckle and take another heathy swig of scotch. "I often wondered if this were not the basis for the Scheherazade stories in the *Arabian Nights*."

He took another sip and continued, "Kidnappers stole her on her wedding day, before he managed to bed her.

"Enraged, he sent his soldiers and emissaries in all directions, declaring, 'When she is found–kill the kidnappers and bring her home. On her successful return, I will bless her, reward the finder, and have all my soldiers to fire their weapons in rejoicing.'

"This monthly celebration commemorates her return. My young staff will fire the same weapons . . . ten old 'blunderbusses,' all that remains of original hundreds. Today, they fire them at arms' length as we have lost too many boys to their explosions." He invited us outside, then, to see the highly stylized ritual.

[91] Most ranking Moslems (sheiks, emeers, etc.) have four wives, with as many concubines and hand-maidens as they can afford. (I always wondered about the "hand-maiden" connotation.) When traveling, the higher the rank, the more they carry with them–including family members, parents, children, brothers, sisters, cousins, etc.–plus servants. Princes and kings of the Saudi family travel in hordes. Though I visited Upper Volta, drank and dined repeatedly with the Mahdi, I never saw or met any wife or concubine . . . yet he had a vast supply of young servant boys always at his beck and call. (?)

Outside the "Mahdi's" residence, Ouagadougou.
The raised, circular area in the center is the dais
where the Mahdi sits on his throne (brought out via the
dark wood door in the wall, also centered). From there
he presides over the gun ceremony.

Outside, he waddled[92] up onto a dais and perched precariously on another makeshift throne. A young boy led a bedraggled horse from behind the building and to the Mahdi. He blessed the girl riding in the saddle (hidden by robes and veils).

Ten young boys (ages ten to twelve), ran out and tried to shoot

[92] The Mahdi is one of those to whom the Moslems "pay tribute," literally and annually, They place in front of his palace, once a year, a big scales. (It had to be big, he obviously weighed somewhere between four- and five-hundred-pounds, maybe more.) They then weigh him and give him his weight in gold–coins, jewelry, chains, small ingots . . . whatever they were able to amass. He lives on that for the next year–and very well too. If, perchance, he *does* become "strapped," all he needs to do is call for another "weighing" and his followers cough-up another load of gold. (This is really pretty sad when you think about it. Most of "his people" are ignorant, itinerant nomads who earn less than fifty dollars a year, and some never see coins, solely trading and bartering their way through life. While he lives in the lap of luxury, year-around, traveling worldwide, dining at Maxims and La Tour D'Argent in Paris, they scrounge through the sand and heat, gathering money to assure his continuing affluence– and he's not even a "good Moslem.")

the ancient, muzzle-loaders. Only three of them fired–another exploded, injuring the boy (but not seriously). The others threw theirs to the ground and ran off. The boy led the horse and girl back behind the quarters . . . and this concluded the ceremony. We returned to the Mahdi's quarters where he thrust upon us another drink before he let us leave.

The Mahdi said his goodbyes in flawless English, adding, "That was a jolly good show today. Last month, three boys were killed and the month before one of them shot the horse the symbolic girl was riding."

On another of our trips, this time within the Ivory Coast, we carried several of the Peace Corps Volunteers around the country at Ambassador Wine's request. Here, I met a young attractive blonde who often came into Abidjan regularly for parties and to discuss her work with the country's Peace Corps Director. Their Peace Corps doctor also headquartered in Abidjan, and required volunteers to have physicals as often as possible because of the diseases they acquired "in the bush." (This girl and her associate contracted amoebic dysentery.)

This girl, Jule Anne Tadevic, (about twenty-two at the time) was the youngest of the Peace Corps group. During language training in Quebec, Canada, her French instructors heard her name as "Jewel"–*Bijou*" in French–so "Bijou" she became . . . and that is what everyone called her.

I met Bijou again on my next trip north when she and her fellow teacher in the city of Korogo, hosted a dinner for the ambassador, the Peace Corps Director, Barry and me. Unknown to us, that afternoon, as they began the meal, their propane tank showed "empty." They had neither the time–nor money–to replenish its contents.

Without gas for their stove, the two girls were up a creek without a paddle! They had no way to prepare the meal, and they had planned as their center piece, unusual, African-style omelets, and hash-brown-type fried potatoes with mixed vegetables.

Showing inherent ingenuity, the two girls borrowed clothes' irons from everyone around them (and there were only three mud houses in town with electricity).

Turning the irons upside down, they cooked the pastas on them as if using a griddle. (I learned about all this from Bijou's associate before we left, when I commented on how harassed they seemed. I thought they had found another mamba in their house, as they mentioned during dinner.)

This visit was memorable for another reason. Both the ambassador's and the Peace Corps Director's French skills were abominable, to say the least. (A joke among their staffs, but mine were only a bit better.)

The ambassador, when he finished dinner, slid back his chair and patted his stomach, saying, in French, *"Je suis plein!"* (The ambassador believed he was indicating, "I am satisfied." But this sentence, in French, is normally used only with reference to pregnant farm animals. When used in reference to humans it is a gross vulgarity. He had just told the girls and other guests the equivalent of, "I'm knocked up.")

Everyone roared, except the ambassador–who looked startled–and the director, who thought he had spoken correctly. I bent forward and whispered, "Mister Ambassador, I will explain later, but–for now–just laugh with us and say, 'I wanted to compliment you on such an excellent meal . . . I am more than satisfied.'"

A few weeks later, Barry and I managed to find an excuse (another "IR") to visit all the airfields in the Ivory Coast. And again the ambassador wanted to haul some of the country's Peace Corps workers around with him. (The ambassador declared that, as a former close friend of John Kennedy, he wanted to give the Peace Corps as much support as possible. Secretly, Barry and I believed he had "a thing" for either Bijou or her associate, because of his pointed request to pick them up and carry them with us . . . a four-day excursion.)

On this tour of the country, my first, Barry showed me how to find the airfield at "Man." This was a tiny village with a narrow airstrip carved from the densest jungle, located on the eastern side of a mountain in the far western part of the Ivory Coast, near Liberia.

To get there, we flew over the field going north, then around the small mountain to our left, descending all the way and readying for landing (gear and a quarter flaps down, props forward).

Barry warned me we would not see the field again until we passed over the huge trees at the southern end. We then had to "dump" the nose, add full flaps, and hope we could round-out and land . . . before reaching the trees at the other end.

Everything worked beautifully . . . except . . . he had *not* warned me there were three humps in the field–small hillocks. I touched down on the first . . . and went back into the air. I touched down on the second . . . and bounced again. I finally held it down on the third rise, and screeched to a halt with no more than a hundred feet ahead to the tree line.

I make an issue of this landing (in my years of flying I did a lot of bouncing, so this was not terribly unusual) solely because Bijou never let me forget it. Anytime she flew with us after that, she always held up three fingers as she entered the cabin. "Are we going to do three again, today, Colonel?"

Ilogene and I invited Bijou regularly to our Abidjan parties when we needed an extra, young, unattached girl. (All the female embassy secretaries were older–some much older–or married.) So, when a new officer or airman reported-in, or we had an odd young male with no companion (and Bijou was in town), we recruited her to fill-in. She also, on occasion, stopped by and had lunch with us, and our children. Ilogene, Bijou and I, therefore, became well acquainted. But I never even imagined we would see her again after leaving.

Immediately after my first attaché tour, the Air Force assigned

233

me as commander of the Chicago USAF Recruiting Squadron. After my arrival, Bijou was the first person to call and welcome me to the city. (My picture, with a write-up, had appeared in the local newspapers and a TV station interviewed me.) During my two years in "The Windy City"–before I returned to Africa for my second attaché tour–I met both Bijou's parents and her brother (a truly sharp young man, killed a few years later, flying helicopters for the US Army in Viet Nam). Today, Bijou, sporting a Master's Degree, is a stock broker and Vice President for Smith Barney in Chicago, handling my itsy-bitsy account.

Yet, on that same visit to the western side of the Ivory Coast, Barry and I flew over those extra-big trees growing there in the tropical rain forest. Since this was my initial exposure to this area, Barry pointed them out. "Look down there, Colonel. Some of those trees are even more than three-hundred feet high."

I stared out the window, marveling. But I wanted to know their names. I asked him, "What do you call trees like that, Barry?"

He thought long and hard, then laughed. "T-a-l-l trees."

 * * *

The African landscape, so spectacular it never ceased to amaze, shock and astound, also offered us magnificent opportunities to relax . . . when we had the time. Our job stretched across the days and hours, still we managed a few days here and there to "hit the beach."

From an African Chieftain near Abidjan, I leased a stretch of the sand five hundred feet wide and five hundred feet deep, extending from the rolling waves of the Gulf of Guinea in,and to the highway. (It cost me twenty-dollars in the local currency and a fifth of Johnny Walker Red scotch, annually.)

To collect, the chief swaggered down the sand, exactly one year to the day, hand out to greet us, fingers snapping for his loot. Dressed in his full regalia–a headdress of white egret feathers thrust through his thick white hair, his black, almost purple, tall (six-foot-plus), but thinning body, wrapped in a long, sarong-like

cloak of bright, red, blue and brown, hand-woven cloth, interwoven with silver and gold befitting his rank—he clutched and waved his sign of authority (a hand-carved, gold-topped shaft, shoulder tall). His neck, ringed with heavy gold chains, showed his wealth. His crinkled, wizened shining face trying to produce a toothless grin demonstrated his friendship. (Rumors claimed only a few years before WWII he had been a head-hunter and cannibal. His always grasping my upper arm and squeezing, as if testing the quality of the meat, made me edgy. At least he did *not* lick his lips.)

Our greetings and the payment protocols were ceremonial. We shook hands, embraced, kissed on the cheeks. We pounded each other on the back and shoulders. We bowed. I scraped. I offered the scotch. He tossed it to a member of his twenty-person, male, female and child entourage, tucked the money into a hidden spot under his wrap, waved once more (I always sort-of expected a "high-five"), and moved regally down the beach to his next renter.

By a trade-off (some more of that Johnny Walker Red plus a few bottles of cognac from our diplomatic stores), we, in addition, managed to talk the local Italian contractor into using his native laborers to build us a woven wall on each side and at the back of "our property," and a beach hut (complete with thatched roof, walls, a covered porch, benches and tables for picnics). A little more cajolery produced a tap of fresh, potable running water, underground from his offices two thousand feet away. (No one else even thought of doing that.) He even paved us a road to our back wall. (It was amazing what a little liquor accomplished in Africa!)

With those we had the prize location on the beach and even ambassadors fought to join us. (The only problem—the waves off our shore, a mile east of the Vridi canal, produced a dangerous undertow. Swimmers had to be careful. Any swimmer could be rolled up onto the sand, dragged out to sea, or shoved eastward a

thousand feet.)

This site turned out to be the best investment we ever made in Intelligence-gathering terms. Members of the diplomatic community flocked there. Among them, one of my best "sources" and "contacts" was Junkeer Leopold Quarles Van Offret, ambassador from the Netherlands. He and our Mike became great friends. Here, too, we entertained the Rogets, a French businessman and his wife who ran an extensive French fishing fleet out of Abidjan, covering the Atlantic as far west as Dakar, Senegal, and as far east as Gabon. (His data on what was going on "sea-wise" in this part of Africa was gold to the US Navy.)[93]

* * *

Trips "Around the Horn," as Barry and I called them (from Abidjan, Ivory Coast, north to Ouagadougou, Upper Volta, east to Niamey, Niger, southeast to Cotonou, Dahomey, then west across narrow Togo to Accra, Ghana) took us through the major, central countries to which we were accredited. With a communistic government in Ghana, the USSR exerted a strong influence. (We kept a close watch on their camps in the jungle. They were training natives to infiltrate the surrounding nations and "bring political enlightenment" via the teachings of Lenin and Stalin.)

Early on, in Ghana, a Russian general acting as an attaché (but was actually the president's political mentor), pretended he did not speak English. I let him get away with it for a while, communicating through his interpreter.

[93] My assistants, our wives, and I dealt with and entertained individuals, couples and personalities ranging (in the Ivory Coast alone) from President Houphet-Boigny, through his assistants, his Defense Secretary and staff, to the French generals, ambassadors of the major nations, and their known (and some not-so-well-known) covert spies. They were all colorful. There is no way to adequately describe more than a few–to do otherwise would make this a multi-volume set. Let me, therefore, summarize in a few words what demands millions: I found these people–from the Africans to the French to the multi-nationals from around the world, of all ranks, grades and backgrounds to be universally interesting, some fascinating, and none repulsing. I made many true friends, people who could call me in the middle of the night and I would respond solely with, "What can I do for you? Where?" I enjoyed their company, even when it was work.

Finally tiring of the facade, one night I said, "General, I have a dossier on you this thick –" I held up my fingers an inch apart. " – it says you were a military attaché in London and speak fluent English."

"Yeah? Well, ours on you is this thick." He held up his fingers, two-inches apart.

"That's bigger than the one my own government has!"

He grinned and waved for his interpreter to leave. "I would hope so."

After that we became relatively close friends. We were always wary, but he was helpful. He seemed as leery as we were of Ghaddafi, just then beginning to make noises in Libya, to the north on the Mediterranean.

Half the data I had on the Russian general came from the local British Brigadier Attaché, the other half had come from the French attaché. Not only did we attachés gather info as an intelligence community, but coordinated and traded it with others for our mutual benefit.

Ghana's two attachés' and the Russian general's data on Ghaddafi proved to be of great value when I went to Chad. There, Ghaddafi gave us fits[94].

During this first assignment while still in Abidjan, Barry and I made many "contacts" and grew quite close to some. On a trip to Upper Volta, we came out of our room in the Hotel Independence (Ouagadougou) to see the Lebanese ambassador crouched on a sofa in the lobby, head in his hands. We stopped and touched his shoulder. "Sir, is there anything we can do?"

He removed his hands and looked up. His face was so swollen it was unrecognizable. His left eye protruded to the point it

[94] Ghaddafi grew more and more greedy every year. He wanted to take over Chad and get his hands on the vast oil dome our astronauts discovered in Chad's bordering mountains during their satellite passes over the area, verified by my crew on the ground, with samples and test lines. He began sending infiltrators and insurgents into Chad to conduct random attacks, and terrify the natives. This eventually succeeded and he then began a full-scale war to integrate Chad into Libya.

appeared ready to pop from its socket. He nodded. "I can hardly see. I have some kind of gross infection and the pain is excruciating. There are no doctors here. I need to get to Abidjan at once–but the airlines are booked solid."

Barry and I immediately gathered him up, bag and luggage, and placed him in our plane, canceling all local plans. We flew the ambassador to Abidjan as fast as our old C-47 could honk along.

Luckily, his doctors caught the disease in time. He recovered (but it took several months). After that, this ambassador kept us up-to-date on all the intelligence info on any area (Africa, middle East, wherever) to which he had access, and any time he received fruit or wine from Lebanon, he shared them with us, case after case. (Lebanese oranges, apples and wines could not be beaten . . . then.)

Both Barry and his wife, Mickey, as well as Ilogene and I, enjoyed dinner after dinner at his home. He had a lovely, attractive wife and a daughter to drool over. My middle son, Patrick, took one look and had trouble getting his tongue back in his mouth.

The United States then sent me a Jewish assistant to replace Barry. That very day, the Lebanese ambassador came to my office in the embassy with dejected apologies.

Such is the complicated life within the diplomatic community and its invisible restraints, for he had to tell me, "I am sorry, Rod, but my country forbids me to associate with you any longer, now that you have a Jewish assistant." Occasionally, though, Ilogene and I still found packages on our doorstep we knew were from him. But in public, as far as he was concerned we were now anathema.

When I left Chad, a few years later, this same Jewish assistant was sent to replace me in Fort Lamy–which brought up another problematic situation. This former assistant was also a former fighter pilot, as had been my last assistant in Chad. And neither of

them was ever completely at home in twin-engine aircraft.

The first of these two assistants, the Jewish[95] boy, always had trouble landing the C-47, as did the pilot in Chad. I warned both of them that–if they did not "get with the program"–one day they were going to end up on their noses.

But the first one also had trouble monitoring the systems of a C-47 (which were actually quite simple). He never seemed to learn he had to switch fuel tanks from time to time, and pump fuel around . . . to keep the plane level and the engines running.

On a trip from Abidjan, via Dakar, he screwed-up when we were flying at ten thousand feet over the Atlantic Ocean, inbound to Tenerife in the Canary Islands. (This was another trip to Europe for our periodic aircraft refits and inspections.)

I left him alone in the cockpit so I might speak briefly with Ambassador Estes, his wife, and mine, in the passenger compartment. I pointed out that, to balance the plane, he had to stay alert. (He already had let one tank become unbalanced while I previously conducted some measurements in the rear and we were currently running both engines off one tank.) When the levels equaled again, he was to shift the other engine back to its corresponding tank.

I was delayed in the rear for thirty minutes longer than anticipated, talking with the ambassador. Suddenly, both engines quit.

By the time I reached the cockpit three pairs of hands were outstretched, ready to make the control adjustments necessary to avoid ruining the engines and get them running again. (My hands, my crew chief's and my radio-operator's–both of whom held commercial pilots' licenses and were "checked-out" on the C-47–

[95] Lest someone think I am castigating this young officer, I am not–nor do I hold any bias against Jews. My daughter is a converted Jew, two of my grandchildren were raised in the Hebrew religious tradition, and I have attended temple services and sung in both temples and synagogues. Also these officers demonstrated outstanding potential, they merely showed a lack of experience in larger aircraft during these periods.

groped for the throttles.) But, my assistant sat there as if "hit by a whirling blivet," apparently shocked into an unmoving stupor. (Meanwhile the plane–on autopilot–was slowly starting to lose altitude in a flat configuration, nearing a stall.)

My illustrious assistant had done nothing. He had NOT pulled back the throttles. He had NOT turned on the fuel pumps. He had NOT switched fuel tanks . . . (I could go on, but you get the picture.)

We did everything needed and had the engines running smoothly in a few seconds. After that, I never left him alone in the cockpit and insisted either my engineer or crew chief sit in the right seat to monitor his every move (or failure to move).

My other assistant, the one who became my assistant in Chad, showed many of the same failings. (Fighter pilots are accustomed to fuel tank switches and pumps being automatic, not a source of concern.) Also both these men continued to make landings the "hard way"–bouncing, then braking, when they landed. This worried me.

On my return to the States and I found out my former assistant was going out to replace me, I told General Carroll (then head of the DIA), "General, you better switch one of them and assign the colonel in Abidjan–the one who had that C-47 before I traded planes. Those two young fighter pilots, flying together, will dump that ship on its nose, sure as God made little green apples."

The general nodded. "Excellent idea. I'll do it at once." He lifted the phone from its cradle and dialed while I sat there.

While the general made the call, it was already too late.

My two former assistants, now flying together as an Air Force Attaché and his assistant, had crashed the C-47 on one of their first landings in Fort Lamy (putting it up on its nose). The aircraft was ruined . . . and it was *not replaced.*

Africa, however, has its own scary way of reaching into all flying operations, and bringing along its own gremlins to boot.

Since I was ill, the USAF air-evacuated me to the States, out of

our American hospital in Wiesbaden, Germany, directly to the hospital at Wright-Patterson Air Force Base, Ohio. Ilogene and Mike had to come home alone . . . commercially.

Their flight went south, out of Fort Lamy, across the mountains to Yaoundé in the Camerouns, then southwest to Douala. About to land at Yaoundé, their four-engine, *Air Afrique* plane lost an engine.

The pilot notified his passengers, but assured them there was no real problem, except they must overfly and *not* land at Yaoundé. (This was because Yaoundé lay in the mountains and they needed to have all four engines to take-off. It would be repaired at Douala.)

Then they lost a second engine a hundred miles south of Yaoundé.

Again he reassured his now-edgy planeload of passengers. "No problem we still have two good engines."

But when the third engine quit several hundred miles from Douala, no matter what he did the aircraft maintained a steady descent toward the mountains. Now things became really dicey. (Ilogene felt certain this held true not only for the passengers in the cabin compartment, but also for the pilots in the cockpit.)

Still, the French pilot *did* get them onto the runway at Douala . . . using a straight-in approach and putting down his gear and flaps at the last instant. (A duplicate of my own, oft-repeated maneuvers—only I did *not* have my family aboard, and he did!)

From there, everything went swimmingly. Ilogene and Mike[96] climbed onto a TWA flight out of Douala, and changed again at Dakar. They arrived in Ohio only a few days after I did. (Remember, early on I claimed a little black cloud with rain and lightning hung *over the entire Cron family's heads* . . . not just mine. This verified it.)

Before I left, however, an up-front, personal and direct

[96] For accuracy, my youngest son, Michael (Mike), has checked all the discussions herein regarding events in which he participated.

involvement with Ghaddafi's bands of insurgents came about unexpectedly. One day, when we had flown to an eastern conservation park, carrying our American ambassador to Chad, his wife, my wife, and a small contingent of his embassy staff–way out in the Chadian boonies–they attacked us.

In this remote park, the natives claimed extensive African wild life still lived. They swore the fauna still numbered high in the thousands–buffalo, rhino, even one of the last big herds of old, long-tusked elephants the poachers had missed.

We left the crew with the plane to protect it and climbed into three waiting vehicles the Chadian president provided. Bumping across the rough, uneven ground, dodging tree limbs and skirting mud holes around a small disappearing pond, we found our elephants. (See below.)

The angry male is on the right here. He attacked
soon after we snapped this picture.

I leveled my motion-picture camera and began cranking away, focusing on their lifted trunks, waving ears, and simulated attacks, approaches and retreats. Then the lead elephant–a huge, aggressive old male, with massive ivory six-feet-long–started getting serious.

Rearing his head and lifting his trunk even more threateningly, he stomped nearer. Only at the last minute did he stop, hesitating as if undecided whether or not to continue. His snorting and bellowing went on, however, and he began swaying back and forth, swinging his trunk from side to side, ears flapping even more.

Our native guide warned us, "Back up! He's angry."

Back-pedaling as fast as the trucks were able to maneuver on the uneven terrain, we slipped away. Simultaneously, a volley of shots sounded behind us from the direction of our aircraft.

I raised my hand and pointed. "Mr. Ambassador, that signals trouble. We must return to the ship at once."

Driving even faster and bumping even harder, we made a headlong dash for the landing strip. Nearing the field, I saw our men, machine guns already out, firing regularly at a mass of rag-tag men crouching behind clumps of weeds and hillocks at the edge of the strip, shooting back and edging nearer.

I hopped out of the truck, waving the embassy people and Ilogene, along with the ambassador and his wife into the plane. Grabbing up a machine gun, I added my firepower to my crews'. I then had our engineer break open a case of hand grenades and we tossed as many as we could throw at the attacking group.

The assailants scattered.

We still saw them, huddling in the bushes, but they appeared to be withdrawing (at least for the moment). Immediate retreat appeared to be the better part of valor.

My aircrew continued firing, first from the ground, then from the side door while we loaded up and prepared to leave. They continued shooting even as I started the plane and taxied to the take-off position. We closed the door and "buttoned-up" only when we were well into our take-off roll.

Once aloft, I made a quick turn away from the area where the last of the guerilla fighters disappeared, nevertheless we sustained several bullet holes. Whether we took them before or after take-

off we never knew. Yet no one was injured.

I debated silently all the way back to Fort Lamy, *If I report this, exactly as it happened, this can compromise our diplomatic mission and may cause an international incident. What can I do?*

Before landing, I elected to take the problem to my French friend, Colonel Jacques Hascöet. *Maybe he,* I reasoned, *can help.*

Jacques invited me to meet him at once in the office of the French general, Morlet. Between the two of them they agreed to issue an official communique (in French), "This afternoon, one of our French flying patrols encountered a pocket of Ghaddafi's insurgents, infiltrating Chad." They added the figures for the number killed and wounded their scouts learned at the scene.

Transmitted via diplomatic, military and news channels, his message got us off the hook. Our ambassador was everlastingly grateful to both the general and the colonel.

Such is the life of the military and attachés, everywhere. But most especially in the volatile areas of the world. Still that was not the last we heard from Ghaddafi.

Not long after, we flew our plane for its fifty-hours inspection–completely across the Sahara from south to north, for cripes sake![97] to our last Air Force Base in Tripoli, Libya. While there, things got really sticky!

The Israelis launched the "Six-Day War" and there we sat, surrounded by a somewhat-less-than-friendly Moslem nation. The natives tossed bombs over the fences at us. Protesters daily paraded outside the gates. Local vendors disappeared and, those that did not, refused to honor their contracts to supply the base mess halls with vegetables. We began running low on food.

The base commander, with due consideration, confined all military and their dependents to the base. He doubled the

[97] Going north, we flew directly over the area where our charts showed the "Lady Be Good!" had wrecked. Even with the detailed checkpoints identified, no one on our plane could find the B-24 downed in WWII (and we used several pairs of binoculars). Then and there, I vowed, "No more flying across the unmarked Sahara with my family on board."

perimeter guards. He armed troops with heavy fire power and prepared for possible attacks and an invasion.

This situation made it imperative we return to Fort Lamy at once. But, first, I had to take my newly installed propeller out for a test flight.

The Base Commander warned, "If you have any trouble in the air . . . do everything you can to return to the base. If you must land elsewhere, even King Idris's airport, you will very likely be incarcerated. And we have no idea how long it may take to get you released, assuming we can."

Heeding his advice, I took-off, climbed to ten thousand feet before beginning my test procedures. (Standard Operating Procedures called for feathering and unfeathering the new propeller at least ten times, then flying with it in various configurations for so many hours). Great plan . . . reality sucked!

The first time I feathered the new propellor, it refused to unfeather. It turned 180-degrees and froze. There I was ("at ten thousand feet, both engines shot out, hanging by my throat mike . . ." No! That's another story), but we *were* on the horns of a potentially disastrous dilemma.

A propellor's hanging up in that position gives a pilot a problem equal to a huge barn door erected on one wing–no lift, no power, no positive benefits, just lots and lots of drag. *We were going down–no question! At 500-feet per minute. But where!*

The air base lay some miles behind us. King Idris's airport was almost beneath us, but that was O-U-T! (I had no desire to sit in an Arabic prison for who-knew-how-long.)

Electing to try for the air base, I asked my co-pilot to call the tower, alert them to my problem, and request an immediate, emergency landing clearance. (If we made the field, we would be coming in on a whisker, mere feet above the ground when we crossed the fence, and we would not be putting down the gear until the last second–if we did not have to "belly" it in before we got there. If the remaining engine did not blow up from the strain.

If–and there were a thousand other "ifs" I could enumerate–but we had no time.

It sounded to me like a case of, "If we had the eggs we could have ham and eggs, if we had the ham." None of the prospects looked encouraging. Anywhere we landed, but at the Air Base, we would be behind bars.

Now, described on paper, it sounds easy. But then, we perspired away ten gallons of fluid making that single approach.

Yet everything worked as if it had been rehearsed for the big screen. Crossing the air field's fence with but one engine and ten feet clearance left, we snapped-down the gear and banged the plane onto the near edge of the runway, on its wheels.

My co-pilot and I went straight to the Officer's Club bar.

The engineers had to come out and tow the plane to the hangar for more rework. Three days later we repeated the test procedures and experienced not a single problem. (But I flew solely back and forth over the air base, just in case.) In a few days, the tension eased, but we were long gone.

On our return flight across the desert (my avowed last), fate contributed a strong tail wind. We flew non-stop from Tripoli to Fort Lamy (seven hours and twenty-odd minutes). Stretching it? Yes, but we avoided landing, unprotected, thereby, on an isolated Arabic air strip in the middle of the Sahara to refuel.

The Base sort of "got even" with the Libyans when Ghaddafi ordered the USA to leave a few months later. Ghaddafi thought he would acquire an entire USAF military installation, completely intact, with all its technological equipment, all its expensive dependent and military housing . . . everything.

Our Air Force Base Commander fooled him.

Bringing in huge transport aircraft from the States, he transferred-out, first, the dependents. Then, as they were no longer needed, he sneaked out the military and civilian personnel. At the same time, he stripped every set of quarters, the offices, and the hangars . . . to the last bathtub, toilet, lavatory and

heating/cooling outfit. Carefully, as they finished each one, the engineers buried bombs throughout the buildings and the entire length of the runways and taxiways.

When the last plane took-off–the Base Commander's–they flew back over the field once more and triggered the bomb array by radio. Gleefully the commander and his crew watched explosions demolish every inch, every stick, and every structure Ghaddafi wanted so badly.

On learning what the commander did, all who had been in Libya applauded, "Way to go, Colonel!"

CHAPTER SIXTEEN

▲

As noted before, between our two attaché assignments, I commanded a recruiting squadron in Chicago with hundreds of recruiters and offices scattered from "hell to breakfast" –throughout Chicago proper and its suburbs, Illinois, Indiana, etc. The powers-that-be who gave me the job considered it the absolute pits in recruiting assignments. They were right, and I agreed.

Yet I had asked for it . . . deliberately.

I bragged earlier–when I was Director of Plans and Programs at Group Headquarters, Chanute AFB–"I can make Chicago boom. All it takes is hard work and incentives for the men."

On my return from Africa, Headquarters finally said, "Okay, sucker . . . she's yours. Go for it!"

I would like to be able to say, "I made Chicago a roaring success, that we met every quota, no matter how high, or how difficult. That we established all kinds of records, won prizes, earned medals and promotions. That we became the outstanding recruiting unit in the USA."

Oh, I can *"say"* that . . . but it would *not* be true.

My men and I did, though–working full time, on weekends and nights, by introducing a "Top Hat Cub"[98] and giving frequent

[98] We designed the "Top Hat Club" (with exclusivity) specifically to give each recruiter a strong incentive to make his quota. Officers and recruiters earned the real opera hat, cane and sumptuous dinner I bought them (awarded with great ceremony), along with city- and statewide publicity, a large engraved plaque with a certificate (with a photo of his indoctrination into the "club"). Recruiting leaped. Records soared. Morale shot through the roof. This put us "Over the top," for the first time . . . ever! (Other groups adopted the program and, by the time I returned from

partics for the men "on the firing line"–make Chicago a winner far beyond recruiting headquarter's greatest expectations and any previous records since its inception in 1952. We achieved an assigned quota, for the first time–ever!–and we repeated it. (Not regularly and not every month, but we did it from time to time. But no one had done it previously.) We set records still unmatched.

I also would like to be able to say, "We recruited all the special people the Air Force needed." That too would be a lie.

And I would like to say I always succeeded where my men failed, but I can't do that either. One outstanding incident shows my personal weaknesses.

One month our group badly needed one *nurse–just one more nurse!*–to sign-up as an officer trainee. We and the Air Force had to have her ink that application before midnight, if we were to fill our quota.

Called in to do it–my men erroneously believing (and I sharing their belief) I could accomplish the task where they had failed. But I pulled a "Casey at the Bat!" We stayed up with the recalcitrant young nurse to the witching hour . . . and thought we had the quota "in the bag" (please forgive this: literally and figuratively). At the last minute, she said, "No! Give me a few more days to think about it."

We (or rather, I) missed our quota–by one. She signed-up three days later. (I could have cut my throat . . . and gave serious consideration to cutting hers.)

While I was in Chicago my usual mix of good and bad again crept over the horizon. As I had for years now, I was called upon to speak every two days or so at some military or civilian activity–a breakfast club, a service club, a promotion–I even awarded Bobby Orr a trophy. From this, our squadron garnered sheaves of publicity photos, inches of newspaper columns, and

Africa after my second attaché tour, it was becoming popular nationwide.)

hundreds of word-of-mouth compliments . . . all of which generated even more speeches for me, and additional commitments. (Being on the stage, singing and acting, I grew accustomed to applause and publicity, but only my published books inspired more lionizing.)

Rodney L. Cron in costume, on stage, singing the title role, Dr. Falke, "The Bat," in "Die Fledermaus."

(See next page for another role.)

Speaking at various places and seeing hundreds of strange faces in the audience at every gathering, I noticed one person standing out. He appeared regularly, at all kinds of activities. *Certainly*, I asked myself, *this man can't be a member of everything!* But he seemed to be. He popped up everywhere.

Ah, I thought, *he represents Mayor Daley[99] . . . and he's*

[99] Invited to meet the mayor soon after my arrival in Chicago, I went at once to his office. (No one kept Mayor Richard Daley waiting–NO ONE!) An administrative flunky ushered me into the long room, All I could see was his desk at the far end before a broad window, looking out on the city, the light behind him. I trudged three-quarters of the distance (it seemed like a hundred feet), wading through deep-pile carpet, before I could make out something other than a dark blob. He paid me the compliment of coming around his massive desk to greet me. Even shorter than I, the older Daley carried a quiet sense of authority and assured confidence I had not seen even in some generals wearing four stars. He damn-near over-awed me. I went

checking to see if what I am saying affects him positively, or negatively.

Close, in one way, but no cigar!

Nell Foster, Soprano,
New York City Opera,
and Rodney L. Cron,
singing the leads in
"Smoky Mountain
Lovin'."
(1952)
(World Premier.)

Finally, after my presentation and breakfast, this stranger came forward. He took out an elegant, engraved card and handed it to me. "Colonel, will you be available for lunch tomorrow? I'd like you to be my guest at . . . (he named the most prestigious, exclusive location in the Chicago). "

"My plate is full, if you want me to give a speech in the near future," I told him.

He grinned, a youthful, disarming smile. It should have alerted me. "Let me assure you, what I want to discuss has absolutely nothing to do with your giving a speech . . . at least not right away."

away feeling honored . . . and, perhaps, a bit intimidated. (And I believe that was precisely his intent.)

Agreeing to a time and meeting place, I pocketed his card.

The next day at lunch, my new acquaintance eyed me closely throughout the meal, questioned me at length about my family . . . and ended-up exploring even the depths, lengths and breadths of my personal beliefs and prejudices. All in all he was a remarkable person, evidently quite skilled at this type of . . . then I recognized what was going on–this fellow was interviewing me as if for a classified position.

I sat back and folded my napkin. "Sir–(I won't insert any name, the reason will soon be apparent)-whatever you have in mind, I am fully committed to the United States Air Force."

"It's your name and honest record we want. What if I offer you one hundred thousand dollars to start . . . and assure you, you will be making far, far more annually after three years . . . would that stir your blood?"

I immediately thought of a better life for Ilogene, college tuition for our children, and a bridal dowry for Melodie. (We had been able to give her only five hundred dollars when she and Don eloped.) But I also realized sums like he just mentioned do not come without strings. Lots of big, long, sticky strings. (And I was right.)

I asked. "Who do I have to kill?"

He winced and bent nearer, whispering, "This is for your ears only. I want you to be our front man in a completely legitimate insurance business. You'll have a big office, lovely secretaries, a town car–later, perhaps, a limousine–all the perks."

Lifting my eyebrows, I said, "You didn't answer my question. And –?"

"I represent a well-known family preferring to remain behind the scenes. Some people call them 'Mafia,' but of course they aren't." (Hah! Hah!)

"Okay, let's suppose I resign my commission and take the job. If, in a few years, I don't like what I see, can I resign this one, too–with no questions asked, no repercussions?"

He frowned. "Not usually. But no one ever leaves us like that."

I stood and tossed my napkin onto the table. "Thank you for lunch, but 'no, thank you' on the job offer. I'm like the cowboy leery around Indians, 'I prefer keeping my hair on my head.'"

He did not show again at any of my speeches (that I saw). I was also never again invited to such an exclusive site[100] for a meal . . . not even by another representative of the Devil . . . or the Devil himself. (I worried, though, *did I now know too much? I guess not . . . I'm still here.*)

My flying out of Chicago's O'Hare Airport those years and, sometimes, from the Navy Base in the center of Chicago, managed to keep me current on my aircraft qualifications. But my singing skills and appearances went by-the-board.

I accrued my hours in C-47s and C-119s at O'Hare, with the Air Force Reserves. Flying the slowest aircraft in the Air Force inventory and doing it from one of the nation's busiest civilian airfields made for continuing complications. Those are big, dangerous . . . pitfalls!

Take-offs presented few difficulties. The tower took our radioed requests for taxiing and line-up, and put us in a complicated queue, much like our mission preparations during WWII. Coming from all sides and all taxiways, we lined up ahead

[100] We had an "exclusive" restaurant of our own in Chicago, the "Cloak and Dagger Room." It branched off the cloakroom of a larger restaurant. To get in, we had to pull-down two coat hangers simultaneously (they were levers opening a hidden door). But also we must have been approved previously, as there was no cash register and not a price in the menus. (A patron signed his statement and they billed him at home, once a month,) The menus themselves were affixed inside the front of hard-cover mystery novels (Carrying-on the "Cloak and Dagger" theme.) The room sported a small bar (excellent wine, liquor and cognac selections), and held no more than thirty seats, arranged in clever little secluded booths and alcoves (perfect for an assignation or tete-a-tete). The limited menu offered gourmet specialities, my favorite was their lobster thermidor. I never saw their chef's kitchen bested. The room was closed some years ago. But before they closed it, I visited it again–after being gone some thirty years. My name and credit were still on file and they welcomed me with open arms. I enjoyed–for the last time, without knowing it–one more order of the lobster and a Beefeaters's martini, with my usual white wine. Now there was a loss worth mourning.

of and behind huge commercial 747s, small executive jets, other little private planes, and clunkers like ours. We took-off, in turn, on the tower's call. After take-off we disbursed, flying-off in set departure patterns at various altitudes, in directions designed to keep us separated and aimed toward different destinations.

The problems arose when circumstances, such as a high influx of aircraft, tight commercial ETAs, or low fuel, forced O'Hare's tower to put that same motley mixture of ships back into the same traffic pattern *for landing*, one behind the other. My airspeed, for example (if I flew at "full blower," keeping up my wheels and flaps to the last second–illegal and it gave the tower fits), was limited to no more than 135 knots. Those 747 monsters flashed in at around 175 to 180 knots (and higher), the smaller jets only slightly slower. (Far too many times those 747s were right on my fanny and I had to get out of their way–and quickly–or be eaten alive.)

This situation so confused and frustrated one Reservist he lost control and put his C-119 on its back, skidding along a runway. (He effectively closed down that strip for two hours.)

My aircrew and I nearly "bought the farm," too, while making an approach one night in terrible weather (storms, rain, lightning). Every aircraft in the pattern was flying solely on instruments in a pea-soup mix of clouds and thick mists, guided solely by ground radar and tower controllers.

Invisible aircraft kept jostling us as they passed. Finally, the controller sent me off on an "immediate 45-degree angle to the right!" A 747–right on my tail– needed to land ahead of me.

I had no more than reached the new heading and we were bounced a hundred feet from the turbulence of the passing 747's huge engines. And that presented another glitch in the landing procedures: If we landed too soon after a huge jet, its engines' created vortices making smaller planes uncontrollable and causing crashes. At high speeds the vortex magnified–during take-offs and recoveries (forced go-arounds.)

Also because various aircraft sizes and speed differences so limited their landing methodology, our O'Hare controllers frequently diverted us (smaller craft) to secondary runways. This put us in a position where often we had to land in heavy crosswinds and shifting gusts. This increased our accident rate. (O'Hare, we believed, must be the place earning Chicago its name, "The Windy City.")

The Navy flew only their planes from their field–no 747s, no monster jets. Their runways were safer and far better supervised. (Now it is gone!) While it existed, I went out and flew with them most often as I neared the end of my Chicago assignment. The Navy was always most considerate of us "poor Air Force slobs." (They had tried to fly from O'Hare, too, and encountered the same grief.)

The overall weather near Lake Michigan also left much to be desired. Though it had its history of a rare tornado, the sudden rain squalls and snow flurries (approaching blizzards), reduced visibility, low clouds, sudden wind shifts, and "lake effect" made O'Hare and Midway pilots scream. (Also the air fields at Milwaukee and Minneapolis-St. Paul–our usual alternates–often suffered some of the same handicaps.)

Our flights were diverted frequently to airports, some many miles away, snowed in for days when snow-blower equipment was overwhelmed or failed, and snow-removal operators were stranded at home or on the road. Aircraft in this climate tended to be unreliable anyway, especially when the temperatures dropped below zero . . . and virtually unusable when they went sub-sub-zero and stayed there. Washing the wings with solvent helped, when done just before take-off (long lines often rendered this virtually impossible), but did not prevent icing after take-off. Some military aircraft (the B-26, for example) had no de-icing capability for wings or propellers.

While we were in training in Europe, one of our neophyte pilots had asked the civilian engineer assigned to teach us to fly the B-26

(actually, now the A-26, Invader), "How much ice can an A-26 carry?"

The engineer smiled, then turned serious. "It all depends. If you stuff it in the bomb-bay, it can carry at least 6,000 pounds . . . the same as a bomb load. But, if you put it on the propellers, about fifty pounds will kill you."

Pilots flying out of O'Hare into ice storms and high humidity-low temperatures, during the 1960s, regularly left widows behind. Every airplane can quickly become a tricky little beast when the wings turn white and the propellers begin flicking ice shards into the cockpit and fuselage.

Yet it is the tornado that stands firm as the most dangerous weather phenomenon to avoid. Hurricanes are fairly well defined and well advertised. Tornadoes sneak up on you when least expected.

One fall afternoon, on a shuttle run between San Antonio, Texas and Orlando, Florida, the weatherman predicted my flying at 6,000 feet would be, "In a calm, stratus, overcast cloud system, no storms, no cumulus . . . no problems."

My sergeant and I climbed-out from the Texas runway, and took our assigned altitude of 6,000 feet. The clouds were thick, flat and smooth, as predicted. They stayed that way until we neared Jackson, Mississippi.

Suddenly we began to encounter turbulence and increasing static. I suggested we remove our ear phones for a period.

I had no more said that and we apparently entered the funnel of a tornado hidden in the clouds. Our aircraft abruptly shot upward to *more than sixteen thousand feet.*

Slammed, banged and inverted, the unexpected storm tossed us out, spinning, from the top of its towering cumulonimbus. I recovered control only with extreme difficulty. To level the aircraft and keep flying, required crossing controls and holding one rudder pedal halfway forward.

The ship obviously had suffered major damage.

Prepared to order my sergeant to bail out, I looked over to see he was incapable of leaving. He was unconscious. He had banged his head against the aluminum baffle around the window. Slumped over, he was bleeding like a stuck hog.

Unable to jump out, I had to put the aircraft on the ground ASAP and get him to a hospital for medical attention. Calling an emergency, "MayDay! MayDay!"–I alerted the nearest tower (at Jackson) and made a straight-in approach. Barely keeping the faltering aircraft upright and under control, I fought it through the clouds and onto the ground.

We pulled up and parked in front of the control tower only to discover we could never have bailed-out, anyway. The canopy was crammed shut. The fuselage was so twisted, the ground crews had to use crowbars to free us.

As I stood on the wings helping remove my sergeant, both wings went "c-r-e-e-e-c-k" and settled about ten inches at their tips. I checked the rear, vertical stabilizer–it was bent to one side at a thirty-degree angle the reason for the in-flight control problems.

The weatherman came running out of the terminal, shouting, "Are you the pilot who just reported over Delhi to the west?"

I nodded.

"They just reported a tornado. Did you see anything unusual?"

Pointing at the twisted tail and drooping wings, I nodded. "What do you think?"

That aircraft never flew again. The last time I was in Jackson it still sat there, sagging more each year.

For years after that I experienced regular, recurring nightmares which really bugged me. I dreamt I was on the ground with a tornado rapidly approaching and no place to hide. I threw myself into a ditch . . . but the funnel came straight at me (sort of like the one in the "Wizard of Oz"), sucked me up into its maw . . . and I was dragged skyward. The dream always ended before I went further. (No Toto. No Wicked Witch. No ruby slippers . . . No

Judy Garland . . . *damn!*)

I suppose this dream haunted me because I saw so many tornadoes, and even looked up inside one a few miles inside Texas.

Driving alone en route to San Antonio on a dark and fitful afternoon, just outside Texarkana the weather abruptly turned sour. Low clouds skittered out of the southwest. It began raining buckets.

I had been following another car, perhaps too closely in the rain, yet even then I barely made-out its red taillights through the gloom. Suddenly, they blossomed. I slammed on my brakes too.

Abruptly, the rain stopped and the clouds lifted. We had stopped in a narrow cut (this was only a two-lane road then) between rock-covered banks. Immediately to our southwest, coming straight at us and sounding like a freight train, was a narrow, twisting tornado. Too late to get away, I dived to the floor of the front seat (I was smaller then). The funnel lifted up, out of the field on my left and passed directly overhead.

Briefly, I looked upward through my windshield into the twister's green, swirling opening filled with debris and lightning flashes. It came down again in the field on my right, exploding like a cannon . . . and continued across the open range toward the city. As it passed over, the car lifted, turning light as a feather, air whistling through the four open, window vents (no air-conditioning, I had put down the windows about an inch, protected by plastic window shields). I was certain I was a goner. I just knew the car and I were about to get sucked up into that huge, gaping mouth. Luckily, the open windows seemed to exhaust enough air to break the hold on the car, though my eardrums ached from the rapid pressure changes. The car dropped back onto the pavement . . . and I burst into a sweat.

The driver of the other car climbed out and came staggering back. Passengers of other, following cars, gathered around, talking.

"Did you see that?" Still shaking, the first driver pointed at the receding cloud to our northeast. "That scared the hell out of me."

All of us agreed.

Then the first driver looked down. His trousers were soaked. "It also scared more then the hell out me, I guess." He reeled back to his car and slid in, brushing at himself.

Now, I had been in tornadoes at least twice. But that was not to be the last.

General Snavely and I flew to Oklahoma City–the motherland of all tornadoes and the heart of "Tornado Alley"–to assess the damage from one that had danced along the Air Base's ramp and mutilated a dozen B-29s and B-50s. Our inspection finished, we were in Operations filing our flight plan, ready to leave, when the weatherman dashed out to tell us, "Better hurry. My predictions say we're going to have another one, just outside the base."

The general and I leaped into our B-25 (a twin-engine Mitchell, one of Doolittle's former toys) and scurried for the runway. While lifting off, a funnel dropped out of the clouds directly ahead. I hurriedly cranked the plane onto its left wing and swung to the south to avoid its path.

The tornado followed exactly the same route as the previous one . . . up the airport's ramp, by-passing the tower and Operations Terminal by a hair . . . tossing huge aircraft right and left as if it were a runaway bulldozer. I looked over at the general. "What do you think, sir?"

"Well, we're already here. May as well stay and make a new assessment. It'll save us another trip."

Later that afternoon, the area reported two more . . . but none hit the base.

Though my flying-training stint at Lubbock AFB, Texas, following my return from Korea, was not too long, tornadoes there were all-too-common as well. The twisters seemed to have a particular affinity for our base's mobile home community (we were still calling them "trailer parks," then) sited to the northeast

of the base.

Standing in Operations one early evening, I marked time before a flight with some of my students because the weather was on the cusp. The weatherman came out and invited us in, to look at his equipment. (Some new trainees had not seen the working section of a weather station.)

Inside, he pointed to and explained the extensive array of measuring and observation instruments covering his tables. He stopped speaking when he considered the long-range radar scope. He then pointed his finger at a bright, distinctive, comma-shaped blip moving our way, southwest of the field, not more than ten miles off.

I said, "Is that what I think it is?"

He stared an instant longer. "Yep! That's a tornado . . . sure as hell!" He reached across his counter and flipped on the base's warning sirens only recently installed. He added, "I better call the trailer park manager–it's headed that way."

All of us went outside and watched. The funnel approached in a straight line, to the edge of the air field. As if following a map, it then skirted the field's outer fence, and drove like an fired arrow toward the trailer park. Within two minutes it destroyed twenty trailers, ruined several dozen cars, and injured more than thirty people. Thank goodness no one was killed . . . by that storm!

A month later, another tornado followed the same path. This one, however, came across the airfield and did some aircraft damage as well.

This storm was a "maxi." It killed several dependents and came very close to eliminating the entire trailer park. (We and the weather people became convinced the vast field of metal provided by the acres of grounded trailer tops, when considered in toto, created an electrical attraction. Inasmuch as tornadoes regularly hit mobile home parks even today–apparently at a rate still exceeding other sites– this remains a viable theory.)

For a while, tornadoes appeared to dog my path.

Flying across the Gulf of Mexico, four waterspouts dotted the sky around us like a picket fence.

On a trip through southern Illinois, I was about to turn north to Chicago . . . but chose another route when a huge finger dropped from the clouds two miles in front of me and began groping along the ground, exploding everything in its path, leaving behind a mist of debris.

Later, planning to land at the fighter base west of Phoenix, one afternoon, flight service diverted me to the south, claiming a tornado was sitting farther west– churning, but unmoving–a few miles east of the mountains. This one, I had to see.

I flew over there. Sure enough, there sat this isolated storm, still in the same place. It lasted long enough for weather people from the base to drive out with motion-picture cameras and photograph at least a half-hours' worth of film. (That was a really rare phenomenon. Likely it was caused by cold air's spilling over the eastern side of the mountains into the hot air over the desert, and falling to ground into the different temperature/moisture gradient. It remained in one place as long as the wind and air temperature combinations sustained the triggering engine.)

Though confronting tornadoes seemed for a time to be my bag, there was enough hurricane experience to go around as well. At least I had enough to raise my blood pressure.

Hurricanes hit Orlando, Florida, 1948/1949, when I served as aide to General Snavely. Whenever the weather bureau reported incoming storms, the base immediately dispatched its aircraft to Marietta, Georgia, to avoid wind damage.

General Snavely always stayed until the final moment. He kept me on stand-by in my B-26, ready to go (sometimes, for hours). We had "go, no-go" procedures: I would wait until wind speeds reached a steady 45 knots, then either the general joined me and we took-off, or I took off and he stayed. That meant my plane was always the last to leave the ground.

On one occasion, when the wind reached 40 K, I alerted the

general. He said, "I'll be right there."

At forty-five knots, when they were rising fast, I called him again. He said, "I can't get away . . . you go ahead."

We had cut it too close. By the time I got back to the plane, fired up, and taxied to the runway, the wind speed already exceeded sixty knots and was accelerating rapidly. The hurricane was approaching much faster than expected. We expected harder winds any minute, with heavier rains and stronger gusts, plus lightning and possible tornadoes.

I started my take-off roll ASAP, and experienced severe wind sheer in the first one thousand feet. The plane shuddered and leaped from side to side. It required me to keep both hands on the controls, to stabilize the ship and hold it on the runway, I thrust the gear handle (past the protective detent) into the upward position.

With the gear lever in that position, the wheels would stay "down" only so long as pressure was maintained on the tiny solenoid affixed to the left main gear. Thus they would remain down only as long as the aircraft's weight held it there.

When I reached the runways' intersection (where there was a slight bump), three simultaneous events occurred: (1) the plane hopped upward a few inches, (2) a gust of wind slammed into the plane, and (3) the combination lifted the fuselage off the solenoid. My gear vanished into the nacelles.

Suddenly, I had no gear under me. Only a few inches off the ground, I was barely flying. Halfway through my take-off roll and halfway down the runway, I felt certain we "had it."

Easing up the nose . . . just a smidgen . . . to keep my prop tips off the concrete, I prayed. But the rapidly increasing wind speed, added to my take-off acceleration, kept the plane flying. I began to climb, ever so slowly, bouncing up and down as if driving along a rough country road. The plane, though, was still close to the ground.

The tower called at that point, "Air Force 1012, did you just

lose your landing gear . . . or did you plan that?"

I gulped. "I sure as heck did NOT plan that."

Flying on to Marietta I was certain I'd be hearing from the FAA . . . but at least I was not going to be credited with "pilot error" for an accident. (True, I might have claimed weather as a contributing factor. But the review board would never have bought my gear's folding based on weather. What occurred could happen only under the circumstances I had created–which was a take-off "No-No!")

Maybe the tower operator was generous, or maybe the controller thought it was due to the weather too. But I never heard anything more from that example of my stupidity.

Today, instruments can fly the aircraft all the way to the runway, while the cockpit panel provides visual GPS locations with arrows and pointers showing where the beam center is on any approach (again up or down; left or right), and a set of cross-hairs indicating constantly where one is relative to the invisible flight path one needs to follow . . . all the way to the ground. What's more, flight paths can be programmed into an aircraft's auto-pilot computer and, when turned "on," built-in electronic equipment round out . . . and land–"hands off."

Rodney L. Cron

For anyone who has not heard what went on while flying an instrument approach in those days, permit my explaining:

A pilot had a single radio beacon as a checkpoint. This transmitter sent out an "A" (in Morse code–a dot and a dash) to one side of the beam and an "N" (in Morse code–a dash and a dot) to the other side. A pilot determined his initial direction, relative to the radio transmitter (going toward or away from it) by turning down his radio so he only faintly heard the signal. If it faded, he was going away; if it became louder, he was approaching. The intent then was to find the center of the beam (where the two signals blended into one solid, continuing, unbroken sound, increasing in volume). Many pilots failed on this point, alone.

When the pilot flew over the beacon at–say–two thousand feet, there was a momentary "cone of silence" showing us he "hit the station." We then had a precise location and pattern to follow. (Usually he flew straight ahead one minute, on the "away" side of the beam, made a one-needle-width, 180-degree turn, and returned letting down all the way, but watching closely to avoid going "below minimums.")

This procedure was designed to bring a plane in, headed toward the airport. He would again cross the "cone of silence" (hopefully) at a very low altitude. If he correctly calculated the time to the station on that heading (taking into consideration wind speeds and directions at that new altitude, he reached the field (about a half-mile away) at a height allowing for making a visual landing.

(This lower "cone of silence" was so abrupt it could be missed–like the blink of an eye. A colonel once gave me, as a first lieutenant, the most devastating insult I ever received from a senior officer. He told me, "Son, I've got more time over the lower cone than you got in the air." Obviously, that hit me hard–to this day, I never forgot it.)

* * *

Landing at Marietta AFB was seldom a picnic . . . if it were necessary to make a let-down on instruments. The approach pattern to the airfield, north of Atlanta, lay from north to south, next to a radio tower jutting a thousand feet into the sky. Beside the tower itself, there were invisible guy-wires making the near-passage, even in the daylight and clear visibility, a guessing game. In the dark or under instrument conditions, when the pilot saw only his cockpit's flight dials, it was one of those hair-raising

264

episodes. (This was before precise needle indicators and other guides provided crisp visual instructions regarding descending flight paths and directions, up or down, right or left. These let-downs were done aurally, by sounds, listening to the "As" and "Ns" (in Morse code) that blended only in the center of the narrow beam. This created a steady signal. Yet a little increasing wind from one side or the other might send a pilot slipping off at a crucial moment. (See preceding "text box," previous page.)

It was difficult enough staying in the center of the radio beam under the best of conditions, but a cross-wind made the critical flight treacherous as the aircraft descended and entered a new air stream. ["Killing the wind" (as we called it), meant holding a compass-heading slightly to the right or left of the beam-heading (always into the wind). That balanced the wind force pushing the aircraft away.] Changing conditions kept a pilot on his toes and fighting constantly to keep up with the necessary alterations. I always admired the men who appeared to have a built-in instinct for this. I had to work at it.

The next time I made this approach, I held to the right side of the radio beam . . . regardless. Ending my flying career as part of this radio tower's permanent decorations held absolutely no appeal.

The next spring, a B-25 (Mitchell) *did* hit the tower, and the entire crew died. Following that accident, the FAA shifted the approach, and made it west to east . . . something we had clamored for, for two years. (That also made possible a "straight-in" instrument approach. Again see the previous text-box.)

Those months in Orlando we "bugged-out" to Marietta four times. Not once did General Snavely accompany me. Nor did Ilogene and the children. They always had to remain behind in Orlando. That was a constant worry. We eventually worked out a routine to insure their safety.

Though Mrs. Snavely invited Ilogene to come to the base with the children and stay with her, we elected for Ilogene, instead, to

go to Major and Mrs. Stanhope's (from Columbus, Ohio), only a couple blocks away in Orlando proper.

The general's quarters on Orlando Air Force Base were more than sixty years old and built of wood. They stood on four-foot stilts in an open area, surrounded by small lakes and orange trees.

The Stanhope's lived in a new, well-constructed, concrete and steel cottage, amidst a close surround of other buildings and a thick grove of trees. Neither, however, suffered any damage while we were there. But, when they closed the base and tore down the general's house, they found it was infested with termites and ready to collapse.

CHAPTER SEVENTEEN

▲

While in Fort Lamy (now N'Djamena), Chad–as said before--
Ilogene and I developed a close, intimate friendship with the
French Colonel Jacques Hascöet and his wife, Suzanne. Among
his many duties, he was assistant to Chad's president.

The four of us regularly played bridge together. We dined
together often–alternating between our homes–and helped each
other in every way possible. Our children ran around in a tight
little group of embassy and military kids. (Mike was the only one
with us on this trip. Melodie was married; Rod III was in
submarines, diving under the poles, chasing Soviet subs, or
whatever, as a nuclear reactor operator; Pat was attending high
school in France.)

Jacques and Suzanne's trio of boys, Jean-Jacques, Patrick and
Thierry, were a handful. Jean-Jacques (today an M.D., and
oncologist in Caen), liked wine, women and song. (Girls literally
fell on him, even the French prostitutes.) Patrick was more sedate;
he acted as a buffer between Mike and Jean-Jacques, (Mike was
too young for the French waywardness). Thierry was but a lad.
(Jacques, the colonel, died a few years ago. Patrick and Thierry
are now both excellent dentists, also living in Caen. Suzanne, as
attractive as ever, travels.)

Colonel Hascöet suffered his entire his life from his POW
terms and eventually died from them . . . though the government
hospitalized him annually and did their best. During the war, the

Nazis arrested this man three times (each time under a different
name). He headed-up the French underground in Normandy, yet

the Germans never discovered who he really was. (Knowing, they would have shot him instantly.) Twice he escaped. The third time, we released him. By another of those strange coincidences–he was one of those we removed from the POW camp when our aircrew was in the front lines. Of course, I did not know that.

I told him and Suzanne of my up-front experiences one evening. during a bridge game at our house. Jacques suddenly leaped to his feet, excused himself, and drove off in his car.

In a few minutes, he returned. "I knew I saw you before!" He thrust a photo at me. It showed an American flying officer carrying the bottom rungs of his stretcher, putting him in the medical truck at the POW camp. I was the young officer!

The chances of that are about a million to one–against. That bonded our friendship even more.

Jacques came to my rescue a few week later, when Ghaddafi's Libyan troops attacked our diplomatic aircraft. He, along with General Morlet, took care of it (reported elsewhere in detail).

My second attaché stint came easily for both Ilogene and me, except at the house. Our predecessor had told his servants that, "As long as there's a Defense Attaché in Fort Lamy, you have a job." (With that he ruined their boys for us!)

They were snotty, arrogant and discourteous to Ilogene, even while our predecessors were still there. The instant we waved goodbye to the colonel and his wife on their commercial plane, Ilogene went straight home and fired every one of them. She then drove to the French Attaché's quarters and spent the afternoon playing bridge with his wife and a group of other embassy wives.

The ladies gathered around as she nonchalantly played cards, nibbled on canapes, and sipped at her gin-and-tonics. "Aren't you worried, Mrs. Cron? You just arrived and now you have no servants?"

Ilogene grinned. "Not at all. By the time I get home there will be a line around the block . . . of boys and cooks wanting jobs."

There was. She hired three that night, on trial. The next day she

tried three more. By the end of the week, she had sorted through those showing the most promise, and pretty-well sifted the ashes for the best. By the following weekend, she had assembled a satisfactory cadre. They worked well for the remainder of our tour.

The assignment went even better for me.

The first morning after the other colonel departed, I received an invitation to join Jacques, General Morlet, and his staff at the French Military's Regional Headquarters. General Morlet (although only a colonel at the time, but slated for stars) commanded the entire, French Foreign Legion forces in Africa.

Morlet, personally, escorted me into their briefing room and dramatically unveiled their secret wall charts (showing the total distribution of the French military by types, numbers and locations throughout Africa). He then welcomed me to sit in on their weekly briefings and conferences, and add any comments or questions. He assured me they would keep our office up-to-date on anything we wanted to know that they could supply.

Their briefing was comprehensive and valuable. (In one sitting I gained enough information to fill a dozen Intelligence Reports. If a person is not charged with gathering military Intelligence from an entire continent, it is difficult to appreciate what a coup this was. Imagine our CIA calling a foreign agent into its Headquarters at Langley, Virginia, and offering to brief him regularly on all our troop data, numbers, status and objectives!)

I asked Morlet if they had so-briefed my predecessor? (None of my readings in D.C. had shown this level of information).

Morlet smiled at Colonel Hascoet, then at me. "I hate to say this, Colonel, but Colonel (and he named him; I won't), was aloof, overbearing, and a pain in the *derriere*. I never once considered bringing him in here."

For whatever the reason, we had "fallen into the outhouse and come out smelling like a rose." We were most fortunate . . . and I told him so. He and his staff gave us, thereafter, every support we

could want.

One night not long after, I had a chance to reciprocate to a small extent. A young French paratrooper who had been at the bars and enjoyed one too many, climbed into a window of the dormitory housing our incoming Peace Corps volunteers. He had a special and very attractive girl cornered.

The Peace Corps Director called for my help.

Dressing in full uniform (which I seldom wore except for formal affairs), I drove downtown to the dormitory and ordered the young soldier out. He took one look at my gaudy white uniform, my rank, my pissed-off look . . . and skedaddled.

He apparently (and willingly) had taken a girl's friendliness as an invitation for fun and games, yet he had done no harm. (The girl told me this and pleaded for him.) I proposed, therefore, to leave things as they were. (She agreed to that, too.) So I made no complaint to the French.

The next morning, Morlet and Jacques came to my office. "We heard about last night's problem. We have the soldier's name. To what extent do you want us to prosecute?"

Explaining my perspective–and the girl's (I believe she realized she had been basically at fault)–I told him, "Though it is not my prerogative to say what you should do or should not do with your men, I suggest only a mild oral reprimand."

They appreciated my viewpoint and hesitancy. They did *not* take away his stripes as intended. The eager young, very horny soldier evidently cooled-off his battalion comrades too. No one hassled our girls after that. (At least, none complained.)

Colonel Morlet received his promotion to two-star general the next week. He told me about it when we were dining together at the local Vietnamese Restaurant (Le Lotus), complaining, as I mentioned earlier, he might lose a job previously offered.

When we finished the soup (my son always kidded me about this, a specialty of the house, costing twenty-dollars a bowl), I reached out and fingered the stars on his collar. "*Tien!* I suppose

you could give them back . . . or to me."

"*Non! Non! Non!* I worked too hard, fought too many battles, and took all that *merde* off DeGaulle for that fiasco at Dien Bien Phu. Never will I give them back. *Jamais!*"

I do not know what job Morlet had "lined-up" originally– and lost. But I *do know* the one he took after retirement paid him a bundle annually and included perks like his own private jet. (I offered to come over and fly it for him. The twin-engine, French-made commuter they were to give him was a real beauty.)

There were some other humorous events as well. Soon after our arrival, Ilogene and I were invited to dine at General Morlet's home. Everyone in the French Embassy wished they could take our place. The reason? The general's wife had learned to cook in Viet Nam and had with her an outstanding Vietnamese chef. The general's wife's personal specialty was "Nems"–the ones we call "Spring Rolls."

I wanted to arrive early for the general's dinner. Since this was the French commander's party, I claimed he would expect it. Ilogene disagreed, based on our experience in Abidjan[101]. On this occasion I won out. (Thank goodness!)

At the general's house, I parked and noted the street full of cars. We thought they were empty.

When we climbed out and started across the street, Jacques caught up with us. "Wait, Rod! We all go in together."

This, I had never seen before. Everyone debarked from their vehicles and gathered in a group on the front steps.

[101] Our first social invitation, in Africa, had come from an American and his French wife who lived at the dead-end of our street in Abidjan. (Really CIA, he worked undercover as an Evenrude outboard motor salesman.) The invitation read, "Six o'clock." So I wanted to be there at six. Ilogene said, No! That's too early for a French community." I argued, "I'm a military officer, they'll expect us on time." (Boy, was I wrong!) We knocked . . . and knocked. With the servants gone on a Sunday afternoon, his wife answered the door–finally–clad only in her very, very scanty French bra and panties (so tiny, the latest thongs only recently introduced seem like "Mother Hubbards" in comparison). Of course, henceforth, I *always* wanted to be early . . . but Ilogene insisted on our being at least one-half-hour, fashionably late. (There were times when Ilogene could be a real "spoil-sport.")

The ranking French officer stood at the door, one hand up-raised to knock. He held the other outstretched so he could read his wrist-watch. At precisely the time on our invitations (seven o'clock, if I remember correctly) he pounded *once* on the door.

The door opened as if the servant had been waiting, hand on the door handle. We vanished inside with a speed I have seen matched only by young fans attending a favorite rock-and-roll star's concert.

The French embassy was right. The food was delicious. Madame Morlet had worked for three days in preparation and it showed. Each course was perfection itself. So were their accompanying selections of fine French wines from Morlet's *cave privé* (his private wine cellar).

Precisely two minutes before nine, the group abruptly stood and hurriedly said their goodbyes. They departed en masse with the same dispatch by which they entered. We went along.

Ilogene and I talked about it for days. Every later visit–other than on those occasions when Ilogene and I went alone–the French conducted in the same manner. (I wanted to give their "quick-in, quick-out" performance a name, believing it unique enough to merit identification. Both Jacques and Ilogene discouraged me. I still think something like, "another in-and-out-er" would have captured its essence. Jacques did not grasp the ribald significance, but Ilogene did–so that was out.)

The French Airbase Commander in Chad–a pilot with almost as much flying time as I had–and his wife, became our close friends as well. They, like the Hascöets, were an active couple that became involved in our social lives, both formally and informally. The Base Commander and I flew together regularly. Sometimes we tried one of his ships, sometimes we went out in our old "Gooney Bird." He learned quickly to fly it well.

His tour ending, the French military recalled him to France for training before reassignment. Surprising him, they entered him into French Attaché school.

He returned to Fort Lamy, eyes open to the new vistas his training's enlightenment inspired. "Why, I never knew what you did," he exclaimed.

"It's no secret, Colonel. I thought you knew."

We spent many hours before he left, discussing our mutual "open spy" methodologies and techniques over dinner, drinks and card games. He had long-since introduced me to his other officers and issued us a standing invitation to all their Squadron parties. Ilogene and I also were welcomed as members of their exclusive Officer's Club. (Here is another place where my predecessor had lost out. They never once invited him into their inner sanctum sanctorum, citing the same reasons Morlet had. That was unfortunate[102].)

[102] Not to abase my predecessor, but, instead, to ameliorate his record, during the first year Ilogene and I were in Chad we obtained an entirely new picture of what had gone on before. I believe my predecessor was not so aloof and overbearing as the French thought. (I had known him and his wife previously.) I believe –since he originally went to attaché school with me when I was training for Abidjan, and had been "on station" this entire time (having moved his base office, house, staff and aircraft from the Congo to Chad)–this much "older" man was tired, losing his eyesight and hearing. As a specific example: when we went out for our "swing around" the countries to which I was now accredited, he wanted me to do all the flying (and the aircrew breathed a sigh of relief). Only as we approached Fort Lamy on our return, did he ask to take the left seat (the main pilot's position) and make that one landing. (He knew he was going home to retire.) He said, "This may very well be the last landing I will ever make." I am convinced he never flew again. He made such a very poor landing, actually dangerous–bouncing the aircraft so hard and high, and making no attempt at recovery–that I actually had to take over from the right seat, recover, and land. After he left, the aircrew confided in me that his flying was what they had worried about constantly. They believed he was unable to see or hear well, and kept trying to hide it until he finished his tour. (I later contacted him and his wife in Albuquerque when we were there a couple years later, but he was already a semi-invalid and talked only hesitantly on the phone.) Another negative factor was their thick Texas accent. Even my youngest son, to this day remembers their phone number in Chad–"Tront-day-urn, tront-dur." (That was their French for, "Trente-et-une, trente-deux"–31-32.) That undoubtedly played a part in the French's dislike. For it is true, "The French don't really care what you say, just as long as you pronounce it correctly."

I passed on as much of my knowledge to him as I was permitted (all unclassified, of course). And we shared "trade secrets" of the Intelligence game wherever possible. (I learned some of the latest European systems and how best to work with Interpol–the major European Police Organization.) Yet I am sure he held back as many tidbits as I was forced to conceal.

Upon leaving Africa, he received a really "difficult" attaché assignment. Some place like the Bahamas, if I remember correctly. (I know it was tropical, with blue water and gentle waves, white beaches, thatch huts, dulcet breezes, natives dancing seductively around fires, and lots of willing, brown-skinned, sloe-eyed maidens. I know this because he sent us photos and rubbed our noses in it with his little slang comments, like "Nyah . . . nyah . . . nyah . . . nyuh, nyah, nyah! That's me you see lying on the hammock in the shade of the palm tree, sipping a tall cool one. Rough, huh?"

Like Morlet's promotion, we fired back a letter saying, "Yeah, we should have it so tough. You lucky *chien* (dog)! They should have stuck you with Washington, D.C."

CHAPTER EIGHTEEN

▲

"Of all the places in all the world . . ." (that opening sounds like Humphrey Bogart's comment about "gin mills" in *Casablanca),* BUT Africa was *not* the spot to develop a negative attraction for animals. Yet, *I* did.

Ilogene had no such problem. On our initial Abidjan tour, the first time we drove into the savannas ("lion grass" country), Ilogene saw animals by the dozens, lying hidden amongst the tall ground cover. Lions, leopards and hyenas crouched there in prides and small family groupings. Where I was blind to their presence, Ilogene saw them all—every one, without fail. She picked them out, even when they did *not* twitch an ear or flick a tail. She did this when no one else could, neither our old hands nor our native African guides. (We attributed this noteworthy talent to her American Indian heritage. She was one/eighth Shawnee.)

For me to gain this ability, at even the most basic rudimentary level, required three months of continuing practice. In the meantime, we discovered I also tended to draw animals to me . . . animals eager to "have at me."

I had heard about President Jimmy Carter's hassle with an "attack rabbit" while out in a boat, fishing. (Supposedly on the prowl it swam right toward his boat). But my introduction to the aggressive nature of normally shy animals occurred one evening while I sat on an eight-foot log by our campfire, out in the boonies.

A large bird[103] flew down and perched on the log beside me. We stared curiously at each other.

After a few moments, it began edging toward me, hop by slow hop. Raising a hand, I waved at it, thinking it would fly away. (It *was* fairly large . . . now appearing to grow larger.)

The bird acted as if I were beckoning it closer.

I rose to my feet and kicked at it.

Did it fly off? *No way!*

It hopped from the log, dropped to the grass, and attacked my foot. It drove its long slender beak into the end of my flying boot. Thankfully, it did *not* pierce a toe.

Thinking it might have rabies (rampant in wild animals in Africa), I jumped away, jerked out my .22 pistol (just right for this "huge, threatening beast") and fired three times . . . quickly and perhaps fearfully. Not being Annie Oakley, I missed with all three shots at a distance of six feet.

The bird fluffed its wings disdainfully. It then gave me a haughty look and flew away. It may have thought I was unfair, resorting to firearms when we had been going at it mano-a-mano. (I did not see it again. But I kept a sharp lookout, and that had everyone chuckling behind my back. I heard them laughing.)

My next two encounters were also out in the boonies during safaris. Our car dealer-friend from Piqua flew into Monrovia, Liberia. We picked him up in my plane, flew him to Abidjan, and hustled him north to Upper Volta.

Up there we had laid-on a two-week hunting safari in the wilds, covering most of the country's southern area–part rain forest, part savanna, part desert. In Upper Volta, he had a good chance to shoot a lion . . . and he badly wanted a set of lion claws[104]. We

[103] Our reference books suggested it may have been a kind of tern.

[104] Real lion claws–done up with the native goldsmiths' filigree and made into necklaces and bracelets–were all the rage in the USA. If the husband could also brag he killed the lion himself, it was an even better conversation piece. (Like

also had a chance at water buffa,o, wild boar, and a wide range of horned animals. We needed no licenses with our special "Presidential Privilege" granted by Maurice Yameogo. We needed only find an approved hunting area (not a Reserve) and native helpers. This was all arranged by Ambassador Thomas Estes through his staff. Tom wanted to come with us. He would have, too, but, at the last hour, a diplomatic flap developed and he could not get away.

The first day, in the gloom under the trees, we trudged along, separated by about a hundred feet, searching for game. Gun on my arm, with my native beater/gun-bearer/general factotum a few yards behind me, I came across a hulking figure barely visible through the early morning mists. I had no idea what it was, but it looked tall . . . and broad.

I raised my loaded rifle and sneaked nearer. The meandering, shadowy object abruptly stopped, as if suddenly aware of my presence. Slowly it turned and moved toward me. (Reminding me of the aggressive tern on the log.) I grew wary.

When we were fifty yards apart I recognized in the thinning mist I had been stalking a "Grand Bustard," a huge bird, towering some inches over my height. Unlike the tern, Grand Bustards were noted for their aggressive nature when disturbed during mating season, and I was not about to interfere with nature's most intimate and demanding drive. Since I saw no others of its ilk about, I worried he also might be mistaking me for a female. That, too, I could do without.

I aimed and fired at its feet. Unlike the tern, this bird took the warning as intended and vanished in the other direction. (Of course, my shot alerted all the nearby game. So we called it a day.)

Jonathan Winter's "dog with the infected ear.")

Driving back to our tent site[105] (I was riding in the rear of our open truck), we encountered a King Cobra of unbelievable size. It stretched completely across the track ahead of us . . . and appeared no less than eight inches in diameter.

The driver brought the truck to a rapid halt ten feet away. We all leaped from the truck bed and cab. (Another big mistake! This thing was *huge!*)

Eager to kill it as a prize trophy, I made a fast draw of my handy .22 revolver[106]. For my next gross error, I shot at the cobra.

My bullet slug hit the road only inches before its nose. It instantly coiled like a set of bed springs and raised itself to our eye level. The hood spread, two-feet-wide. The monstrous head, mouth agape, tongue flickering, would have covered a large-sized dinner platter. Its fangs glistened in the fading light as if they were a saber-toothed tiger's.

Everyone around me fired their big-caliber hunting rifles. One Frenchman even blasted away with Ted's elephant gun. The barrage struck the snake in the center of its hood, a foot or so beneath the head, cutting the snake into two segments.

For us to photograph it, a native gun-bearer/beater, tall and lanky enough to be a Watusi, lifted the body by its severed neck (with both hands, as it weighed a ton) and held it over his head. The snake hung down and lay strung out across the road like a fire hose. We estimated fifteen feet long (at least), without the part we

[105] We were really "roughing it." The five men of the embassy staff who had come out to help us and hunt too–brought coolers of ice, cases of scotch and beer, and crates of food. They had set-up their tents on the front lawn of a German whose hunting concession we were using. Ted and I stayed at the German's cottage, sleeping in beds with mattresses and mosquito netting, on his outside patio . . . twenty feet from his filled and inviting swimming pool.

[106] I took a lot of verbal abuse for carrying this "itsy-bitsy, teensy-weensy" hand-gun. Everyone swore (first) it couldn't kill anything of significance and (second) it would simply make an animal angry if I shot at it. Riding on my right hip, though, it gave me false courage and, despite my acknowledging the validity of their arguments, I refused to substitute a 9mm or .45 on this trip. (But I changed my mind that very night.)

shot away.

I did *not* get my trophy, though. The natives took the snake home to their nearby village, cut it into small pieces, cooked it in a delicious sauce, and fed their entire tribe. They had enough left over to bring us a wooden platter loaded with little cubes saturated with the sauce, on thin bamboo slivers, much like our shish kabob.

To repay us for shooting them so much meat, they also brought along their finest delicacy. They held out and opened a broad damp leaf. Inside lay a number of white, writhing worms, actually grubs, five inches long and as big around as my thumb. These, only our Frenchman would try. Of course, he said, "It tastes like chicken." (Hah! I didn't care what it tasted like, I would have none of those creepy-crawlys.)

That same safari, as I noted, Ted and I slept on the German's patio, in the open air, under the wide, clear panoply of stars. No pollution here, the sky resembled Texas's–each planet and twinkling star so close we felt we might reach out and steal one. But we did not sleep. Not really. We dozed-off for short periods, awakened every few minutes to the raspy cough of a persistent, nearby lion, only feet away in the jungle.

This time I had my 9mm P-38 under my pillow. A .22 would not have given a bee-sting to a full grown lion.

I opened an eye in the middle of the first night when I heard a nearby snuffling and thought it was Ted. Instead, I saw, standing between our cots, the side of a king-size civit cat[107]. He sniffed at Ted, smelled me, then went back to Ted.

My heart in my throat, I thought it was a leopard. I wondered, *Is he trying to decide which of us to eat first?*

Chills chased each other up my spine while the rank odor of

[107] A civit cat can grow to be as large as the panther it resembles. This one stood about four-feet-tall at the shoulders. Its small head jutted out in front of its slim, well-muscled body, its canine teeth plainly visible. In the light of the moon, just then rising, I was certain it was a leopard. If it had been a leopard, he might very well have killed one, or both, of us. But civit cats are usually fairly docile. Africans and Europeans often make pets of them.

carrion on its breath nauseated me. As quietly as possible, I gulped down the bile rising in my gorge and eased a hand under the pillow for my handgun.

About then, its curiosity apparently satisfied, the cat lost interest. It meandered off the patio and returned to the jungle. I did not tell Ted until morning.

The next night–and thereafter–we slept *inside*. It was hotter in one way, inside; but a lot cooler another. There, I got some sleep.

Ted's safari in Upper Volta yielded additional mistakes . . . on everyone's part. The day after the cobra incident we came around a turn and burst from beneath the trees. In an open field to our right a magnificent, elk-like animal with a five-foot-tall rack of curved horns posed regally, head up-raised as if listening to our truck's approach, and curious.

This African antelope must have weighed-in at more than 2,500 pounds! Immediately our natives began shouting (in their language), "Shoot! Shoot! Shoot! We need the meat."

In unison, our "Intrepid Great White Hunters" snatched up their rifles, aimed through their expensive telescopic sights, and started firing. They threw out a barrage of slugs, ranging from bird shot to solid deer-rifle bullets, heavy enough to sink the Bismark.

Not one struck the poor startled creature. Still he did not run.

Ted, realizing his gun sights were unreliable, fired over the top of his and brought the antelope down. The beast dropped to its knees, then forward onto its face, falling like a mighty oak.

Our native boys leaped forward, eager to skin, gut and carve the carcass into chunks small enough to put into our truckload of coolers. On the other side of the road, all this activity scared up an entire family of wild boars. They charged away from us at full speed–from the huge, six-hundred-pound+ males (with long tusks curving up and back almost into their brains), to a group of large, breast-dragging females, to a trio of babies. The little ones ran along behind, their tails in the air like tiny television antennae topped by flags (tufts of hair).

Again everyone raised their rifles and poured out another volley. Again no one hit a single animal.

Still standing in the truck with Ted's elephant gun in hand, I raised and aimed it. This one had iron sights (no telescopic lens to shake loose while rattling around the floor of the truck), and carried shells loaded with heavy-grain ammo. Following Ted's lead, I merely sighted across the top of the barrel (the pigs were now about a hundred yards away, leaping over some fallen timbers) and fired once. I had no expectations of hitting anything more than the others did.

The biggest boar of them all suddenly rolled end over end. Four of our boys went out to bring it back. (Being Moslem they could not eat it for it had cloven hooves. As a matter of fact they were not even supposed to *touch* it, but that did not seem to bother them.)

Bringing it back to the truck, the lead boy pointed-out the exit wound (on the side of the boar's neck just under the jaw), but could find no entry point. Then he laughed, and opened the boar with his knife to show me the bullet's route through the body.

The large slug had entered through the boar's anus (up-raised and a perfect target when jumping over the log). The bullet then continued boring through its intestines and heart, exiting by the head.

The natives jumped up and down, and began chanting, their chanting songs praising me for being such a good shot. No matter what I said, assuring everyone it was pure, unadulterated, dumb luck–and it was!–they refused to believe me. From then on I was "Dead-Eye-Dick" in their tongue.

Yet cats gave us all fits, from time to time. My crew always slept under the wing of our plane when we landed any place where we had no other military around, as there was seldom any security, or housing for the aircraft. On another trip to Ouagadougou, sleeping rough like that, though on the nightly shut-down airport, a *real leopard* inspected them the same way

the civit cat did Ted and me.

Both men froze in place. Neither had a gun. They were in the plane. Again the animal slunk away without attacking.

Armstrong, our radio operator, swore that, before the panther disappeared into the brush, it stopped, looked back as if undecided and licked its jowls as if about to change its mind. Lucky for them, he said, it majestically pranced off into the night, leaving them unscathed[108]. (Maybe they needed a bath?)

Later still, while visiting Dahomey (a tall, slim country between Nigeria and Togo), Madame Soglo (the president's wife) invited Ilogene and me on a photographic safari. Her drivers (there were two vans and a truckload of soldiers, her personal covey of hand-picked body guards) scoured Dahomey as far north as Niger, looking for the unusual.

Entering the tsetse fly area we got our initial indoctrination into what those little buggers look like and can do. A tsetse fly appears much like a horse fly, only bigger, with a longer body. Yet every other fly I ever saw, disappeared when you swung at it. Not the tsetse! They sink-in their teeth and hold on.

Ilogene and I seemed to be exempt for some reason, but they loved Madame Soglo. (It must have been something she "et.") She

[108] Though we saw a number of huge animals in Africa, we missed by thousands of years seeing what lived there in an earlier age. The day I visited President Houphuet-Boigny's home in Yammassoukro he took great pride in telling me about the mastodon tusks he had implanted in concrete to each side of his broad doorway. ("The basic symbol of 'The Ivory Coast,'" he said.) Almost two feet in diameter at their base, they rose majestically to form an arch over his double doorway's frame. Under a special high roof, the tusks crossed in the center and stood some twenty-odd-feet tall. He patted one of them and asked, "Colonel, how would you like to have fought one of these when they were alive? Big, eh?" I agreed and was properly awed. He patted the tusk again and gave a pretend shudder before leading me inside to lunch, his eyes gleaming. **Later, we dined on golden dishes, not gold-trimmed ceramic, but solid gold. I lifted one and found the serving plate weighed about five pounds. At the same meal, his house boy serving our wine became fascinated with my wings and ribbons . . . he filled my glass and kept on pouring. The President said something in his native dialect and the boy fled from the room, white pale. (Later rumors said he ended up in one of the President's crocodile-filled ponds just outside the door.)**

was sitting on the seat in front of us in the leading van when the first tsetse landed on the back of her neck.

I waved at it. It did not move.

I flicked my fingers at it. It stayed put.

I slapped it with the palm of my hand. It budged not an inch.

I grasped its body with the tips of my fingers and pulled. Still no joy!

I grabbed it again–more firmly this time–and twisted. It came loose, struggling to get away like a trapped mouse (and not much smaller). It left a raw, bleeding wound on Madame Soglo where it had been chewing into her skin.

Since Madame Soglo was their prime target, we drove quickly through the fifty-mile-belt of the tsetse fly region, and soon she had relief. But when we stopped for lunch she was a pattern of red welts and weeping bites.

Early that same afternoon, we came upon a female baboon carrying a tiny baby in her arms. Madame Soglo screamed for a picture. To oblige I crawled out with my Leica and 135mm lens, and edged cautiously nearer.

The baboon mother bared her teeth, but let me come close enough to take several good shots. Yet I had not been truly careful.

I glanced up at the sudden silence. Close by, on each side, stealthily moving nearer and about to surround me, a gathering of male baboons, teeth bared, prepared to attack and protect their female with child.

Back-pedaling as fast as my short legs managed, I dashed into the van, and we sped off.

Because of these incidents, one night after we were assigned to Fort Lamy I came close to blowing-away our gardener-guardian. Yet his sole intent was to protect Ilogene and Mike.

Our gardener-guardian had been cutting grass in our rear yard

when I returned from a trip[109]. As a result he did not know I was home.

Not long after Ilogene and I went to bed, he and his faithful goat (he slept with the stinking thing), plopped themselves onto the cement patio outside our bedroom's French windows. When they inadvertently banged against the window, I awoke, leaped to my feet, drew and cocked my .45 automatic, ready to let fly.

Ilogene saved him by yelling just as I aimed through the glass. "Don't! That's only Adama!" (She had to explain about the goat.[110])

The next day I warned Adama to alert me anytime he was going to sleep out there. He promised he would. Then I told him how I almost shot him.

He bowed and salaamed, "Ah, yes, Patron, but that was *not* Allah's will."

Serenely, he gathered his tools and resumed his labors. (He made me wish I had that kind of confidence.) A week later, our boys had a great feast celebrating the conclusion of Islam's Holy Month of Ramadan.[111] And the goat "got the axe."

It was not necessary, however, for us to leave our homes in

[109] He trimmed the lawn with his extra-sharp machete so close it looked like the finest putting green.

[110] This was what the natives called a "mouton." Half sheep-half goat it could easily have passed for one of Doctor Doolittle's animals. Its front half was solid white, its rear solid black, the division between the colors as straight-edged as if drawn with a ruler. It stank like a slaughter house and reached taller than Adama's shoulder. Supposedly it had been bought to scare away snakes. (It never did.) I always thought the servants conned Ilogene into buying it solely so they might have a nice big feast at the conclusion of Ramadan. Well, they did. I even had a bite. When cooked, they called it "mish-wee."

[111] Ramadan is a sacred period for Moslems (thirty days). During Ramadan, from dawn, the moment they can distinguish the difference between a white and black thread, until they can no longer do so in the evening, they cannot eat, drink, have sex, or even swallow their own sputum. This makes for a tense and edgy period among the followers of Islam. Its conclusion triggers extensive and elaborate religious celebrations and feasting. (Here is where our former "goat," became the center piece for our Moslem boys's big meal.)

either Abidjan or Fort Lamy to be stalked by animals. Some benign, some dangerous, some pets.

Because of Africa's persistent heat, our diplomatic community conducted many of its cocktail parties outside in the open air. In Abidjan, the gardeners kept the lawns immaculate and close-cut (as did ours). The servants erected flaming torches around the perimeters for light and carried outside the movable bars with liquor, mixes, ice and food. These attracted insects.

While standing on the back lawn at one of the first parties Ilogene and I attended, something struck me in the chest. (I thought someone had hit me with a ball bat, it was that violent.) An enormous insect fell to the ground, stunned.

I picked it up and examined it. It was an Emperor Beetle larger than my closed fist and about the same shape, weighing a pound or so, with a wing-span of more than ten inches on a side. I had never seen an insect so huge and those few I had seen were in museums. It flew away as soon as it recovered. (It astounded me—its ability to get that much weight airborne.)

A nearby secretary from the British embassy saw me rubbing my chest. "Got you one, did he, old chap? That's a problem with these outside parties. Happens all the time." He squinted into the torch flames close by. "The bats'll be out soon. Then the bugs'll ease up." He stared over the tip of his drink at the lawn surface. "Gotta keep an eye out for the creepy-crawlies too, you know. A fellow stepped on a viper last week at a party."

Everyone not only groused about the insects, but also used them as reliable indicators for telling how long a newcomer had been in Africa.

Since we were outside so much, the liquid in our drinks attracted a variety of the flying "critters." A newcomer, one in Africa less than a week, on finding a bug in his drink, tossed out the contents and demanded *a new glass and a new refill.*

During the second week, through the end of the first month, the newcomer tossed out the drink and used the *same glass for a*

refill.

The second and third months, a newcomer *reached in and removed the insect, then drank the drink.*

From the third month through the sixth month, the newcomer was becoming an "old-timer," so he *reached in and held the bug to one side and drank the drink.*

After the sixth month, African veterans *drank the drink, insects and all.*

I thought this was just one of those tales told by the embassy staffs to scare new arrivals. But I watched. The varied responses became a fairly accurate guide for a newcomer's behavior and for the length of time a person had been "on-station." I even saw one "old hand" at the French embassy actually chewing-up his drink's insect accumulation. [NOTE: Ilogene and I never got beyond the stage where we "held-the-bug-to-one-side." The French chided us with, "You are unnecessarily fastidious." But we both hated the idea of eating insects. So we didn't . . . normally.]

In our Abidjan compound, Barry and I (and our wives) counted a wide variety of animals–dogs, cats, monkeys, boas, green mambas, rats, small and middle-sized deer. (Though we had the space, if I had not put my foot down we also would have had a baby elephant . . . maybe two. Their mothers had been poached and my aircrew planned to abduct them from the local zoo. I told the boys to forget it– unless they were prepared to stand a thirty-day watch, caressing, feeding and stroking them around the clock. The vet told us any new baby elephant will die without that continuing attention.)

But, first, you must visualize our Abidjan garden. Two hundred feet wide, three hundred feet deep, enclosed on two sides by stone and concrete walls, eight feet high, the rear wall consisted of steel cyclone fencing fastened to ten-foot posts. (The Danish Ambassador later moved in behind us–a real "show place.") All were topped by concertina barbed wire. A single gate behind my house (under our second-floor balcony) led from the garden past

our downstairs' rooms to our three-car carport[112]. The only other gate, behind my assistant's house next door, opened onto the same vista.

A broad stand of bamboo at the rear sheltered the deer . . . and a family of green mambas. The boa lived beside the house and ate the rats. The rats lived above us in our double-roof arrangement. They came down nightly to feed . . . and be shot and/or eaten. (I shot them or the boa ate them.)

Three, waist-tall deer lived in our bamboo patch (at night we heard the bamboo growing–its squeak audible from our balcony). Briefly, we also enjoyed two tiny "dik-diks," deer so small they were no larger than the two-pound Chihuahua we took with us to Fort Lamy. The monkey lived beside the house, in a tree.

For the most part, we left the mambas and boa alone . . . and they reciprocated. Only when Ilogene went into the bamboo–once!–to check on a newborn deer did we become apprehensive. But she got away with it. (The bite of a mamba–green or black–is usually fatal.)

Our gardener-guardian kept the lawn immaculate, including the thousands of blossoming flowers, the grass, shrubs and stand of bamboo. Visitors exclaimed over his work as if it were a

[112] The French called houses like ours, "villas grand standing," which meant they were imposing and affluent. We also had a short front drive–and a large iron gate between two more walls–leading into the carport. This provided a front parking area large enough to accommodate ten cars. We lived on the second floor. Up there we had two skimpy bedrooms (the French believed bedrooms served solely for sleeping or "on-the-bed" romps), two and a half baths, a tiny kitchen, a storage area (8' by 8' with strong locks),and a long, broad, combination dining and living area. This latter room stretched across the entire house from front to rear. At the rear it opened onto our balcony overlooking the garden. At the front, a line of windows faced the parking area. This room was so large (28' by 28') we held dinners for twenty-four guests at one long table, under the windows. Nearer the balcony, an arrangement of four sofas and ten chairs, four coffee tables, and a miscellaneous assortment of lamps and end-tables did not even crowd the floor space. Bookcases lined each of the other two walls. Oil paintings, including the one President Yameogo bought and brought to President Johnson, hung on the walls and over the doors. Downstairs, there was a primitive laundry room, two toilets, water heaters, and two more guest bedrooms. (We put Patrick in one and gave the other to our gardener/ gardien, his wife, and young son, "Dow-Dow".)

horticultural exhibit.

Our best remembered pet in the Ivory Coast, though, was "Sam," a green monkey weighing about twenty pounds. He stayed in a tree out back on our guardian's advice. We originally planned to bring "Sam" into the house to live, but our gardener dramatically held his nose and shook his head. (He was right. "Sam" was really ripe most of the time.) We talked to him from our balcony, and also brought him in regularly, for brief periods. (He loved Mike and Ilogene. He never gave me the time of day until we took him to a Frenchman on our departure. "Sam" then ran, not to Ilogene, nor to Mike, but to me and jumped into my arms and cried. So did I.)

We kept "Sam" fastened to a tree with a cloth parachute riser wired to a chain. Adama brought him in for parties (the ladies loved him). But, if it had not rained recently, he carried a distinct tang of urine and worse.

The girls liked him because he, too, was very fond of the ladies. He sprinted forward and at once ran his little hands up inside their legs, grinning. (So did they.)

"Sam" also had a trick everyone loved to watch. He straightened out his chain and riser, keeping most of it in his fists. He then threw some of the bananas and other fruit he saved just for this, under his tree.

The deer dashed over, grabbed-up the fruit with their mouths. Sam" timed it exactly. He dropped to their backs, and held on, while they ran around the tree until his chin grew taut and jerked him off the deer. The deer then scurried to a far corner of the garden and ate the fruit.

Ilogene, Mike and I watched this repeated performance so often we were convinced the deer enjoyed it as much as Sam did, and acted like suckers solely to give him a ride. "If not," we argued, "Why didn't they run straight away as soon he landed on their backs? Like they did when the chain grew taut?" (Their inherent animal intelligence and deliberate, mutual cooperation had to be

the only answers.)

My assistants (and their wives) liked pets, but most harbored felines. Inasmuch as Mike and I are highly allergic to cats we tried to keep our distance.

Yet, in Abidjan, my assistant, Barry Whittier, and his wife, Mickey, owned a Persian short-hair they called "Griô." (Pronounced "Gree-Yoh.") The native vet in Africa ruined it during his sterilization procedure. (Without giving the cat any anesthetic, the vet slitted the cat's scrotum, reached in, grabbed the poor cat's testicles between his fingers . . . and jerked!)

A week later the cat tried to eat a poisonous toad. (I wondered if he were trying to commit suicide.) Though he vomited before ingesting enough to kill him, he did become quite ill. For weeks after that, the cat sat around, sucking in water and spitting it out, as if saying, "Wow! That was really . . . r-e-a-l-l-y bad!" He never "tasted" another toad.

Ilogene and I, having both Mike and Pat with us in the Ivory Coast, relented early-on to their begging and purchased an African dog. A pretty, brown- and golden-colored mutt, Pat and Mike named him "Fang" (for obvious reasons). This nondescript, but playful pup grew like a weed until he was two feet tall and weighed approximately forty pounds. He never grew to match those five-inch fangs, though, nor did he ever become housebroken. This forced us to keep him outside where he became our gardener-guardian's pet.

What we never understood was "Fang's" change of heart. Though he lived with blacks before (we bought him from an native family), within ten days he hated all blacks (except our guardian), growling and snapping at any passing by. We also had to spend a wad of dough on his ears. They became infected, flies literally eating them away, and we had to have them clipped like Mr. Spock's (of *Star-Trek*).

In Abidjan, my second assistant and his wife, brought with them a much more precious pet–their baby son, barely a year old.

He was the center of attention throughout the remainder of our tour. And good reason: his bright little eyes promised a sharp brain and his quick grasp of new challenges assured he had the intelligence to go far.

Once we were sent to Fort Lamy, we battled other animals as well, and my second assistant (married to an attractive girl who resembled Jackie Kennedy–too closely, actually, because it caused her problems) raised "Blue Point" kittens. The kittens were so alluring I even wanted one, though I would have had to take antihistamines constantly. But they sold all their kittens quickly, removing the temptation.

Of all my people, though, it was Sergeant Alvin (Al) Batman who fought the greatest and longest battle with the local animals. I mentioned earlier the mambas, gaboon vipers, and scorpions, but did not give specifics until now.

One evening, Al slid into his small Two-Horsepower Citroen truck and there, coiled up, next to him on the passenger seat, lay a four-foot gaboon viper. They were not noted for their speed, only for their deadly poison, so he slipped out as quickly as he climbed in. It took fifteen minutes to oust the snake and urge it out of his walled-in front yard.

The day he drove me to his house to show me his snake and scorpion problems, for a moment I actually thought he "salted" the place with the critters. When he opened the front door, a mamba dropped to the floor from either the top of the screen or the door casing. We leaped back and gave it room to skedaddle. When he opened his bedroom dresser's top drawer, another mamba–lying among his socks–slithered away down the back. In his kitchen a third snake lay half under his refrigerator. In his bathtub, we found four black scorpions, each more than eight inches long, and another scampered out from under his bed when we entered. (That was enough! I immediately gave him our house until he went back to the states, while Ilogene, Mike and I moved into the departed administrative officer's.)

To top this off, the first Saturday following our arrival, while Al was fishing alone in a twelve-foot rowboat on the Chari River, he caught a fish more than fifteen-feet-long (about one quarter mouth with teeth four inches long). Natives in pirogues, fishing near him, gathered around and assisted his "landing" the fish on the shore (it was far too huge to even attempt pulling into his boat). The entire local village turned out to exclaim over its size. Al donated the fish for their help and they conducted a celebration dinner in his honor. I attended and six of the natives who helped him stood shoulder to shoulder, arms out, to brag about its length. The chief showed me some of the teeth and held open his arms to simulate the mouth. (Despite this, Mike water-skied on the river, regularly, while Ilogene and I wrung our hands. We just knew that one day he would be eaten alive. But he wasn't.)

Compared with Al's daily threats (and he had lived with them until I arrived), Ilogene's and my problems seemed almost a picnic. Still, there were moments . . .

Every morning in Chad, before breakfast and prior to opening the embassy, for example, I took a short dip in our pool.

Our two house boys went out even earlier, scooping out the pool and beating the nearby bushes for the night's accumulation of wild life–snakes, insects and small animals. When I came out, the area was supposedly clear and safe. (Hah, again!)

I dived in one morning and a strange creature matched my pace all through my initial laps. No one ever figured out exactly what it was. All I know it was black, more than six inches in all dimensions, had long legs–and lots of them–no hair, but fangs to die for . . . literally.

I shouted. Our nearest houseboy scooped it out with one of our nets on a pole.

It scrambled out of the net as he lifted it to one side and hit the grass running. It either vanished into a hole in the ground or ran into the next field. It was fast and ugly . . . enough to give us all pause. Yet never again did we see its like.

291

One afternoon. while we swam in the pool, a dark-green snake stuck his nose out of the surrounding hedge. Obviously not poisonous (his nose was too long and thin), he measured more then twelve feet in length. But he had an odd, wrinkled skin, like the crinkle finish on those old NCR cash registers. Non-poisonous, I insisted the servants carry him to the airfield (a quarter mile behind our home) and release him.

Later, during an early evening in the brief twilight hours, Ilogene, still in her swim suit, wearing only that, a small shirt, and sandals, headed for our separate storage room at the rear of our garage. Looking down at her hands, trying to separate its door key from the dozen others, she walked blindly up the laterite[113] pathway from the house to the garage in the dim light.

Walking right behind her, I reached out and grabbed her arm, saying, *"Don't put your foot down!"*

She froze! Beneath her upraised foot a long, Gaboon viper crawled away, slowly, toward the garage.

Her foot would have landed in the middle of its back. Now, gaboon vipers may be slow, but they react violently when threatened. Another microsecond and Ilogene would have been struck on her bare leg. In another few seconds, she'd have died.

She made it a point after that to watch more carefully.[114]

That was outside. Inside our houses, small gecko-type lizards lived behind our wall hangings, paintings and clocks. They were an important adjunct to life in Africa. They ate the spiders, the mosquitos, the cockroaches (as big as those in Texas and Florida),

[113] Gaboon vipers are striking in appearance. Presenting diamond-like designs on their backs they are almost exactly the same, reddish-sandy color of the laterite. With this as a background they were always difficult to see, especially in diminished light.

[114] Looking back, now, on our two African tours, I believe it must have been a minor miracle that none of us—neither my family, nor my men, nor any of our dependents—were ever bitten by a snake or spider, nor stung by scorpions. For they lay all around us on every side, day and night.

and even small snakes. No one in Africa more than a week killed one intentionally. (We needed them too much to keep down the insect population–like the fruit bats on Abidjan. The bats there swarmed by the millions each night, cleansing the air of flying bugs.)

The day we moved into my former administrative officer's housing (Al Batman lived in my assigned place up the street), we discovered a little gecko–so small and transparent we watched his blood circulate and heart beat. He lived in our shower basin, a four-inch-deep, tiled opening, four-foot square, cut in the bathroom floor (no stalls there).

Every time I showered, I reached down and carefully picked him up, placing him on the window sill. When done, I returned him to the shower basin.

Ilogene followed the same routine.

The little lizard grew accustomed to the change of location. He even crawled into my palm one day from the window sill, when I coaxed it.

But, on our new administrative officer's arrival, I moved to Al's old place and forgot to tell the new man about our little gecko. At our staff meeting the next day, he expounded about, "Killing a scorpion in our shower this morning . . . and I did not know they actually bled."

I said nothing, nor did I tell Ilogene. We had come to think of that little lizard as a family pet.

In our yards, though, dozens of nasty creatures lurked in the ground, some I had never heard of. The "scorpion-spiders," as a prime example, sneaked from their hidden lairs at some kind of interval, motivated to do so by no-one-knew-what.

Ilogene saw the first one. It was chasing my sergeant's little six-year-old boy around our drive as if bedeviled. The creature seemed, "For all the world," as Ilogene described it, "determined to catch him, bite him, or sting him." She went on to say, "They were odd looking, covered in a light-grey skin and no hair. Legs

more like a tarantula's than anything else, except the two front ones were as much antennae as legs.

"When it caught up with the boy, it used those front antennae (legs) to feel the toe of his shoe . . . then tried to bite him. He kicked at it and it chased him again for a while. Suddenly this insect (or whatever?) stopped as if tired of the sport, and disappeared into the lawn covering."

I did not see any of this. But two nights later we had an unusual wind storm. The wind blew so hard our front door (which we thought was locked) flew open, banging against the wall. The big shocker came, though, when one of those scorpion-spiders flew (or leaped) through the open door and did not land until it reached the center of our livingroom. (Some leap, even if the wind did help!)

Holding a magazine at the time, I ran forward and conked the spider with the rolled-up pages. As tough as any tsetse fly, the spider ignored the assault . . . and headed for my feet. I slammed down the magazine atop the spider . . . and jumped on it with both feet. Despite my 165 pounds of solid muscle and bone (That's a joke!), the spider was not the least bit fazed by the treatment. Before Ilogene managed to close the door, it took off like a scalded eagle. It flashed back through the opening and was gone.

We never saw another one. The embassy told us, however, how fortunate both my sergeant's boy and we had been. The embassy said the scorpion-spider's bite can sicken and kill, like a tarantulas', and they were unusually strong and aggressive. (No one needed to tell us the last.)

There were other pets and animals, too many actually, all remembered, but none compared with my assistant's little boy. So, like they once said while closing those old travel log films, " . . . As the sun slowly sets in the west, we must leave the mysterious cities, deserts and jungles of Africa . . . its exotic animals, pets and . . . " (With that, the final credits flashed across the screen until "The End" appeared and all went black.)

CHAPTER NINETEEN

▲

Foreign countries of primitive development, like most of Africa–except, maybe, Egypt at one end and South Africa at the other–offered limited entertainment possibilities. (Let's face it, none of my African countries matched the most backward of Europe, or even those behind the Iron Curtain.)

Abidjan, for all its being called "The Paris of the South," at the time boasted only a soccer field, the lagoon for boating, and one large, public swimming pool–no golf courses, but lots of bars and bistros . . . and a broad-scale "Red Light District" (serviced by native, French and Arab, girls and boys, from Europe and Africa.)

There was one, more or less open-air theater. (Half under the stars, half under a covered canopy, it had a small, fifteen- by eighteen-foot screen and a ten- by twelve-foot stage.) Since it had no air-conditioning, patrons welcomed any little breeze (when there was one), but detested the flies, mosquitos and other crawling/flying insects this milieu made available.

Yet here is where Gene Kelly, the American actor-dancer of "Singing in the Rain" fame, brought his cartoon movie and danced for us. He even spoke a sort-of French patois. (The natives loved him. The French lionized him. The Americans housed, fed and entertained him. Our Pat and Mike rode down with him in the elevator at the Hotel Ivoire. They talked and shook hands–then did NOT want to wash their hands, *ever,* they were so proud.)

Still the US government did its best for us "diplomatic soldiers out there on the front lines." Both the embassy and defense attaché systems distributed, on world-wide routes, a continuing array of

Hollywood's latest (and sometimes oldest) 35-mm movies. The reels arrived in protected cans once a month. We showed them, then sent the cans on by diplomatic pouch to the next embassy.

They were not always first-line films, and sometimes the selections were really bad. But, we were so desperate for entertainment, we watched them all, regardless. (We never quite reached the point where we had to show "Birth of a Nation," yet we did not miss it by far.) Some of the other embassies–France, Britain, Holland, German and Spain–had similar film exchange procedures. When there were subtitles, we traded our choicest offerings. When really desperate, we watched *anything* that moved, spoke or sang. (There were times when Chinese and Urdu might have been acceptable, if the action were interesting. *That* was really desperate.)

The Defense Attaché's office also received monthly "Care" packages (as we called them) from the USA. These were boxes of books intended for our office libraries, usually as many as fifty books at one time–hardcover, trade and paperbacks. Included were large-size, old-style 33 1/3 rpm recordings produced by the Armed Forces Network (AFN), copied directly from their radio show broadcasts.

All of us enjoyed the latest "Best Seller" books, and liked the music, but many of us ate-up the westerns as well as the horror stories, adventures and romances. (Here is where Ilogene and I first developed our taste for Harlequin and Silhouette romances . . . an urge prompting us to write several series ourselves after retirement[115].)

Some of the books were real howlers. Evidently, these were "remaindered" products the publishers felt they might foist off onto us poor schumcks way out in the boonies, solely in a last ditch effort to make a buck on their dogs. We even received sex

[115] See "My Books," in the Addenda, for the last of these, *At Cross Purposes*. This one my wife and I were writing when she died. I was unable to touch it for almost six years. Then I finished and published it.

manuals and some purple prose. And, often, the poetry was not merely obscure, it was unpalatable. (And I like poetry). We passed around the good books until the pages were dog-eared and the covers were worn away.

Here, also, is where I first discovered Louis L'Amour's tales of the Old West, and grew to admire his tale-spinning skills and brilliant use of words.

When again teaching at Ohio University ("Writing Salable Fiction"), after retiring from the military and Hobart, I used Louis L'Amour's books as good-writing examples. As an opening gimmick, I gave my students only the first sentences from two dozen books, and asked them to identify any they could. Once, out of a class of fourteen, one girl named, without hesitation, everyone of L'Amour's entries, plus their titles and dates of publication. (Yet she did *not* know the opening lines of "Rebecca," nor even Dickens's, "It was the best of times, it was the worst of times . . . ")

* * *

Air-evacuated by C-5 to the United States from Chad (actually from the hospital at Wiesbaden, Germany) my military career ended far more abruptly than it began. Hell, I wasn't ready to retire! If you do the math I was but forty-six-years-old in 1968. I had no plans for retirement. I had no job "lined-up," like General Morlet. Nor did I envision, like some men, sitting on the front porch in a rocking chair . . . and, after a couple years, slowly beginning to rock. I was too young, too eager, too . . . everything.

Yet, disgusted with the military, one afternoon I folded my tent, stole away into the night, and called it quits. At the time, I lay abed in the hospital at Wright-Patterson AFB, Fairborn, Ohio. The medical staff had gone too far and angered me.

Still fighting debilitating physical problems, I wanted only for the short-sighted doctors to agree I suffered from extreme gall bladder attacks–and operate to remove it. Living in French

communities (Ivory Coast and Chad), eating gobs of rich sauces daily and drinking vintage wines, the environment had been ripe for such repeated crises. Despite all the classic symptoms–nausea, pain, abrupt paleness, diarrhea, dizziness, and I had them all–the doctors could not prove my gall bladder was at fault since nothing showed up on their dye tests. They believed the symptoms were psychosomatic or I wanted out of my attaché assignment. Nothing could have been further from the truth–I held a lush "plum." We lived like general officers. We had servants. We had parties. We had friends in Africa. I had my own plane. Who would want more? (They even thought I was crazy. *I thought they were!*)

I put in my papers for immediate retirement. That same afternoon, three general officers (all two-stars), came personally to talk me out of it. Each insisted he needed me to work with him. (Good for my ego, but they left me cold.)

One came from the Pentagon, one from MacDill AFB, Tampa, Florida, and one from HQ, USAF Recruiting, right there on Wright-Pat. (This sounds far more grandiose than it was. There happened to be a general officer conference going on in Fairborn and they were all attending, anyway. They simply knew me and found out I was in the hospital.)

The Pentagon representative wanted me to return to D.C. and work in the attaché office, taking charge of the African units. Major General Thomas McGeehee, asked me to join him in Florida and take over the African chair for military Intelligence. The two-star from recruiting, urged me to reassume command of Chicago and again "work my magic" there.

I turned down all three.

The medical staff had rankled me–especially their taking me off flying status. One doctor in the Wiesbaden Hospital had even suggested I was insane–since he was unable to verify my symptoms were gall-bladder-related. (Oh, I might have been crazy all right. Their too-oft-repeated tests to no avail, and their unwillingness to take positive, corrective action so disaffected me

298

I felt like pulling out what little hair remained. I became as angry *with the service,* as I had been *with civilian life* when I accepted their Regular commission in 1947.)

General McGeehee sweetened the pot, suggesting he could get me put back on flight status . . . and see I wore stars. Even that did not "hack it" for me.

I told him, "Thank you, General. But I made a vow, years ago–'When they take away my wings . . . I quit!' They did . . . and I have." (And I truly liked Tom, whom I'd known since he was a major. But the military had suddenly soured for me.)

(See the next page for my official retirement photograph.)

Nearing the end of my three-week-wait for retirement orders, I took leave and went to Piqua (thirty miles to the north). Ilogene and Mike had just returned from Africa. We could not buy a house or relocate permanently until my retirement was assured, but we looked for and picked out a place.

In anticipation of my retirement, a "Head-hunter[116]" sought me out with several job offers. From among them, I tentatively accepted a position in Findlay, Ohio, with a large, nationwide manufacturing plant, as their new personnel director. There, among other tasks, my staff and I were to recruit other executives, administer psychological testing to, select and train, all new employees, of all ranks. I drove to Findlay, oriented my new staff (and myself) and agreed to come "on-board" the following week . . . after I retired.

[116] "Head-hunter" is the name given to an executive recruiter who searches the country for the specific skills, talents and experience needed by corporations for their management positions

299

Rodney L. Cron

Rodney L. Cron
Official retirement
photo (1968)

The next day I received a far more attractive offer from the Hobart Manufacturing Corporation, Troy, Ohio. They invited me to become their first National Service Manager for KitchenAid. I accepted and aborted my Findlay move.

The better salary and shorter distance from home were significant factors. Ilogene's parents had been ailing, we wanted to be near them, and we wanted to give them a rousing Fiftieth Wedding Anniversary Celebration. (Ilogene had already returned twice to Piqua–only seven miles from Troy. Once, while we were in training and again after we arrived in Fort Lamy, when her mother suffered increasing strokes.)

At Hobart, hiring some of my former military staff whom I knew were good administrators, I applied my basic management rule: "Surround yourself with people who are smarter than you are, and you prove you are the smartest." Together, Al Batman, Bill Bonaker, and I developed an office cadre and a network of regional managers, plus a ten-year operational plan which ran the company's service support activities like a charm for the next

decade . . . long after I left to write books. We developed and instituted systems integrating technological innovations never tried before (but were rapidly adopted by other company divisions). With my two helpers, we achieved unheard of rapid, customer response times and degrees of satisfaction[117]. Answering letters within twenty-four hours, using electronic typewriters, then computers, we created multiple letter forms and flexible paragraphs so we could call-up answers quickly for any query. We arranged regional managers in central locations. We trained them to, in turn, train and supervise our service outlets and distributors. This made for a startling efficiency. The results earned kudos for our team from the company president, our board members, our distributors, and our thousands of customers. My management and working teams made me more proud of them each day.

When the company exhausted our ten-year-plan, they called me back to prepare another one . . . but I declined (unless they paid me big bucks – and they did not want to do that.)

Ignoring some of our management warnings to the company president, another corporation bought them out as predicted (using Hobart's own liquid assets). That company then sold KitchenAid, realizing millions. I had already sold my stock options. A good thing too, because the stock went "down the tube." Not long after, KitchenAid was again bought out, this time by Whirlpool. (It is still there.)

Two facets fell by the wayside–my singing and flying. I managed to do some singing, in churches, but far too seldom. The chances to fly were even fewer. There were some rare occasions when an instrument instructor was needed, but no chance to do any major, cross-country flights.

A manufacturing corporation in Dayton, Ohio (twenty-odd

[117] These successful management innovations and methodologies are explained in detail in my three management books, *Assuring Customer Satisfaction, Survival and Success in a Shrinking Economy*, and *Let's Do it Now!* (Van Nostrand Reinhold, first two, and Condor Publishing Company, the last.)

miles south of Troy) bought an airline's DC-3 (the same as my old C-47). Their executives spent more than a hundred thousand dollars to bring it to tip-top shape inside and out–new paint, new avionics, new engines, a new chic interior . . . the "works." Then they put it on the market–not having flown it one hour–and bought a new executive jet.

They asked only twenty-five thousand dollars for the DC-3. I wanted it so badly I could taste it. Ilogene was against it. KitchenAid was luke warm. So someone else bought it. (I have kicked myself ever since. That plane would have been perfect for our company's–and my use–dashing about the country, visiting distributors and my regional managers.)

My flying then became an "on again-off again" affair. With some hard work I managed to push four people through the necessary training and tests until they qualified for instrument and commercial-pilot ratings, and–as one man did–an airline pilot ticket.

While with Hobart, Ilogene and I moved three times. Into a new home in Piqua, then to Troy, then–when Ilogene's mother became critical–back to Piqua, across the street from her parents'. Mike, meanwhile, dropped out of school and joined the Army. (See next page.) Patrick graduated West Point, went into the Air Force as an officer, and to flight school as a pilot trainee.

Ilogene's mother lived only long enough to see Pat graduate West Point. (We thought she deliberately held on until she saw him achieve that long-awaited goal, before giving up. Pat had been her favorite, the one she took fishing, day in and day out, whenever she was able.)

Morris and "Babe" Mays
(Thaddora Mercedes)

Ilogene's father and mother

Swearing Michael into the
US Army–his second
enlistment.

I do not have photos of my swearing-in Patrick at West Point,
nor of my swearing-in Rod III for one of his enlistments.
Somehow, they were lost in the shuffle. I can show only two of
the four swearing-in ceremonies, Melodie's (when she became a
Second Lieutenant in the Army Nurse Corps and one of Michael's
reenlistments).

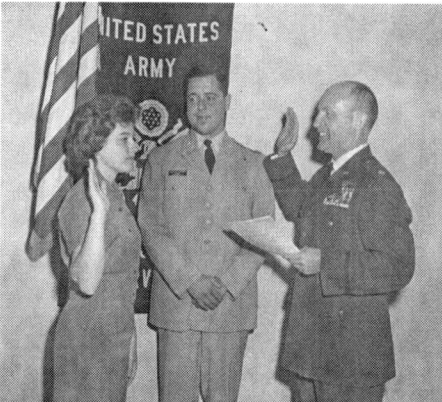

Swearing Melodie into the
US Army Nurse Corps.
as a second lieutenant.

Soon after, Ilogene and I moved again . . . to southeastern Ohio. We bought fifty acres in the country as a summer place. We elected to move there and build a house when I quit Hobart to re-embark on my writing career and again teach at Ohio University.

Leaving on a planned trip to Florida, and taking with us Ilogene's Dad (right out of the hospital after an extended bout of pneumonia), he abruptly died with no warning while we awaited lunch at a restaurant in Troy. Ilogene and I buried him with her mother (and arranged a place on the other side of the tombstone for us).

Working in Piqua for two weeks, Ilogene and I cleared out and sold his house, and everything we had in Piqua. With no longer any reason to stay in the area, we decided to live permanently in Logan.

Everyone wondered why we chose Logan, when we could go anywhere in the USA and had friends everywhere. In the final analysis, it was Ilogene's decision, with which I concurred.

She said, "Logan is small and inexpensive, with little traffic or crime. We have friends there. You can teach at OU, if you want–it's not too far way. But I don't want you even thinking about moving to Athens (OU's location). They play 'musical beds' down there, and I don't need the competition." (Though there would have been no competition as far as I was concerned, Logan it was!)

Developing our fifty acres–completely forested with second growth timber–we cut out a space for a driveway and installed a 40-foot by 28-foot pole barn (which we used for a garage, a site for Ilogene's ceramic oven, and storage). We leveled another, smaller spot, giving us enough room for temporary housing. There, we poured a tremendous concrete pad seated on three huge footers, and placed thereon a 14-foot by 78-foot mobile home. Intending this to be temporary, we cut more timber and cleared a site, behind and above the pad, for a planned retirement home atop the hill behind us.

Unfortunately, a new resident up the road ruined our 378-foot well when he did *not* encase his well when he drilled. Our water became unpalatable. We replaced filter after expensive filter to no avail. Finally, we sold out and moved to Albuquerque, New Mexico. Before we left, though, we earned some thirty-five thousand dollars selling off fifty-six, black walnut trees for harvesting. (Another sixty-eight we left for the new owner.)

Julius Katona (Tony), a former Air Force officer-friend, and his wife lived in Albuquerque. I always liked the high altitude and dry heat, but Tony was dying of Alzhiemer's. We knew we could not alleviate it, but we might be able to help his wife, Millie, through this trauma. (Ilogene really disliked the area, but indulged me–as she so often did.)

There, we largely visited Indian sites, traveled, even drove to Las Vegas and gambled several times. The Sandia Air Force Base gave us medical and commissary support, and I took a job managing a mobile home park. But most of our time we devoted to Tony's care and Millie's.

Tony quickly failed. Soon he was no longer ambulatory. We had to use wheel chairs. He quickly lost his ability to speak coherently and, finally, lapsed into a semi-awake-type, virtually unresponsive coma. Then, one night, we inadvertently happened on a technique momentarily arousing him to coherence and alertness.

I brought to their house one of my favorite movies, of Nelson Eddy and Jeanette MacDonald. Tony became enraptured with the music. (Early-on in his military career, he played in the band and was quite a musician). He sat upright. His eyes opened and he watched avidly throughout the entire performance, waving his hands in time with the singing, and beating the tempo on his wheelchair armrest.

When it was over, he spoke clearly for the first time in weeks, "Now, *that* was *really* good!"

Two minutes later, he relapsed into his semi-coma. Nothing we

did roused him—not even replaying the music. He never came alert again . . . until the end

Several months after this episode, Tony slid deeper into this insidious disease—and went into the fetal position. He died soon after in the Veterans Hospital in Albuquerque.

Two interesting sidebars came from this. Tony's oldest son, Steve, was finishing his residency as a Physician's Assistant at the VA hospital. The night Tony died, the duty nurse called for Steve to go to his father's room—purportedly Tony had awakened from his coma and wanted to talk to him.

Steve hurried in and found Tony wide awake. Tony spent the next fifteen minutes detailing what he wanted done for his burial . . . then died. Steve followed his father's instructions, amazed he had enjoyed such a fluke, having those last moments to see and talk with his father as he once had been.

As another odd facet of this, some years before, Tony and I had visited the Veterans National Cemetery at Santa Fe, where he was later buried. Standing by his grave, I sighted-in the landmarks, all familiar[118].

I told Millie, "This is the exact spot Tony and I climbed to, all those years ago. Tony dug his heel into the earth, right here—or within a few yards—and said, 'Here is where I want to spend eternity.'"

Millie swallowed. "Well, Rod, he's getting his wish. And, soon, I'll be right here with him."

In National Cemeteries they now place the first grave some fifteen-feet down, so they can bury the wife and children on top in a stack. Millie, therefore, eventually will be there as well. The best part is Tony's place in the cemetery affords a view of snow-covered mountains, the desert, a few trees, and nearby Santa Fe . .

[118] While at Brooks AFB, in 1948—when I first returned to active duty, working in the Fifteenth Air Force Headquarters—I assisted in the first mass burial of bodies returned from overseas. We buried the remains of an entire B-17 crew at Santa Fe, in five graves, while this cemetery was comparatively new to WWII veterans. On that occasion, Tony and I tromped the hills, admiring the site and view.

. even the opera house is only a short jaunt up the road. Those were the vistas Tony loved best.

Soon after Tony died, a telephone call asked me to return to Logan as secretary to the Hocking County Airport Authority. Ilogene, eager to go back to Ohio, massaged my ego, saying, "You must go–they *need* you!"

A week later we were in Ohio. Not that the secretarial job paid all that much, but I did not care. I planned to teach at OU anyway, do some flying, and write books with Ilogene.

Still, we forgot that little black cloud. It continued to hang over our head. It soon burst forth and lightning struck once more. The bank president who called me back for the secretary job (a man I'd known since he was a young pup starting out in the banking business at seventeen) experienced a massive heart attack on his way to the office. He died a week after we returned. He and John Tansky had been the "spark-plugs" behind the drive to build a local airport. The proposal, without the bank president, slowly but surely went defunct. (As the secretary, I was forbidden by law to take any overt action. My job limited me to providing guidance, counseling–I had to know the laws–recording and representing.)

Sometimes, the many parts of life's puzzle fall into place. Sometimes, they fall apart.

Ilogene and I had been proposing a trip to Europe. Now we elected to do it. My son-in-law and daughter asked us to take along Andrea, our granddaughter, and give her the "Grand Tour." (Like parents did in the old days). I, in turn, obtained a commission from Air West to write an article for their magazine, with photos, of the trip's main points–mainly the New Hebrides islands.

With Andrea acting as our third traveler, we flew to London, did a concentrated tour of lower England, then went to Scotland. There, we completed a combination train, bus, ferry tour of Scotland and the New Hebrides, falling in love with the people, their food and customs. (Their only off-putting offering was

"Haggis." If you do not know what that is, I won't enlighten you. Just skip it, if given an option.)

Hopping over to Paris, the three of us did all the touristy things there, too (for Andrea). We climbed the Eiffel Tower, tramped the Champs Elysee from one end to the other, explored Les Invalides (where Napoleon is buried), shopped Le Printemps (the major department store), saw four stage shows . . . and, of course, took-in Le Louvre museum.

Andrea entered Le Louvre with a notebook in hand and a list of items to see. At the foot of the stairway to the second floor, Ilogene pointed out the statue of "Winged Victory" on the landing. Andrea hurried forward, eyeballed it . . . and marked it off. On the next floor, Andrea sought out the "Mona Lisa," paused for a minute in front of it, cocked her head to one side, scratched a checkmark in her notes, and moved on to the "Venus de Milo."

Within ten minutes she had seen and checked-off every item she had planned to see. Now she was ready to leave.

I grabbed her arm. "But, honey, you haven't seen a thing. This building contains art treasures from around the world. Billions of dollars worth of great masterpieces–from Egypt, Africa, Asia . . ."

She shook her head. "Nope. That's all. Let's go."

She *did* like Paris's French fries and wines, though.

The following day we took her to Caen and Etoupe-Four in Normandy where Jacques and Suzanne Hascöet lived (only a block from Yul Bryner). While there, we visited Saint Michel and the American Cemetery holding all those thousands who gave their lives on D-Day. (See the earlier photo taken there.)

Jacques and Suzanne wanted to keep Andrea for the summer . . . but they scared her with threats of serving frog legs and snails. She refused to stay. (Now she likes both foods.)

Next, we visited my son, Michael, his wife, Karen, and son, Jeremy, in Germany. There we relaxed for a few days (Andrea marked time, impatiently.) From Munich we took the bullet train through Switzerland (enjoyed the penthouse suite atop a hotel in

Lucerne overlooking the lake), then charged on for Italy.

On the southbound train leaving Germany, we picked up a young girl. An American exchange student (only a few years older than Andrea), her stint in Germany completed, she was taking a final peek at Europe before going home.

We found her sitting in our seats in a "reserved" car. Andrea and this girl hit it off, right way. (Andrea was obviously growing tired of us older types, so we invited the girl to stay with us to Lucerne.)

She did, then went on with us to Milan. She left only when we headed for Venice. (She had to make plane connections from Paris to the States, or she might have gone farther with us.) She later invited all three of us to her wedding near Indianapolis.

In Milan, we again became gawking, photo-scrounging American tourists. Dashing from the Duomo, to La Scala (across the square), to Leonardo da Vinci's "Last Supper," we re-embarked on another train for Venice.

(This is reading a lot like a travel log. Hang in there, it's almost over.)

While in Italy, Andrea tired of drinking fruit juices at every meal and shifted to Coca Cola. This was a bad decision–not for her or for us, but for her Dad. He was paying the tariff for his little girl's "Grand Tour" . . . and coke, in Italy, cost four dollars a bottle. The same size bottle of wine, what Ilogene and I drank at lunch and dinner, cost thirty-five cents. In Italy, even the children drank wine . . . all except Andrea. We tried to talk her into becoming a "wino." She wouldn't have it.

For her favorite lunch she also quickly focused on a cold salad consisting of asparagus and ham . . . and not just any kind of ham, but the most delicate, the most fragile, the most tender prosciuto. That, of course, was also the most expensive. Andrea's regular lunches on the road cost more than twice what Ilogene's and mine did, added together.

Again we urged her to sample other foods. Again, she refused.

(I believe I might have been able to buy the Rolls-Royce I always wanted with what her meals cost in Italy alone.) Don, her father, understood, though, when we returned home. He had run into the same stubborn streak himself.

Yet, overall, Andrea provided continuing delights. Seeing Europe through her eyes opened new perspectives. We did not know it, but we had grown blasé, too accustomed to the sights, the sounds, the views, the smells and the tastes. Andrea made the trip more exciting . . . even for us "old fuds."

But Italy had its down side. In Venice, our tour company quartered us in an old hotel (which one isn't?) on the Grand Canal. The Grand Canal outside our window was a mad house, day and night–with all its comings and goings, its singing, yelling, arguing, selling, stinking, and its biting, voracious mosquitos. Our rooms were not air-conditioned and our open windows invited (and we were prey to) every hungry insect within fifty miles. The mosquitos ate Andrea like a ripe tomato. But, with her nearby, they left us alone. (See a later comment on this.)

Yet, as Andrea said, "Once you've tasted the sea food (scrumptious and well-prepared), seen the canals (they all look alike) and the Bridge of Sorrows (so what?), smelled the stench (ugh!), ridden in a gondola (Ah!), and heard the lousy tenors who think they're Caruso or Pavarotti (shudder, shudder!) . . . what else is there?"

Andrea also had the answer, "That's it. Let's go . . ."

So, we did.

Humble and tiring, which we were, we trained on to Naples. From there we visited the ruined cities on Vesuvius (Pompeii and Herculaneum), submitted to the usual gouging by the local tradesmen hawking ten-cent cameos for fifty dollars, boated out to see the Isle of Capri and the Blue Grotto, then boated back and once more bused–to Rome.

Only the Isle of Capri and the Blue Grotto impressed Andrea. She promised to return there on her honeymoon (remember she

was only thirteen at the time). But, married twice since, neither honeymoon included the Isle of Capri. She still vows, like MacArthur, "I SHALL return!"

In Rome we hit all the usual spots–from St. Peters to the Vatican to the catacombs (that Andrea hated), to the Sistine Chapel (which Andrea wanted to take home)–and rapidly eyed most of the other ancient and largely ruined Roman monuments spread across that twenty-mile scene.

We had a considerate (and Catholic) tour guide who helped Andrea locate all the Jewish symbols on every cathedral. (Her mother had recently converted to Judaism. So also, by default, had Andrea and her younger brother, Jarrod.) The guide showed Andrea those symbols to prove the Jews provided the money for every Christian building in ancient Rome. (In those early times, Holy Christians could not handle money.)

Our days in Rome finally passed and we readied for home.

Standing in line for thirty minutes at Rome's Leonardo da Vinci Airport (the computers were "down"–when aren't they?), awaiting departure to the States, we had one final "taste" of Italy. A zippy, handsome young man came dashing through the double doors off to our left, ran up to our line towing his towering piece of luggage on wheels. Momentarily sizing-up the weary passengers, he barged in ahead of my granddaughter–the first of us three.

I went up and tapped him on the shoulder and motioned for him to go to the end of the line. Pointing at its end, twenty people behind us, I said a few words in French he did not like.

He scowled and moved. At the back, I heard him complain in Italian, something about those "damned Frenchmen."

Again I left the line to confront him. In English, I read him the riot act, ending with, "As Hercule Poirot might say, 'I am *not* a "damned Frenchman," I am a "damned American."' And we're much worse!"

Everyone who heard and understood, laughed. That made him

even more angry . . . then he, too, laughed. In English, he said, "You're right."

Ilogene's final and most memorable comment on Italy hit the nail on the head, "If God ever decides to give earth an enema, He'll insert it somewhere around Rome." In a nutshell, Ilogene captured the essence, the heart and flavor of our viewpoint regarding Italy, Rome and the southern foot of the boot–to all true Italians, "the old country."

On returning I complained, "They don't even make good pizza or spaghetti." (Only to learn neither originated there.)

<center>* * *</center>

Ilogene and I returned to Europe several times after this trip. But we avoided Italy. Once was enough. Like the description we heard another lady give, "I spent six months there one day."

We preferred England, Scotland, France, Holland, Spain, Portugal and Germany. Our favorite, though (next to Paris) were the New Hebrides Islands.

From the edge of Glasgow, Scotland, David Dean operated a set of tour buses called "Classique Saloon Luxury Coaches." (You have seen them often on television and in the movies. BBC uses them almost exclusively for any vintage movies demanding buses, "Inspector Morris," "Hercule Poirot," etc.)

These were 1950s coaches, refurbished and narrow-beamed, able to drive over the narrow, twisting, sometimes unpaved, single-lane roads and tracks on the islands. They were also small enough to enter and leave the teeny ferries with no problem. The buses hauled tourists where none of the big, fat monsters could ever have reached. Lean, sleek and beautiful–inside and out–they were surprisingly comfortable. Their only draw-back–they carried no bathroom facilities. Sometimes it was necessary to "rough" it, when the lonely landscape showed no village in sight.

Ilogene and I were on one of Dean's initial trips to introduce a new tour. Following obsolete maps we drove along a truly rocky, rough-tough road, as a short-cut. (I was recording and

<center>312</center>

photographing all this for Air West. This was a once-in-a-lifetime event and I got it all.) When we reached the other end, after having driven up the center of the entire island, we stopped a farmer. "Hey! This road was in pretty bad shape. What's the story?"

He pointed back the way we had come with a gnarled finger. "Yar darn't come across't there . . . in that bus, did yar?"

We nodded. "Sure did!"

"That road's been closed for neigh on ter forty yars. Seems a bus drove off the pavement, one night, and disappeared. Yar be the first since them days."

David thanked the farmer and climbed back inside. "From now on, folks, we're sticking to known highways."

The passengers growled. "It isn't very often a tourist gets to open up an old road like that. Can we turn around and go back?"

David shook his head. "Not on your life. Anyway, we have to keep on some kind of schedule, if you want to see what's on our itinerary."

Every evening, we stopped at a new inn. Every evening we had some kind of wild animal for our major entrée (venison, wild boar, pheasant, grouse—we might even have had bear, the meat one evening was so gamy). Every evening we had at least two different types of potatoes (one night we had four: mashed, fried, boiled, and scalloped). Every evening a piper marched through the inn playing his bagpipes. Every evening the piper played "Amazing Grace" before we ate. (I began to think he was hurrying on ahead just to do this at our every stop . . . like the woman who thought the gas truck refilling the airplane's fuel tanks rushed ahead to be ready at the next airport.) Every evening, after dinner, Dean's driver played his guitar and sang to us in Gaelic. (Quite good too!) He even taught us how to say—in Gaelic—hello, goodbye, and toast our fellow drinkers (claiming those were the only essentials a newcomer need know). We used all three phrases, day after day.

Our first breakfast on the trip, at Tobermory, I made an unwitting fool of myself. I saw "kippers" on the menu . . . and I love kippers.

I called the waitress[119] to our table. "My wife would like the oats and a single poached egg on toast."

The girl nodded and made notes.

"I do *not* want the tomatoes, but I'd like two kippers, with two fried eggs on top. Is that okay?" (My reading of the menu indicated every order included tomatoes, and I do *not* like tomatoes for breakfast.)

The young girl's eyes bugged. "I will have to ask the manager, sir."

I thought this rather strange (*maybe, they have a "tomato" fetish, or something?*), but I nodded. "Fine. I'll wait."

She returned with a smile. "The manager said, 'If that is what he wants, give it to him.'"

When she returned, she served Ilogene her oats and egg, then placed a huge dinner platter in front of me. On it lay two enormous, flounder-like fish, one atop the other, so big they extended several inches beyond the platter at each end and on both sides. On top sat my two fried eggs.

I stared. "Miss, I could not possible eat that much food in a month of Sundays."

"Sir, that is what you ordered."

This confusion resulted from my vision of kippers. My concept came from those we buy Stateside . . . in tiny cans about eight-inches long, two inches wide, three-quarters of an inch deep, containing as many as four or five kippers. "Real" kippers–at least in the New Hebrides–come fresh out of the sea, approximately two feet long, a foot tall, and more than an inch thick.

The waitress kindly took back my order and brought me a sampling with my eggs. (The kippers were delicious, but not so

[119] Note: in Scotland they called waitresses, "waitresses," not "servers." The Scots do not bother with so-called, "political correctness."

good I could ever scarf up two of them weighing more than five pounds.)

Yet this was not the end of the food saga on this tour. I became very picky and asked questions regularly after the "kipper" incident. When, one evening at dinner the menu proclaimed the restaurant had "trifles," I was nonplused. (This is another of those conditions putting my teeth on edge–I was uncertain whether or not I had ever been so much as "plused," even a little bit. But I was pretty sure, this time, I was "nonplused.")

I called the girl to our table and asked what a "trifle" was. She explained how they made the dessert and what it looked like. So, I tried it.

At our table that evening sat a Glasgow native and school teacher, Cynthia Ferguson, with her husband. When we were about to leave, she shyly said, "You know, your asking that question sounded odd to me. In Scotland, we teach our students never to ask questions like that, for fear they will look either ignorant or foolish."

A teacher myself, I gave her my standard classroom response, "We, in the United States, Cynthia, believe just the opposite–we believe everyone *should* ask questions, whenever they don't know an answer. That's one of the ways a person learns. We also believe the only stupid question is the one NOT asked."

All night long, Cynthia thought over my answer. The next morning at breakfast, she said, "I believe you're right, Rod. I've been teaching incorrectly for thirty years."

After Cynthia retired she told us, when we were again in Glasgow, "Things worked better in school after I changed my approach."

(*Was this*, I asked myself, *the attitude of the staid English system? If so, how did they go so far . . .?*) Cynthia truly shocked my belief in English-Scottish schools.

Yet no tale of European travel, largely by air, would be complete without a story about a narrow escape. (Flying *does*

have its terrors–even flying commercial–some real, some imagined, some supposed.)

While in Europe to get around intra-city and between countries, we used trains, buses, taxis, trams, car rentals, and airlines–German, English, French, Irish, Italian and American. Somehow our trip from New York, beginning our three-month-long trek, suffered a last-minute change. Instead of our scheduled US carrier, we flew to London in a BOAC (British Airways) 747.

Sitting in first class and talking with the flight attendants, I commented on how I was an Air Force pilot who flew combat missions from England during WWII. The attendant relayed the info to the captain. He came back and we sat together "telling war stories," (he had flown with the RAF), then he invited me to join him in the pilot's compartment.

Up there, he proudly explained all his latest equipment–some completely new to me. (The electronic GPS, for example, showed where they were at all times and–triangulating the signals of three satellites–assured an accuracy within three feet.) He also said this was his last flight. When we arrived at Heathrow he was to be forcibly retired because of his age.

He nodded toward the man flying as co-pilot and first officer. "Tomorrow, he will be taking my place." He waved his hand at the multiple arrays of complex instruments. "With all this he can safely make take-offs and landings, and fly from London to New York . . . and back."

He bent nearer and whispered, "I can take-off, fly and land this big bird *without any of that*–and I'll bet you can, too–but he can't. If his electronics fail, he's a dead duck." He squeezed my shoulder. "As a clue, starting tomorrow I am not going to fly BOAC, even as a passenger."

I thought about that long and hard. In recent years I have

flown[120] less and taken ships more. My last trips to Europe and back were on the Queen Mary II. I liked it. I enjoyed the leisurely adjustments to the time changes (one hour, each day, going both east and west), not fighting jet lag, and avoiding the virtual "strip-searching" air travel now entails.

With those and the captain's warning as incentives, I will be traveling more by sea and less by air from now on. (The more strict, recent "airport hassles" required by the terrorist protection requirements added a third and final argument on behalf everyone's driving and sailing.)

Oh, I'll fly . . . when I must. But it will never be like doing it in our own *"l'avion privé diplomatique."* (Private diplomatic aircraft.)

[120] If you are wondering where the narrow escapes were, there were two: (1) if we had flown on BOAC the next day, his co-pilot would have been sitting in the captain's seat (but we didn't), and, (2) the other narrow squeak really did occur on our return BOAC flight . . . when this same co-pilot was flying as captain. By his own words, the former captain would not have accompanied us on either flight.

317

CHAPTER TWENTY
▲

Following my military retirement, every one of the years I worked with Hobart as the KitchenAid National Service Manager presented new challenges and new awakenings. Having commanded a large recruiting unit with hundreds of men and dozens of offices in multiple States, and enduring two attaché assignments, each with more than twenty+ country responsibilities, my organizing and managing a national service network was a piece of cake.

As a national service organization, we dealt in only one currency. We worked in but one language. We wrote our own procedures and management guides. For the most part, we were our own authority. No longer did we answer to a list of touchy bosses from D.C., to Wiesbaden, to Fort Belvoir, to Florida, and elsewhere.

Despite all the benefits, my Regional Managers–first six, then ten–scattered across the USA, never ceased to amaze me. Brilliant men? Yes! But, sometimes, they acted stupidly*.

(*One of the rules of writing fiction, for example, is "making smart people do stupid things." Often, this is the basis of good fiction. Shakespeare frequently used this ploy too.)

One fall, my northeast manager invited me to his home just south of Boston, close to Cape Cod. This area and his distributors serviced some of the "biggies"–the Kennedys, Bushes, Biltmores, Astors, etc. He also had trained to be a private pilot and finished in August.

I congratulated him on receiving his "ticket," and he arranged

to fly me out to Martha's Vineyard one afternoon where he was to replace a restaurant's commercial disposer on the island. (This was really out of our bailiwick, but he had the request, the smarts, and the equipment, so away we went.)

Installing the two-horsepower unit proved to be more difficult than anticipated. We were unable to get away until early evening. He rented the plane only for the day, so we had to fly back and could not stay over.

Meanwhile, those little gremlins of mine lay in wait for us among the skies.

We took off from the island into the twilight, diminishing visibility, and an incoming scud layer. I elected to navigate, freeing him to handle the controls.

When we neared the coast we found the mainland (the southeastern tip of Massachusetts) completely obscured with low clouds. I leaned nearer. "Which approach will you use?"

He bestowed on me the familiar, vague stare I'd seen far too often in flying student's eyes who were at a loss. "Approach?"

"Yes," I told him. "This is no longer a VFR[121] flight, you are going to have to obtain a clearance and land under Instrument Flight Rules."

"I can't. I don't have an IFR license . . . I don't have the approach handbooks. There's no let down or equipment at the airport. I don't even know where the nearest radio stations are."

Making a quick examination of the map I was holding, I said, "Okay, I'll take over. But this will be illegal six ways to Sunday. I'll make a part VFR, part IFR approach and try to land . . . *once*. If I can't do it, we go back to the island, come hell or high water."

On our departure from the little field, I had seen no high buildings or hills, nor radio towers, in the airport's vicinity. With a great deal of luck, if we could sight-in one major landmark, and

[121] VFR = visual flight rules (flying where you can see the ground and the open air around you; IFR = instrument flight rules (flying on instruments where you can NOT see the ground or other aircraft flying in your vicinity).

319

calculate from there, we might be able to do it.

By the Grace of God–and I am giving full attribution to that sole source–we hugged the ground, staying in the clear, close above the lower cloud layer gradually thickening under us. When I was about to throw in the towel and return to Martha's Vineyard, I saw through one of the last remaining holes in the merging clouds, a road and a building I recognized on the map. I stood the plane on its left wing, assumed a southwesterly heading, and made a fast let-down through the clouds. We broke out beneath the now-virtually-complete overcast, the single, short runway a half mile in front us. Perfectly lined-up for a landing, I called the tower, lowered our gear, and slammed that little sucker onto the runway.

Bob, my manager, thought I had accomplished a minor miracle. I agreed, but kept my mouth shut. Wanting to impress on him this was a true fluke, I said, "I will never fly with you again, until you know what you're doing and have the gear to do it." I pounded my hand on the instrument panel for emphasis. "What we just did," I said, "was illegal and stupid." Later, I chewed on him again. "What would have happened if you tried a stunt like that while you were up there alone?"

(If you think about it, those were almost precisely the same conditions–flying into poor weather and uncertain visibility without the needed pilot qualifications–that killed John F. Kennedy's son . . . and in the same area.)

I wish I could say this was the sole instance in which ignorance got me into trouble. But I can not.

A couple years before, when I was on leave, my mother insisted Ilogene and I take her to Kentucky to see my distant cousin and his wife. An affluent dentist, my cousin bragged about owning his own airplane–a brand-new, single-engine, tricycle-geared, cabin plane capable of carrying five people. It was a real beauty, I will give him that.

He offered to take us for a ride. Again this was a small, single landing strip with no amenities, sitting isolated in a farmer's

wheat field. Its only distinguishing feature was a huge tree near the opposite end of the runway, about fifty feet to one side. I considered the tree a dangerous hazard to flying. My cousin (three times removed, and if he had not died soon after this flight, I would have been tempted to "remove" him further) said it was the only good landmark they had for locating the runway. (At the time I did not appreciate his perspective . . . an hour later I did.)

Before we got into the plane, while we pilots made the pre-flight inspection (Ilogene and Mom were already in the rear seat), my cousin made another generous offer, "You go ahead and fly. You'll like it."

Warning him I had never been in this type plane before, I took the controls and managed—with his help—to start the engine, check the instruments, and take-off. I then flew around the area, while we examined the sights.

Since this plane was new to me, I elected to try several stall series so I could check on landing speeds. (I warned everyone what I was doing for it can be quite scary–the plane seems to drop out from under you, and you fall rapidly until the pilot recovers.) Thank goodness I did the series, because, as we neared the area in which the field was supposedly located, the ground was dark and we saw nothing.

"How do you get them to turn on the runway lights," I asked.

"Huh? We don't have any."

"Well, how in heck do we find the field?"

"Remember . . . that big tree? The other pilots tell me they use landing lights."

I sat back and said, "Then, I guess you better take over. This is all too new to me –the plane, the field, the runway, and your checkpoints."

My cousin folded his arms. "Uh-huh . . . not me. I just bought this damned thing and I haven't even been up in it before."

It is obvious (since I am writing this) we DID manage to land that night, but it was one of my hairiest excursions. We turned on

our landing lights, searched the area at less than a two-hundred-foot altitude, dodging trees, windmills and barns, bats, owls and night birds as well, until we located that one special tree, and landed. Again I vowed no more flying with him. (But he had a massive heart attack soon thereafter–and died.[122])

That night, though, I could have choked him myself. Our little episode could easily have killed all of us, him, mother, Ilogene and me.

Mother had been biting her nails all through the landing approach. When I asked Ilogene if she were frightened. She smiled calmly and said, "Not a bit. You were flying."

(I could have used some of that confidence, myself. But these two incidents taught me NOT to rely on any civilian pilots' statements, real or implied. From then on, I checked each element myself.)

Another of my regional managers, this one in San Francisco, met me at the airport with his slim, platinum blonde, young wife wearing a silver lamé jump-suit, high heels, and nothing else. (It is obvious I never forgot it.) The "nothing else" was confirmed by the tightness of the suit. It looked sprayed-on. It was so tight there was no question regarding her sex. Her nipples protruded like two tiny fingers from the center of two well-enhanced breasts, and any more-than-half-blind observer could count her pubic hairs from twenty feet away. (Ah, but this was not all!)

Since this was our first meeting, she graciously insisted on cooking dinner at her house. When we arrived at their suburban

[122] My cousin's death was another of those odd stories. This overweight man loved his big thick steaks, his heavy sauces, his bourbon, and his big black cigars . . . and he had them every night. His doctor told him if he did not stop all those–and at once!– he would be dead in two weeks. He said, "To hell with it! Then I'll be dead." And he *was*–exactly two weeks to the day and hour from the time he got the doctor's warning.

cottage[123], she immediately excused herself, ostensibly to change into "something more comfortable." (I expected a skirt and blouse, or an apron and a pair of slacks–dress more appropriate for cooking and serving her husband's boss.)

Instead, the "something-more-comfortable" turned-out to be what I believe is called a "Teddy." In a few seconds, she came prancing out in a flimsy, see-through pair of almost-thong panties with an equally transparent lace over-shirt. Anything missed before was now completely visible.

But this was their home, so I gulped down my objection and kept my mouth shut. (And still this was not all!)

After dinner, in their livingroom, she told me how lonely it was when her husband went off working in the other states (he handled Washington State through southern California). She brought out a box, ten inches long and four inches square. Proudly, she displayed the battery-operated, large-sized dildo, lying inside and filling the box.

Smiling innocently(?), she exclaimed, "This keeps me happy when he's away."

I hurriedly grabbed my coat and had him take me to my motel. Unfortunately, this was not the last time I met this girl. (Yes, there is still more.)

The following year, Ilogene accompanied me when we took a special training course on small appliances around the country to each of my regional managers. Together, with them, we conducted a series of courses for our distributors. (We also brought the wives of the two men helping conduct the course, from our Greenville, Ohio factory.)

In Los Angeles, this same manager and his wife joined us from San Francisco. My wife told me that, from the second the girls met to have breakfast together, his wife shocked the wives from Ohio with her waywardness. Not only was she in garish make-up

[123] A tiny, two-bedroom–they had no children–tucked away among the hills, facing the Pacific Ocean.

so outlandish she appeared ready to walk the streets, but she wore the same silver-lamé jump-suit. If possible, it was tighter than before. (That was the beginning.)

When she whipped out a cigarette, ten men appeared eagerly out of nowhere to light it. She bestowed alluring smiles on them all and took the hand of the most handsome, pulled the flame to her cigarette-end and sucked in the smoke. Then, blowing it in the stuttering young man's face, told him in a sultry voice, "Honey, you can put your hot one against mine any time, and make me burn."

The young men followed her around like they were dogs and she was a bitch in heat. (Which may have been very close to the truth.)

Before leaving the restaurant, she confided to the girls, loud enough to be heard from the other side of the room, "Just wait until you see what happens tomorrow. I won't wear any panties. When I give em a 'shot of the old beaver,' they'll go ga-ga."

Ilogene told me the next morning the men were waiting in droves at the same restaurant. And the wife did exactly as promised. This manager's wife slid in and across the banquette, short skirt riding up to her hips, legs spread wide. The men fell over themselves bending down, dropping napkins and utensils, then flying forward with their tongues and lighters out.

Ilogene took this young lady(?) aside, later that morning. Once alone, she told her, "I know you have the wares to attract every man within smelling distance . . . but–please! –knock it off while we're out here. You already have these naive Ohio girls worrying about their husbands . . . and you're making us look like a covey of prostitutes."

The girl *did* modify her looks and deportment. (So a "word to the wise" was sufficient in this instance.) If it had not been, my west coast manager would have been looking for another job. (I originally wrote in that previous sentence, "Looking for work"–but I figured that was wrong. He already had his work cut

out for him, at home.)

Some of my men, envied her husband. I did not. Ilogene and I decided this woman really spelled, as they said in *The Music Man* . . . T-R-O-U-B-L-E!"

Another regional service manager embarrassed me in Athens, Georgia, when I flew down to spend a week with him. Ilogene and I had known his wife in Troy, Ohio—a retiring sort of mouse, but faithful and devoted. We were not, therefore, strangers.

He had the gall to show up and bring a woman along to stay with him in his motel room putting all her costs—as well as his—on our company's expense account. As if that were not bad enough, he wanted me to accept her as a guest at our dinner meetings, knowing I knew his wife.

This was too much. I demonstrated my "straight-arrow" prudishness when I fired him on the spot and denied his expense account for the trip. In addition, I called for an audit of all his previous expense accounts for the last year. The auditor, in due time, found he had been taking this woman with him, as his wife, doctoring his meals and room reports to cover for her.

When his wife called to find out why I fired her husband, I told her, "You will have to ask him. He knows." (This man also was a private pilot—and I began to wonder.) But I was not about to let him, or any of my people, involve me in a family dispute. (I counseled many couples, but stayed away from allowing them to squeeze me between them. When, as a supervisor, you let that happen—or you begin to agree with one against the other—you are worthless as a manager, a mentor, and a counselor.)

Occasionally, I flew to one of my regional manager meetings. And, once a year brought them all together in Troy. I tried to spend a week with each one in the field, twice a year.

I managed to accomplish this only after Al Batman (from my Fort Lamy, Chad, attaché office), joined me and shared the management load. I told Al, who had been a master sergeant—and I wrote it into his final effectiveness report earning him a

promotion–"I would be happy to place silver oak leaves on this man's collar, promote him to lieutenant colonel, and work side-by-side with him as an equal," he was that good.

From the beginning, I trained Al to be my replacement. I had my sights set on leaving Hobart, teaching again at the university, and writing books.

Al, however, refused the promotion. Yet, a few years later, he went with the KitchenAid name when Whirlpool bought it . . . and accepted the service manager's job there. Brain cancer took Al from us shortly after his early retirement. He married late in life, a girl we knew and loved, and became a father long after we thought there was no chance. His son, a replica of Al, shows Al lives on through him and his son's children.

But back to my regional managers: I do not want to leave the impression these men were "oddballs." They were not. They were, one and all, intelligent, hard-working, talented . . . and underpaid. I fought constantly to raise their salaries.

The northeast manager learned to be a good pilot. The west coast manager's wife calmed down (maybe he cooled her off). The Georgia/Florida man I replaced. Another slot I filled by hiring a second of my former master sergeants–Bill Bonaker. He had been an outstanding recruiting supervisor in Rockford, Illinois. But he required continuing "jacking up."

When I commanded the Chicago squadron, I called him in regularly from Rockford, some distance west of Chicago, to give him a good chewing. When I did, I told him, "I want to see you standing in front of my desk at 0700 hours tomorrow morning."

His half-growled, "Yes, sir . . ." assured me he would bust his buns to get there ahead of me. This became a game we played.

My headquarter's office normally did not open until 0800. But, the first time I ordered him in, he arrived at 0600.

I was sitting at my desk when he came through the door expecting me to come in later so he could smirk. His disappointed expression showed his surprise. (But he said nothing about it.)

The second time he arrived at 0500. Again he found me waiting. I heard his teeth grinding from across the room.

The third time, he flew through the door at 0300 hours. Once more I was waiting.

This time I had brewed coffee. We sat and drank it together, laughing about his driving so hard and so fast to get there ahead of me.

"Okay, Colonel, I give up." He grinned across his coffee mug. "Just how early do you get here when I'm coming in?"

I smiled. "I will always be here one hour before you . . . no matter what time you arrive." I tapped the side of my head. "I've the gift."

Actually, I knew this man so well it was easy to anticipate his every move. It kept him on his toes in Chicago and when we were at Hobart. (But the day I left Hobart he began slacking off. Though I told my replacement his weaknesses, he never learned how to handle Bill.)

Leaving Hobart, I did several years' of management consultancies, too, and once worked with a sorority wanting to go national. (Oh, yes, I did that in my spare time when I was not writing, singing or flying). At the sorority's convention, Ilogene and I again met Bill Bonaker's daughter, an officer in the organization. We had not seen her since Chicago.

This girl died abruptly–and quickly–a few months later with a rare type cancer. The following year, her father, my friend and employee, died with the same disease. (Neither his wife, nor son have had any similar problems.)

But that meant both my most trusted and loyal assistants had been taken by the same condition, and within a few years of each other. I began to wonder about our work and life styles.

Maybe it was best I left Hobart.

CHAPTER TWENTY-ONE

▲

Together, you and I have now come to the last chapter of this book, just as I am coming to the last chapter of my life. These are no longer my "twilight years," nor "early evening hours," nor even the "late evening period." I am past all that. Full darkness has crept in around me and I approach the midnight hour.

As for the "golden years," they were–and are–*all* golden. Every moment of every life. Every day. Every hour. Each should be cherished. No one can foretell tomorrow or how much time you have. One must make the most of each day.

Being realistic, I acknowledge I am no longer young or middle-aged–I am *old* (I do *not* believe in sugar-coating it). I am still short (an inch shorter for having had my knees replaced), and now I am also fat, wizened, wrinkled, liver-spotted, and white-haired (what's left). My eyesight is great, though. (When they replaced my lens because of cataracts, my vision jumped back to 20/20. With glasses correcting my astigmatism, I can read 20/15 in the distance, but need reading glasses for close work.) My knees are made of steel and plastic. My heart has three stints. My blood pressure, cholesterol and triglycerides require daily medication (one small tablet each). I easily become emotional. Where once I cried at bad commercials, now I cry at good ones, a favorite piece of music, a lovely sunset, a sky of azure blue, and a new baby. Their tiny fingers, toes and nails still amaze me–and some people say God does not still perform miracles! (*Hah!*)

During my life I have demonstrated repeated, multiple weaknesses and deficiencies. My feet are clay. I am egotistical,

chauvinistic, and inconsiderate. Of these I am not proud.

I tend to be single-minded, meaning that, when I begin a project, such as this autobiography, I thrust all else aside. Once I begin working, nothing matters but "the job."

While a work is in progress, I concentrate on it to the exclusion of all other tasks, requests and persons, as if they did not exist. I often do not eat or sleep. When I do sleep, I rise up at odd hours to type, hunch over a keyboard, squint at the little, teeny weeny letters . . . and miss commas and periods.

During the act of creation (writing), to an observer I seem deaf, dumb and blind until I finish. My wife used to say I went away to "Live in another world," one which she was not part of and could not penetrate. For that, too, I am sorry. (But, if I could do it over again . . . I'd . . . I'd . . . well, I'd probably do the same thing.)

On the good side, my "plumbing," my hearing and reflexes remain above-average. I am not, as yet, diabetic, and I still stand straight (fairly so). But others must attest to my idiosyncracies and mental status, vis-à-vis advanced senility or Alzhiemers.

Yet I consider myself "blessed" for I am largely without pain or restrictions. I can eat virtually anything I like, walk, climb stairs, and drive. I do not drool, except when confronted by extreme examples of youthful, nubile femininity.

I still adore and appreciate the loveliness of women and I am a true romantic. I dote on candles, flowers, poetry, perfumes and gifts, cards and celebrations. I try to be a gentleman, polite and gracious. (Admittedly, I do not always succeed . . . but I try!)

I still have a "sex drive," but age has stolen away the opportunities and capability, leaving only vain, unrequited desires. (Ah, youth, so wasted on the young!)

Knowing the time had to come inevitably, some time ago I made three major decisions. So far, I have held to them:

I vowed that—when I *should* no longer continue . . . (by my own reckoning, not at the whim of others) . . . I would stop singing, flying and driving. (George Bernard Shaw even went so far as to

decide when he would die . . . and did it.)

First, *I quit singing*–therefore, some fifteen years ago, when I began braying like José Carreras. (Tape recorders do not lie. Why do singers go on?)

Second, *I gave up flying*–when I needed a waiver for my commercial pilot's license because of mild, high blood pressure. (Maybe that was an excuse too. Though I flew jets using all the latest instruments, the world passed me by. Flying is a young man's game–like the military–and I was no longer young.)

Third, I WILL stop driving--the minute I sense, see or know I am no longer safe, for whatever reason. Oh, I miss a stop sign every now and then . . . but so do my children, twenty to thirty years younger. (But, for this "driving" decision, I may have to accede to the criticisms of others. This assessment is often too difficult for the involved individual to be completely objective. Similar to being insane, you are always the "last to know.")

Though I am not yet of an age where *all* my friends have preceded me in death, many have. Others will soon. And, more to the point, I know I am scheduled to do so in the near future.

Reading through these pages, however, I am astounded at how many, many times, circumstances forced me to open with, "For the first time," "In the beginning," etc. This did not mean no one else had ever done or saw what I was describing. These phrases signaled only this was the first time I (or we) had done this or that. So many adventures were new to Ilogene and me. So many places. So many people. So many vistas. Though they had been there for millions of years, and had been witnessed or done by millions before us, they were pristine as far as we were concerned. In thousands of ways, then, we found our lives a constant adventure into newness. So we went "boldly," as they say in Star Trek, yet NOT where others had never gone before, but where *WE had never gone before.* (But isn't that what life is all about–from birth, to and including death–seeing, feeling, tasting, smelling, hearing, each day, some new element of the universe? Isn't this is what

gives life its color and dimension, its flavor, its excitement, its "*reason d'etre*?" I still have it . . . and hope I will still have it when I breathe my last.)

Beginning last year, I again started off in a new direction–exploring my own personal philosophy about life. I am calling it, "What I believe." So far, it is more than seventy pages long, single-spaced . . . and I am still going full blast, astounded at what I find out about myself at every turn. Yet, very likely, it will remain unfinished when I shuffle off this mortal coil. (This type exploration is not a single afternoon's activity.)

The "belief" exploration I highly recommend (like all fanatics) to everyone–Jew, Christian, Moslem, agnostic, atheist . . . whatever. Forcing one's self to face your beliefs –what you *do* believe and what you *do not* believe, is a sobering experience–if you are honest and forthright. It requires your delving into the depths of your soul, sifting and weighing your most coveted perspectives. It forces you to examine closely, all the dark shelves and hidden pigeonholes of your psyche, pulling out everything you have kept undercover . . . even from your conscious awareness.

This shocks, surprises and disturbs. But also rejuvenates.

An in-depth exploration unveils hidden biases, prejudices and discriminatory viewpoints you did not even know you held. Knowing them, you can atone, apologize or excise. And knowing them, then taking corrective action, can provide new satisfactions and a greater confidence in the future.

Friends have asked me, "What do you 'know' about what happens after death and where you will go?"

I have consistently told them, "I 'know' nothing . . . but I 'believe' . . . in God, an afterlife, and humankind's ultimate value. I 'hope' I will be with my God, my wife, and my loved ones." This, to me, is about all any of us can say, ask, or hope for.

My wife believed that this life, here on earth–was *hell*! She had a list of well-thought-out reasons, too, for her evaluation. (Part

Shawnee Indian, she inherited from her ancestors some of their beliefs. Many believed, after this life, there is only the "Happy Hunting Grounds.")

So, perhaps, soon I will share with her an eternity in the "Happy Hunting Grounds." (I can imagine far worse places.)

I am an acknowledged sinner, yet I have only a few regrets. Looking back now, I see how helpless I was to either prevent or resolve, the major ones.

Taken chronologically–*not* in the descending order of their effect or depth of emotion–I regret, first, my always odd, love-hate relationship with my mother. I cannot say I hated her, but I *can* say I never really loved her. Only when I was older and Ilogene showed me what a true, selfless and unselfish, "giving" love really was, did I recognize I never had that from Mom. Oh, I suspected I didn't–seeing other parents' and children's interactions. Mom's life experiences skewed her emotions and I truly believe she loved only one person–herself. They caused her to be aloof. To me, she was always "just there," like a cold statue. Perhaps, she "tried," but I felt only "used," a "thing" . . . not her son.

Second, I regret my father's death, so early–at forty-one. He gave me the love I never received from Mom. From the moment he died, I resolved to discharge my obligations to Mom, but began subconsciously seeking a life and his missing love elsewhere. (Perhaps, this is the motivating factor for my abrupt interest in marrying?)

Third, I regret a number of less earth-shaking personal failures, for example, for having accomplished so little in life. I should have been more generous and more considerate. But I do *not* regret there will be no monuments to my achievements, no stone or metal plaques attesting to my service, no scrolls honoring my largess, my generosity, or even my few kindnesses. Those I consider–like acts of charity–to be solely between my God and me. I can only pray and hope (there's that word again), someone,

somewhere, has had a better life for what I did, said, gave, or wrote.

Like everyone else, there have been times I spoke when I should have listened; I sat when I should have stood, expressing my chagrin, my distaste and my disagreement; I did not volunteer when I should have, and, instead, let others take the lead, the burden, the "hits." I have hurt people, knowingly and unknowingly–for that I am truly sorry. I did not "chip-in" when I should–and could have–keeping my hands in my pockets.

I have hated, when I should have loved. I have struck out in anger, when I should have "turned the other cheek." I stood fast, when I should have "walked the extra mile." I moved to the other side of the road, avoiding responsibilities, when I should have stopped and helped like the "Good Samaritan."

The Holy Bible is a litany of all those things "I should have done." I can only confess and ask forgiveness . . . saying those positively worthless words, "I am only human." *(For that is no excuse.)* We *are* responsible–always. We are not expected–not really!–to be perfect, but we *are* expected to try, to strive, and to move toward perfection, and to accept responsibility for our actions while working constantly to do better. I have not always done those either.

My family (and I, particularly) used to kid my wife, saying she must believe I was personally responsible for everything *bad* that happened in this world. (I thought that was going a little too far, though . . . maybe "in the family," "locally" – or even "in Ohio." That I would have "bought"–but "everything in the world?" Huh-uh!)

We also claimed she must believe, "All the 'bad' things came about solely because *of something I did do, or I failed to do.*" (Who can resist an argument voiced in such specific terms?)

So far, I have been talking pretty much here about the "down side" and the "far side." What say, in conclusion, we turn it all around and extol the positives for a change?

I would like to end on this high note:

One of the facts life taught me has been the abiding value of *love*. (Dad, "Grandpa," Ilogene, her parents, and our children did this.) A few years ago I wrote a romance in which I included a sermon on love (a young female minister finally fell in love and was able to preach about it for the first time). Here is what I wrote for her sermon, and here is what I believe:

"Love is a continuing contrast.

"Love is difficult; love is easy.

"Love is understandable; love is incomprehensible.

"Love is hot; love is cold. Love is hard; love is tender.

"Love is demanding; love is giving. Love is glory and ecstacy; love is sacrifice, tears and sorrow. Love is tragedy and comedy.

"Yet, for all its costs . . . love's worth and value cannot be measured in earthly terms. Only God can judge, and only God can give, take away, provide, remove and exalt.

"Love is God's ultimate gift, and lesson, to humans.

"Love takes us as close to heaven as we can ever come in this world."

Fate, God, or whatever your belief system includes, has sprinkled our earth and our lives with a near-infinity of tools and provided a lush, fertile field of opportunities from which to fashion our dreams. People, with positive and "Can-Do" attitudes will succeed, overcoming unbelievable handicaps. Humans are tough. They can survive hardships and tortures–of the mind and body–far beyond the realms of their very worst imaginings . . . and still plow through them to be a better person.

As a final admonition, I urge everyone to face your fears, overcome deficiencies, accept personal responsibility for your actions and inactions, and GO OUT AND DO YOUR VERY BEST! I did . . . still do . . . and *will* continue to try . . . 'til the last toll of the bell.

ADDENDENA

▲

Friends and acquaintances have frequently asked, "Did you do anything on active duty you'd call out of the ordinaiy?"

Biting my tongue to prevent saying, "In wartime, what is NOT 'out of the ordinary?'" and "Hell, yes!" or "I like to fly, but who likes shooting and bombing people–and getting shot at, yourself? I don't!"

So, in answer to these questions, I developed the following descriptive responses.

#1–FLYING UNDER & "LOOPING-AROUND" BRIDGES.

In the nineteen-forties at least, cadets loved to perform "daredevil" feats. (Bill Prentiss said they also were popular way back before and during WWI, too–as shown in "The Blue Max.") This is what made novice pilots think they were such "hot rocks." But both tricks quickly became routine . . . as did "hedge-hopping" and "cattle- chasing."

Flying under bridges was "apple-pie-easy." Just line up with the bridge a mile or so up- or down-river, aim the plane's nose between the bridge's foundation columns, and fly low enough to miss the span above, and high enough to clear the water below. This was a snap. Child's play.

Ah, but "looping-around bridges" was another matter, entirely! Getting under the bridge in preparation for the loop required only doing what I described above, plus lots of airspeed. To get the "sight picture" scaring off those who refused . . . look up–right now–at the ceiling above your head.

If you will, imagine yourself, upside down, on your back, approaching the river, bridge and ground. You have just completed most of the loop. At this point, you are seeing the bridge and river *above your viewpoint* (as you now see the ceiling). For the moment, your motions seem reserved. Yet you MUST still *pull back* your control column . . . far enough to keep you out of the river . . . but *push it forward* far enough to avoid hitting the unforgiving steel-and-concrete structure you hope to fly under. (Doing this gets easier as you come out of the loop and things fall into their more-natural positions . . . the river below and the bridge above.) You finally whiz through between the critical limits, breathing a sigh of relief, but still scared, asking yourself, "Whew! Did I just do that?"

#2 – FLYING UNDER THE EIFFEL TOWER.

I refuse to verify I did this. A retiree is still subject to military court-martial. So, let us say, *if I were to have done it,* oh, say, sometime in early June, 1945, here is the way I would have gone about it, some of the factors involved, and the anticipated results.)

First, as they say on television, "Do not try this at home." For one, it would be impossible–you can *not* have a full-sized, "Eiffel Tower" in your backyard.

For another, if you go to Paris today, you will find it equally impossible. Trees, brush, monuments and a park now block an approach to the tower from the land-side. On the curbside, a tour-bus stop at the sidewalk is usually filled with a long line of tall, diesel-exhausting monsters. (This is on the opposite, "street and river" side, and also prevents exiting there.) All those items, plus the kiosks, people and "stuff" under the lowest arch were not there in 1945.)

Also, to attempt this feat, it could *not* be a "spur-of-the-moment" decision. This forbidden act required detailed prior preparation and organized assistance from a number of others.

Setting a date and time were easy. With most Catholic Parisians

336

attending Mass at 1000 hours, each Sunday morning, that was
when the fewest people would be around. This resolved that
option. (Even then, some people had to be on hand, under the
tower, to shoo-away those who were there.)

Detailed calculations next demanded careful scrutiny. Every
library contained pictures and engineering manuals providing the
exact dimensions needed–the height, width and curvature of the
lowest arch. One also needed to know the A-26's precise profile
height while in level flight, from the lowest sweep of the
propellers to the top of the vertical stabilizer, and its breadth, from
wing tip to wing tip. With these in hand it was then possible to
determine if an A-26 could make the transit–get down quickly
enough on the approach to fly through the arch, then fly through
(without hitting the top of the arch with the tail, missing the sides
with the wingtips, and still remain high enough to avoid the
propellers' digging into the turf). Following the penetration, could
a pilot then climb fast enough to pass over the bridge lights and
either between or above the two buildings of the Museum of Man
across the river? (A few minor factors also entered in here, too:
Would this require a quarter flaps, full flaps, or no flaps?
Carburetor mixture rich/lean? Airspeed fast/slow? What are the
optimum prop rpms and engine pressures? What changes in
aircraft flying characteristics occur with each option?) Here is
where a project like this begins assuming prodigious proportions.

All objective questions answered, two subjective items
remained: Would the crew go along with such a scheme? (and)
What might be expected if the try were successful? (If it were *not*
successful the crew had no worries, they would be dead!) The
crewmen would be putting their lives on the line . . . and the pilot,
if he lived, most certainly would be chastised, face a court-
martial, and a possible fine, with his rank reduced.

Would, one day, an eager, confident crew elect to take such a
chance? Yes! A pilot, rather errant and about to leave the service,
for example might. Some idiot willing to take the risks.

[Extended and repetitious rehearsals, previously flying under bridges and looping through them, might prove to be excellent preparation.]

Interestingly enough, all this actually happened in June 1945. The pilot, as they approached Paris, gave his crew a last-minute opportunity to call it off.

Everyone shouted, "Go for it!"

The A-26 descended, heading under the tower arch from the land side. At that time, the approach path was bare of trees, a flat area the Germans had used for parades. The pilot made the penetration without a hitch. Afterward, climbing out over the Seine River, rejoicing in success, the crew looked back, smirking in triumph.

What they saw wiped away the grins.

Behind them a P-47 fighter had flown through the tower's *second tier* only milliseconds behind them. And his passage sucked out the napkins and tablecloths from the restaurant, then at that level. The fluttering shower of white made a noteworthy, colorful display, focused everyone's attention on the fighter.

The P-47 pilot *was* court-martialed. He also created such a spectacle no one reported the A-26 (until much later, when it showed up in the Air Force's archives). The A-26 pilot and crew did not receive so much as an oral reprimand.

#3– LANDING WHERE ONE COULD NOT TAKE-OFF AGAIN.

These were oft-repeated dilemmas to which I willingly admit.

While I was a general's aide, one of our Twelfth Air Force pilots landed an A-26 (Douglas Invader) in a farmer's small field near Tuscaloosa, Alabama. It sat there for days. The pilot refused even trying a take-off.

At General Snavely's request (he thought I could do everything!), a friend flew me up there from Orlando and I looked over the situation. I decided I would try it. I drained all but a few

gallons from the tanks (leaving just enough to get me to the nearest airport for refueling). Common sense also dictated my removing everything else I could–those items I sent back to our base by truck.

With help, we backed the plane till its tail protruded across the fence at the end of the longest field dimension. I climbed in, alone, and using Doolittle's method for taking his B-25s off the carrier . . . revved the engines until the plane shook, released the brakes . . . and went safely across the fence at the other end, wheels just entering the nacelles. (No sweat! I had more than six inches to spare!)

General Snavely forced me to do this again, a month later, when he insisted I fly him into a wee-little New Orleans airport on the south side of Lake Pontchartrain, surrounded by a six-foot dike. This time I crossed the dike's concrete wall, when leaving, with slightly less clearance. Even the general was white-knuckled. He never asked me to land anywhere else I did not recommend. (The New Orleans tower issued a special bulletin the same day, forbidding any but small planes from landing there, henceforth.)

In Africa, one of my ambassadors wanted to visit a city deep in the Sahara with no nearby airfield, with not even a smooth strip of sand close by.

Each time I was assigned as a Defense Attaché I dealt with at least ten ambassadors. Each presented some kind of problem. This man had a bad back and did not feel he could sustain a fifty-mile trek across the rough bad lands in a truck (the only other transport available).

I scoured the charts and located a long-unused WWII reconnaissance strip, barely 600 feet long, marked out on a lava bed and used solely by small aircraft. It showed on the map, sitting at the very edge of the fortress-type city!

No one thought we could land there.

I practiced three, short-field landings and take-offs at Fort Lamy, then said, "Let's go!" The others drove. With only the

ambassador and my crew, we flew down and landed on that tiny airstrip–after we found it. By this time the wind was kicking up sand and the faded yellow markers were virtually invisible. Astounding even me, I made the best, three-point landing I ever made. When we checked the runway (the lava-based field stood about five feet above the surrounding area), we found the tail wheel had touched down *one inch* before the yellow boundary strip and we had stopped before reaching the halfway "circle." (Landing in fewer than 300 feet.) The thirty-five-mile headwind and a landing speed of seventy-five helped.

When we left the next day, the winds still blew. I put the entire embassy contingent on board and flew home, getting off again before the midpoint.

Lest you think this is bragging, let me assure you it is *not*. Attachés in remote locations were called upon constantly to do far more difficult tasks. These were mere every-day requests.

Remember, back in WWII, when I left three B-26s (Martin Marauders) in the center of Brussels? That field proved to be too small for any take-off. Not much longer than the one on the lava bed, the tall buildings of Brussels formed an unscalable boundary on all four sides.

During both WWII and the Korean "Police Action," my crew and I returned regularly with shot-up hydraulic systems requiring crash landings on the runway. One might even lump my single-engine-on-take-off episode in this category.

Another time, returning from a seven-and-a-half-hour flight, on one of my last weather "recon" missions in Korea, I arrived over Kimpo (our Air Base, a few miles northwest of Seoul), tired, short on fuel, with my right engine showing a hydraulic leak. (We had sustained several "hits" as we passed over a North Korean Army location en route in from the Yellow Sea.) But we were unable to land right away, so I adjusted the engines for maximum endurance and hung in there, chomping at the bit.

We shared Kimpo with the 4th Fighter Wing, Korea's most

famous American fighter group, commanded by Colonel Gabreski. His new operations officer, after many calculations, had sent off the entire fighter wing in different directions that morning, planning to bring them back at exactly the same time! (Not the most brilliant decision.) Now, they (all of them) . . . and I . . . had arrived.

When I called-in for landing instructions, I heard a returning fighter pilot scream for permission to make an immediate emergency landing. The tower calmly told him, "Air Force 1289, you're number ten in the flame-out pattern."

Finally, the fighters all landed. Their planes lay scattered about the field like my lead soldiers when I was a kid, on every taxiway, parking strip, and grass verge.

When I started my approach, I saw my right gear dangling loosely under the engine nacelle and knew it would fold on landing. Alerting the tower to "another" problem, I landed, touching down as if I had a gross of eggs in my lap.

I held up the nose wheel as long as possible, and prepared to use the compressed air braking system, certain the wheel would collapse. But, before I jerked the air lever, I killed and feathered the engines. Using the starting switches, I aligned the propellers with a "Vee" at the bottom, so, when we fell to the runway, we would hurt the engines least.

Finally, I pulled the lever and—as anticipated—the gear collapsed. By then we had slowed so much the plane made but a 30-degree turn to the right and knelt gently onto the runway. Neither engine required replacement. The plane was in the air the next day.

I did not know it at the time, but the Base Photographer "caught" the whole scene on motion-picture film—the approach, landing and stop. At the subsequent enquiry and hearing, the safety board found not a pilot error. (This is a worry every pilot sustains: being adjudged "pilot error" for an accident. Luckily, I never earned a point.)

#4–WHAT WAS A TYPICAL MISSION LIKE?

Movies and TV programs have sketched-in what happened during WWII Air Corps combat missions ("Ten O'Clock High" and "Command Decision" come to mind), but many interesting (and maybe to some, boring) aspects have been ignored, overlooked or deliberately skipped. (In Europe, a medium bomber pilot's "full tour" consisted of fifty missions; the same for Korea, so I had plenty of experience.)

One evening, when I was telling a "war story," a group of friends requested more information, professing, "We never heard *that* before." During the same evening, a member of the group wanted to know the details of missions and formation flying.

> Providing more information than you ever wanted to know on the subject, here is a not-so-quick "run-down," of a typical WWII sortie. (If this does *not* interest you, go on to the next entry.) But, if you are interested, I will try to "put you there," showing the sights, sounds, smells, tastes and feel of a mission, with its emotional trauma and internal thoughts.

So here's the nitty-gritty:

A normal combat mission began hours before our squadrons aroused us pilots and crew members for briefings. Visualize, then, our Group headquarters, in an old French farmhouse on the north side of our airfield. The time–near midnight. The house, chilly, as the wood and stone walls were uninsulated. The fires were banked.

Inside, near the phones and Telex, the staff duty officer sat alone in the creaking building, mice rustling in the walls, the air smelling of cigarette smoke and garlic from dinner. In an uncomfortable chair by a desk, chosen solely so he would not fall asleep, one lamp burning, he read a lurid French novel forbidden in the States.

Yet he was alert, one ear cocked for the telex to begin

chattering. If 9th Air Force were to send "Operational Orders," it had to be within the next few minutes or the Group would not fly a mission the next day. *It was time!*

The telex whirred. The "mission order" spewed from the unit (in our case, relayed from Operations Planning, 9th Air Force, Major General Hoyt S. Vandenberg commanding). Seldom did the order offer more than bare bones: The day's target, the bomb load (100- to 1000-pounders, explosive- or incendiary-types, designed to destroy personnel, bridges, buildings or large structures), and a prime directive–the mission was to be either "Maximum Effort" or a lesser number of planes would be demanded from the Group.

The staff duty officer at once called the 391st Group Operations staff. (He would call the Group Commander later. Navigators and bombardiers came staggering in, eyes grainy from lack of sleep, clothes grubby from no dry-cleaning, grabbed up coffee mugs and lit their first cigarettes. The colonel awakened, slipped in, and lighted up. His arrival added the aroma of a good, Havana cigar.

Together, they read the "Ops Order." Discussing it briefly, they went to the huge wall chart and began planning the details. The room quieted as pens scratched, scissors snipped, airmen typed, and officers scribbled.

Each staff member had his own special task: one laid out the routes, in and out, based on the latest Intelligence reports telling which German fighter fields and flak emplacements to avoid. Another calculated fuel loads and the fighter escort needed (if available). The latter required instant coordination with Fighter Command. (A short, terse telephone call.)

Operations determined the time of take–off and worked backward, preparing the list of all the other, pertinent times (for awakening crews, briefings, breakfast and take-off). They selected the specific crews (who was best at this type target) and the planes (from those "in-commission" and "air worthy"), designed each ship's arrangement in the Group's formation, and the order in which they were to take-off. (This was not as simple as it sounds.)

Meanwhile, the pace increased as did the staff's coffee consumption, smoke, and nervous sweat. The stench worsened as the minutes passed.

Inasmuch as each plane sat alone on its own separate "hardstand," in isolated locations scattered around the field's single runway, an Ops Officer had to chart their intricate assembly procedure–and the field boasted only one encircling taxiway. [To avoid traffic jams, each ship had to be aligned behind its primary squadron or flight leaders (those carrying Norden bombsights, and the principal squadron and flight bombardiers/navigators), for all planes did not have either.] The "back-up leaders," loaded with the same components, must also "fall-in" at the right place.

The resulting, written instructions looked a lot like those Japanese booklets for assembling complicated toys–put "A" into "B," stick in "F," screw "F" into "X," "Y," and "Z," joining "C," "D" and "E," etc.) Pilots puzzled over them for minutes, and usually ended-up merely watching, then trundling their planes out and falling in behind the preceding aircraft in the chart.

The flights, squadrons and entire group had to fit together like clockwork. Not a piece must be out of place or fail to perform its function. ("Ops" novices sweat some more.)

The end result put all the Group's participating aircraft in the air, quickly, forming a "flight" pattern like this (from above):

▲ (Group, squadron, or flight leader)
▲ ▲ (Wing-men/no bomb sights)
▲ (Backup leader/"slot" position)
▲ ▲ (Wing-men *on* second leader)

(The above drawing fails to show the third dimension. In this flight configuration–when flying Marauders–the wing-men flew slightly "above" the level of the leader. In Invaders, they flew slightly "below." Cockpits, seats, windshields and a pilot's visibility, made these differences a requirement. Nor does the above drawing demonstrate the true, "bomb run" closeness of this

set-up. To show this accurately would require drawing in an overlap of the wing-men's wing tips, over or below the leader's fuselage, also showing them flying farther forward, nearer the leader's wings. In addition the "slot man's" nose would be (*for both B-26s and A-26s*) UNDER the leader's tail. *In all instances,* the second group of three of the six (as shown above) flew below the level of the first six's "slot man."

A horizontal view of the above configuration–from behind– would have shown the "flight" (the name of such a grouping of six) like this:

▲▲▲ (For A-26s, "stepped down")

 (Leaders higher than wing-men)

▲ ▲ (For B-26s, "stepped up.")
 ▲

 (Leaders lower than wing-men)

Multiply by four the above picture of six (called a "flight"), and put each of the "flights" in the same double-triangle arrangement, as shown above for the single planes, and you have a "squadron." (See below)

▲
▲ ▲
▲

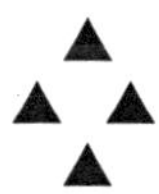

Put four of the above "squadrons" into the same diamond pattern and you have a "Group."

This is the pattern Groups produced during "join-up," and held throughout entries and exits from enemy territory for maximum protection from the Group's cross-firing machine guns. The Group held this position even on bombing runs when attacking large targets. For bridges and small targets, the Group broke itself down into smaller units (sometimes no more than a "flight" or a single aircraft) and each squadron flew in tandem, reforming as above after releasing their bombs.

A "Maximum Effort" mission demanded the Group put every

available plane and crew into the air–usually no more than forty-eight to fifty-two. Sometimes a Group looked pretty "rag-tag," missing a plane here and one there from each "Flight." Occasionally, when a previous day's mission resulted in heavy losses, headquarters assigned the Group to either "fill-out" another Group's ranks, or told the Group to "stand-down" (no mission until it again built up its strength.) On rare occasions, as during the Battle of the Bulge, the Group flew day and night, regardless, with single planes following single planes, hitting targets of opportunity. "Ending the war" fast and with the smallest number of casualties was the "name of the game"–always!

Minor determinations, such as the times to awaken the "troops," pick them up for transporting to the briefing hall, conduct the mission briefing, begin pre-flight breakfast, and haul them to their planes, also included the times for engine-start up and take-off. Headquarters designated some ships and crews to act as spares (if the number available and "on-hand" permitted). These crews and aircraft took the place of those whose engines or systems failed.

But back to "the mission profile":

Most often, the crew briefing came at 0400 hours, breakfast at 0500, and take-off at 0600 hours. A hot meal consisted of powdered eggs, greasy bacon, cold, hard toast, a shot of "battery acid" (grapefruit juice) . . . and coffee–whole bunches of coffee. We needed the caffeine to wake us up and keep us awake. (The coffee always hit my bladder just before the "IP.")

Crew briefings began with a quick, pithy "Go! Go! Go!" spiel by Colonel Gerald (Jerry) Williams, Group Commander. The Operations officers followed.

A sergeant first closed the window shades. The room hushed.

"Ops" began by dramatically pulling back the curtain covering the huge, wall-mounted, detailed chart showing England, Belgium, Holland, France and Germany (as far east as Berlin . . . at that time far beyond our flight capability). Stretching from the

left wall to the right wall, and floor to ceiling in bright multi-colors, the map, each time, revealed a new set of white, air-route lines overlaying the basic pattern of cities, railroads, roads and battle fields (friendly and enemy).

The audience gasped on seeing the target.

The route-in also inspired moans. (A few enemy targets had earned "deaths' heads" as potential killers. Even a few enemy fighter bases and anti-aircraft emplacements were also on the "Oh, God, No!" list.)

The "Ops" Officer always tapped a long pointer against the target and opened his part of the briefing with the fateful words, "Today . . . (brief "pregnant" pause) we are bombing . . . (*name* of target city, railroad yards, petroleum plant or storage areas, etc.)"

Here is where men began clearing their throats, hanging their heads, swallowing hard, and panting. Some mumbled prayers. A few began visibly shaking.

Sketching in the route, the Intelligence Officer told the airmen what to avoid and what his reports anticipated they might expect in fighter and flak opposition. He reiterated the basic written data everyone now held in their hands (called "flimsies," issued on entering the briefing hall), and pointed out the auxiliary fields where we might land for any of a number of reasons—usually weather-, injury- or damage-related. (At this point I always thought about the tiny field in the center of Brussels and wondered how the British colonel was doing nursing my three stranded B-26s.) By now the room, despite its size, was stifling from body heat, odor and developing fear.

The movies may portray all aircrews as stalwart he-men who never trembled, perspired, or had their mouths go dry and stomachs ache . . . *don't believe it!* It was not unusual for the rank scent of feces to permeate the room when a scared airman's bowels "let loose."

"Ops" returned to the platform. Now he gave us the calculated

length of the mission from take-off to landing, our fuel and bomb loads, any special "join-up" instructions, today's codes and designators for aircraft and squadrons, and the meaning and use of visual signals (flare colors). These were always the same: One yellow for "start engines"; one green for "begin taxiing (in the assigned order)"; two green for "start take-off"; three red to "abort the mission"–at any stage. One red on return from a plane, meant "wounded on board" and two reds proclaimed a "dire emergency"–such as "I need to land immediately." This latter signal was normally used *only* when a single remaining pilot was barely conscious and fading fast.

When an aircraft was failing and not the pilot, the signal was a red, a yellow, and another red. These last two conditions were also the only "authorized" reasons for breaking radio silence, although many did for minor potentially hazardous situations (as I did when I warned Colonel Williams about his gas shortage).

Following the Ops briefing, the Group weather man gave us his forecast. This included weather expected at base on take-off, on our return, and along the route.

This always brought a chorus of hee-haws from the by-now-really-stewing aircrews. (I believe a gambler at roulette stood a better chance predicting winning numbers than weathermen scored on the weather.) Most of the time, pilots, trained in meteorology, made guesses as accurate. (In Korea, I served as a meteorologist, flying "weather recon.")

I recall only two outstanding successes: the weather for D-Day and the beginning of the major snowfall ushering in the German's attack at the Battle of the Bulge.

Finally, a master sergeant "hacked" the time. We all set our watches . . . to the second!

The chaplain gave us his blessing and everyone returned to their trucks and mess halls for breakfast. (Between breakfast and assembly at the planes, the chaplains provided individual blessings and, sometimes, confession opportunities.)

After eating and prior to our conducting the pre-flight inspection of our aircraft, we dressed for the flight while reviewing every detail on the chart showing where we were to fly in the "grand scheme of things" that morning.

At the plane, the pilots shared the "pre-flight" with the engineer. This was NOT a mere tire-kicking exercise. Together we examined all the guns to see if they were installed properly and the ammunition racks were full. We made certain each fuel tank was filled to the brim and there were no leaks, (oil, gas or hydraulic fluid). All bombs had been loaded and secured. The bomb bay opened and closed. Wheels, flaps, wings, tail and tires appeared okay. The windshield sparkled–clean and clear. All repairs, previously written-up, had been completed and were acceptable. In this, pilots cross-checked the engineers; they, in turn, cross-checked the pilots.

No one smoked around the refueled aircraft. Conversation was sparse, confined to, "Does that tire look okay to you" as one bent to examine a suspicious tread. Or, "I see the new guns are in the rear turret. Have you tried them?"

An answering grunt, growl or brief "Yeah" or "Nah" often was enough. Few officers took offense at the absence of military protocol–these were members of "our" crew, about to share a life or death experience with us, such petty things were ignored and unimportant now.

Nothing–and I mean *N-O-T-H-I-N-G!*-was left to chance and no one was careless, haphazard, or lackadaisical. This plane was our lifeline, our way "home." Every one of us wanted to add the greatest possible assurance to that hope and prayer. (For some, however, this was not enough. A few usually did *not* make it back. These were our friends, our buddies, our roommates. Not a one will be forgotten as long as those of us who shared their valley of woes, still live.)

Crews carefully watched the clock. Five minutes prior to the time scheduled for starting engines, they climbed into the ships

and "buttoned up." (Closed hatches, fastened seat belts, arranged paperwork, charts, etc.)

The yellow flare shot high over the field.

From all sides, engines roared in unison, exhausts blatted, fire shot out of the nacelles . . . and the Group, in one moment, ceased to be an inert mound of steel, flesh and aluminum, and merged into one giant, living entity about to "go in harms way" with deadly intent.

On the green flare, lead planes taxied from their hardstands. Wing-men followed, one behind the other, lumbering along the taxiway like elephants in a parade. The gasoline exhausts grew suffocating. Excitement suppressed all noxious sights, sounds and smells.

Some crewmen might have been thinking, "Will I come back?" or "I can get killed doing this!" But most pilots were too busy scrambling into position, checking gauges, switches and instruments to worry. (For most of us, worry came later, with the flak and fighters. Others never worried, assured by their religious beliefs or–erroneously–like all over-confident young men, certain they would "live forever."

I was amazed during my first few missions at how well everything worked. Only one plane out of our Group's forty-two took off too late, but it managed to squeeze into formation in its correct spot during the squadron's first swing around the field.

The flight east was one long climb, dodging shells and enemy ships. Now soaking wet under our heavy clothing, regardless of the cold, we edged nearer and nearer, approaching the "IP." (See next entry for "formation flying" and the "Preface" for the flak[124],

[124] "Flak," the visible, bursting shells fired by ground-based anti-aircraft batteries came usually from 88 millimeter guns. A battery consisted of four guns arranged in a circle around a central tracking and firing unit. This central unit tracked the planes, set a shell's bursting altitude in terms of time and distance, followed the aircraft's path, constantly transiting the four guns to bear on the central unit's computations, and initiated the firing signals. The guns fired at 1-second intervals, not simultaneously. This spread the pattern and increased the possibility of hits. The shell bursts exploding below an aircraft were more dangerous than those above, as the pattern of each shell explosion was more mushroom-shaped than globular. At a

fighter, rocket ship hazards.)

From the "IP" to the target we usually crowded together as close as possible without hitting each other. (Some exceptions: when bombing large, broad-scale petroleum installations, railroad yards, personnel encampments, or munitions factories we often used "scatter-bomb" techniques to assure, instead, maximum coverage and blowing up as much/many as possible.)

The shout on the interphone of "Bombs away!"[125] and we made an immediate turn (left or right), usually dropping a thousand feet or more, at the leader's whim, and headed for "home." (The immediate turn put our leaders' on-board cameras in the proper position to best record the "strike"–hit or miss. This proof determined some group's next mission, maybe ours.)

Still, we were not "out of the woods." The Group suffered the same hazards exiting enemy territory as entering. Those planes barely limping to the target and through the "bomb drop," began falling behind, and/or crashing far below. With luck the crews made it to a friendly field. Some landed in the "no-man's-land" between enemy and friendly lines. Some parachuted behind enemy lines. (Many of these airmen were killed by irate townsmen or the military. Some managed to hide and sneak back

distance of five hundred feet or more, explosions appeared as mere puffs of black smoke. Closer, they showed a bright red core. Within fifty feet the resulting shrapnel rattled the fuselage; aircrews heard the "crack" and "bang." (Explosion and force wave.) Nearer, the shrapnel penetrated the thin aluminum skin of the wings and fuselages, leaving holes, spilling fuel, and injuring crewmen. Closer bursts also penetrated engines and bodies, killing and maiming. and disabling aircraft, Explosions sustained *inside* an aircraft's compartments, engines or bomb-bay usually destroyed the aircraft instantly. "Flak" was never taken lightly – really – though airmen scoffed at poor and distant shots (like "whistling in the dark,"). More B-26s and A-26s went down from "flak" then fighters or rocket planes, yet most aircrewmen appeared, from their discussions and critical assessments, to fear them more.

[125] The bomb release signals varied. Some leaders instructed the flights and squadron to "drop," on seeing their bombs fall; some triggered two clicks on the radio microphone; some flicked-on red lights installed on the fuselage or tail, just as the bombs released. All intentions were aimed at a "drop" in unison, for a single flight, when flying in tandem. For large, broad-scale area bombing, "dropping in unison" meant the entire group released their bomb loads as close to the leader's release as possible.

to our lines. More ended up in Stalags–aircrew prison camps. A few died, shot while descending in their parachutes, or from the fall.)

Reaching our home base, the commander gave priority to the red and red-yellow-red flares, and the radio alerts. One by one the planes landed.

Here again all did not usually go well.

Hydraulic, brake and electric lines failed. Gears collapsed. Injured pilots and planes lost control, running off to the runway's sides and off the end, or spun in uncontrollable circles. Ambulances raced up and down gathering the "fallen."

Undamaged aircraft and crews returned to their hardstands where trucks picked up survivors and sped them to a debriefing by the "Intelligence" staff. Here, too, the Flight Surgeon poured the liquor shots designed to relax frayed nerves and restore circulation.

After that it was back to the mess hall for more coffee, a meal, and to unwind further. Here, crewmen refought and reflew the mission with loud, raucous descriptions and hand gestures. Here, too, the Group and Squadron commanders did their congratulating and reporting on the "strike."

The men eventually ran down quickly and ran out of anything to say. Tired, they quieted, grew sullen and morose, then traipsed away to their cots. This is the time hidden problems manifested themselves.

Following one particular grueling sortie, three of us pilots were trudging tiredly toward our quarters in the former hospital. At the first turn in the road, two of us trailed along the rutted, curving tracks. The third pilot continued walking straight on, into the snow, fell on his face, and kept on making walking motions with his hands and feet. We quickly pulled him onto his back . . . his eyes were blank. He never recovered. The Flight Surgeon shipped him home, literally a vegetable.

He was not alone. Everyone worried this might happen to him

too, but no one knew how to prevent it.

Seldom did any of us stay up late, over-drink, or hold lengthy gab fests. Most of us were too tired, too disgruntled, or fretting too much inside. We "hit the rack" early and slept hard. For, tomorrow morning was another day . . . and, perhaps, another mission. (The determination to lay aside worries did not always work–the dreams and nightmares often took over when the mind should be at rest.)

#5– HOW DID WE FORM UP & FLY SO CLOSE?

Since we had our little chart showing where we belonged–who our leader was, who preceded and who followed us on take-off, who flew to the leader's right and left when in flight, we had some flexibility, even if we goofed.

We took off in twenty-second intervals. Then chased our preceding aircraft until we caught it.

Each engineer sat on the floor behind and between the two pilots–*in the Martin Marauder, B-26.* If we were *not off the ground and flying 35 seconds* after we went to full throttle, he levered up the gear and we skidded off the end of the runway. Neither we, nor the plane, went on the mission. (The plane and crew might both require complete replacement–dead, injured or destroyed.)

Assuming we got off the ground okay, we pulled up the gear, and eased up the flaps, climbing toward our already-turning predecessor. We flew largely at full throttle until we caught up with him (just ahead of us).

We managed this by "cutting inside" his sweeping left turn, which he began thirty seconds after take-off. The leader reduced his airspeed to minimum cruising, to give us a chance to catch up and conserve fuel. All of us had to use a minimum amount of fuel and time assembling the group; we had neither to waste.

When we caught up, a matter of a few minutes, we eased into formation, either staying where we were (on his left), or slid under

and took up our assigned position (on his right). We stayed close (about ten feet away, during this phase) and slowed to match his speed.

[In jets this was tricky, they are so streamlined and their engines so aerodynamic, they seem to take forever to slow down—one reason it was necessary to remain alert and anticipate each of the leader's moves. In jets, dropping a little dive flaps helped. On prop-driven planes, a pilot merely jerked back his throttles and his plane slowed immediately. A-26s, however, were almost as sleek as jets.]

During this massive join-up, the group usually had to make two turns over the field to gather its "flock" (the fewer the planes, of course, the fewer the turns and shorter the time).

Pilots used this time to adjust to the leader's flying, set throttles and air speed, get a feel for the turbulence, and relax a bit. Gunners tested their guns and bomb-bay doors. If guns refused to fire, turrets refused to move, or the bomb bay doors did not open and close, the aircraft returned to base and a replacement took its place.

Normally, no one flew really close formation until we crossed enemy lines, then we did it for mutual protection. Crossing enemy lines we moved into what I called our "secondary flight profile"–this was closer, but not too-close, maintaining a distance of about four feet from the leader.

What was the closest we flew in formation? Soon after I joined the Group I found out that, whenever the Commander (Colonel Williams) scheduled himself to fly a mission, my crew would be on his right wing. (He told me he liked our exceptionally tight formation, as it guaranteed the best possible chance to take-out a target with a single sortie. I called that our "third formation profile!")

One morning, during our return flight, flying B-26's ("stepped up"), I was near enough to look down into the colonel's cockpit and read his instruments. I broke radio silence to warn him he had

to switch tanks, at once, or his right engine would quit. He did, and waved his thanks. Neither he nor his co-pilot had noticed the lapse. Now *that* was close flying. Though I cannot speak for all pilots, flights or squadrons, I doubt if many other Groups flew in such a configuration, except perhaps on the "bomb run."

Formation flying like this, however, was extremely tiring. A number of pilots did not do it well. A wing-man must, subconsciously, develop a "sight picture" of his leader's aircraft and know in an instant when he is sliding "out"—or "in"—when he is creeping higher or lower relative to the leader's plane, and when he is pulling ahead or falling behind. Keep in mind, formation flying is always a highly draining, three-dimensional activity. I always thought it four-dimensional as "time," also played a major role. (See the next paragraphs.)

The most minute movement of any control surface, such as a rudder or aileron, slowed the aircraft and had to be balanced by a touch of throttles. This made for white-knuckle flight. Hands grew numb. Backs ached. Feet and legs trembled. Eyes teared (especially at high altitudes where the temperatures reached fifty to sixty degrees below zero.) There was no heating in combat aircraft in WWI or WWII. Aircrews wore heavy gloves, fleece-lined boots and trousers, down jackets, flak helmets (obscuring their vision), parachutes and flak jackets. The flak jackets did little but give a false sense of security regarding hits. Yet, men often sat on two, folded-up flak jackets "to protect the family jewels." (I did!)

Ten minutes at the controls, flying close formation, and a pilot lost track of time and space—the lead aircraft and its relative position became the central focus of his being, and his aircraft's controls became his life. Within twenty minutes muscles screamed, demanding he remove his hands, one at a time, from the controls and begin flexing his fingers (to regain circulation and warm them.) After half an hour, it was necessary to pull away from the leader for a few seconds and relax the feet . . . and,

concurrently, recheck the instruments to see how much you have been slipping and sliding, cross-controlling, making the plane fight itself. Resetting the aircraft– neutralizing the controls–you again slid the plane back in close and started over.

If you had a good co-pilot who could fly while looking across the cockpit, he might be relied upon to "spell" you at the formation-flying chores. But experience was a crucial factor. Co-pilots who "gave good formation" the first time out–or even the second and third time–were rare, worth their weight in gold . . . and soon promoted to "pilot" status. Those who could *not* "hack the program" stayed co-pilots. Some headquarters shipped out or gave other ground/desk jobs.

Considering all this, is it any wonder the Air Force and Navy aerobatic stars, like the "Blue Angels," burn out quickly and must be replaced? They fly at nearly a thousand miles an hour and nearer than we ever did . . . and they do it through turbulence, clouds and close to the ground. Only a very few aviators qualify for the duty–now you know why. [At my very "best"(?), I doubt I could have matched their standards . . . but, daredevil that I am, I would like to have tried. I believe any pilot worth his salt feels the same. We are not only an egotistical, but a super-confident lot. If we were not, we would never have climbed into those infernal "flying machines" in the first place.]

A pilot must be a little crazy and a lot stupid to be a success. Also, to be an "old"pilot – as contrasted with, or also, a "bold" pilot–demands skill, extreme concentration, "guts," training, experience . . . and whole bunches of luck. As an alternative, one *might* get away with it, with a special "guardian angel" riding on one's shoulder. In my case, I believe in the "angel."

#6 – GLENN MILLER, "AND THE BAND PLAYED ON . . . "As I mentioned earlier, I wrote a fictional short story about Glenn Miller, titled as above. Here, for those interested, is a copy of that story:

* * *

Beneath the afternoon's sodden skies, December 24, 1944, my aircrew and I waved goodbye to a single-engine aircraft. The plane, leaving London for Paris, boasted but one passenger. England's chill breezes whipped damp flight suits about our legs, while we thought about the lucky fluke–our getting to talk with him at length in Operations before he left.

A nearby RAF pilot called out, "Hey, Yank! Who was the VIP?"

"Didn't you recognize Glenn Miller, the famous 'Big Band' leader?"

A few minutes later, we too took off in our B-26 (a Martin Marauder, twin-engine, medium bomber). Figuring we must leap into the skies at dawn on another combat mission, we scurried eastward with our colonel's Christmas gifts, already running late.

Over the English Channel we caught up with Miller's plane.

It flew below us, between cloud layers. The aircraft's heading, however, appeared even more northerly than ours. Yet we were headed for Royé, seventy-five miles northeast of Paris.

Radio silence prevented my querying Miller's pilot. So, instead, I asked my navigator, "Shouldn't we be flying about the same course?"

"The pilot may be approaching the French coast on another vector to avoid German fighters. After all, his courier plane is unarmed."

Ten o'clock that night, Christmas Eve, the entire world heard the shocking news. Major Glenn Miller *never arrived.*

My crew and I mourned Miller's lost talent, then helped look for him.

Christmas day, we Americans flew low-level passes over the North Sea. The British fleet and Royal Air Force scoured the English Channel. Allied ground troops, though fighting the Battle of the Bulge since December 16, tramped snow-covered fields, scanning allocated sectors. None found a trace of the missing

plane.

Generals and admirals washed their hands of the tragedy and returned to wrapping up World War II. Frustrated, navigators returned to their charts. Disheartened ground and air forces quit the search.

Still, many of us believed Major Miller still lived out there–somewhere. Some swore he crashed in enemy territory. More prayed he landed in friendly hands. No one *knew*.

Under wraps, we went on looking. Yet, due to the still-raging battles, messages barely dribbled in.

Bit by bit a chaotic pattern formed. The press contended Miller vanished in the North Sea. Fragmented radio and telephone calls, even telegrams, claimed his plane crashed, on an isolated shoreline or among tree-covered hills, hidden by deep snow drifts. Some said his plane landed in the no-man's land between the conflicting armies, with cannon fire and shell bursts precluding any news. Aircraft spotters in Belgium and the Netherlands reported a plane flying by, very low. All cited poor visibility. All blamed the snow-filled clouds and thick fogs.

"Certainly," everyone assured, "his plane came down somewhere nearby."

Not a single fact confirmed any one of their observations.

Only when the Battle of the Bulge ground to a halt and the defeated German armies retreated from their "last-gasp-effort," did the military resume its search. Giving the missing celebrity one, last, "full court press," our generals enlisted, once more, the aid of every military and civilian presence in the suspected areas . . . all to no avail.

The navies folded their hands. Headquarters, ETO (General Eisenhower's office), called off the troops. Only a few–all us die-hard, Miller fans–did not give up hope.

In March 1945, on completion of my crew's fifty combat missions, our group commander assigned us a small personnel carrier (a s-all, pickup-type truck with one bench seat for the

driver and a passenger, plus room in the cloth-covered rear for three more men, luggage, gasoline and food packs). "Get away for a little R and R (Rest and Recuperation)," he suggested. "I'm attaching your crew to the staff of a front line general, as 'observers' and 'liaison.' But go wherever you want, within reason." The colonel knew our intentions.

My aircrew and I left on a Sunday morning.

We pursued the path marked earlier on our maps, based on our last sightings of Miller's aircraft. Though we gave the same information to the "powers-that-be" on December 25, they discarded it as unconfirmed. But we all *felt certain* Miller was out there. "And, by George!" we vowed in unison, "We're going to find him!"

The next day we drove north through France. We weaved our way through the remnants of the British Army and ours. We passed hordes of Germany's dead Tiger tanks and Patton's. We struggled through the mud and blood across Belgium and into the Netherlands.

Once there, we trudged up and down beach after beach, careful of land mines. We talked first with one family, then another–all kind and helpful. We interviewed police, veterans, and soldiers. We trekked over farms, sloshed through snow, and paddled across pond upon pond south of the Zuider Zee.

In places we needed Hans Brinker's ice skates. In others, we commandeered rowboats and coracles. Yet, our efforts produced "no joy." Allotted only two weeks for our little diversion, we finally counted but a few days remaining.

One morning, we happened upon a quaint, isolated farm house on a North Sea shore. Though the entire trip had been bone-chilling, that last day forever etched itself in our minds as the worst. Huddling around an open fire beside the personnel carrier, we blew on freezing fingers and flapped our arms like headless chickens.

"Let's explore that cottage," I urged, pointing with an elbow.

"Captain," my crew argued, "this is a waste of time."

"Come on, Captain, let's go back to base."

"Major Miller must've deep-sixed in the drink, sir. He's a goner."

"Okay." I nodded. "If we find no clues by noon, we head south."

We poured in our last Jerry cans of gasoline, fired up the vehicle, and approached the lone farm house. I stopped our driver outside the enclosed courtyard.

Amazed to see an actual thatched roof, I waded through the muddy slush to pound on the heavy door, inset in a thick, sparkling-white, stone wall.

A young girl of about thirty answered. Cheeks so bright red they seemed false, she wore the traditional outfit we call "Dutch" . . . down to the wooden shoes.

I didn't understand a word of her rapid, multi-voweled Flemish. In the end we spoke fractured French and mangled English.

"Did you," I asked, "see a small American plane last Christmas Eve?"

She nodded with enthusiasm. If possible, her cheeks turned more red. She exclaimed, "Ah, but yes! He is here."

"Major Glenn Miller?"

She nodded again. She also waved both her hands, as if directing a band. "He is a be-e-e-g musician . . . no?"

"Is he all right"

Her lips turned down.

Hoping her moue indicated only a misunderstanding, I squeezed out another mutilated French question concerning his condition.

This time, she wiggled an open palm in the age-old Gallic gesture meaning, "So-so."

"May I see him?"

She smothered my enthusiasm with apprehension, when a flicker of dour expressions crossed her ruddy face like passing

storm clouds over the nearby sea. Then she stuck out her lower lip once more and urged me into the house.

I turned to the waiting crew and gave them a "thumbs-up."

The young girl led me across a cramped, living-dining room with a roaring fireplace. Still chilled, I felt tempted to pause. But the chance to rescue Major Miller took priority and I dragged my frozen feet onward.

Opening a bedroom door, the girl ushered me inside.

There sat the derelict of the once-great band leader. Emaciated to a mere skeleton, Miller tottered on the edge of a cot, dressed in worn "pinks" (at the time an Army officer's dress trousers) and some sort of colorful robe, probably the girl's.

He never turned. Incessantly fluttering his hands before his face, he directed an imaginary orchestra playing music only he heard. The vacant eyes and a deep, still-angry-red groove across his forehead attested to his mental state . . . and the reason. From Miller's scars, I figured the pilot must be long dead.

I eased in and passed a hand before Miller's eyes. He never so much as blinked.

Protective, the girl hustled forward and smoothed his hair like she might a small child's. She then made circles beside her forehead and motioned me to the door.

Once we were in the living room, she whispered, "The doctors say he is dying. My husband is already dead–killed by the war. I have no one, and I am so alone. Can't you leave him with me these last few days . . . to care for . . . until the end?"

Her pleading voice and welling eyes got to me.

Right or wrong, in view of Miller's hopeless condition I made an instant, command decision. I nodded mutely and left.

Outside, my men were smoking their last cigarettes on the far side of the road, their backs turned to me. I gathered an armload of "C" rations from our stores. Carrying them to the girl, I returned to call everyone back to the carrier.

"All a mistake, guys. She confused Major Miller with another

pilot downed locally. And her doctors give him only a couple more days to live."

Pointing forward and pumping my fist in the "Go" signal, I forever closed the door on our search for Major Miller.

"Men, you're right; we've had enough disappointment. Let's go home."

<div align="center">* * *</div>

#7–WHAT HONORS HAVE I EARNED?

As I grew older, the honors, commendations, citations, medals, degrees and plaudits of my fellow man came to mean less and less, until I now avoid discussing them if I can. Examining mine in the cold light of day, they served their purpose, in their time, yet I have discovered–as I believe all older people eventually do–it is *not* what you have done, or what someone patted you on the back for, nor the number of certificates hanging on your walls, or the awards gracing your tables, shelves and desks . . . but the *people whom you love and who love you, that count.* Parents don't teach that enough. Adults don't stress that enough. Everyone plods on, focusing on their toes and ignoring the beauty of the lives around them.

Like most military officers who flew combat, I earned a chestful of ribbons and medals. Like most who attained higher rank, I worked for and obtained degrees from schools, colleges and universities (military and civilian, undergraduate, graduate and post-graduate). Like every military man I have a stack (mine is about two inches thick) of graduation certificates, commendations and citations. (All three of my boys have similar files.)

Around my house, cluttering book cases, desks, and shelves like so many what-nots, stands a host of awards, some plastic-encased, some mounted on wooden bases with pretty little flags, some up-right and attention-grabbing, many hidden in drawers. Do they make any difference?

Not a one will buy a cup of coffee at Starbucks, nor even a

coke at McDonalds. Can I take them with me when I "go." They will not, either individually or in toto, pay–or pave–my way into heaven . . . and I doubt they will even contribute to a hell-bound passage.

I have found the stones upon which a happy, successful life is built are quarried from the height, depth and breadth of human affection, flavored by hugs and kisses, and sprinkled with the warm glances added by parents, spouses, loved ones, children . . . and friends.

Not a single piece of those papers will get me out of jail, if I am arrested. Nary a one will provide evidence to prove I am innocent or guilty of a crime. There is not any that will make me rich, a better person, or more loved by others. *Nor will any bring back my wife from the grave.* Then why do we make such a fuss over such irrelevant items?

For status! So we can brag about what we have done. So we can declare it to others and show how important we are. They are our "proof" we are alive!

So, let's be practical and evaluate what will happen when you do this. Expect to encounter three types of people: those who have not as much as you, those who have equally as much, and those who have more, maybe much more. (Bill Gates comes to mind, here. Want to compete with him . . . in anything?)

If you show to and compare your holdings with the first group, you will be putting them down. If that is your intent you will succeed, and they will resent you and your inconsiderate actions.

If you show to and compare your holdings with the second group, they will think, "So what." They may also be affronted by your having stated the obvious.

If you show to and compare your holdings with the third group–the ones having more than you–*you* will be affronted and put down. Then you will know how the first group felt.

Are these the reactions you want to engender? If so, why? (Are you a masochist or sadist?) None of these are fruitful or

friendship-building endeavors. These approaches are best . . . when avoided.

For *there is no answer*. But there should be *no question* or, if there is, we should *not* ask it–directly or by implication.

While teaching at Ohio University I was astounded at the status level structure and its internal segregation, though the faculty and staff would be the last–if ever–to admit it. (I thought the military was bad . . . but I enjoyed an unusual place as a general's aide and became spoiled, expecting to be accepted as an equal by everyone.)

At OU, during President Baker's first "indoctrination and get-acquainted" gathering, Ilogene and I mingled and talked with each level. We found out quickly, instructors talked with instructors and–maybe–assistant professors. Assistant professors talked with professors–unless the professors were the heads of the department or emeritus (then that too was a "No-no!"). Professors talked solely with deans, and the deans (thinking themselves "God-like") talked only with "God"– President Baker.

I really tossed a monkey wrench into the works, when I dashed up to Mrs. Baker and Mrs. Hunkins, wife of the Dean of Men, introduced Ilogene (as I might have done, as an aide, to any general and his wife). We engaged President Baker in a heated conversation about the weaknesses we had already seen on campus! Woo-wee! It was very nearly as bad as my comments on our return from that horrendous mission in Europe–those lower levels wanted to tar-and-feather me, and ride me out of town on a rail. But it *did* break the ice."

#8–THE "BIG QUESTIONS":
Recently, a friend's questions stimulated a great deal of introspection and speculation for me. His questions included: *"Who were the truly great people you met in your life?* (and) *"What made them great?"*

These questions floored me. I had never looked at my fellow

man (or woman) in this light. But I tried . . . and found the second question preceded the first. Before I could measure greatness, I needed a yardstick. Electing to make my appraisal as objective as possible, eliminate as much subjectivity as I could, I also wanted my own decisions inherent in the task, not a compilation of other thinkers', philosophers', or lists from popular magazines or books.

After much stewing and fretting, it became obvious neither of these questions was easy. (It began to look like answering the eternal philosophical question, "What is truth?")

First, I tried to determine the basic characteristics of a "great" person (man or woman) . . . and found my own viewpoint warping my choices. To make such an objective assessment I had to set aside prejudices and biases, and all preconceived opinions. (I do not expect everyone–or anyone–to agree with my conclusions. I suggest everyone develop his own, then compare them with mine.)

Here is what I–finally!–arrived at ("In my opinion"):

First, I decided a person to be "great" must *be modest, unassuming and civil.* I started with those as basic. I was not going to try ascertaining what a "perfect" person might be, but only what a "great" person must live up to. There lies a world of difference. (To find a "perfect" human, I felt was an impossibility. I wanted to keep this as realistic as I could.)

Second, the person must *show reasonable intelligence.* (Again I was not looking for a genius–or, if a genius, then that might be his/her single qualifying factor.) It seemed to me, a certain amount of brains must go along with any modest, unassuming and civil nature. (The latter demanding the former as a prerequisite.)

Third, whoever it might be–man or woman–the person must also care about others, (not necessarily more than himself or herself, as that is an oft-stated, unreasonable expectation). Yet, to me, a truly "great" individual must show valid altruism– demonstrating a real caring for others' welfare, a broad-scale sacrificing nature as shown by efforts to help improve the world in

some way, and a willingness to let someone else accept the credit.

I saw, at once, this ruled out braggarts and limelight hogs. (This one critical element alone, banned from consideration most politicians, presidents, generals, and other "under-the-spotlight" notables, including movie, TV, theater and music idols, as well as stage personages, "stars," "superstars," divas, prima donnas, etc. Since I fell in the egocentric category, I ruled myself out.)

Using those as my primary points of departure, I began sifting my memory, knowing full well I'd develop more criteria and greater detail as I progressed.

I scrutinized those people I had known to whom I felt most attracted. *Is this a factor?* I asked myself. *Do I have to "like" the person to consider him or her to be "great?"*

My answer was a solid "No!" That should *not* be a factor. Anyone–even an enemy, a person I actively dislike, someone I might even hate–A-N-Y-O-N-E should be considered, if he or she "fits the bill."

Nor did one have to "give his life for his country," to fall into the "greatness" category. That, as far as I was concerned, already included all the usual "heroes"– military and civilians who did. (I am thinking about Pearl Harbor, D-Day, Beirut and 9/11 here–and these were but a few of the many, many possible examples.)

If death, sacrifice and renown did not count, then what did?

Finally, I had to beg the issue. I discovered *there was no one in my entire acquaintance whom I could honestly rate as being "great."* There were those I admired and did *not* admire, to varying degrees.

Among those few I truly admire is Rev. Benjamin Edwards. This man is the epitome of goodness–and shows all the positive factors making up a "great" personality. Yet I cannot say he is "great," solely because his effect, though scattered broadly, did not move everyone he touched. (I guess, using "universality" as a criterion, only Jesus, Moses, Buddha or Mohammed, or perhaps some other biblical or historical characters, earn that accolade.)

Yet Ben would be the first to tell you his deficiencies–one of my other elements of "greatness." He and his wife have given unstintingly throughout their lives . . . to their family, their friends, their churches, and their parishioners. Both he and his wife may, very well, qualify for sainthood, but not greatness. (Yes! I'm a tough judge. It is a good thing I do not sit at God's right hand.)

I cannot evaluate George Washington or Abraham Lincoln–I did not know them and, perhaps, "greatness" can be assessed only in the fullness of time. But I can say none of the Presidents . . . Roosevelt, Truman, Kennedy, Johnson, Nixon, Ford, Clinton nor the two Bushes, fall in the ballpark. (I met only a few, FDR through Kennedy.) General Dwight Eisenhower, an oft-maligned president . . . did NOT have a war, ran the government when seriously ill, and balanced the budget while in office. His highly praiseworthy accomplishments, though so-far-inadequately-acknowledged, fall short for other reasons I will not enumerate. (Remember: this is *my* opinion.)

I admired each of the above for some factors, disliked them for others. The same applies to Thomas Estes, our ambassador to Upper Volta; Bill Lear, Jimmy Carter, General Ralph Snavely, General Curtis Lemay, and hundreds more I have known, more or less intimately.

Sifting the sands again, I admire most, next to Ben Edwards, my now-deceased friend, Colonel Jacques Hascöet. A Frenchman, despite all the stories to the contrary he was true to his wife through thick and thin. He also served his country above and beyond, accomplished notable goals, and died as a result of his sacrifices–like so many. [Jacques escapes "greatness" solely for one remembered episode: while we hunted meat for the president's table in Africa, I injured an eland with my first shot, but did not kill it. It ran into the brush. When the bushes jiggled at the point of entry, Jacques shouted, "Shoot!" I waited, saying, "Not until I see what I am shooting at." Out of the jungle an African shepherd urged on his flock of mouton. I pointed. "See! I

could have killed him."

Jacques waved away the nonsense. "There are plenty more like him in there." (I credit this answer to Jacques' extended and multiple imprisonments, and the subsequent harshness of his life. I saw his words, not as an exception, but as his standard viewpoint. Admired? Yes, in many ways. But great? No!

It is an arrogance, I decided, to try and assess my fellow men and women for "greatness." Yet, because I was asked, I tried. So far, that completes, my list . . . two people (three if you include Carolyn Edwards, Ben's wife). (See below, this page.)

Thus, in a way, I am much like the priest who was asked, on going home after forty years in Africa, "How many souls did you save for Christ while here, Father?"

He thought for a moment and held up three fingers. Then he turned one down, leaving only his index finger and the next one upright. "I was going to say I am sure of three . . . but that other one was sort of . . . " He stuck out his hand and wavered the open palm in the classic Gallic gesture signaling *"comme si, comme ça."* (Meaning he was undecided, it could go either way.)

Reverend Benjamin and Carolyn Edwards.

For some specific examples:

We visited Dr. Albert Schweitzer's hospital at Lambarené, Gabon. There we also toured his office (untouched since his death, except where they place a fresh rose daily on his desk).

His grave lies just outside his former office window. The cross bears his name and pertinent dates in German (born 1 January, 1875; died 4 September 1965).

Dr. Albert Schweitzer's grave. The cross gives the details.

We flew into Bilma, Niger, one afternoon and actually got to see and smell the herd of more than twenty-thousand camels. *Take it from me–they really stink!*

A few of the more than twenty thousand camels assembled near Bilma. Their owners bring them here to get shipments of salt from the salt mines shown below.

These salt mines, now some thirty feet below the surface of the sand and worked for five thousand years, show not one sign of giving out.

The surface of these brine pools, colored dark red like iodine, skim over with salt every day. The nomads take out this salt in a form like a man's peg leg, only shorter. This form is easiest to load on a camel's back. Each will carry some twenty or more.

In addition, we had an opportunity to participate in a wedding party while assigned to the embassy at Abidjan. I translated the French wedding service in the Mayor's office.

Wedding party for "Roberts couple," 1st line, centered.
1st line–Amb. Wine, Bill & Jeanne Roberts, 1st Secty Rood.
2nd line–Col. Cron, two embassy secretaries (bridesmaids),
Mrs. Wine.
(Taken at the ambassador's residence, since Mrs. Roberts
was his private secretary the Wines provided the reception.)

We also visited some of the finest restaurants and dined with some of the finest people. The above photograph shows the former wine cellars at Botin's, Madrid, Spain, 2 Feb 1965. This Spanish restaurant is known the world around for its famous pheasant, baked piglet, and superb wine list.

371

Seated at the table and listed from left to right are:

Col. George Hughes (Wing Commander, Torrejon AFB); Mrs. Ruth Estes (wife of Ambassador Estes), Ilogene Cron; Capt. Allen S. Gindoff; Mrs. (Leah) Gindoff; Col. Rodney Cron; Michael Cron; Ambassador Thomas S. Estes; and Mrs. Jean Hughs (wife of Col. Hughes).

EPILOGUE
▲

This is "mea culpa" time. Writing these reminisces stirred-up memories filled with trauma, guilt and remorse. It forced me to relive incidents and events I preferred to forget. Yet these are now a part of me and who I am. These events permanently dyed the pattern of my life's fabric with browns, blacks, greys and deep purples (representing the sad and the bad).

It is difficult to put a cheery face on any year filled with war, death, injury, near-misses, struggles to live and earn an income, and scraping away to buy my family the basic necessities. Yet, continuing the analogy of "life as a tapestry," there were many bright colored threads as well–reds, greens, blues, yellows and oranges. These colors represented the elements of joy, delight, glee and warmth Ilogene, our family, and loved ones brought into the weave.

In this history, I realize there has been too much "I, my, me" (ego). There has been too little, "we, us, our" (sharing) and "they, them, their" (acknowledging the parts others played). In my omissions I may have treated Ilogene and my children much as my mother treated me.

I asked myself, then, "How can I–ever!–show my true awareness and deep abiding appreciation for all Ilogene and our children did? How can I acknowledge their infinite value, and meaning to me?"

My answer was a resounding, "I can not." In Ilogene's case, it is too late. In my children's, it is impossible. No one can redeem the past, nor make amends for past failures or hurt. These pages can but hint at the golden treasures they represent and I cherish.

My early years warped me, as mother's did her. I grew up under a cloud; she suffered trauma . . . and passed on her suffering to me.

Mentioned earlier, we are not "who we are" solely because we sprang from the loins of certain parents, but because of those with whom we rub elbows, and the experiences we sustain along our pathway through this vale of tears and laughter.

"Who I am *now*" resembles very little the young man Ilogene rescued from my earlier malice, egocentricity and selfishness.

Oh, all those character flaws are still there and I sometimes lapse, but let us accredit my saviors–principally Ilogene and my children–for making me *even resemble a human being.*

When I met Ilogene for the second time, we were both nineteen. I was searching for something, but did not know what. Ilogene, with an inherent wisdom far beyond her years, took me carefully in hand. She taught me to love, not withdraw. She taught me to care, not ignore.

When Ilogene died, I went into a spiraling depression. I lost my balance wheel, my *reason for being.* Though concerned about *my* loss, I felt Ilogene was cheated. She had so very much to live for: her children, grandchildren, and great-grandchildren, a world of plans, a spectrum of hopes, an infinity of undone things, a wealth of unspoken words, a universe of unseen places she would never do, hear, say or see. One moment she was a vivacious, loving wife and doting mother, the next she was empty, a shell. The spark of "soul" gone forever.

I felt certain I should feel some sort of communication from "beyond," we were so close. I reached out. I groped. I searched. Not one of my prayers, my meditations, or my wait, produced a single hint or clue. No feeling of warmth crossed the infinite gap between us. Her death cost her everything, as death does us all. Even at the age of seventy-six, it was too soon, too sudden, too much. I felt it was without rhyme or reason. Then, I realized, isn't that the way we feel about any death?

I lost sixty pounds in three months. I lost my drive, my

incentive, my purpose. I found I had been working not for myself, but to give her a better life, to make things easier for her, to give her those things she never had, to repay her for her earlier sacrifices. I was no longer the self-centered egoist she married, but intent on doing what I could for her. Without her to live and care for, I was nothing.

I tried to find a meaning to continue. Finding none, I shoved the barrel of my automatic into my mouth, ready to join her.

Only then, at the very last minute, did I think–since I was still here and not Ilogene–there must be a reason. Perhaps I had a job yet to do. Some unseen, unrealized duty to perform–for Ilogene, for our children, my community, my universe.

Ilogene and I discussed death often in those last years, and planned financially. We had talked about death in intimate terms, expecting her to outlive me by years. When she died first, I realized that . . . no matter what we had done, no words we had said, no amount of prior intellectual conversation ever prepared a person for the shock and trauma occurring when it actually happens. The person left behind enters a new, strange and frightening world. Now bereft, one sees the once-friendly ambiance as subtly hostile. I saw the world differently. Only my religious beliefs, my children, and my supportive friends ushered me through the darkness to the light beyond.

I threw myself into my writing–again. Yet I made a number of stupid mistakes Ilogene would have prevented. I *did* follow our decision not to sell our house, or move, under a year. (I waited for more than two years.) But I bought automobiles I did not need, did not want, and resold. I tried travel and found everything had paled. I lost money on the stock market. I did not drink or womanize, as some men do. But I *did find* a woman I wanted to marry–someone I had found attractive for years.

That was my third–and perhaps biggest–mistake. I led myself into believing she would marry me. (I must give some credit where credit is due, however, she fostered this belief, so my expectations

were not all one-sided.) Though I entered the situation with my eyes at least partially open, her final change of heart traumatized me.

I must credit her, however, with giving me a new reason to live, a central incentive I had lost. Our brief interlude relit the fire in my soul and rekindled the fuse to my ambition. A single life is a barren existence, ask any widow or widower. But I would have gladly proved the adage that, "A person who deeply loved his/her spouse will remarry quickly."

So, what have I done since Ilogene died? My children and I took a long, Caribbean cruise. I have gone to Europe five times. I have written a number of books[126]. I have done what I can do, to help my children, and I have provided for them after I am gone. I am now laying the ground work to "shuffle off this mortal coil" as easily and as unobtrusively as possible.

Beginning a year ago, I started putting on paper "My Beliefs." And, this year–for the second time–I have begun this, my memoirs/autobiography. (This time, "God willin' and the crick don't rise . . . " (sic) I will finish it.)

Though I would like to complete more books, they are not a priority. I really do *not* care much about anything, anymore –not fervently. Maybe this is a new maturity. But I never cared much about "things," anyway– only people. I can be hurt by only those I love . . . the more I love them, the more they can hurt me. Like everyone, I am vulnerable only to the ones I love.

I tell friends, "I can walk out the front door and everything can vanish behind me–all my possessions, my house, my car, my furniture, all my work and all my writing (even this) . . . any hint I ever existed–and I would not care." Few people understand.

"Things" are meaningless. Valueless. People put far too much store in "stuff." Sure, we need those items to live, but *not to love*.

My oldest son, Rod III, would like to start a church with the

[126] See Addenda ("MYBOOKS") for books published since Ilogene died, and those "in the mill."

central theme, "God is love . . . all else is do-do!" He expresses my philosophy.

What else have I done since Ilogene died? I worked in various churches . . . and became frustrated by pettiness. Some ministers speak out of a corner of their mouths and sin, doing precisely what they criticize. Some parishioners, under the guise of helping, feather their own nests at the church's expense. Some, under the guise of altruism, maneuver the church's funds and activities to their own benefit in other ways . . . ignoring the church's needs. Some want only to warm pews, but not to work as a disciple, congregant or parishioner. I am certainly nowhere near perfect, but I believe a person who acts in such a contrary manner should, first, change his/her behavior to be more helpful . . . or withdraw. No one should perpetuate nor compound a felony, especially in a church.

Now I live in a small, modest two-bedroom home near the center of town. I do not exercise enough, eat too much, and indulge my tastes when I should not. (I discovered why the elderly grow fat–*eating is often the only pleasure still available to them*.) I eat and drink (alcohol) less. I love good wines and cognacs, but limit myself to small sips and small glasses. I cannot read at length. I need brighter lights.

Every year my friends grow more sparse. I help anyone I can. I have an extensive library and reread favorite books periodically, enjoying again the stories and nuances, maybe because they are so familiar.

Rodney L. Cron

ILOGENE[127]

Deliberately, until now, I described Ilogene only superficially. Her memory is impossible for me to confront without a deep emotional response.

From my perspective, I see not one, but a million "Ilogenes." I see her with a lover's eye, an artist's, a workmate's and a husband's (but, now, I see her through tears). I see her as a young girl of thirteen, as a single girl of nineteen, as a newlywed, as a mother, as a parent, grandmother and great-grandmother, as a sharer of trials, tribulations and pleasures, as an advisor, as my soul mate and life's companion. I see her happy and sad. I see her well and ill. I see her now as a long line of herself, like images reflected in two facing mirrors, stretching into infinity. To me, Ilogene was not one person, but a multitude. Yet I will always see her--and she will forever remain in my memory--in the bright light of her vivacious youth. The figure I saw last, lying in the casket, was beautiful, even in death . . . but that silent, unmoving clay was no longer Ilogene. The Ilogene I knew, and know, lives on forever in my memory as an active, fiery spirit of our mutual love.

Statistically, Ilogene stood but five-feet tall and weighed but one-hundred-twenty. Even at seventy-six she had a shapely body, with the firmly muscled legs and small, highly arched feet of a ballet dancer–which she was. Her once-brown hair grew thin, then thinner after sixty; and, though fading, showed virtually no gray. Her near-sighted, golden-flecked, brown-hazel eyes needed glasses from the time she was twelve. Her hands were small, slim and well-formed; her nails, always unpainted, were well-cared-for. Her oval face showed the characteristic high cheek bones and molded forehead of her Indian ancestry, yet the only other clue to this

[127] I wrote this entire manuscript before the comments about Ilogene. Even now I write in tears, eyes clenched, gasping. But this, the last entry in my memoirs, I wanted to reflect my life not only as one of eternal love for Ilogene . . . but also as a testament to my love for God, my fellow man, and my military compatriots.

heritage was her uncanny ability to see unmoving animals in the wild.

Ilogene had a quiet, though steadfast personality. Her broad-spectrum intelligence shone forth in her love for others, her delight in cross-word puzzles, her quick retorts, and her vast reading capabilities. She preferred new relationships to move slowly. She tended to hold strangers at arms' length until they proved their mettle, then she quickly thawed. But she always loved children, ours and others'.

Yet these are mere, writable identifications–cold, factual, unwarmed by the many facets of her out-going personality and uncolored by her immeasurable depth, breadth and soul. Though all humans are individual and unique, Ilogene possessed special qualities I imbued with even greater value because I loved her so very much . . . and because I always will.

I reached the absolute abyss of despair when I last looked at her body in the casket, before they sealed it. To our son, Pat, who stood by my side, I said, "I should be lying there, not her."

His words actually gave me my first urge to live again, "No, Dad. You would not have wanted Mom to go through this."

Pat was right. The pain, anguish and utter hopelessness of her death were personal, unendurable tortures. I never would have wanted Ilogene to experience them. And she didn't. That was the sole solace of her death. It still is.

(*Our children, I know, felt her loss almost as keenly as I. The reason I do not say, "*as keenly*," is because not one of them lived with, cared for, or loved her for as many years.)

This did not happen overnight and Ilogene's reconstruction of me remains unfinished. When she died, fifty-five and a half years after our marriage, she was still remolding the clay making-up Rodney L. Cron.

It was Ilogene who nudged me into visiting my mother after she slapped Ilogene and following a lengthy, three-year estrangement (during which mother, also, made no attempt at reconciliation). It

was Ilogene who counseled me, gently but forcibly, on my dealing with our children. Though I was often gone for extended periods, I expected to return, instantly take over the reins of family leadership, believing our children should leap at my commands like trained puppies, demonstrate adult discernment, and–despite what they saw as my meanness–love me, cater to me, show me the unmitigated warmth and friendliness of doting children. It was Ilogene who sanded off the roughest edges of my abrasive personality.

It was she who polished the rawness of my stone and gave it whatever luster it may have acquired. She stimulated warmth where there was little. It was her comforting love that brought out what faint vestiges of color lay sequestered beneath my hardened and tarnished exterior.

I know now, too late, Ilogene saw some obscure character and strength in me– where there was little to find. But she made the most of what there was, or tried to. I honor her virtually infinite spectrum of positive facets.

Since 1 January 1989, without her guidance and quiet hand upon my steering–though I am fighting it–I am slowly reverting to what I was "B.I." (Before Ilogene). Now there is no one who can, or will, save me.

Ilogene sacrificed her time, her health, and her energies constantly, to assure our family's welfare. Husbanding my meager income as a cadet, she starved while I ate lavishly in mess halls. She lived (cold, hot and miserable) in shacks and cockroach-, scorpion- and ant-infested rooms, just to be near me (while caring for a child). She scrubbed clothes and diapers until her hands bled and she could not sleep.

She walked miles in snow and rain, wore rags she mended and patched. She pushed a baby carriage or carried a heavy child in her arms, so I could hold our children for a few minutes.

I can recite a list longer than both my outstretched arms in tribute to Ilogene's unrelenting courage, consideration and

demonstrations of love. Still, there were many times, focused on "my" needs and not seeing all she was doing, I hurt her with angry words and stupid actions–walking out, slamming doors, driving off. But I always came back to apologize, try to do better, and worship her accomplishments.

There was–and is–*no* way I could ever repay her. Yet, if she were here today to read this, she would say, "Love requires no repayment."

That was Ilogene.

ILOGENE
(This is the girl I
married.)
(1942)

ILOGENE
(This is the girl I
buried.)
(1998)

Also, I have barely sketched-in my children's part in my life. Yet, they too, worked–and are still working–to scrape off my hoary accumulation of negative barnacles. They are now trying to take over the reshaping job Ilogene began. They are adding the love I need.

L to R: Me, Patrick, Melodie, Mike, Carrie (Pat's daughter), and Rodney III.

Melodie, our oldest, living in Cincinnati married to her second husband, is brilliant, but all our children are. (Aren't yours?) She works far beyond what is necessary to prove it. (She did this from the first grade on. Making straight "As," she constantly thought she was failing.) Lovely from birth, her only physical handicap has been acute myopia.

At twelve, in San Antonio, when we again took her in to strengthen her glasses, the optometrist suggested contact lens. She left wearing them, refusing to remove either one until bedtime.

Outside, she looked up and said, "Why, those trees have *leaves*! I always thought that was just a green haze."

Ilogene and I gasped. "How," we asked, "could we have been so cruel?"

Melodie's life, too, has had its ups and downs. Briefly an Army nurse, she now works in a "Psych" ward at one of Cinci's major hospitals. She tries to visit her grandchildren regularly in Pennsylvania and concurrently appease her second husband's, (Doug Robinson's), self-centered demands (as Ilogene did mine).

Melodie and her first husband, Dr. Don Levi, gave us two exceptional grandchildren, Andrea and Jarrod (both now married).

To Rodney III, intelligent like Melodie, life came easier. More laid-back, Rod retired from the military as a Master Chief (E-9). He was one of those who "ran the Navy, answering only to God and Admiral Rickover," and, sometimes, still thinks he's God. Rod III, an accredited teacher of mathematics and computer science, holds several degrees, and is an ordained minister, licensed by Ohio's Secretary of State to perform weddings. A published author as I am, Rod's sole purpose in life, now, is to help small churches get their feet on the ground, become solvent, and g-r-o-w. Though he was once married–a disaster for a submariner–he is now single and lives in Logan, Ohio. But the northern cold exacerbates his back injuries and he says he will return soon to Corpus Christi, Texas (where it is warmer, and he can swim and fish year-around in its tepid waters).

Patrick Morris, our number two son, lives in San Antonio, married to his second wife, Becky. He is our only West Point graduate. (One does not graduate from "The Point" with nothing on the ball.) Because I was a senior Regular officer, at his request I wangled him a transfer to the Air Force. He tried flying, but his eyes, even with a waiver, gave him too little confidence in landings. He ended-up in communications and even directed the USAF Recruiting School, a job I once held. He retired as a major after twenty years. Cathy, his first wife, gave him one daughter–Carrie–who also lives in San Antonio.

Our youngest child, Michael Dennis, came sort-of unexpectedly.

While I taught at Ohio University (1949-1952)–a "given" three years in one location–Ilogene and I tried to have a fourth child. For a long time it remained a pleasure-filled, but futile effort.

On our first date in 1942, I asked Ilogene, "How many children do you want when you get married?" She said, "Four!" I responded, "Great! So do I, let's get married." So our OU stint seemed just the place to fulfill our plan. But no luck.

When time began to run short (anticipating the end of my tour and a trip to Korea) we initiated a speeded-up program to adopt a baby girl. The very day the hospital approved the paperwork, I hurried home to tell Ilogene.

She exclaimed, "Boy! Do I have news for you!"

Yep, the doctor just verified number four was on the way!

Ilogene gave birth to Mike in Nelsonville, Ohio—the only one of our four children not delivered in Piqua. Michael also retired after twenty years from the Army—as sharp as any of the others (there is no IQ competition among them). He has a rare and special wife, Karen, who is too good for him. (Even he admits it.) Her character, wit and warm consideration are matched only by her generosity. There were times when Ilogene and I, and the other boys as well, wished we might clone two more Karens, one for Rod, one for Pat. Mike and Karen, now living in Logan, produced the sole members of our family who will perpetuate the Cron name—Jeremy (now married) and Joshua. (Both college graduates—Jeremy with a B.A., Joshua with a two-year diploma.)

This brief recital of Ilogene's and our children's names, talents and skills does not do justice to any of their unique personalities. That would require a separate set of tomes, lengthy, detailed and earthy. But they merit my heartfelt thanks and appreciation for burning away my crustiness, for their continuing support, for "being there" when I needed them (when Ilogene died)—and here, too, Karen was one of my main braces.

More important, each has a gift. All the boys served as middle-managers and teachers—military, high school, or university. Melodie is a nurturing care-giver with a penchant for medicine, taking under her wing every living creature she ever saw.

Rod III is predominantly a teacher, though he is also much more—a minister, a planner, a super-manager. He is the family's "rock," steadfast, reliable, assured . . . and our computer guru, repairman and builder.

Patrick is also a teacher. Like Rod III did, he teaches

mathematics to high school students. He also teaches management to college graduates. An avid golfer he suffers physical problems similar to mine–heart and knees. Pat is the family wit, always ready with a joke.

Michael is a born manager, forced by stress to let his skills languish. He was our only baby I was near at birth.

Even then, fate mitigated against my actually being present.

At the hospital, expecting Ilogene to deliver in an hour, the doctor took her to the delivery room. He told me to finish breakfast then come in. I put on a gown and mask, and watched the birth. (A girl!) I left, but met the doctor in the hall. When I told him what I saw, he told me to keep it quiet . . . Ilogene had given us Michael, fifteen minutes earlier.

Michael (Mike) and Karen, parents of Jeremy and Joshua, whose pictures appear below.

Amber and Jeremy
Cron
(Mike's older son.)

Christie and Joshua
Cron
(Mike's younger son.)

Each of our children, including our grandchildren and great-grandchildren, is a treasure. Each is different. All are precious. I am proud of every one.

David and Andrea Bilicic, with Danielle, Griffin and Avery. (Andrea is Melodie's daughter, the girl we took to Europe with us when she was but fourteen.)

Jarrod and Susan Levi ("Jay" is Melodie's son by her first marriage, as was Andrea.)

Yet I, too seldom, expressed my true feelings. Too often I did not say, "I love you." Too frequently I did not stroke or pat their heads. Too many times, to them, I must have appeared withdrawn, introspective, aloof or cold. More often than I like to admit I did not listen to grievances and examine school papers. I am sure many times I seemed hard, harsh and mean. There were episodes when I did not–as they felt I should–talk or act as they wanted me to. (But

what parents do? Yet that is not an excuse.)

I have been remiss–No! I *failed!*–to be a good father in many ways. I am unable to offer excuses. There are none that are valid. But I tried.

Today, thanks to Ilogene, more than to me–and to their own efforts– our children are responsible, brainy, praiseworthy and trustworthy citizens, well-educated, and good parents (better than I). Each is a credit to his/her family, his employer, and our country. I would not trade any of them for any person or any thing . . . not even a promise of eternity in heaven. They may not be perfect–but no one is–yet they stand head and shoulders above the crowd (any crowd), honest, forthright, "straight-arrows." I can give them no greater compliment than Ilogene did with her unstinting love and unshakeable confidence in their assured future.

Our grandchildren and great-grandchildren also merit kudos, from Andrea and Jarrod, to Carrie, Jeremy and Josh–and our great-grandchildren, David and Andrea Bilicic's Danielle, Griffin and Avery. *(See photos, preceding page.)*

Maybe none will ever be rich. Maybe none will ever set a world record, earn a Nobel prize, or achieve everlasting fame. But posterity, as represented by our family's progeny, appears to be in good hands.

I leave them our world without hesitation.

FINAL CONCLUSION:

Let me add one final observation. These pages contain an additional, hidden and recurring theme. Not as overt as the flying and terror elements of my life, but one more subtle. This I shared with my father.

He believed, as I do, that life and love intermingle.

I want, therefore, the same song sung at my funeral (or memorial) he wanted at his, "Ah, Sweet Mystery of Life."

If you examine the first two lines of the song, you can see why both of us felt this was the perfect coda to our existence:

Rodney L. Cron

"Ah, sweet mystery of life . . . at last I've found you,
"Ah, at last . . . I know the secret of it all . . . "
(For is not death–and love–the great secrets of our lives?)

B-26, "loaded for bear."
(Note the rockets and guns under each wing and the
guns in the upper turret).

It seemed only fitting to end my narrative with a photo
of the aircraft I flew . . . and liked . . . most,
what we once-called an "A-26" (with a glass nose).

Printed in the United States
210597BV00003B/76-105/P

9 780980 037845